Islamic Financial Contracts

Islam encourages business and financial transactions as a way of securing the basic needs for all human beings, but these need to be conducted in accordance with the principles contained in the Qur'ān and Sunnah. However, these legal concepts are not classified subject-wise, and the verses on commercial law, like all other topics, are scattered throughout the Qur'ān, making it difficult for readers to gain a full understanding of the topic. This, therefore, is the first comprehensive book to demystify Islamic contract law and specifically Islamic financial contracts, and to examine its roots and history.

The book is written in a clear style to allow for a greater understanding of the more challenging and misunderstood areas pertaining to Islamic business and financial contracts. It also contributes a series of chapters which address the market niche and need, concerning *Shariah* compliance for Islamic financial products and services. The book is divided into 16 chapters in order to provide a holistic and thorough overview of Islamic law of contract. It covers the objections and misconceptions surrounding Islamic business and financial contracts. It also includes the key features and guiding principles of Islamic law of contract and offers technical know-how, illustrating the concept of formation of a contract, as well as the essential elements of a valid contract. The authors also offer a discussion on the system of options under Islamic business and financial contracts and potential solutions to breach of contracts.

The book will serve as a handy reference for scholars and students of Islamic business and finance and Islamic commercial law and will also be beneficial for practitioners as well as legal and judicial officers. It will open new doors for further research in the field of Islamic financial contracts.

Hussain Mohi-ud-Din Qadri, PhD, is a Deputy Chairman of the Board of Governors of Minhaj University Lahore and an Associate Professor at the School of Economics and Finance at MUL. He is also the President of Minhaj-ul-Quran International; Chairman of the Minhaj Education Society (running 650 schools and colleges all over Pakistan); Chairman of Aghosh Orphan Care Homes; Chairman of Al-Mawakhat Microfinance; and Chairman of Minhaj Halal Certification. He has also been affiliated with the University of Melbourne Australia as Senior Fellow for many years. Dr. Qadri is an author of thirty books, writer of over 50 research articles and a reputed international speaker.

Nasir Iqbal is a senior Advocate High Court. He is Legal Advisor of Minhaj University, Lahore, Minhaj Halal Certification and Al-Mawakhat Microfinance. He is also managing partner in law firms "ABNAQ & Co. Advocates/Solicitors/I. P Attorneys" and "Nadeem Saeed & Co." dealing in civil law and commercial law. He is also a visiting lecturer for commercial and business law in Minhaj University. He has more than 20 years' experience in the field of law and is an expert in the area of business and financial contracts/commercial law and intellectual property laws, particularly in trademark and copyright laws.

Islamic Business and Finance Series
Series Editor: Ishaq Bhatti

There is an increasing need for western politicians, financiers, bankers, and indeed the western business community in general to have access to high quality and authoritative texts on Islamic financial and business practices. Drawing on expertise from across the Islamic world, this new series will provide carefully chosen and focused monographs and collections, each authored/edited by an expert in their respective field all over the world.

The series will be pitched at a level to appeal to middle and senior management in both the western and the Islamic business communities. For the manager with a western background the series will provide detailed and up-to-date briefings on important topics; for the academics, postgraduates, business communities, manager with western and an Islamic background the series will provide a guide to best practice in business in Islamic communities around the world, including Muslim minorities in the west and majorities in the rest of the world.

Islamic Monetary Economics
Finance and Banking in Contemporary Muslim Economies
Edited by Taha Eğri and Zeyneb Hafsa Orhan

COVID-19 and Islamic Social Finance
Edited by M. Kabir Hassan, Aishath Muneeza and Adel M. Sarea

Islamic Fintech
Edited by Sara Sánchez Fernández

Islamic Financial Contracts
A Research Companion
Hussain Mohi-ud-Din Qadri and Nasir Iqbal

Benchmarking Islamic Finance
A Framework for Evaluating Financial Products and Services
Edited by Mohd Ma'Sum Billah

For more information about this series, please visit: www.routledge.com/Islamic-Business-and-Finance-Series/book-series/ISLAMICFINANCE

Islamic Financial Contracts

A Research Companion

Hussain Mohi-ud-Din Qadri
and Nasir Iqbal

Routledge
Taylor & Francis Group
LONDON AND NEW YORK

First published 2021
by Routledge
2 Park Square, Milton Park, Abingdon, Oxon OX14 4RN

and by Routledge
605 Third Avenue, New York, NY 10017

Routledge is an imprint of the Taylor & Francis Group, an informa business

British Library Cataloguing-in-Publication Data
A catalogue record for this book is available from the British Library

Library of Congress Cataloging-in-Publication Data
Names: Qādrī, Ḥusain Muḥīuddīn, author. | Iqbal, Nasir, author.
Title: Islamic financial contracts: a research companion/Hussain Mohi-ud-Din Qadri and Nasir Iqbal.
Description: Milton Park, Abingdon, Oxon; New York, NY: Routledge, 2021.|
Series: Islamic business and finance series | Includes bibliographical references and index.
Identifiers: LCCN 2021001015 (print) | LCCN 2021001016 (ebook)
Subjects: LCSH: Finance (Islamic law) | Finance—Law and legislation. | Finance—Religious aspects—Islam. | Contracts (Islamic law)
Classification: LCC KBP940.2 .Q23 2021 (print) | LCC KBP940.2 (ebook) | DDC 346/.08—dc23
LC record available at https://lccn.loc.gov/2021001015
LC ebook record available at https://lccn.loc.gov/2021001016

ISBN: 978-1-032-00506-5 (hbk)
ISBN: 978-1-032-00509-6 (pbk)
ISBN: 978-1-003-17447-9 (ebk)

Typeset in Times New Roman
by Deanta Global Publishing Services, Chennai, India

Contents

Introduction xii

1 Some basic legal terminologies and concepts 1

1.1 Concept of Islamic law 1
1.2 Shariah 1
1.3 Qur'ānic basis of Shariah *2*
1.4 Fiqh 2
1.5 Qur'ānic and Sunnah basis of *fiqh 3*
1.6 Islamic jurisprudence 5
1.7 Islamic concept of law 6
1.8 The significance of trade and commerce in Islam 7
1.9 Underlying philosophy of commercial transaction in Islam 9
Notes 11

2 Historical evolution of contracts and codification of Islamic law of contract 14

2.1 Historical evolution of contracts 14
2.2 Pre-Islamic era 14
2.3 Post-Islamic era 15
2.4 The historical origin of the English law of contract 17
2.5 Codification of Islamic law of contract 19
2.6 Definition of code and codification 19
2.7 Shariah *and other legal systems 20*
2.8 Reasons for no codifications till the date 20
2.9 Origin is different 20
2.10 Nature is different 21
2.11 Sources of law are different 21
2.12 Territoriality aspect is different 21
2.13 Two views about codification 22

2.14 Efforts of codifications 23
2.15 Efforts in the sub-continent 24
2.16 Efforts in Java, Indonesia 24
2.17 Efforts by the Ottoman Empire 25
2.18 Efforts in Egypt 26
2.19 Efforts in Saudi Arabia 26
2.20 Malaysia and other countries who adopted English law of contract 27
Notes 27

3 General Theory, nominate contract, freedom of contract and the juristic person 30

3.1 Nominate contracts 30
3.2 The general theory of contract 32
3.3 Freedom of contract 35
3.4 The juristic person 40
Notes 43

4 Key features of business and guiding principles of Islamic contract law 46

4.1 Key features of business 46
4.2 Earning a living 46
4.3 Moderation in earning 48
4.4 Freedom to work 49
4.5 Creation of wealth 49
4.6 Sharing personal resources 50
4.7 Timely payment of wages 50
4.8 Social welfare 51
4.9 Justice and benevolence 52
4.10 Guiding principles of Islamic contract law 54
4.11 God-made laws 54
4.12 Mutual consent is necessary 55
4.13 Sanctity of contracts 55
4.14 Awareness of rights and duties 55
4.15 Principle of general permissibility 56
4.16 Justice, equity and equality 56
4.17 Prevention of violence and excessive gains 57
4.18 Removal of difficulty 57
4.19 The prohibition of *riba* (interest) 58

4.20 The prohibition of *gharar* (risk) 59
4.21 The prohibition of *Maysir* (gambling) 59
4.22 The prohibition of fraud and cheating 59
4.23 The prohibition of two mutually inconsistent contracts 59
4.24 A contract should not be contrary to Maqasid al-Shariah 59
4.25 The prohibition of dealing in certain forbidden commodities 60
4.26 Prohibition of trickery in contracts 60
4.27 Encourage and development of business 61
4.28 Principle of profits and loss sharing 61
4.29 Public welfare and no exploitation 61
Notes 62

5 Meaning and definition of contract in Islamic law 65

5.1 Literal and lexiconic meaning 65
5.2 Legal and juristic meaning 66
5.3 Technical and jurisprudential definition of aqd 66
5.4 "Contract" as defined in different codes of Islamic countries 68
5.5 Some similar terms to aqd 69
5.6 Distinction between contracts and some other terms 70
5.7 Sunnah basis of contract 75
5.8 Purposes of the Shariah *doctrines of contract 77*
Notes 79

6 Constitution or formation of a valid contract 83

6.1 Essential elements of a contract 83
Notes 97

7 Parties and their legal capacities 100

7.1 Introduction 100
7.2 Classification of Ahliyyah or different aspects of Ahliyyah 100
7.3 Ahliyyah al-Wujub 101
7.4 Types of Ahliyyah al-Wajub 101
7.5 Ahliyyah al-Ada' 101
7.6 Types of Ahliyyah al-Ada 102
7.7 The stages of capacity under Islamic law 103
7.8 How to determine the capacity 104

7.9 *Division of capacity for the purpose of transactions* 105
7.10 *Circumstances or factors which prevent the legal capacity of a person* 106
Notes 109

8 Subject matter 110

8.1 *Conditions for a valid subject matter* 110
8.2 *Subject matter should be fit for transaction* 110
8.3 *It should be a "property" or "usufruct"* 111
8.4 *It should have some value* 111
8.5 *It should be ownable* 111
8.6 *No charge should be attached* 111
8.7 *Existence of subject matter* 112
8.8 *Possession and deliverability of subject matter* 113
8.9 *Knowledge of the subject matter* 114
8.10 *By inspection or examining* 114
8.11 *By description* 115
8.12 *Legality or suitability of subject matter* 115
8.13 *The object of a contract* 115
Notes 116

9 Mutual consent and intention to create legal relationship 117

9.1 *Free mutual consent* 117
9.2 *Literal meanings* 117
9.3 *Definition* 118
9.4 *Consent under Islamic law of contract* 118
9.5 *Qur'ānic and Sunnah basis of mutual consent* 118
9.6 *Ways/modes to express the consent* 119
9.7 *Factors which vitiate the mutual consent* 121
9.8 *Intention to create legal relation* 122
9.9 *Offer and acceptance* 124
9.10 *Free will (*iradah*)* 124
9.11 *Choice (*khiyar*)* 124
Notes 125

10 Vitiating factors 127

10.1 *Mistakes* 127
10.2 *Literal meaning* 127
10.3 *Definitions of mistake* 128
10.4 *Qur'ānic and Sunnah basis of mistake* 128

10.5 Classification of mistake 128
10.6 Legal effects of the contractual mistake 128
10.7 Rendering the contract void 128
10.8 Rendering the contract voidable 129
10.9 Misrepresentation 130
10.10 Qur'ānic verses regarding misrepresentation 130
10.11 Kinds of misrepresentation 130
10.12 Legal effect of misrepresentation 131
*10.13 Coercion (*ikrah*) 131*
10.14 Literal meaning 131
10.15 Definitions 132
10.16 Qur'ānic verses regarding coercion 132
10.17 Ahadith *regarding coercion 133*
10.18 Conditions for the presence of coercion in a contract 133
10.19 Kinds of ikrah *134*
10.20 Effects of a contract under coercion 134
Notes 135

11 Forbidden elements 137

11.1 Introduction 137
11.2 The relation between purposes and prohibitions in Islamic law of contract 137
11.3 Usury/*riba 138*
11.4 Gharar *146*
11.5 Qimar *and* maysir *(gambling) 151*
11.6 Fraud and cheating 154
11.7 The contracts contrary to maqasid al-Shariah *166*
11.8 Two mutually inconsistent contracts or contingent contracts 167
Notes 170

12 Classification of contract 175

12.1 Classifications of the contract according to its nature 175
12.2 Unilateral contract ('aqd infiradi*) 175*
12.3 Bilateral contract ('aqd thuna'i*) 176*
12.4 Multilateral contracts 177
*12.5 Quasi-contract (*shibh al-'aqd*) 178*
12.6 Classification of a contract according to its legal consequences 178
12.7 Classification of contracts about the time of completion 182

12.8 Classification according to the purpose of contracts 183
Notes 184

13 Cessation and dissolution of contract 186

13.1 Introduction 186
13.2 Dissolution of a contract 186
13.3 Cessation of contract by performance 187
*13.4 Cessation of contract by assignment of debt (*hawalah*) 188*
*13.5 Dissolution of contract by mutual agreement (*iqalah*) 189*
13.6 Dissolution of a contract automatically 189
*13.7 Dissolution by revocation and termination (*al-Faskh*) 190*
13.8 Unilateral revocation of contract 191
*13.9 Dissolution for the impossibility of performance of the contract (*istihalah*) 192*
Notes 193

14 System of options under contract 195

14.1 Introduction 195
14.2 Kinds of options 196
14.3 Khiyar al-majlis *(during the sitting/meeting) 196*
14.4 When the parties declare their approval of the contract 197
14.5 Jurists view regarding khiyar al-majlis *197*
14.6 Khiyar al-shart *(option of condition) 198*
14.7 Contract in which khiyar al-shart *is applicable 198*
14.8 Contracts in which khiyar al-shart *is not applicable 198*
14.9 For whom the option is stipulated 199
14.10 Period of khiyar al-shart *199*
14.11 Effect of the contract with khiyar al-shart *200*
14.12 End of the option 200
14.13 Khiyar al-ru'yat *(option of viewing) 200*
14.14 Contracts in which khiyar al-ru'yat *is applicable 201*
14.15 Opinions of jurists regarding option of viewing 201
14.16 Effects of the option of viewing 202
14.17 Khiyar al-'aib *(option of the defect) 202*
14.18 Conditions for exercising the option of defect 203
14.19 Effects of the option of defect 204
Notes 204

15 Remedies for breach of contract 207

15.1 Rescission 207
15.2 Difference between rescission and repudiation 208

15.3 Grounds for rescission 208
15.4 Damages 209
15.5 Kinds of damages 209
15.6 Specific performance 210
15.7 Injunctions 211
15.8 Restitutionary remedies 211
15.9 Quantum meruit *211*
Notes 211

16 Some important contracts 213

16.1 Contract of sale 213
16.2 Conditions for validity of sale contract 213
16.3 Kinds of sale transactions 214
16.4 Musharakah—*the contract of partnership 214*
16.5 Mudarabah—*limited partnership 216*
16.6 Murabahah—*deferred payment sale 218*
16.7 Ijara—*Contract of Lease 219*
16.8 Sukuk—*issuer's certificates 221*
16.9 Takaful—*contract of insurance 222*
16.10 Istisna—*contract of manufacturing 230*
16.11 Contract of salam *231*
16.12 Contract of partnership 233
16.13 Contract of agency 234
16.14 Contract of arbitration 234
16.15 Contract of gift 234
16.16 Contract of suretyship 235
16.17 Contract of guarantee 235
16.18 C.I.F. contract 235
16.19 F.O.B. contract 236
16.20 Contract of mortgage or bailment 236
16.21 Contract of compromise 237
16.22 Contract of employment 238
Notes 238

Bibliography 243
Index 251

Introduction

Writing on the subject of law in general and Islamic law in particular is a technical and difficult project. We took the initiative to write a comprehensive masterpiece entitled *Islamic Financial Contracts: A Research Companion* and this book is in your hands by our joint efforts.

A number of classical and modern works and scattered literature in Arabic in the field of Islamic law of contract are available written by great Islamic jurists. Among them are Dr. Wahabah al-Zuhaili, Dr. Abdul Razaq al-Sanhuri, Dr. Husain Hamid Hasan, Mustafa Ahmad al-Zarqa, Imam Muhammad Abu Zahra, Abd al-Salam Madkur, Dr. Abd al-Karim Zaydan, Dr. Yusuf Musa and many other scholars.

A very few works were also developed in English by some orientalists. But unfortunately, they have tried to degrade Islamic concepts of contract law in their literature in "sugar-coated style." They have tried to bracket the pure legal, financial, commercial, social, economic and political works of Islam within the religious aspect only. Among them are Anderson, N.J. Coulson, Joseph Schacht, Baillie, Dr. E.S. Rayner etc. There are also some contributions made by a few Islamic scholars in this field in English, namely, Prof. Dr. Abdur Rahman I. Doi, Dr. Liaqat Ali Khan Niazi, S. Sitti Salwani, Dr. Masum Billah, Dr. Muhammad Tahir Mansuri, Dr. Ala' eddin Kharofa and so on. Muhammad Masum Billah has also mentioned some of these names in the preface of his book.

Students often face conceptual difficulties in learning and understanding the complex concepts of contracts and other areas of commercial and business law. This handbook of Islamic business and financial contracts is written with the aim of setting out, in a manner that can be easily understood and explaining in greater depth the more challenging and misunderstood areas particularly of the Islamic law of contract. An attempt has been made to produce a write-up that could serve as a reference book for students and all others who have a desire to understand the principles and different concepts of Islamic business and financial contracts. However, this book is not intended to be the last word.

In preparation of this book, we benefited basically from the Holy Qur'ān and Sunnah and from traditional classical works of jurists on Islamic jurisprudence and the academic literature available on Islamic contract law and business transactions. References have also been made from classical contract texts and articles written by different modern authors relevant to each area of the Islamic law of contract. The works of orientalists have also been consulted.

It is hoped that this book will be a useful contribution to the Islamic legal literature and more importantly to the Islamic law of contract in Pakistan. It is our hope that this book will be beneficial for practitioners, legal and judicial officers along with those in academia. It may be taken as a text book for students studying Islamic law of contract in their BS programme in Islamic Banking and Finance and as a handy reference on the basic principles of the Islamic law of contract.

All praise be to Allah u whose help and guidance has sustained us to bring this 1st edition of the book. We pray to the Almighty Allah for His acceptance of this humble effort, related to Islamic concepts and knowledge of the Shariah in business and commercial dealings and to make this work a useful addition in Islamic contract law.

0.1 Scheme of the chapters

The book has been divided into 16 chapters in order to have a synoptic and comprehensive view of Islamic law of contract.

The first chapter provides an introduction to Islamic concept of law. It also deals with some important legal terminologies of Islamic jurisprudence, such as *fiqh*, Shariah and jurisprudence.

The second chapter presents a detailed discussion on the historical development of Islamic contract law and the common law of contract. This chapter also deals with the concept of codification of Islamic contract of law.

The third chapter attempts to provide an overview of the generally misunderstood concepts of Islamic law of contract such as general theory, nominate contract, freedom of contract and juristic person.

The fourth chapter attempts to provide an overview of the key features of business and guiding principles of Islamic contract law. The eight most important key features of business and commerce in Islam along with 19 guiding principles for making contracts in Islam are discussed with Qur'ānic and Sunnah proofs.

The fifth chapter provides the meanings and definitions of contract in Islamic law. Eleven definitions defined by classic and modern jurists have been collected along with definitions defined in codes of eight different Islamic countries. Twenty-four Qur'ānic verses and 13 *ahadith* related to concept of contracts in Islam have also been selected.

The sixth chapter deals with the constitution or formation of contract and essential elements of a valid contract. A detailed discussion has been made on *sigha*, i.e. offer and acceptance as the first and most important element to constitute a valid contract in Islamic law of contract.

The seventh chapter goes deeply into the details of the contracting parties and their legal capacities to enter into a valid contract. In this chapter, classification of legal capacity, the different stages of capacity and its determination and circumstances which prevent the legal capacity are discussed.

The eighth chapter discusses the subject matter of Islamic law of contract which is a vital element of a valid contract. Conditions for valid subject matter are also discussed in detail.

The ninth chapter discusses in detail the core element of mutual consent of the contracting parties along with the intention to create a legal relationship between the parties. The Qur'ānic and Sunnah basis of mutual consent, modes of expressing, and factors which vitiate the mutual consent are also discussed.

The tenth chapter deals with vitiating factors which may affect the performance of a contract, such as mistakes, misrepresentation and coercion etc.

The eleventh chapter goes deeply into dealing with forbidden or prohibited elements which make a contract void. The purpose of forbidden elements is discussed. *Riba* and its prohibition by Qur'ān and Sunnah, its kinds, *gharar* and its prohibition along with *qimar* and *maysir* are discussed, along with fraud and cheating and their prohibition by Qur'ān and Sunnah. Another four prohibited elements are also discussed.

The twelfth chapter discusses the classifications of a contract according to its nature, legal consequences, the time of its completion and according to the purpose of a contract. Their further subdivisions are also discussed.

The thirteenth chapter deals with the cessation and dissolution of a contract. In this chapter cessation of a contract by performance and by assigning of debt is discussed along with dissolution of contract by mutual agreement, automatically, by revocation and by the impossibility of performance. Similarly, termination of contract is also discussed.

The fourteenth chapter discusses a very critical topic, i.e. the system of options under Islamic law of contract. Only the four most important kinds of options—*khiyar-al-majlis*, *khiyar-al-shart*, *khiyar-al-ruy'at* and *khiyar-al-a'ib*—are discussed in detail.

The fifteenth chapter is the smallest chapter, consisting of remedies for breach of a contract in which rescission, damages, specific performance, injunctions and restitutionary remedies are discussed.

The sixteenth chapter is the last chapter of the book in which some important contracts are discussed. A total of 20 important contracts have been selected, such as contract of sale, contract of *musharakah*, contract of *mudarabah*, contract of *murabahah*, contract of *ijara*, contract of *Sukuk*, contract of *takaful*, contract of *istisna*, contract of *salam*, contract of partnership, contract of agency, contract of arbitration, contract of gift, contract of suretyship, contract of guarantee, C.I.F contract, F.O.B contract, contract of mortgage or bailment, compromise contract, contract of employment.

Hussain Mohi ud Din Qadri
Nasir Iqbal Qadri

1 Some basic legal terminologies and concepts

1.1 Concept of Islamic law

The expression "Islamic law" is commonly used in legal literature written in the English language to refer to four different Arabic terms, namely *fiqh*, *Shariah*, *qanun* and *urf.*[1] *Fiqh* has been loosely translated into English as "Islamic law" and so has *Shariah*, but these terms are not synonymous either in the Arabic language or to Muslim scholars.[2] Some authors refer it as "Islamic jurisprudence" and others confuse it with "ethics" of Islam by equating it with *Shariah*. "The general precept of the Islamic *Shariah* is conveniently referred to as a guide to moral conduct"[3] rather than a law that is enforceable in a court of justice. In our view, it is a misconception. The term Islamic law is a generic term, which may be applied to the whole set of laws connected to Islam. So it is necessary to understand some Arabic terms in their legal perspective as used in Islamic academic literature. As this book is not on the topic of Islamic law or Islamic jurisprudence, we will describe the terminologies very briefly but to the extent that the meanings of the terms are clarified. We begin with the term S*hariah.*

1.2 Shariah

Literally, the term *Shariah* means "the way", or "the clear path", which Muslims should follow to be guided rightly.[4] *Shariah* is an Arabic word meaning the path to be followed. Literally it means "the way to a watering place." It is the path not only leading to Allah, the Most High, but the path believed by all Muslims to be the path shown by Allah, the Creator Himself through His Messenger, Prophet Muhammad a.[5] "Shariat," says Sir Abdur Rahim, "which may be translated as the Islamic Code, means matters which would not have been known but for the communication made to us by the law-giver."[6] The *Shariah* itself is a vast network of injunctions and regulations which relate the world of multiplicity inwardly to a single centre which conversely is reflected in the multiplicity of the circumference.[7] In the theological discussion, the word *Shariah* is referred to as divine revelation *in toto*. It provides all humanity, of all nations, a multidimensional body (compendium) of faith and belief, and laws and regulations. So, in this way, it is viewed; *Shariah* as the embodiment of the "Divine Will", and God is seen as the "supreme legislator" whose laws sanctify human life.[8] In Islam, Allah alone is the sovereign, and it is He who has the right to ordain a path for the guidance of mankind.[9]

1.3 Qur'ānic basis of Shariah

In the Qur'ān it is mentioned, "He (Allah) has ordained (*Shariah*) for you the same religion (Islam) which He ordained for Noah, and that which We have inspired in you (O Muhammad) and that which We ordained for Abraham, Moses, and Jesus."[10] "To each among you We have prescribed a law (*Shariah*) and a clear way."[11] "Then We set you on the open path of *Shariah* in your affairs. So follow it persistently. And do not yield to the desires of those who are simply unaware (of the glory, dignity, and trueness of your Din [Religion])."[12]

Shariah is broadly classified into two strands: Ibadah (worship and devotional practices) and mu'amalat (civil transactions).[13] It is composed of abstract rules that are laid down in both the Qur'ān and the Sunnah of the Prophet Muhammad a. God has revealed these abstract rules to Prophet Muhammad a. The Prophet (PBUH) received and practised them in his own life, educating his companions, and also guiding the whole of humanity for the future. "Islamically, however it refers to the sum total of Islamic laws which were revealed to the Prophet Muhammad a, and which are recorded in the Qur'ān as well as deducible from the Prophet's divinely guided lifestyle (called the Sunnah)."[14] The *Shariah*, being a complete system of life and an all-embracing social order, prescribes directives for the regulation of all spheres of life, be it the individual or the collective life, religious, political, social or moral aspects of life. It encompasses the economic, administrative, judicial and criminal aspects of life, as well as the national and international life, including the questions of war and peace. It is an organic whole not to be isolated from its universal elements.[15] Islam signifies the entire scheme of life and not an isolated part or parts thereof.[16]

Hence the concept of *Shariah* is broader than the concept of law in its counterpart. The closest Islamic term to the modern concept of law is, however, the *fiqh* which includes legal interpretations that can be found in various academic books, fatwa, and court decisions.[17] The concept of *Shariah* in the Islamic legal system is unique as no such concept exists in any other legal system of the world. Since the *Shariah* is dynamic and evolving with the progressing society and culture, it has the power of adaptation, assimilation and modification, provided they are not in conflict with the spirit of the Qur'ān and Sunnah.[18]

1.4 Fiqh

The dictionary meaning of the term *fiqh* is understanding or knowledge. The word *fiqh* has been typically defined as "knowledge of practical revealed rulings extracted from detailed evidence" (*al-ilmu bi al-ahkam al-shariah al-amaliyyah min adillatiha al-tafsiliyyah*).[19] Thus, *fiqh* is related only to "practical" (*amaliyyah*) and not to the tents of faith, i.e. theological (*itiqadiyyah*) issues. Hence, *fiqh* is the knowledge of the *Shariah ahkam* (legal rules) pertaining to conduct, that has been derived from their specific evidence. The author of "Touzih" defines *fiqh* as

> the knowledge of laws (Ahkam) of the *Shariah* which are intended to be acted upon, and have been divulged to us by revelation of determined by concurrent decisions of the learned jurists, such knowledge being derived from the sources of law with the power of making current deductions therefrom.

Fiqh means a true understanding of what is intended. Jurists generally define *fiqh* as the outcome of human "understanding" (*fahm*)[20], "perception" (*tasawwur*),[21] and "cognition" (*idrak*)[22] in the form of derivations from defined sources of law, i.e. Qur'ān and Sunnah. Technically, however, *fiqh* refers to the science of deducing Islamic laws from evidence found in the sources of Islamic law. By extension, it also means the body of Islamic laws so deduced. Hence *fiqh* refers to the result of the human activity of exploration, interpretation, analysis and presentation of the textual sources of *Shariah* (detailed evidence).

In cases where there is no clear injunction or directives in the Qur'ān and Sunnah, jurists are allowed to legislate and use their faculties of juristic knowledge (*ijtihad*) to frame laws.[23] The *fiqh* is the further extension of *Shariah* (revealed in primary and secondary sources) which consists of legal research of jurists and the Islamic schools of law's wealth of heritage. The vast collection of laws in books of *fiqh* is based on juridical reasoning that was given by scholars and jurists from various schools of thought for their own environments and times in regard to the application of *Shariah* to real-life situations, issues and cases. The jurists derived the laws from the primary (Qur'ān and Sunnah) and other authentic (*ijma*, *qias*, etc.) sources of Islamic laws by adopting rigorous methods of derivations in the light of the principles given in Qur'ān and Sunnah for the derivation and legislation of laws.

1.5 Qur'ānic and Sunnah basis of fiqh

The word *fiqh* is used in the Qur'ān and *hadith* in various forms to refer to understanding, comprehension and gaining knowledge in general. Qur'ān says as:

وَمَا كَانَ ٱلْمُؤْمِنُونَ لِيَنفِرُوا۟ كَآفَّةً ۚ فَلَوْلَا نَفَرَ مِن كُلِّ فِرْقَةٍ مِّنْهُمْ طَآئِفَةٌ لِّيَتَفَقَّهُوا۟ فِي ٱلدِّينِ وَلِيُنذِرُوا۟ قَوْمَهُمْ
إِذَا رَجَعُوٓا۟ إِلَيْهِمْ لَعَلَّهُمْ يَحْذَرُونَ

> "And it is not possible for all the Muslims to set out (together). So, why should a party from within every group (or tribe) not go forth in order that they may acquire deeper knowledge (i.e., thorough understanding and insight) of the Din (Religion), and warn their people when they return to them so that they may guard themselves (against a life of sins and disobedience)?"[24]

Qur'ān further says:

وَمَا كَانَ ٱلْمُؤْمِنُونَ لِيَنفِرُوا۟ كَآفَّةً ۚ فَلَوْلَا نَفَرَ مِن كُلِّ فِرْقَةٍ مِّنْهُمْ طَآئِفَةٌ لِّيَتَفَقَّهُوا۟ فِى ٱلدِّينِ وَلِيُنذِرُوا۟ قَوْمَهُمْ إِذَا رَجَعُوٓا۟ إِلَيْهِمْ لَعَلَّهُمْ يَحْذَرُونَ

"Say: '(In fact,) all comes from Allah.' So, what has gone wrong with these people that they do not feel inclined to understand anything?"[25]

At another place, Qur'ān says:

وَمِنْهُم مَّن يَسْتَمِعُ إِلَيْكَ ۖ وَجَعَلْنَا عَلَىٰ قُلُوبِهِمْ أَكِنَّةً أَن يَفْقَهُوهُ وَفِىٓ ءَاذَانِهِمْ وَقْرًا ۚ وَإِن يَرَوْا۟ كُلَّ ءَايَةٍ لَّا يُؤْمِنُوا۟ بِهَا ۚ حَتَّىٰٓ إِذَا جَآءُوكَ يُجَٰدِلُونَكَ يَقُولُ ٱلَّذِينَ كَفَرُوٓا۟ إِنْ هَٰذَآ إِلَّآ أَسَٰطِيرُ ٱلْأَوَّلِينَ

"And amongst them are (also) some who keep their ears towards you, and (in view of their evil intentions). We have wrapped their hearts in veils. (So, it is not possible for them now) that they may understand it (the Qur'an) and (We have) plugged their ears."[26]

At another place Qur'ān says:

قُلُوبٌ لَّا يَفْقَهُونَ بِهَا وَلَهُمْ أَعْيُنٌ لَّا يُبْصِرُونَ

"They have hearts wherewith they understand not."[27]

The concept of *fiqh* also narrated in Qur'ān as under:

أَفَلَا يَتَدَبَّرُونَ ٱلْقُرْءَانَ ۚ وَلَوْ كَانَ مِنْ عِندِ غَيْرِ ٱللَّهِ لَوَجَدُوا۟ فِيهِ ٱخْتِلَٰفًا كَثِيرًا

"Do they not ponder over the Qur'an? Had this (Qur'an) come from anyone other than Allah, these people would have found in it many contradictions."[28]

يُؤْتِى ٱلْحِكْمَةَ مَن يَشَآءُ ۚ وَمَن يُؤْتَ ٱلْحِكْمَةَ فَقَدْ أُوتِىَ خَيْرًا كَثِيرًا ۗ وَمَا يَذَّكَّرُ إِلَّآ أُو۟لُوا۟ ٱلْأَلْبَٰبِ

"He blesses with wisdom whom He wills. Moreover, he who is granted wisdom (and reason) receives tremendous good. And only those who are endowed with wisdom and insight receive direction and guidance."[29]

An example of this usage can be found in the *Ahadith* also. The Holy Prophet Muhammad a said: "To whomsoever Allah wishes good, He gives the Fiqh (true understanding) of the religion."[30]

The Holy Prophet (PBUH) while praying for His cousin Abdullah ibn Abbas; said **اللهم فقه فى الدين** O Allah! Bless him with the understanding of religion.[31]

"Fiqh, according to traditional authorities, is knowledge of the practical regulations and rules of the *Shariah* acquired by reference to and detailed study of the sources." "The detailed practical rules derived by reasoning from the corpus of *Shariah* are known as Fiqh."[32]

Fiqh is distinct from *Shariah*. "*Shariah* is the wider circle; it embraces in its orbit all human actions. *Fiqh* is the narrow one and deals with what is commonly understood as legal aspects."[33]

1.6 Islamic jurisprudence

It is defined as فهو العلم بالاحكام الشرعية من ادلتها التفصيلية "It is knowledge of the laws of *Shariah*, relating to men's acts and derived from specific sources."[34] According to Maliki jurists, "it is the science of the commands (laws) of the *Shariah* in particular matters deduced by the application of a process of reasoning."[35]

> Islamic jurisprudence is a broader term that is applied to mean all that is covered by Islamic law. It is sometimes applied to mean the study of *usul al-fiqh* or legal theory. This restricted application of the term emphasises the importance of the discipline of *usul al-fiqh* because *usul al-fiqh* is indispensable for the study, practice, and teaching of Islamic law and is also a prerequisite to the study of *tafsir* and *hadith.* If it is to be confined to issues covered by *usul al-fiqh,* it may be titled as 'Islamic Legal Theory.' The term includes both *usul* and *fiqh,* i.e. legal theory, legal concepts, and substantive and procedural law.[36]

The term *usul al-fiqh* is broken up into its two components—*usul* and *fiqh*—and by understanding their meaning, we understand the meaning of Islamic jurisprudence. The term *fiqh* we have already explained. Now we explain the term *usul.*

The term *usul* is the plural of "*asl*". The literal meaning of the "*asl*" is "something from which another one originates". Thus, the origin of a thing is its *asl.* Technically, the term *usul* here means principles. These may also be referred to as *qawa'id.* There are several types of principles, but here it means principles used for the interpretation of the texts of the Qur'ān and the Sunnah. Thus, the term *usul al-fiqh* means the principles of interpretation used to derive the knowledge of the legal rules of conduct from the specific evidence. Muslim jurists define the term as follows:

> They are the principles by the use of which the *mujtahid* arrives, through the specific evidence, at the legal rules of conduct.

This definition states that the *usul al-fiqh* is a body of principles of interpretation by the help of which the *mujtahid* can derive the law from the detailed evidence in the Qur'ān, the Sunnah, *ijma'* and *qiyas.*[37]

It is also worth noting here that Muslims were the pioneers in the known world in the field of science of law. In the West, jurisprudence was seriously treated as science only in the 18th century. In Islam, it had acquired that status by the end of the second century *Hijra* viz. about 1,200 years ago.[38]

According to Anwar A. Qadri "The science of Islamic jurisprudence is considered as an evergreen system, vigorous and vital in nature and features. It has a methodology out of which solutions for new problems of law in the light of changes in people's habits and modes of living can be drawn".[39]

The Muslim scholars worked very hard for jurisprudence. Especially Imam Abu Hanifah, along with his disciples compiled judicial works that are unparalleled in the world. Even the British jurists could not compete with this school. That is why Imam Abu Hanifah is regarded as one of the greatest jurists. He possessed a remarkable power of reasoning and deduction. The other three Imams, viz Malik, Shafi and Ahmad bin Hanbal were also endowed with talents of an exceptional nature. They enjoyed an excellent reputation as jurists. Due to the combined efforts of the above-noted Imams, it can be safely said that Islamic jurisprudence has become more scientific than British jurisprudence.[40]

1.7 Islamic concept of law

The literal meaning of the word "law" is "foundation" or "root": root of every knowledge, rule or "*dastur*". The word "*Kanun*" has Greek origin.[41] In Arabic, this word was used in the sense of "foot-rule". Dr. Sobhi Mahmassani writes "In Arabic *qanun* means the measurement of everything. From this meaning the general use, denoting any law, lato sensu, was derived, so one can say, 'the laws (*qawanin*) of health' and 'the laws of nature' etc.".[42]

The expression "law", in Islamic legal terminology, signifies the word "Hukm" or "Hukm-i-Shari", which is defined as:

> Law is a rule of human conduct established by a communication from God, expressive either of demand or indifference or mere declaration.[43]

The term "*Hukm*" does not signify the words and the letters literally contained in the commandments of Allah, communicated in the form of Qur'ān. It is the rule or legal value established by the communications of Allah. The "*Hukm*", in its exact technical sense, is "what is established by communication, not the communication itself (words of communication)".[44]

The same is expressed by Mahalli in Shahrah Jam il Jawame by Qazi Azd-ud-Din in Sharh-ul-Mukhtasar, by Asnawi in Sharh-ul-Minhaj, by Amidi in Sharh-ul-Haj, by Amidi in Al-Ihkam, by Fazil Qarabaghi, Allama Bihari, Qanuji and many other authorities on Islamic jurisprudence.

It is pertinent to mention here that what is the established from the communication from God does not mean only explicit text of Qur'ān, but all legal rules and juristic values based upon Prophet's Sunnah and definite *Ijma* and other authentic sources of Islamic law are also included. Hence the standard definition of "law" in Islamic legal science is that "Any rule, established, directly or indirectly from the communication of Allah, which pertains to human acts, whether it be to demand a choice between alternative or a simple declaration is known as *Hukm* or 'law'."[45]

It is worth noting here that a law or a legal system is a system of communication that is also recognised in the modern age though the Emitter or the Communicator may be different.[46] In the case of the Islamic legal system, the Emitter or Communicator is "Allah", and in the case of its counterpart, the Emitter may be King or any other sovereign or body so authorised.

Therefore, the "law" in Islamic concept is a body of rules regarding human conduct, established:

From Qur'ān (because it is an explicit and manifest version of Allah's communication);

From "Prophetic Sunnah" (because it is an implicit version, practical denotation and physical demonstration of Allah's communications); and

From "Definite *Ijma"*, (because it is an authoritative device of knowing and inferring what has been divinely communicated to humanity). This also included other authentic sources of Islamic law.

In Islamic legal science, the concept of "law" is unanimous among all the jurists and the schools of law right from early periods till today. No dichotomy or conflict of opinion upon this issue exists in Islam. Therefore, in Islamic jurisprudence, the term "law" possesses a permanent and universal character, which is not subject to any alteration,[47] as opposed to its counterpart, where there exists no single definition of the word "law".

1.8 The significance of trade and commerce in Islam

Islam is a holistic way of life for the whole of humanity as it caters to spiritual and worldly needs. The importance is attached to commerce and trade in the Qur'ān and the Prophetic Sunnah. The Qur'ān gives clear directives and regulations for running businesses. The Messenger a himself demonstrated the worth of trade by choosing it as an occupation.

Before the arrival of Islam, an Abrahamic monotheistic religion, many Arabs were traders. Qur'ān describes the trade journeys of the Arabs in various seasons as Divine grace towards them. The social and economic prosperity of the people of Mecca depended on their trading caravans. Their two annual trade caravans, one to Yemen in the winter and the other to Syria in the summer, have been described.

لِإِيلَٰفِ قُرَيْشٍ ١ إِۦلَٰفِهِمْ رِحْلَةَ ٱلشِّتَآءِ وَٱلصَّيْفِ ٢ فَلْيَعْبُدُوا۟ رَبَّ هَٰذَا ٱلْبَيْتِ ٣ ٱلَّذِىٓ أَطْعَمَهُم مِّن جُوعٍ
وَءَامَنَهُم مِّنْ خَوْفٍۭ ٤

> "To awake drive amongst the Quraysh, they were acclimatized to the summer and the winter (commercial) trips. So they should worship the Lord of this (Sacred) House (Ka'ba, to give Him thanks), who has fed them in hunger (i.e, provided them sustenance in starving conditions) and secured them from fear (of foes i.e, blessed them with secure and peaceful life)".[48]

The Allah Almighty also says وَوَجَدَكَ عَآئِلًا فَأَغْنَىٰ

> "And He found you seeking (closeness with your Lord), and (then blessed you with the pleasure of His sight and) freed you of every need (forever). Or And He found you compassionate and benevolent, then (through you) made the destitute non-liable."

The following verse is also an excellent example of choosing to trade as a career.

يَٰٓأَيُّهَا ٱلَّذِينَ ءَامَنُوا۟ لَا تَأْكُلُوٓا۟ أَمْوَٰلَكُم بَيْنَكُم بِٱلْبَٰطِلِ إِلَّآ أَن تَكُونَ تِجَٰرَةً عَن تَرَاضٍ مِّنكُمْ ۚ وَلَا تَقْتُلُوٓا۟ أَنفُسَكُمْ ۚ

> "O believers! Do not devour one another's wealth unlawfully amongst yourselves unless it is a trade by your mutual agreement and do not kill yourselves. Surely, Allah is Kind to you."[49]

Another verse urges the Muslims to seek Allah's grace—that is, trade and business.

فَإِذَا قُضِيَتِ ٱلصَّلَوٰةُ فَٱنتَشِرُوا۟ فِى ٱلْأَرْضِ وَٱبْتَغُوا۟ مِن فَضْلِ ٱللَّهِ وَٱذْكُرُوا۟ ٱللَّهَ كَثِيرًا لَّعَلَّكُمْ تُفْلِحُونَ

> "Then after the prayer is offered, disperse in the land and (then) look for Allah's bounty (i.e., sustenance). And remember Allah much so that you may attain prosperity."[50]

Even after performing pilgrimage (hajj), it is allowed that Muslims may engage in sale, purchase and trade to fulfil the necessities of life. On deriving material benefit from the hajj activity, Allah says in the Qur'ān:

لَيْسَ عَلَيْكُمْ جُنَاحٌ أَن تَبْتَغُوا۟ فَضْلًا مِّن رَّبِّكُمْ ۚ فَإِذَآ أَفَضْتُم مِّنْ عَرَفَٰتٍ فَٱذْكُرُوا۟ ٱللَّهَ عِندَ ٱلْمَشْعَرِ ٱلْحَرَامِ ۖ
وَٱذْكُرُوهُ كَمَا هَدَىٰكُمْ وَإِن كُنتُم مِّن قَبْلِهِۦ لَمِنَ ٱلضَّآلِّينَ

> "And it is no sin on you if you (also) seek your Lord's bounty (through trade during the Hajj days). Then when you return from 'Arafat, celebrate the remembrance of Allah near Mash'ar al-Haram (Muzdalifa). And remember Him as He has guided you. And you were certainly wandering disorientated before."[51]

Ibn 'Abbas (R.A) reported:

> Dhu al-Majaz and 'Ukaz were the markets of the people in the time of ignorance. When Islam came, people did not really like to trade in them until it was revealed: And it is no sin on you if you (also) seek your Lord's bounty (through trade during the hajj days) [Qur'ān 2:198] in the hajj festival.[52]

It is worth mentioning here that seeing the optimum economic, strategic and diplomatic potential in the hajj season, Muslim governments should organise and manage this activity as a large-scale project. Not only does the hajj stimulate various economic sectors in Muslim lands, but the centrality of the Ka'ba contributes to anchoring the Muslim community in a world of increasing globalisation and cross-border financial transactions. Moreover, the economics of the hajj may play a decisive role in strengthening relations and fostering brotherhood among the Muslim countries.

It has been observed that when the hajj is celebrated, through its impact on investors' sentiments, it boosts the stock market as well.

Prophetic traditions also place emphasis on the significance of trade and merchants; some of these are:

Rafi' b. Khadij (R.A) narrated that Allah's Messenger a was asked, "What type of earning is best?" He replied: "A man's work with his hand and every business transaction that is approved."[53]

According to Jabir b. 'Abd Allah (R.A), Allah's Messenger a said:

> "May Allah show mercy to a man who is lenient when he sells, lenient when he buys and lenient when he asks for payment!"[54]

According to Sakhr al-Ghamidi , Allah's Messenger said:

> "Allah, bless my nation in their early morning!"
>
> He (the narrator) said: "Sakhr was a trader, and he used to send his goods out at the beginning of the day, and his wealth grew and increased."[55]

Once Allah's Messenger a saw the people doing business, so he said: "People of the trade!" and they replied to him, turning their necks and their gazes towards him, and he said:

> "Indeed the merchants will be resurrected on the Day of Resurrection with the wicked, except the one who has a fear of Allah, who behaves charitably and is truthful."[56]

'Umar b. al-Khattab (R.A) narrated that the Messenger a said:

> "The importer is blessed with the provision and the hoarder is cursed."[57]

Ibn 'Abbas (R.A) reported that Allah's Messenger a said there are 20 ways of making a livelihood. Nineteen of them are inclusively for traders, and only one way is open to industrialists.[58]

1.9 Underlying philosophy of commercial transaction in Islam

As we know, all human beings are also social beings and are not self-sufficient to fulfil all their needs individually without help from others. Honourable livelihood is the essential need of human beings to live and lead a practical life. Many people complain of a paucity of resources and find it challenging to live within their means. For this, they need to interact, trade and cooperate with each other. They also need to make and develop relations between them based upon business transactions and matters of debt and credit etc. Commercial activities are vital for fulfilling one's responsibilities and reducing destitution in society.

The underlying philosophy of commercial transactions in Islamic commercial law is to encourage lawful earning through recognising the right to earn a livelihood. Qur'ān says:

أَحَلَّ ٱللَّهُ ٱلْبَيْعَ وَحَرَّمَ ٱلرِّبَوٰا۟

"Allāh u has declared trading (buying and selling) lawful and riba unlawful."[59]

Similarly, seeking good things in the life of this world in addition to the life after death is endorsed in Qur'ān:

وَمِنْهُم مَّن يَقُولُ رَبَّنَآ ءَاتِنَا فِي ٱلدُّنْيَا حَسَنَةً وَفِي ٱلْأَخِرَةِ حَسَنَةً وَقِنَا عَذَابَ ٱلنَّارِ

> "And there are others of them who submit: 'O our Lord, grant us excellence in this world, and excellence in the Hereafter (as well), and save us from the torment of Hell.'"[60]

A renowned author named A.E. Libber states: "Islam is perhaps the one great religion which affords the merchant a highly honoured place in society."[61] Another author commented that

> there are religions whose sacred texts discourage economic activity in general, counselling their followers to rely on God to provide them with their daily bread, or more particularly, looking askance at any striving for profit. This is certainly not the case with the Koran, which looks with favour upon commercial activity.[62]

People are encouraged to earn a living through lawful means to cater for both their mundane wellbeing and their livelihood. Islam encourages business transactions to secure the basic needs for all human beings, and these should be within the general ambit of permissibility transactions in order to effectively manage the resources that God has bestowed upon the world.[63] Similarly, regardless of a person's gender, Islam gives an unfettered right to the acquisition of property to all, subject to the general rules of the *Shariah*. As the propensity to earn or acquire property is an innate character of humans generally, Islam regulates this right for the benefit of all. The regulations placed on lawful earnings in Islam are not meant to retain the legitimate acquisition of property but are there to guide people in the proper manner to do so to avoid rancour and chaos in society.[64]

The right to earn legitimate earnings through wages or doing business transactions is embedded in the higher objectives of the *Shariah*. This right was conferred on everyone—male and female—more than 1,400 years ago through the divine legislation in the Qur'ān and Sunnah. Men and women are considered equal in matters of this kind; both have the right to enter into lawful transactions through contracts that are in accordance with the general principle of the *Shariah*.[65] The Qur'ān says:

وَلَا تَتَمَنَّوْاْ مَا فَضَّلَ ٱللَّهُ بِهِۦ بَعْضَكُمْ عَلَىٰ بَعْضٍۚ لِّلرِّجَالِ نَصِيبٌ مِّمَّا ٱكْتَسَبُواْۖ وَلِلنِّسَآءِ نَصِيبٌ مِّمَّا
ٱكْتَسَبْنَۚ وَسْـَٔلُواْ ٱللَّهَ مِن فَضْلِهِۦٓۚ إِنَّ ٱللَّهَ كَانَ بِكُلِّ شَيْءٍ عَلِيمًا

> "And do not long for the thing in which Allah has made some of you superior to others. Men will have a share of what they earn, and women will have a share of what they earn, and keep begging Allah for His bounty. Surely, Allah knows best everything."[66]

This verse clearly explains that people have the right to earn legitimate means of livelihood. The next verse reveals how Allah Almighty rewards those who are vigilant about the affairs of both worlds.

أُوْلَٰٓئِكَ لَهُمۡ نَصِيبٞ مِّمَّا كَسَبُواْۚ وَٱللَّهُ سَرِيعُ ٱلۡحِسَابِ

> "It is they for whom there is a share of their (virtuous) earning, and Allah is Swift at reckoning."[67]

It is the Divine intention that humans should look for means of sustenance on land and sea. The Sustainer subjected canals, seas, rivers and oceans to them. The treasures of the deep waters, as well as the marine creatures, are there for human benefit. Furthermore, we may get numerous other benefits from the great body of water that covers a large portion of the earth. Regarding the beneficial nature of natural streams of water, Allah says:

ٱللَّهُ ٱلَّذِي خَلَقَ ٱلسَّمَٰوَٰتِ وَٱلۡأَرۡضَ وَأَنزَلَ مِنَ ٱلسَّمَآءِ مَآءٗ فَأَخۡرَجَ بِهِۦ مِنَ ٱلثَّمَرَٰتِ رِزۡقٗا لَّكُمۡۖ وَسَخَّرَ لَكُمُ
ٱلۡفُلۡكَ لِتَجۡرِيَ فِي ٱلۡبَحۡرِ بِأَمۡرِهِۦۖ وَسَخَّرَ لَكُمُ ٱلۡأَنۡهَٰرَ

> "Allah is He Who created the heavens and the earth and poured down water from the sky and then by means of this water produced fruits for you as provision. And He has made vessels subservient to you so that they may sail in the sea by Allah's command, and He has (also) put rivers under your control."[68]

The following *hadith* highlights the significance of earning one's keep. The Prophet (PBUH) said if someone enters the morning tired as a result of working (diligently) with his hands, his sins are pardoned.[69] This also has been explained by the Prophet (PBUH). Rafi' ibn khadij narrated:

"It was said: 'O Messenger of Allāh a what kind of earning is best?' He said: 'For a man to work with his hands and every honest transaction'." In another narration, Al-Miqdām (R.A) reported that Allah's Messenger a said:

مَا أَكَلَ أَحَدٌ طَعَامًا قَطُّ خَيْرًا مِنْ أَنْ يَأْكُلَ مِنْ عَمَلِ يَدِهِ وَإِنَّ نَبِيَّ اللَّهِ دَاوُدَ عَلَيْهِ السَّلَام كَانَ يَأْكُلُ مِنْ
عَمَلِ يَدِهِ

> "No one eats any better food than someone who eats from what he earns by the work of his own hands. Allah's Prophet, Dāwūd (peace be upon him), used to eat from what he earned by the work of his own hands."[70]

Notes

1 Muhammad Abdul Khaliq Omar, Reasoning in Islamic law, 3rd ed. (Cairo: M. Omar, 1999).
2 Dr. Abu Ameenah Bilal Philips, The Evolution of Fiqh, p. 1.
3 Ahmad bin Mohamed Ibrahim, Sources and development of Muslim law, p. 1 (1965).
4 Muhammad Hashim Kamali, Shariah law: An introduction, 2008, p. 14.
5 Abdur Rahman I. Doi, Shariah: The Islamic law, p. 2.

6 Sir Abdur Rahim, The principles of Muhammadan jurisprudence, p. 50.
7 Seyyed Hossein Nasr, Sufi essays 43 (1999).
8 Muhammad Hashim Kamali, Shariah law: An introduction, 2008, p. 14.
9 Sayyid Qutb, Hadha al-Din (this religion of Islam), USA, I.I.F.S.O. Publication, undated, p. 19.
10 Qur'ān, 5:48 (English translation from 'Glorious Qur'ān' by Shaykh-ul-Islam Dr. Muhammad Tahir-ul-Qadri).
11 Qur'ān, 42:13 (English translation from 'Glorious Qur'ān' by Shaykh-ul-Islam Dr. Muhammad Tahir-ul-Qadri).
12 Qur'ān, 45:18 (English translation from 'Glorious Qur'ān' by Shaykh-ul-Islam Dr. Muhammad Tahir-ul-Qadri).
13 M. Kabir Hassan, Rasem N. Kayed & Umar A. Oseni, Introduction to Islamic banking and finance, principles and practice, p. 4.
14 Muhammad Shalabee, al-Madkhal fee at-Ta'reef bil-Fiqh al-Islaamee, p. 28.
15 Syed Habibul Haq Nadvi, Islamic legal philosophy and the Qur'ānic origins of the Islamic law, p. 26.
16 Khurshid Ahmad, Ed. *The Islamic law*, p. 19.
17 Bernard Weiss, Interpretation in Islamic law: The theory of Ijtihad, (1978) The American Journal of comparative law, 203.
18 Syed Habibul Haq Nadvi, Islamic legal philosophy and the Qur'ānic origins of the Islamic law, p. 189.
19 Muhammad Abu Zahra, 'Usul al-Fiqh (Cairo: Dar al-Fikr al-Arabi, 1958), p. 5.
20 Ibn Taymiyah, Kutub wa Rasa'il wa Fatwa (Books, Letters and Legal Opinions), vol. 13, p. 113.
21 Al-Subki, Al-Ibhai fi Sharh al-Minhaj, vol. 1, p. 39.
22 Al-Haj, Al-Taqrir, vol. 1 p. 26.
23 Syed Habibul Haq Nadvi, Islamic legal philosophy and the Qur'ānic origins of the Islamic law, p. 189.
24 Qur'ān 9:122 (English translation from 'Glorious Qur'ān' by Shaykh-ul-Islam Dr. Muhammad Tahir-ul-Qadri).
25 Qur'ān 4:78 (English translation from 'Glorious Qur'ān' by Shaykh-ul-Islam Dr. Muhammad Tahir-ul-Qadri).
26 Qur'ān 6:25 (Eng. trans. from 'Glorious Qur'ān' by Shaykh-ul-Islam Dr. Muhammad Tahir-ul-Qadri).
27 Qur'ān 7:179 (Eng. trans. from 'Glorious Qur'ān' by Shaykh-ul-Islam Dr. Muhammad Tahir-ul-Qadri).
28 Qur'ān, 4:82 (Eng. trans. from 'Glorious Qur'ān' by Shaykh-ul-Islam Dr. Muhammad Tahir-ul-Qadri).
29 Qur'ān, 2:269 (Eng. trans. from 'Glorious Qur'ān' by Shaykh-ul-Islam Dr. Muhammad Tahir-ul-Qadri).
30 *Sahih al-Bukhari* Arabic-English, vol. 4, pp. 223–224, No.346), Muslim, Abdul Hamid Siddiqi, *Sahih Muslim* (English trans.), (Beirut: Dar al-Arabia, n.d.), vol. 3, p. 1061, No.4720).
31 Ibn Saad, *Tabqat ul Kubra* II, p. 363.
32 Syed Hossein Nasr, The Heart of Islam, Enduring values for humanity, p. 123 (2002); Eric Winkel, Islam and the living law: The Ibn al-Arabi approach 15 (1997).
33 Asaf A.A. Fyzee, *Outlines of Muhammadan law*, p. 21.
34 Abu Zahra, Usul-ul-Fiqh, p. 1.
35 Abdul Rahim, Mohammedan Jurisprudence, p. 50.
36 Imran Ahsan Khan Nyazee, Outlines of Islamic jurisprudence, p. 29.
37 Imran Ahsan Khan Nyazee, Outlines of Islamic jurisprudence, p. 29.
38 Justice Aftab Hussain, "Sources of Islamic law-classicism and contemporary problems" published in 3rd Pakistan France Colloquium Islamabad, 1982, p. 42.

39 Anwar A. Qadri, Islamic jurisprudence in the modern world, p. 214.
40 Dr. M. Rashid Ahmad Khan, Islamic jurisprudence, 19–20.
41 Encyclopedia of Islam, II, p. 723.
42 Dr. Sobhi Mahmassani, Falsafa shariat-e-Islam, p. 8.
43 Sadr-ush-Shariah, At-Tauzih, pp. 36 as quoted by Prof. Dr. Muhammad Tahir-ul-Qadri, Islamic concept of law, p. 1.
44 Sadr-ush-Shariah, At-Tauzih, pp. 40; Taftazani, At-Walweeh, p. 50.
45 Prof. Dr. Muhammad Tahir-ul-Qadri, Islamic concept of law, p. 1.
46 Antony Allott, The limits of law, p. 5 (1980 Ed).
47 Prof. Dr. Muhammad Tahir-ul-Qadri, Islamic concept of law, p. 1.
48 Qur'ān, 106:1–4 (Eng. trans. from 'Glorious Qur'ān' by Shaykh-ul-Islam Dr. Muhammad Tahir-ul-Qadri).
49 Qur'ān, 4:29 (Eng. trans. from 'Glorious Qur'ān' by Shaykh-ul-Islam Dr. Muhammad Tahir-ul-Qadri).
50 Qur'ān, 62:10 (Eng. trans. from 'Glorious Qur'ān' by Shaykh-ul-Islam Dr. Muhammad Tahir-ul-Qadri).
51 Qur'ān: 2:198 (Eng. trans. from 'Glorious Qur'ān' by Shaykh-ul-Islam Dr. Muhammad Tahir-ul-Qadri).
52 Narrated by al-Bukhari in al-Sahih, 2:628 #1681.
53 Narrated by Ahmad b. Hanbal in al-Musnad, 4:141 #17265; al-Hindi in Kanz al-'Ummal, 4:124 #9861.
54 Narrated by Ibn Majah in al-Sunan, 2:742 #2203.
55 Narrated by Ibn Majah in al-Sunan, 2:752 #2236.
56 Narrated by al-Tirmidhi in al-Sunan, 3:515 #1210; 'Abd b. Humayd in al-Musnad, 1:299 #966; and al-Mundhiri in al-Targhibwa al-Tarhib, 2:365 #2745.
57 Narrated by Ibn Majah in al-Sunan, 2:728 #2153; al-Darimi in al-Sunan, 2:324 #2544; and al-Bayhaqi in al-Sunan al Kubra, 6:30 #10934.
58 Narrated by al-Hindi in Kanz al-'Ummal, 4:16 #9874.
59 Qur'ān 2:275 (Eng. trans. from 'Glorious Qur'ān' by Shaykh-ul-Islam Dr. Muhammad Tahir-ul-Qadri).
60 Qur'ān, 2:201 (Eng. trans. from 'Glorious Qur'ān' by Shaykh-ul-Islam Dr. Muhammad Tahir-ul-Qadri).
61 Libber, A.E. Eastern, *Business practices and medieval European commerce*, p. 21, *Economic history review*, p. 230.
62 Rodinson M, (1987) '*Islam and capitalism*' in Ghai LS (ed), *The political economy of law: A third world reader*, Oxford University Press, pp. 70-71.
63 M. Kabir Hassan, Rasem N. Kayed & Umar A. Oseni, Introduction to Islamic banking and finance, principles and practice, p. 43.
64 M. Kabir Hassan, Rasem N. Kayed & Umar A. Oseni, Introduction to Islamic banking and finance, principles and practice, p. 44.
65 M. Kabir Hassan, Rasem N. Kayed & Umar A. Oseni, Introduction to Islamic banking and finance, principles and practice, p. 44.
66 Qur'ān 4:32 (Eng. trans. from 'Glorious Qur'ān' by Shaykh-ul-Islam Dr. Muhammad Tahir-ul-Qadri).
67 Qur'ān, 2:202 (Eng. trans. from 'Glorious Qur'ān' by Shaykh-ul-Islam Dr. Muhammad Tahir-ul-Qadri).
68 Qur'ān, 14:32 (Eng. trans. from 'Glorious Qur'ān' by Shaykh-ul-Islam Dr. Muhammad Tahir-ul-Qadri).
69 Narrated by al-Tabarani in al-Mu'jam al-aswat, 7:289 #7520.
70 Narrated by al-Bukh¥rÏ in *al-ßa^Ï^*, 2:730 #1966; al->abar¥nÏ in *al-Mu¢jam al-KabÏr*, 20:267 #631; and al-BayhaqÏ in *al-Sunan al-Kubr¥*, 6:127 #11471.

2 Historical evolution of contracts and codification of Islamic law of contract

2.1 Historical evolution of contracts

Now we discuss the development and evolution of contracts and other commercial transactions in Islamic law as well as its counterpart.

The principles of contract and commercial transactions do not arise today, but they did before Islam and until today. Although the fundamental procedures in a contractual dealing remain the same in all of the periods, there are still some differences in the nature, scope and additional principles of the contract which can be found in a different era, societies and places.[1] We describe them under the headings of the pre-Islamic and the post-Islamic eras.

2.2 Pre-Islamic era

Before Islam, *Quraish* used to be involved in trade and Macca was the commercial city.[2] It is, however, indicated in the Holy Qur'ān: لِإِيلَٰفِ قُرَيْشٍ ١ إِۦلَٰفِهِمْ رِحْلَةَ ٱلشِّتَآءِ وَٱلصَّيْفِ ٢

> "To awake drive amongst the Quraysh. They were acclimatized to the summer and winter (commercial) trips."[3]

A renowned exegete wrote: "Macca it's relation with the important trade route to India from Babylonia, from the ports of Persian Gulf as well as from Yemen, flowed rich products of the Middle East; from Syria, those of Mediterranean world."[4]

Many Arabs had obtained their livings from the camels, horses, cattle and sheep while the rest of them engaged in commerce and their caravans set out at regular intervals to the east and west.[5]

The idea and practice of contract have been popular in Arab society since the pre-Islamic era. Surveys on the commercial background of the pre-Islamic era were done in the sixth and seventh century in Arabia.[6]

Makkah and Madinah were trading centres and market transactions were governed by the customary law of property, contract and obligations.[7]

The cities of Macca and Madinah were well-known commercial cities during the pre-Islamic period, and these two cities had fostered a strong relationship with the Nimads in the area of trade and commerce.[8] Trans-regional trade was prevalent in the then Arabian Peninsula, which involved trade caravans from Macca to Syria and vice versa. Macca was the centre of interregional trade in the Arabian Peninsula.[9]

Macca was one of the richest cities among the Arab states, which established transactions in trade and commerce between the Indian Ocean and the Mediterranean.[10] According to Tabarani, once Hashim bin Abd Manaf (the great grandfather of Holy Prophet (PBUH) travelled to Palestine, bought some flour and brought it to Macca. This had made him the first merchant to make two trading journeys in two seasons, i.e. to the Sham in the summer and to Al-Yemen in the winter.[11] Gradually, the *Quraish* in the later generation of Hashim bin Abd Manaf established the nature and practices of international trade with different countries. There were mainly two types of commercial transactions during the pre-Islamic period: partnership agreement (*musharakah*) and receiving goods on the basis of a partnership.[12] These two types of commercial transactions extended an unlimited development of the trade in the society at that time. The prevailing modes of transactions during this era included *shirkah* (partnership), whether *mudarabah* (trust financing) or *musharakah* (joint venture partnership), both of which were practised as profit and loss sharing (P.L.S.) transactions. In addition, interregional trade within the Arabian Peninsula involved caravan trades where agents were employed to represent their principals in the business, mostly to carry out specific transactions under the authority of the latter. Agents were sent to Syria and its Mediterranean ports to trade in goods. The agents were compensated either through financial payments or proprietary benefits as agreed by the parties. This form of transaction is known as *wakalah* (agency contract).[13]

2.3 Post-Islamic era

Islam did not erase all pre-Islamic customs and practices. Instead, it removed every facet of corruption and cancelled all customs which were harmful to the society. Trade practices were reformed by making the basis of trade mutual consent, and by disallowing all deceptive business transactions.[14]

At the dawn of Islam, business activities were also introduced through injunctions in Qur'ān and Sunnah. Arabs continued their commercial and business transactions in the post-Islamic era. During the post-Islamic period, the Arabs organised trading caravans to make profits through commercial transactions.[15] The Prophet and his companions engaged practically in commercial transactions that involved financial dealings among parties of different nations and tribes.[16] "It is impossible to think of Macca in terms of other than trade. It was first established as a local trading centre around a religious shrine."[17]

Besides the above-mentioned prevailing modes of transactions during the pre-Islamic era, during the post-Islamic era there were other transactions involved such as contract of agency, contract of *salam*, contract of sale, contract of mortgage (*juala*) (*imarah*) and hire purchase agreement.[18] Furthermore, *qard* (a benevolent loan) was also common during this era. The Prophet (PBUH) sometimes borrowed money from Jews and facilitated some interest-free loans for his needy companions. This form of transaction is a goodwill loan made without the intention of receiving interest or any benefit in making such a loan. The Prophet's approval of benevolent loans can be found in a passage where he was reported to have said: "Whoever gives loans would have the reward (equivalent to the reward) of one of them."[19] In a similar vein, one of the wives of the Prophet (PBUH), *Aishah*, told that the Prophet (PBUH) bought some food on credit from a Jew and gave him his chain mail as security for the debt.

Apart from the above modes of transaction, the Prophet (PBUH) also recognised and his companions practically engaged in *salam* (forward) contracts. According to a tale, Ibn 'Abbas, a companion of the Prophet (PBUH) said that when the latter came to Madinah, they used to engage in *salam* contracts against cash payment until the season.[20] Other widespread permissible transactions during this period include *sarf* (exchange of money that is gold for gold and silver for silver at the same sitting) and *ijarah* (leasing).

In the post-Islamic period, the city of Macca was named as a *Jama'a* or a republic.[21] "Macca consisted of a collection of tribal camps, in which all came into a confederation for the purpose of the development of the commercial transaction, this confederation formed a general assembly wherein the commercial enterprise of Makkan's was planned."[22]

The commodities that were involved in the trade were spices, skins (of animals), perfumes, precious stones and pearls, drugs, irons, hides and furs, timbers and slaves, etc.[23] International trade and business also played an essential role between Arab, China Africa, Europe, Russia[24] and many other countries.

The Holy Prophet (PBUH) himself was involved actively in trade and business from Macca to Sham and other places even before the revelation from Allāh u.[25] In his business dealings, Prophet Muhammad a never engaged in unethical transactions, and he did not hoard commercial goods for the purpose of selling at higher prices when such commodities became scarce. Consequently, Khadija, a wealthy and reputable merchant in Macca, engaged the services of the young and reliable Muhammad a to assist in the management of her business. The Holy Prophet (PBUH) was a member of the attested trading clan of *Quraish*.[26] Even after he was appointed by Allāh u as the Holy Prophet (PBUH) of the world, the Prophet (PBUH) continues to encourage his companions to involve themselves in trade activities.[27]

Sayyidina Abu Bakr (R.A) also had a cloth business. Other companions of the Holy Prophet (PBUH) were involved in many other trades at one time or another in their lives.[28] Many other companions of the Holy Prophet (PBUH) had also engaged themselves in maritime and land trade throughout the whole world. The Prophets' companions earned their living through different legitimate means. Leading companions of the Prophet (PBUH), such as Hazrat Abu Bakr, Hazrat Uthman ibn' Affan and Hazrat Abdul Rehman ibn 'Awf engaged in lawful business and trade. Lawful business and trade was the most common form of work and was considered to be the best mode of earning during the era and was carried out in accordance with laid-down principles governing the contract concluded by the parties then involved. Some migrants and residents in Madinah were also engaged in agriculture, and some were also reported to have owned farmland while others were involved in skilled crafts such as smithery and carpentry. There were also professional jobs connected to the state, such as teaching, the giving of compulsory alms (*zakat*), and adjudication of disputes.

Montgomery Watt wrote: "Macca, Mohammad's home for half a century, was entirely a commercial city, set amidst barren rocks. Geographical conditions were also in its favour; it stood at the crossroads of routes from Yemen to Syria and from Abyssinia to Iraq."[29]

Hence, the Islamic law of contract, which forms the core of all trade and business transactions, had gone through rapid development. This encouraging development owes its existence not only to the Holy Qur'ān and *Ahadith* of the Holy Prophet (PBUH), but also to the jurists through the other important sources of Islamic law such as *Ijma'*, *Qiyas*, *'Urf* and *Masalih al-Mursalah.* It is also important to note that the rapid development of the Islamic law of contract takes place in two ways: Principally and practically.

2.4 The historical origin of the English law of contract

Now we explain the historical origin of English law and the English law of contract in a little bit of detail.

It is a fascinating fact that (unlike Islamic law) the English law is not very old and historical study shows that it has no origin of its own, but it originated entirely from European law.

The history of English law starts from the Babylonian era. Frederick Pollock and Frederic William Maitland, state that

> Truly speaking the history of English law got its identity only after the Norman Conquest. From the eleventh century onwards the common law started taking its shape. We can say that common law began in this century. Until the sixteenth century, common law played a very vital role in the development of English law. For almost five centuries common law was at its zenith. Then from the sixteenth century onwards, statutory law took the upper hand on common law.[30]

The same is the case with English contract law. The history of English contract law commences with the reign of Henry II.

> In Babylon people were governed by the Hammurabi Code. It is believed that the Babylonian law of contracts was the first highly developed system on this branch of jurisprudence in the history of the world. During that period, many formalities were to be followed in making a contract.[31]

It is pertinent to mention here that the "Western law of contract developed during the 18th and 19th centuries and grew of the economic and legal theories."[32]

It is interesting to note that in the above references that "Babylonian law of contracts" is used rather than "Babylonian law of contract" (without "s"). It is objected to and criticised in the case of the Islamic law that "Islamic law is the law of contracts and not contract."

Again, another quote is about the contracts which existed in the Roman Empire. W.H. Buckler states in his book that the following are the list of contracts that were prevalent in the regal period of the Roman Empire.[33]

- *Ivsivrandum.*
- *Sponsio.*
- *Nexum.*
- *Dotis* dictio.

W.H. Buckler further explained about these contracts: "*insivrandum* is the contract in which, promisor swore and had to call upon the gods and declare verbally that he will behold his good faith, in case if he breaches the promise, he shall be punished." *Sponso* is the form of contract which deals with a sacrifice of wine in three different stages.[34]

The *nexum* form of contract concerned sales and loans.

> In a loan contract, the borrower was supposed to declare himself as indebted for the some weighed amount. A sale could be made only in the presence of five Roman citizens as witnesses, the amount to be paid was weighed out by an official weigher, and the purchaser could then take possession. The sanctions for breach were violent measures. The creditor was at his option to choose any of the violent measures.[35]

The *dotis dictio* form of contract was considered to be a dowry contract.

Along with above-mentioned four types of contract following are more three contracts, which were also prevalent during the Roman era.[36]

- *Lex Mancipi*: This contract was like a covenant for the transfer of property.
- *Fiducia*: This form was ancillary to *Lex mancipi*.
- *Uadimonium*: This form was similar to the present-day law of guarantee.

Hence it is clear from above that in the ancient period the English law of the contract was based on Roman law. The two renowned authorities on English law, namely Ranulf de Glanvill, Chief Justiciar of England during the reign of King Henry II, and Henry de Bracton, the famous author of books on English law, did not deal with contract as a separate stream of law. Both of them in their works gave little place to the law of contract. This seems to be the same story as that explained previously in nominates contracts of Islamic law. However, it is evident that Islamic law and Islamic law of contracts have their origin 1,400 years ago.

When orientalists discussed the same issue regarding Islamic law of contract, they said that Islamic law is not the law of contract, but the law of contracts (nominate contracts) and Islamic law has no general theory of contract law, etc. They alleged it to be a "drawback" and a defect in the Islamic law of contract. However, in the case of the English law of contract, they do not treat it in the same way as in the case of Islamic law of contract.

It is pertinent to mention here that the Islamic contract law existed and started taking its shape in the 7th century i.e. about ten centuries before its counterpart (English law of contract).

> In contrast to Islamic law, the Western common law of contract, which developed during the 18th and 19th centuries, grew out of the economic and legal theories of the period in which it was formulated. In its nascency, it was formulated by natural law theories and later by *laissez-faire* economic theory both these theories have undergone considerable revision over time.[37]

Islamic contract law, by contrast, started taking shape in the 7th century. It is fair to assume that at this time in human history, commerce was limited to market overt (an open public market) and that goods consisted of surplus farm products or handicrafts. The Islamic law of contracts reflects and addresses the transactional reality of this period. The Anglo-Saxon common law of contracts was reshaped in the wake of the industrial revolution of the 18th century. The Muslim world, in general, did not experience the challenges of the industrial revolution. However, in recent years the sudden oil-based prosperity of some Islamic lands has put the Islamic law of contract into full gear. We find that through its history its responses are reminiscent of the common law tradition. Hence its growth should also be responsive to changing needs and times, as has been the case with common law.[38] The detailed study or discussion of this topic is beyond the scope of this book.

2.5 Codification of Islamic law of contract

Codification of Islamic Law of Contract is related to the codification of other Islamic laws as both are based on *Shariah.* We want to discuss and explain first the "codification of Islamic law" and then the "codification of Islamic contract law".

2.6 Definition of code and codification

Code literally means the act, process or result of arranging in a systematic form, and codification means the act of codifying. It does include, in the view of law, two main aspects, namely: the act, process or result of stating the rules and principles applicable in a given legal order to one or more broad areas of life in this form of code; and secondly, the reducing of unwritten customs or case law to statutory form.[39] The dictionary meanings of codification are: "A systematical collection, in a comprehensive form, of laws."[40] Further, "Codification means action or work codify laws or regulations or to collect into a law book systematically into a code."[41]

The equivalent Arabic term for codification is *Taqnin*. Sanhuri defined the Arabic term as "drafting the laws within arranged texts, in a systematic and consistent form".[42]

2.7 *Shariah* and other legal systems

The first thing which should be kept in mind is that during the early history of Islam, a whole *Shariah* was never collected and specified in a particular "law book(s)", just like other man-made "law book(s)" where the laws are defined and arranged in systematic set of paragraphs and sections/articles to form a *law code*. These law codes are usually written by a specific body, elected or otherwise: a legislative assembly, etc.[43] Secondly, keep in mind that the concept of codification of Islamic laws is different as compared to the codification of other laws of the world. Islam as a "Din" deals in the totality of Islamic teachings and regulates all aspects of human life, including religious, economic, social, fiscal, etc. All the guidelines and governing principles to deal *inter alia* with these aspects are there in the Holy Book of Qur'ān and in the *Ahadith* of the Prophet Muhammad a (although there are other sources of Islamic laws, they all are based on these two). Hence it is not possible to "codify" all Islamic laws in "modern" forms of codifications in a single code applying in the entire or a certain part of the Muslim world. There had never been any codification of Islamic law and Islamic law of contract in ditto form as in another legal system of the world. Because the *Shariah* does not have such a specific form. However, Islamic law and the legal system are there. We may name it as an "unwritten" or "un-codified law". (It is not the only uncodified legal system of the world; the Anglo-American 'common-law' system where the "precedence" of earlier cases defines the law, with codified "statutory laws" as accessories, is another active example.)[44]

2.8 Reasons for no codifications till the date

There may be more than one way of explaining why like other legal systems of the world, Islamic laws never codified till now. The following main reasons may be taken into consideration regarding this.

2.9 Origin is different

One theological reason would be to emphasise its origin as a God-given law, i.e. the origin of Islamic law is different from the origins of other laws of the world. The *Shariah* explains how God wants a man to regulate his life, and this has been expressed in the revelation of the fixed texts of the Qur'ān and Sunnah. When man formulates systematic legal precepts out of this revelation, he necessarily uses his intellect in this process, an intellect that is prone to error. Therefore, what man decides may be right, or it may be wrong.[45] Keeping this view in mind, the early jurists never tried to codify *Shariah* laws in law code form.

2.10 Nature is different

Another historical reason for the lack of codification until now may regard the nature of the authority of the lawgiver. In most countries in the world, the field of law is tightly integrated with political rule. The governments or rulers make the laws through a system of lawmaking. The legal system is an executive branch of the state. Similarly, judges in the courts also form laws in the form of court precedents. Contrary to this, Islamic laws were never made by a Muslim ruler or government nor are the laws made by judges. Islamic laws and their legal system are developed independently from any government but often against the will of the ruler.

In the early Islamic period, the legal scholars (*fuqaha'*), in theory and in practice, were recruited, educated and functioned entirely autonomously from the ruler. To develop the Islamic laws, the first step had to be taken by the jurists to make a list of Qur'ānic laws and prepare an inventory of laws in Sunnah. The next step was the discovery of the juristic principles of *Ijma* and *Qiyas*. Then hypothetical problems, as well as problems of the day, were noted by them and, by use of analogical reasoning, answers or solutions were found differently by various jurists.[46] These legal scholars (*fuqaha'*) and jurists of different localities developed the legal literature in different forms which eventually emerged in different "schools of laws" which are practised now in different Islamic countries. The *fuqaha'* and jurists, again, never tried to codify the Islamic laws in law code form.

2.11 Sources of law are different

The third reason that the codification of Islamic laws cannot be the same as that of its counterpart is because the primary sources of Islamic law, including contracts, are different from the sources of the laws of other legal systems of the world. The primary and fundamental sources of laws in the Islamic legal system are Qur'ān and Sunnah which are unique. The other legal systems of the world have no such sources. So it is difficult to codify the laws given in the Qur'ān and Sunnah in the exact form of law codes as that of its counterpart.

2.12 Territoriality aspect is different

As we know, every country or state codified the laws that are effective within the territory of that country or state. These laws are valid for every person residing within that country or state and do not have an effect beyond the state's border. *Shariah* laws cannot, by their nature, be limited to any territory of a single state. Although a follower primarily is bound to follow his school of thought in no matter which Islamic country he resides, it is not possible to make a single code of laws for the whole world. Due to this problem, early jurists did not try to codify the Islamic laws for the territory where they were residing. Instead, they tried to collect those laws which may apply unanimously to all Muslims, wherever they reside.

For these reasons the early jurist did not try to codify the *Shariah* law as a whole, generally, or Islamic law of contract, in particular.

However, although no codification of divine laws into a law code was made, with the passage of time a dire need for codification remained in judicial minds and effort from the very start. The jurists and Muslim legal experts started many attempts to collect the different laws systematically in forms of books etc. This jurists' law, based on revelation, also continued to develop side by side with the great efforts of the worthy Muslim lawyers and jurists. Scholarly and legal opinions and legal writings of these Muslim legal experts and jurists based upon their interpretation of *Shariah* rulings also expanded with time and were merged into vast volumes of legal compendiums. We may call these the legal books. Now in this sense, the effort of codification of different Islamic law started.

However, it may be reasonable to say that the formulation of the law in the way we have it nowadays, in separate but similar law systems (*madhahib*), was finalised only around or after 900 AD; perhaps even till 950 AD Muslim jurists remained afraid to "codify" the laws.

2.13 Two views about codification

Before discussing the efforts of codification, it is interesting to mention here that regarding the codification of Islamic laws, nowadays, there are two dominant opinions. There is still resistance against the codification of Islamic laws into unified systems, not only from traditionalists but equally from some who defend the concept of personal piety. At the same time, there are now tendencies throughout the Islamic world that if, while Islamic laws cannot be codified, efforts should be made to harmonise common law under broad *Shariah.*

The conservative school objects to the idea of codification. It is led mainly by the scholars of Saudi Arabia and Salafis,[47] A prominent Saudi scholar, who authored a book addressing this issue, concluded that the codification does not apply to Muslims. It is a Western model that cannot accommodate Islamic law, neither in the title nor in content. The nature of Islamic legislation refutes codification and its adoption by Muslims is maladjusted and inappropriate.[48] They want to say that *Shariah* as "divinely ordained" and does not depend on codification; thus human legislation creates a conflict.

The opponents of codification mainly offer the following excuses and arguments as factors of preservation:

i. The fear of distorting the legal rules by the rulers by applying the codes as a device to realise their interests.
ii. The Islamic legal rules have been implemented for more than 14 centuries without official codes.
iii. The universal law system of several developed Western countries, e.g. English Common Law, approves the fact that it is still acceptable to apply laws without them being drafted in systematic codes.
iv. The opposition to the right of free *Ijtihad* granted to qualified scholars.[49]

The argument advanced in point number (ii) above is further elaborated by Dr. Tanzil-ur-Rehman by saying that

> For 1300 years at least more than half of the civilised world was being governed by the Islamic law. If you read the first few lines, of the introduction to Anderson's book on Islamic law in the modern world, you will find that for 1300 years Muslim law was governing the lives of millions of people without any codified law. So the *Shariah* as a whole was being made applicable. The *qazis* were enforcing the law as laid down in the Qur'ān, Sunnah and the books of Fiqh. There was no state codification.[50]

In contrast, Sheikh 'Ali al-Khafif, Sheikh Muhammad Abu Zahrah, Sheikh Hasanain Makhluf, Sheikh Ahmad Fahmi Abu Sunnah, Sheikh Muhammad Zaki 'Abdul Barr, Sheikh Yosuf al-Qaradawi, Sheikh Wahbat al-Zuhayli and Muhammad 'Abdul Jawad, viewed the codification of Islamic law as something necessary.

2.14 Efforts of codifications

The first thing that must be kept in mind is that in the period of the Prophet Muhammad a and during the republican era of the Khulafa-i-Rashidin (632–661 AD) the need for articulating of Ahkam (laws) and the question of codification did not arise. With the passage of time, when a growing number of juristic schools appeared, and the job of the courts was not as simple as before, it was difficult to accept the harmony in scholars' opinions and judges' verdicts, as much as the ruler themselves, began to feel the necessity of a codified law.[51]

The historians refer the very beginnings of codification in the Muslim world to the well-documented event of *Ibn al-Muqaffa*'s dialogue (d.144AH/726CE), with the Caliph *Abu Ja'far al-Mansur* (95-158AH/713-775CE). *Ibn al-Muqaffa*, a famous writer in Arabic literature, was the first to see the necessity of codification. He put a proposal before *Abu Ja'far al-Mansur* in a formal letter named "*Risalat al-Sahabah fi Ta'at al-Sultan*" (Message of Companions in the Obedience of the Sultan) and because it was fruitless it was then called "*al-Risalah al-Yatimah*" (The Orphan Message), stating:[52]

> Codification of Islamic law is the process by which the various legal rulings of the *sharah* (*al-ahkam al-Sharah*) of a specific subject matter (such as property, torts, family law, etc.) that are collected and restated in a clear and concise manner. It is to form a legal code that has a full effect within the range of political jurisdictions.[53]

Codification of Islamic law and contract law is an attempt to collect systematically and comprehensively written regulation in the field of Islamic law and Islamic contract law separately. Attempts at the codification of Islamic laws were started by jurists to codify legal opinions of different schools of thought (*madhahib*) by making them more easily accessible and easier to follow in the practice of daily life. "The different legal rulings were codified in the form of books such as *ikhtilaf al-fuqah by Ibn al-Mundhir* (d.931), *Bidyat al-mujtahid* by Ibn Rushd (d.1198), and *Fatwa Alamgryah* in 1700 century."[54] In addition, the codification process of Islamic law began in the early 19th century and continued throughout the middle of the 20th century. At this time, the majority of Muslim nations completed their legal codification processes and unified their judicial systems.[55]

2.15 Efforts in the sub-continent

Another positive attempt was made under the orders of the Sultan Muhammad Aurangzeb 'Alamgir. The compilation of "*Al-Fatawa al-Hindiyyah/al-Fatawa al-Alamgiriyyah*", within six volumes, was authored, but it did not fulfil the requisites of an official code, owing to the fact that it was not compulsorily applied, nor drafted in a systematical order and it encompassed both the rules of *Ibadat* and *Muamalat* in which some of the rules were only imaginary and abstract truths. Although it was not compiled in the style of a new code, it was an important link in the chain of the works attempted in this direction.

By the end of the 17th century after the occupation of India, under the leadership of Governor-General Warren Hastings, the first experiment with the formal codification of Islamic law took place. Rather than replacing local laws with British laws, the British occupant's administration slowly developed a hybrid legal system. These attempts were made to have easier access to Islamic law; thus they made a series of English translations of key Ahnaf texts. *Al-Marghnns Hidya* was translated by Charles Hamilton in 1791 and in 1792 there was a translation of al-Sirjiyya in inheritance law by Jones. Later on, by 1865, Neil Baille supplemented these early translations with his *A Digest of Mohummaddan Law* (sic), which was a selected translation of other parts of *Fatwa Alamgryah*. Consequently, these translations provided the surface for what was to later on become the Anglo-Muhammadan Laws. It was a complete code of the Ahnaf school of law combined with British laws with the intention of making the latter more prominent than the former.[56]

2.16 Efforts in Java, Indonesia

Moreover, there was another attempt in the codification of *Shariah*, which took place under the Dutch in Java, Indonesia. As in India, Javanese society was ambiguous about this, mainly because local customs and traditions (*Adat*) existed side by side with Islamic law. However, the Dutch, unlike the British, had no interest in a hybrid system or the codification of local laws. Their main intention initially was to create a codification that was suited to given Dutch settlers and subsequently native people. As a result, by 1848, the Dutch had issued codes that governed civil procedures (*Burgelijk*) as well as criminal procedures (*Strafvorderong*). However, the penal code governing locals came later in 1873, and was very similar to the Dutch national penal code. As with the British in

India, the Dutch colonial officials had control of the local *Shariah* and *Adat* (local custom) courts, which gave the final authority to Dutch judges in accordance with Dutch law.[57]

2.17 Efforts by the Ottoman Empire

Further codifications started in the Ottoman *Khilafah*, beginning with legal reforms in the early 1830s. By 1840, there was a codification of penal code (criminal law) founded on Ahnaf law and called *Qanun Namahs*. Their code of commerce originated from European codes which came into effect in 1850. However, the most famous of all the Ottoman codifications was the *Medjelle Ahkam Adliya* issued between 1870 and 1877 which contained 1,851 articles regarding commercial transactions and court procedures (but not covering family or criminal law) based on Ahnaf school.[58]

The compilation of the *Medjelle* was an important event in the history of codification. *Medjelle* constituted the first modern codification of Islamic law of contracts and obligations and was implemented and applied across the territories of the Ottoman Empire and remained in force in the successor states after the dismantling of the empire in 1918. Substantively, the *Medjelle* covered both less and more than a European Civil Code. It dealt with contracts (sale, hire, guaranty, debt, etc.) and some torts, but not with non-contractual obligations and did not regulate other areas of private law, such as marriage, divorce, inheritance and various aspects of genuine property.[59]

Under the Ottoman *Khalifah*, the personal status laws were codified under the basis of the Ottoman law of family rights in 1917. Despite that fact, Turkey officially stopped implementing Islamic law in 1926; the 1917 code was adopted in the formerly Ottoman *Khalifah*. Unlike earlier Ottoman *Khalifah's* efforts at codification, with the exception of micelle, the law of family rights was completely *Shariah*-compliant.[60]

The preceding discussion proves that the laws of the Ottoman Caliphate flowed in two opposing directions:

1. A direction towards Westernisation of the law in the form of adopting the foreign laws, with special reference to French Codes. These sets of laws distorted the Islamic rulings in aspects of estates and penalties, e.g. article 54 in the land law stipulated equal inheritance between males and females. The penal law did not codify the Islamic penal system including the *Hudud* and usury was made legitimate.[61]
2. A direction towards the codification of Islamic law, and this movement was represented by two main compilations:
   i) The issuance of "*Medjelle al-Ahkam al-'Adliyyah*" (Compilation of Principles of Justice) in 1293AH/ 1876CE under the supervision of Cevdat Basha. The compilation covered the rules of transactions (Mu'amalat), the rules of actions and the principles of judicial trials and proofs.

ii) The issuance of "*Qanun Huquq al-'Ailah*" (Family law) in 1336AH/1917CE. The significance of this compilation refers to three reasons: firstly, it is the first historical code in respect of family law on the basis of *Shariah* law; secondly, it stepped outside the Hanafi rite to other Sunni rites of jurisprudence; and finally, it included special rules pertaining to the religious family law of both Jews and Christians.[62]

2.18 Efforts in Egypt

Egypt was a significant centre for legal reformations throughout this period. Just as in many other areas that were under colonial rule and influences, the Egyptian legal system was plural and not unified, including a mixed arrangement of natives and colonial legal jurisdictions.[63]

In 1866, Rifah al-ahw, a highly educated al-Azhar scholar and a reformist, translated and published the French Civil Code and French Trade Law. In 1870, Khedive Ismail requested various *ulama* to share their thoughts on the practicality of codifying Islamic law and adopting aspects of French law. Al-Ahw, who was a minister of justice along with Qadir Pasha, took an interest in codification and ultimately provided three works of codified Islamic laws, namely as *al-Ahkam al-Shariyah fil-ahwal al-Shakhiah* (a collection of Ahnaf rulings which is related to personal law status) published in 1880, *Murshid al-hayran ill ma'rifat abwal al-insah* (a collection of Ahnaf rulings regarding to trade law) published in 1890, and *Qanun al-adl wa al-insaf lil-qada ala mushkilat al-awqaf* (a work seeking to codify rulings on religious Waqaf and donations) that was published in 1894.[64]

In 1876, Mixed Courts were founded in Egypt to provide rulings to non-native people, and it was asserted that it was an enhancement of egregious Ottoman capitulations that Egypt had inherited. Based on that, a different European code was drafted to govern the above-mentioned courts; however, those codes were mostly influenced by the French code. The importance of the mixed court codes can be noticed when it majorly influenced the drafting of Egypt's civil code in the late 18th century.

Moreover, Egypt followed suit with restricting *Shariah* courts from a procedural perspective in 1857. By 1880 there was an order that the *Shariah* courts should follow the most agreed opinions of the Ahnaf school (*arja aqwal al-anafiyah*).

Consequently, the motion was set on the formation of a committee with regard to personal status law with the purpose of creating a codification of these opinions. The committee was a mixture of secular trained lawyers, a profession that became popular in the late 19th century. The established code was modified later on with specific laws throughout the early decades of the 19th century.[65] This effort found its footing in Egypt in 1929 by the promulgation of "Qanoon Ahwal Shakhsia" and then in 1940, the law of Auqaf and in 1943 the law of wills.

2.19 Efforts in Saudi Arabia

Due to the strong literalist view in Saudi Arabia, like other *Shariah* legal systems, shariah law remains uncodified. Despite being the world's eleventh easiest economy to do business in, Saudi Arabia ranks 140th out of 183 economics in terms of enforcement of contracts. King Abdullah took the initiative to make legal reforms to modernise the courts and codify *Shariah* law in Saudi Arabia in 2007. In 2010, the *Ulma*, the religious body, approved a codification of *Shariah* law.

2.20 Malaysia and other countries who adopted English law of contract

Although Islamic law of contract has vast qualities and features, in fact it is not different from the English contract law principles. In English law, "contract is an agreement enforceable by law". In Islamic law, the contract is known as *aqd* which means tie or bond. It means a contract that binds the parties together. To make a contract in Islamic law, there must be an agreement between two parties,[66] and the agreement must be based on the free consent of the parties.[67] To make an agreement legally effective, there must be an offer and an acceptance between the parties. In other words, the offeree must accept the offer from the offerer absolutely and without any qualification.[68] To effect a valid contract, the parties must have the intention of creating a legally binding relationship.[69] All the above-mentioned salient features of Islamic law of contract are the same as in English contract law. Islam emphasises fulfilling contractual obligations. Allāh u says in the Qur'ān: "O ye who believe, fulfil all of your obligations".[70]

This is the reason that Malaysia, Pakistan and some other Muslim countries have adopted the English contract law as a law applicable to contract disputes in their respective countries, just like other criminal and civil codes under which the judicial system is being run. However, it should be kept in mind that in case of any contradiction, Islamic law shall prevail over any foreign law.

Notes

1 Muhammad Ma'sum Billah, Shariah standard of business contract, p. 13.
2 Montgomery Watt, Muhammad at Macca, p. 33.
3 Qur'ān, 106:1-2 (Eng. trans. from 'Glorious Qur'ān' by Shaykh-ul-Islam Dr. Muhammad Tahir-ul-Qadri).
4 Abd Al-Majid Daryabadi, Holy Qur'ān with English translation and commentary, p. 634.
5 Dr. Liaquat Ali Khan Niazi, Islamic law of contract, p. 4.
6 E.R Hards Ivany, Bilateral Contract, Mozley and Whitley's Law Dictionary (1980).
7 Oussama Arabi, Studies in modern Islamic law and jurisprudence, Kluwer law international, 2001, p. 32.
8 Abdullah Alwi Hj. Hasan, *Sales and contract in Early Islamic commercial law*, A thesis submitted to the University of Edinnburg in 1986 (u.p) p. 1.
9 M. Kabir Hassan, Rasem N. Kayed & Umar A. Oseni, Introduction to Islamic banking and finance, principles and practice, p. 9.
10 H.A.R. Gibb, *Islam*, Oxford, 1980, p. 17.
11 Ibn Sa'd. Kitab Al-Tabaqat Al-Kubra, 1. Pp. 75 ff. Al-Tabari, Tarik Al-Rusul wa Al-Muluk II, p. 252 as cited in Abdullah Alwi Hj. Hasan, pp. 4–5.
12 Ibn Hazm, Al-Mahalli, vol. 8, p. 247 and Kasai Badal al-Sanai fi Tartib al-Shara vol. 6 p. 57.

13 M. Kabir Hassan, Rasem N. Kayed & Umar A. Oseni, Introduction to Islamic banking and finance, principles and practice, p. 10.
14 Dr. Abu Ameenah Bilal Philips, The evolution of Fiqh, p. 12.
15 Mohammad Hamidullah. Muslim conduct of state. Lahore 1961 p. 102.
16 M. Kabir Hassan, Rasem N. Kayed & Umar A. Oseni, Introduction to Islamic banking and finance, principles and practice, p. 9.
17 M.A. Haykal, Hayat Muhammad, 13th ed. P. 115, as cited in Dr. S.E. Rayner. Theory of contract in Islamic law, 1991 p. 67.
18 Dr. S.E. Rayner. Theory of contract in Islamic law, 1991 p. 74.
19 M. Kabir Hassan, Rasem N. Kayed & Umar A. Oseni, Introduction to Islamic banking and finance, principles and practice, p. 44.
20 M. Kabir Hassan, Rasem N. Kayed & Umar A. Oseni, Introduction to Islamic banking and finance, principles and practice, p. 44.
21 Waqidi, Kitab al-Mughni, 59, 3. Cited in Dr. S.E. Rayner. Theory of contract in Islamic law, 1991, p. 69.
22 O'Leary, Arabia before Mohammad, p. 183.
23 Dr. S.E. Rayner, The theory of contracts in Islamic law, p. 67.
24 Irfan, Mohammad Raana, Economics system under Umar, The Great, pp. 23–32.
25 Mawlana Fazl Al-Karim, Mishkat al-Masabih, (Trans Eng.), Al-Hj. vol. 2, p. 266.
26 Montgomery Watt, Muhammad at Macca, p. 33.
27 Abd Al-Rahman, Doi, Shariah: The Islamic law, 1990, p. 354.
28 Abd Al-Rahman, Doi, Shariah: The Islamic law, 1990, p. 355.
29 As quoted by Dr. Liaquat Ali Khan Niazi, Islamic law of contract, p. 4.
30 Sir Frederick Pollock & Frederic William Maitland, the history of English law before the time of Edward-I, vol. 1, 2nd ed. 1899, pp. 1–2.
31 Albert H. Utney, Introduction to the study of legal history, vol. 1, Cree publishing Co., Minneapolis, 1908, p. 20.
32 P.S. Atiyah, The law of contract, 4th ed., Oxford University Press, 1989, pp. 1–19 (1961), Cf. ibid at pp. 116–117.
33 W.H. Buckler, the origin and history of contract in Roman law, C.J. Clay & Sons, London, 1895, pp. 3–8.
34 W.H. Buckler, the origin and history of contract in Roman law, C.J. Clay & Sons, London, 1895, pp. 3–8.
35 Sir Henry Sumner Maine, Ancient law, John Murray, London, 1908, pp. 282–287.
36 Sir Henry Sumner Maine, Ancient law, John Murray, London, 1908, pp. 282–287.
37 P.S. Atiyah, The law of contract 1–19 (1961), See also H.C. Havinghurst, The nature of private contract (1961).
38 Makdisi, Legal history of Islamic law & English common law; Origins & Metamorphosis, 34 Clev. St. L. Rev. 3-18 (1985-86).
39 David M. Walker (1980). The Oxford Companion to Law. New York: Oxford University Press, p. 234.
40 L.B.Curzon (2003). Dictionary of Law, 6th ed. Kuala Lumpur: International Law Book Services, p. 72.
41 The American Heritage Dictionary, p. 287.
42 Abdul Razzaq al-Sanhuri, "Wujub Tanqih al-Qanun al-Madani al-Misri wa'ala ay' Asas Yakun Hadha al-Tanqih, Maj. Al-Qanun wa al-Iqtisad, 6(1), p. 3.
43 Knut S. Vikor, The Sharia and the nation state: who can codify the divine law? p. 2.
44 Knut S. Vikor, The Sharia and the nation state: who can codify the divine law? p. 2.
45 Knut S. Vikor, The Sharia and the nation state: who can codify the divine law? p. 2.
46 Justice Aftab Hussain, "Sources of Islamic law-classicism and contemporary problems" published in 3rd Pakistan France Colloquium Islamabad, 1982, p. 42.
47 Muhammad 'Abdul Jawad (1977), *Buhuth fi al-Shari ah al-Islamiyyah wa al-Qanun*, 2nd collection, Cairo: matba at Jami at al-Qahirah, pp. 82–83.

48 Bakr b. 'Abdullah Abu Zaid (1983), *al-Taqnin wa al-Ilzam: 'Ard wa Munaqashah*, 3rd ed. Riyad: *Matbu at-Riasat Idarat al-Buhuth al-Ilmiyyah wa al-Ifta' wa al-Dawah wa al-Irshad*, pp. 99–100.
49 Muhammad 'Abdul Jawad (1977), *Buhuth fi al-Shari ah al-Islamiyyah wa al-Qanun*, 2nd collection, Cairo: matba at Jami at al-Qahirah, pp. 79–85.
50 Dr. Tanzil-ur-Rehman, 3rd Pakistan France Colloquium Islamabad, 1982, p. 177.
51 Amin Ahsan Islahi (2000), Islamic law: Concept and codification, 1st ed. Lahore: Islamic Publications Ltd.
52 Najmaldeen K.Kareem Zanki, Codification of Islamic law premises of history and debates of contemporary Muslim scholars, p. 128.
53 Elgawhary, Tarck A. Citation for codification of law, p. 1 http://oxfordislamic studies. com.ezproxy.princeton.edu/pri.....
54 Codification of Islamic law in the Muslim word, Trends and practices, Sebghatullah Qazizada & Muhammad Zia-ul-Haq Qazizada, p. 162-163.
55 Elgawhary, Tarck A. Citation for codification of law, p. 1 http://oxfordislamic_studies .com.ezproxy.princeton.edu/pri.....
56 Citation for codification of law codification of law, Tarek Elgawhary—Academia.edu.
57 Elgawhary, Tarck A. Citation for codification of law, p. 1 http://oxfordislamic studies .com.ezproxy.princeton.edu/pri.....
58 Citation for codification of law codification of law, Tarek Elgawhary—Academia.edu.
59 Muhammad b. al-Hasan al-Shaybani (1999), Muwatta' al-Imam Malik, 3rd ed. Azamran: Muzaffarpur, vol. 1, pp. 65–66, Sufi Hasan Abu Talib (1990), Tatbiq al-Shariah al-Islamiyyah fi al-Bilad al-'Arabiyyah, 3rd ed. Cairo: Dar al-Nahdah al-'Arabiyyah, pp. 238–239.
60 Elgawhary, Tarck A. Citation for codification of law, p. 1 http://oxfordislamic studies .com.ezproxy.princeton.edu/pri.....
61 Abdul Jamil 'Adhub, *al-Qawanin al-Wadh'iya al-Faransiya wa al-Shariah al-Islamiya*, p. 17; Tariq Ziyadah, *Dirasat fi al-Fiqh wa al-Qanun*, 1st ed. Lebanon: *Dar al-Shimal*, p. 94.
62 Abdul Jamil 'Adhub (2005), *al-Qawanin al-Wadh'iya al-Faransiya wa al-Shariah al-Islamiya*, p. 18; Subhi Mahamasani, *al-Awda al-Tashriiyyah fi al-Duwal al-'Arabiyyah Madiha wa Hadiruha*, 3rd ed. Beirut: *Dar al-Ilm li-al-Malayin*, p. 195.
63 Elgawhary, Tarck A. Citation for codification of law, p. 1 http://oxfordislamic studies .com.ezproxy.princeton.edu/pri.....
64 Citation for codification of law codification of law, Tarek Elgawhary—Academia.edu.
65 Elgawhary, Tarck A. Citation for codification of law, p. 1 http://oxfordislamic studies .com.ezproxy.princeton.edu/pri.....
66 Siti Salwani Razali, Islamic Law of Contract (2010), United Kingdom: Cengage Learning, p. 1.
67 Hasbullah, Abdul Rahman, Offer and Acceptance in Islamic Law of Contract (2000), Journal Shariah, 8(2): 23.
68 Ashshafi, J.A.H.S. *Majlis Aqdi fil fiqhi Islami wal Qanun al-wadi*, Iskandariah (2001), p. 91.
69 O'Sullivan, J. and Hilliard, J. The Law of Contract (2006), Oxford, New York: Oxford University Press, pp. 46.
70 Qur'ān, 5:5 (English translation from 'Glorious Qur'ān' by Shaykh-ul-Islam Dr. Muhammad Tahir-ul-Qadri).

3 General Theory, nominate contract, freedom of contract and the juristic person

Some objections/problems are being raised by some authors and discussed in their academic literature on Islamic contract law. These are as follows:

That there is no general theory of contracts under Islamic jurisprudence (of contract law) but only some nominate contracts are therein. Hence Islamic jurisprudence concerns the law of contracts rather than the law of contract.[1]

That there is no theory of freedom of contract under Islamic jurisprudence of contract law, but there is the doctrine of restriction of contracts. Islamic jurisprudence of contract imposes the restriction incorporating any clauses in nominate contracts which changes its effect.

That there is no concept of the juristic person in Islamic law of contract.

Now we discuss these issues in some detail.

3.1 Nominate contracts

The jurists, after the in-depth study of Holy Qur'ān and traditions of Holy Prophet (PBUH) regarding business transactions and contract, unfolded and developed two types of governing rules and principles concerning the contract law. There are two groups of jurists, the first group advocating the nominate contracts and the second advocating the general theory of contracts along with nominate contracts. We accept the scholarly contribution of academic literature on Islamic law of contract by both sides of great jurists who produced literature on nominated contracts and those who produced literature on the general theory of contract.

According to the first group of jurists, Islamic jurisprudence has the rules only related to specific contracts termed as "Nominate Contracts". They focused their research and developed their academic literature exclusively on specific rules regarding nominate contracts and not on the general theory of contract. According to them, there is no comprehensive general theory of contract under Islamic jurisprudence of contract law. Hence the advocates who supported the lack of general theory concluded that Islamic law is the law of contracts and not the law of contract. On the basis of this Schacht says, "There exists no general term for obligation".[2] It is generally argued by the opponents that Islamic law knows no general theory of contract. Their arguments are based on the method of development of the system of Islamic contracts by the *fuqaha'*(jurists) who categorised each contract into classes of nominate contracts (*uqud al mu'ayyana*) with their own distinctive rules.[3]

Their research is based on the specific rules mainly prescribed in the Prophet's tradition concerning the prerequisites and the effects of several types of contracts that prevailed among the people at the time of the rise of Islam. This is the reason; they concluded that

> The development of Islamic contracts is, therefore, the result of the method undertaken by Muslim jurists to elaborate the comprehensive and piecemeal doctrines of the Qur'ān and Sunnah and to impose them on the pre-Islamic norms of practice. Every so often among the works of the early jurists, it is possible to find a solution or a rule of a specified category which a priori seems restricted to that particular type, but which, if tested on other categories, allows a principle of an absolute generality to emerge. The method followed by the jurists in the development of the system of nominate contracts (*al-'Uqud al-Mu'ayyana*) was by applying the process of *Qiyas* to already existing contracts, and by authorising the resulting category with *hadith* or other legal sources.[4]

They further extended the allegation that the Muslim psychology, therefore, tended to treat the law as paradigmatic:

> made up of individual solutions, handed down from day to day in relation to the specific needs of the moment, rather than of general principles set forth a priori from which the appropriate inference will be drawn for each fresh situation.[5]

Earlier, the basic nominate contracts were four in numbers i.e:

(1) *Bay'* (sale): Where right of ownership passes for consideration (*Tamlik al-Ayn bi-lwad*) (2); *Hiba* (Gift): Where right of ownership passes without consideration (*Tamlik al-Ayn bila Iwad*) (3) *ijara* (hire): Where transfer of possession occurs for consideration (4) *'Ariya* (loan): Where transfer of possession occurs without consideration.

Other nominate contracts include those of *salam* (a contract for delivery with prepayment), *mudaraba* (Sleeping partnership agreement; equity sharing between bank and client), *Sharika* (partnership), mortgage (*Rahn*), *Juala, Wadia* (deposit), *al-Muzara'a* (an agricultural contract where the landlord provides the land, seed and plants and the worker provides the labour) and *Umra*.[6]

The renowned Islamic scholar, Prof. Sanhuri described the following list of six nominate contracts: sale (*Bay'*), gift (*Hiba*), partnership (*Sharika*), hire (*ijara*), piecework (*Muqawala*) and agency (*Wakala*).[7]

If we sum everything up, we get the following list of 20 types of nominate contracts:

(1) sale (*Bay'*); (2) exchange (*Mu'awada*); (3) special settlement (*Sulh*); (4) gift (*Hibah*); (5) hire (*ijara*); (6) borrowing (*'Ariya*); (7) trust or deposit (*Wadi'a*);

(8) loan (*Qard*); (9) mortgage (*Rahn*); (10) guarantee (*Daman*); (11) bailment (*Kafala*); (12) assignment of credit (*Hawala*); (13) partnership (*musharaka*); (14) investment in trade (*mudaraba*); (15) agency (*Wakala*); (16) award (*Ju'ala*); (17) endowment (*waqf*); (18) *Muzara'a*; (19) *Musaqat*; (20) gambling and betting (*qimar* and *Girau Bandi*).

Due to the diversity of these different types of contracts, the early jurists could not agree upon a comprehensive definition of contract in Islamic law of contract. Hence, they considered the "contract of sale" as a model or archetype to which all other contractual arrangements should conform. This is the reason orientalists like Joseph Schacht and NJ Coulson etc. wrongly concluded that the contract of sale is the core of obligation in Islamic law. The most essential nominate contract is that of sale (*Bay'*). Sale formed the prototype contract around which the other classes of the contract were analogously developed. Indeed, it is the chapters on sale (*Kitab al-Buyu'*) in the various legal treatises that formed the basis for the jurists' procedure of analysis: several common principles of contract and laws of ownership may be gleaned from these chapters.[8] Accordingly, it is called a law of contracts rather than the law of contract.

3.2 The general theory of contract

The second group of Muslim jurists focused their research and developed their academic literature on the general theory of contract. The allegation that there is no general theory of contracts under Islamic law, and that the Romans and therefore, the Anglo-American legal system *do* have a general theory of contracts and obligations, is, as a whole, philosophic:

> The rules governing the concrete and the special contracts are deduced from the general theory of contracts. The approach of the Islamic system is scientific. From the concrete cases of special contracts, certain rules of general import are induced which are called the Islamic law of contract.[9]

According to this group of jurists, Islamic jurisprudence of contract has the general rules and regulations governing the contract law which apply to all kinds of contracts and they called it the general theory of contract. This theory is based on the general Qur'ānic injunction: يَٰٓأَيُّهَا ٱلَّذِينَ ءَامَنُوٓاْ أَوۡفُواْ بِٱلۡعُقُودِ

> "O believers! Fulfill (your) promises."[10]

In this verse, the word "contract" is used in general sense and not in a particular sense. This is the general and fundamental principle governing the sanctity of all contracts.

Many other general rules have been laid down in the Qur'ān and the Sunnah concerning contract law, which clearly are regarded as the basis of a general theory of contract. Along with the above-mentioned Qur'ānic verse, the statement of the Prophet (PBUH) saying: "believers must be bound to their stipulations"[11] is also a profound example of the general theory of contract law.

However, it is a fact that most of the early jurists worked much more on nominate contracts rather than unfolding the general theory. Actually, at that time, the business activities and other commercial transactions between parties were limited to sale and purchase, mortgage, hire, loans, agency, guarantees, gift, pledge and bailment. This was the reason which prompted the early Muslim jurists to deal with "nominate contracts of such types only". This was the genesis of Islamic law of contract, which was started to take shape. It is interesting to note here that the genesis of all other Western laws of contract is the same as that of Islamic law of contract. Although we see that at present, Western law of contract and other laws consist of such general theory, they all existed in early times in the same form as Islamic law.[12]

These nominate contracts and particularly sale-contracts have been legislated by the *Shariah* in order to regulate current applications of a general norm of the contract to satisfy the needs of the Muslim people, and to regulate their commercial affairs, precisely as it is done by any relevant statute in modern legal systems.[13]

Another fact or reason for this limited research was that in the commercial law regime of the early period these early jurists only explained the rules of business transactions to people with regard to the particular events and incidents that happened during their lifetimes. Hence, they developed only an array of contract types, the 'nominate contract', each with its own rules and regulations on the foundation of principles, provided in the Qur'ān and Sunnah. They did not pay any heed to developing an all-embracing general theory of Islamic law.[14] But this fact alone does not negate the existence of a general theory of contract.

A *hadith* attributed to the Prophet (PBUH) which says: "Every condition which is not in the Book of God is void"[15] is quoted to develop the idea of nominate contracts and to reject the general theory of the orientalists. However, it is possible to adduce a general theory of contract from this *hadith* by interpreting it another way, saying: "Every condition (or contract) which is repugnant to the Book of God and the Sunnah is void", and therefore it does not indicate that every stipulation which is not dealt with by either of these two sources is void."[16]

The general theory of contract has been advocated by several leading Islamic jurists, who regard the opinions of some earlier jurists as inaccurate.[17] They have firmly rejected the view that the general Qur'ānic contract rule refers only to nominate contracts as being a mere fantasy, which is difficult to accept from jurists and lawyers. They argued that various kinds of transactions are the usual needs of society, in early times as well as in the present. Nominate contracts such as sale, hire, partnership, borrowing and so on have evolved to satisfy these necessities and requirements of society, and there are so many other types of transactions and contracts commonly entered into by people which cannot be categorised as any of the nominate contracts specified in the juristic writings. What would happen to these contracts if we limited the law of contract to nominate contracts only?

This situation to some extent remains until the 13th century. However, in some countries, the Muslim jurists started to give "contract" a general definition, leading towards general theory. They developed and modified the nominated contract concept by adding the concept of accepting a transaction that occurred that did not contravene the Qur'ān and Sunnah as a transaction for a valid contract.[18]

It is pertinent to point out here a fundamental argument that the majority of Muslim jurists have focused on regarding the contract of sale when discussing the rules of the contract. It is very fair to state that, although the scholars do not focus their work on establishing a general theory of contract, or that rare attempts at general theory are to be found among the early jurists, they do not so much formulate watertight theories as deduce several general principles from the libraries of commentaries and exegeses produced by their predecessors or contemporaries[19] by analysing their excellent work in nominate contracts; however, it seems that they are fully aware of the basic general concept of contracting. It is exciting to mention here that the Arabic term for the contract is *aqd* used by all jurists to mean to tie or bind. This is applicable generally to cover a broad spectrum of legal acts and obligations and is not limited to nominate contracts only. The evidence shows that in almost all of their treaties they have presented the discussion on every nominate contract in a standard form, which covers, inter alia:

1. The discussion on the contracting parties,
2. The discussion on the doctrine of offer and acceptance, and
3. The discussion on the subject matter of the contract.[20]

At the same time, they have also presented the discussion on consideration, mutual consent and intention to create obligations in bilateral contracts and many other topics which are also discussed in the Western law of contract. These discussions are the subject matter of general theory, and in this way, much academic literature now has been developed in scattered forms in different works and treaties of the Islamic jurists.

Similarly, there are two ways in which a contract (*aqd*) has been defined in its legal or technical sense (by the majority of jurists). Firstly, in narrow meaning, "the union of the declaration of one of the contracting parties with that of the other in a *Shariah* (legal) manner, the result of which is reflected in their subject matter."[21] In its wide sense, a contract is defined as *iltizam*. The *Medjelle* also defined it in this sense. The aspect is more suitable for the purpose of a theory of contracts.

Various attempts were made by Ibn Taymiyya to generate theory of contract in the 13th century, who separated rules of contract and contract stipulations, discussing them separately from the contract of sale, although it was not full theory; it was the first attempt[22] which is also in our view a serious effort to develop the general theory of contract. Ibn Taimiyah further wrote that "Men shall be permitted to make all the transaction they need; unless these transactions are forbidden by the Book or Sunnah".

Similarly, all four schools of law validated that contracting parties are at liberty to enter into a contract other than that of nominated contracts. Hence, generally speaking, all contracts are permissible to make unless prohibited in the Qur'ān and Sunnah. Again, quoting Ibn Taimiyah, that "The general principle in contracts and stipulations is permissibility and validity. Any contract or stipulation is valid unless there is an explicit text from the Qur'ān, the Sunnah, the consensus or analogy proving its prohibition and voiding."[23] This shows that if any contract can be made outside the nominated contract, it will fall in the ambit of the general theory of Islamic contract.[24]

Nevertheless, the first Islamic theory of contract as a theory in modern-day law took place in the 19th century, during which time the Ottoman's *Medjelle Al-Hkam Al-Adliyyah* was published by Hanafi scholars in Turkey. Murshid Al-Hayran's Egyptian version of the Ottoman's *Medjelle* considered Islamic civil law, including the contract theory, with Muslim jurists subsequently starting to develop a general theory of contract and writing textbooks on the subject. For example, Mohamed Abu Zahra, wrote a book on the theory of contract called *Al-Malkiyah Wa Nadhariyat Al-Aqd* and Abdul Razzaq Al-Sanhuri wrote the book *Masadir al Haqq fi al-Fiqh al-Islami*.[25]

To sum up, the general legal theory of Islamic law of contract *does* exist, and *Shariah* contains the general principle and all necessary detailed rules and regulations on the formation of a contract, related to contracting parties and the properties or the services on which contracts are concluded and which apply to all types of contracts. However, a well-developed Islamic general theory of contract is intended to be laid down. For a long time, and still nowadays, the Islamic law of contract is being studied and elaborated in a modern form, just like a Western contract, keeping in mind all guidelines provided by texts. More deep research is needed to elaborate and discover this theory's incomplete form and to bring it into compiled and codified form. As this is not within the scope of this book, to discuss this matter in detail, however, it can be done as a separate work. Recently, however, within the last four decades or so, works have been produced[26] which impose a continually increasing importance on general theories, derived in abstract hindsight from the series of specific contracts and their regulations formulated by the early jurists.[27] The general theories of today cover such elements as impediments to consent, classification of legal acts and their effects and a resume of the various options (*Khiyarat*) open to the parties for remedy.

It is true that the contract of sale provided a premise for analogy. The majority of legal treatises all contain a chapter on *Bay'*, in which essential ground rules are provided for contracts in general.[28]

After explaining the concept of nominate contracts and the general theory of Islamic law above, we now explain the concept of freedom of contract.

3.3 Freedom of contract

Another allegation levelled is that there is no theory of "freedom of contracts" under Islamic jurisprudence of contract law, but there exists the doctrine of restriction and limitation on contracts. There exist two views regarding the freedom of contract in the Islamic law of contract. Some are against the freedom of contract and some support it.

The main question that gives rise to controversy in this context is whether or not contracts are presumed to be lawful in the absence of a specific prohibition to the contrary, or indeed whether they are presumed to be unlawful unless provided for by Islamic laws. With this in mind, there is consideration towards whether one may create a new contract or add to or vary the terms prescribed by Islamic law.[29]

The advocates who are against the freedom of contracts argue that as the Islamic law is a law of contracts rather than a law of contract, Islam does not recognise freedom of contract. According to them, the list of nominate contracts is closed to new form.[30] They advanced their arguments based on the interpretation of the following texts.

The Qur'ān states:

ٱلطَّلَٰقُ مَرَّتَانِۖ فَإِمۡسَاكُۢ بِمَعۡرُوفٍ أَوۡ تَسۡرِيحُۢ بِإِحۡسَٰنٖۗ وَلَا يَحِلُّ لَكُمۡ أَن تَأۡخُذُواْ مِمَّآ ءَاتَيۡتُمُوهُنَّ شَيۡـًٔا إِلَّآ أَن
يَخَافَآ أَلَّا يُقِيمَا حُدُودَ ٱللَّهِۖ فَإِنۡ خِفۡتُمۡ أَلَّا يُقِيمَا حُدُودَ ٱللَّهِ فَلَا جُنَاحَ عَلَيۡهِمَا فِيمَا ٱفۡتَدَتۡ بِهِۦۗ تِلۡكَ حُدُودُ ٱللَّهِ فَلَا
تَعۡتَدُوهَاۚ وَمَن يَتَعَدَّ حُدُودَ ٱللَّهِ فَأُوْلَٰٓئِكَ هُمُ ٱلظَّٰلِمُونَ

> "Divorce is (revocable) two times (only). Then either retain (the wife) with honour (in marital relationship) or release her with kindness. And it is not lawful for you to take back anything of that which you have given them, unless both fear that (now by maintaining marital ties) they may not be able to observe the limits set by Allah. So if you fear that both will be unable to keep within Allah's limits, then (in that case) there shall be no sin upon either of them if the wife (herself) may give up something as recompense to free herself (from this distressing bond). These are the limits (set) by Allah. So, do not exceed them. And those who exceed the limits prescribed by Allah, it is they who are the wrongdoers."[31]

وَمَن يَعۡصِ ٱللَّهَ وَرَسُولَهُۥ وَيَتَعَدَّ حُدُودَهُۥ يُدۡخِلۡهُ نَارًا خَٰلِدٗا فِيهَا وَلَهُۥ عَذَابٞ مُّهِينٞ

> "But whoever disobeys Allah and His Prophet (PBUH) and exceeds His limits, He will admit him to Hell wherein shall he dwell forever; and there is a humiliating torment for him." [32]

The *hadith* states:

> "How can men stipulate conditions which are not in the Book of God? All conditions that are not in the Book of God are invalid, be it a hundred conditions. God's judgement is more true, and His conditions are more binding."[33]

We are sorry to say that this misconception occurred due to the wrong interpretation of above Qur'ānic verses and Prophet's statement. The majority of jurists understood this statement by the Prophet as denoting every contract or condition that is contrary to the Qur'ān and traditions of the Prophet (PBUH), rather than being a blanket rejection of every contract or terms not cited by such texts.

The statement relates to any contract and stipulation prohibited by Islamic rules; thus, this saying, in essence, does not limit the liberty of the general Islamic principles.

Moreover, the Prophet (PBUH) highlights that "Muslims are bound by their stipulations except for a stipulation which makes the unlawful lawful or makes the lawful unlawful."[34] Such a viewpoint provides parties with the capacity to put forward any stipulations in any contract, stating that parties shall be permitted to carry out all the transactions they need if they do not conflict with Islamic law.[35]

Due to the sea of classic academic literature on freedom of contract in the case of the general theory, it was wrongly concluded by the above jurists that, other than the nominate contracts, new forms of contract cannot be entered into and the contracts which do not fall in the ambit of the nominate contract are not valid. This negates the theory of freedom of contract.

The other group of advocates supports the freedom of contract. According to them, the concept of freedom of contract is also appreciated in the Islamic law of contract. The Islamic contract jurisprudence allows parties a high autonomy over the making and managing of their financial affairs, contract and other private exchanges. All four schools of law validate that contracting parties are free to enter into a contract other than that of nominate contracts.

According to them, along with nominate contracts, all other contracts are lawful unless they are specifically prohibited by the Qur'ān and Sunnah. According to this view, contracting parties are free to make transactions outside the scope of the nominate contracts established by early jurists. This is based on the very well-known principle of general permissibility which means that all things are permissible unless prohibited in the Qur'ān and Sunnah.

These advocates have, like their counterparts, built their arguments on the Qur'ānic verses and *Ahadith* of Prophet (PBUH). They quote the following Qur'ānic verses:

يَٰٓأَيُّهَا ٱلَّذِينَ ءَامَنُوٓاْ أَوۡفُواْ بِٱلۡعُقُودِۚ أُحِلَّتۡ لَكُم بَهِيمَةُ ٱلۡأَنۡعَٰمِ إِلَّا مَا يُتۡلَىٰ عَلَيۡكُمۡ غَيۡرَ مُحِلِّي ٱلصَّيۡدِ وَأَنتُمۡ
حُرُمٌۗ إِنَّ ٱللَّهَ يَحۡكُمُ مَا يُرِيدُ

> "O believers! Fulfill (your) promises. The quadrupeds (i.e., cattle) have been made lawful for you except those (animals) that will be announced to you afterward. (But) when clad in ihram (the Pilgrim's sacred dress), do not presume hunting lawful. Surely, Allah ordains what He wills." [36]

وَأَنَّ هَٰذَا صِرَٰطِي مُسۡتَقِيمٗا فَٱتَّبِعُوهُۖ وَلَا تَتَّبِعُواْ ٱلسُّبُلَ فَتَفَرَّقَ بِكُمۡ عَن سَبِيلِهِۦۚ ذَٰلِكُمۡ وَصَّىٰكُم بِهِۦ لَعَلَّكُمۡ تَتَّقُونَ

> "And that this (Islamic law) is My straight path. So follow it and do not follow (other) paths, because they (the other paths) will move you away from Allah's path. This is what He has enjoined you strictly so that you may become God-fearing." [37]

وَلَا تَقۡرَبُواْ مَالَ ٱلۡيَتِيمِ إِلَّا بِٱلَّتِي هِيَ أَحۡسَنُ حَتَّىٰ يَبۡلُغَ أَشُدَّهُۥۚ وَأَوۡفُواْ بِٱلۡعَهۡدِۖ إِنَّ ٱلۡعَهۡدَ كَانَ مَسۡـُٔولٗا

> "And (also) do not go near the orphan's property, but in a way that is beneficial (to the orphan), until he reaches his maturity. And always fulfill the promise. No doubt, the promise will be questioned about." [38]

The Prophet (PBUH) reported having said: "The conditions most deserving of fulfilment are those whereby you make a woman lawful unto you", which was interpreted as meaning that all conditions relating to contracts deserve to be fulfilled.[39]

They concluded that the injunctions to fulfil all contracts and undertakings is unqualified and absolute.[40] Further, on the basis of the Qur'ānic verse: "He has explained to you that which is forbidden to you", and a *hadith* Sahih related by al-Tirmidhi to the effect that "Every agreement is lawful among Muslims except one which declares forbidden that which is allowed, or declares allowed that which is forbidden."[41]

An argument that is gaining more force in the modern era is based on the Qur'ānic verse: "O believers! Do not devour one another's wealth unlawfully amongst yourselves unless it is a trade by your mutual agreement and does not kill yourselves. Surely, Allah is Kind to you."[42] In this verse, the only condition required according to Qur'ānic stipulation for the validity of any contract is the mutual consent of the contracting parties. These advocates thereby conclude that subject to such consent, and such prohibitions and limitations as yet set down by the law, every contract is valid whether or not they coincide with any of the recognised nominate contracts.[43] Islamic law does not recognise a statute of limitations. There is a *hadith* attributed to the Prophet (PBUH) which states: "The right of a Muslim is not extinguished by the passage of time."[44] In practice, certain limitations have been established. The *Medjelle* stipulates that actions referring to debt, inheritance, real estate held in absolute ownership and others could not be brought after 15 years had elapsed. Modern legislation does recognise a statute of limitations; periods differ depending on the subject matter, and regulations are provided in the relevant sections of the Civil Law Codes of the respective countries. Therefore, it is a reasonable presumption that all contracts are valid subject to their being expressly forbidden by the rule of law, or if they contain voidable stipulations, or contravene Islamic prohibitions (especially those of *riba*, *maysir* and *gharar*), or public policy or morals.[45]

Hence, parties are free to choose their terms and conditions of the contract under Islamic law of contract. There is a maxim: "The contract is the law of the parties", meaning that in general, the parties to a contract are free to agree to the terms and conditions of their own choice, providing that these terms or conditions are not at odds with established principles of Islamic law. It is interesting to note that in Western law of contract the concept of "freedom of contract" is more or less the same as in Islamic law, with the difference that Western law does not concern itself with some prohibited elements, as is the case with Islamic law. The term "freedom of contract", in many respects means the same thing under *Shariah* law as it does under English law, namely that parties are free to choose their terms and conditions of contract, and that the law will rarely intervene to frustrate a lawful contract that has been formed consensually between two parties with sufficient capacity to contract.[46]

Every person has the right to enter into any contract provided that the parties, the contract itself and the subject matter of the contract are in accordance with the provisions laid down in the Holy Qur'ān and the Sunnah of the Prophet (PBUH). Such freedom has been given by Allah u as He does not want human beings to suffer any difficulties. Allah u wants His creatures to have a comfortable life.

He u says يُرِيدُ ٱللَّهُ بِكُمُ ٱلْيُسْرَ وَلَا يُرِيدُ بِكُمُ ٱلْعُسْرَ

> "Allah desires ease for you and does not desire hardship for you."[47]

Another objection regarding freedom of contract raised is that contracting parties in Islamic law of contract are not free to choose which laws should regulate their contracts and which court should settle any dispute that arises. The real fact is that under Islamic law it is permitted to choose applicable law and jurisdiction of the court. To quote here,

> Islam recognises the concept of freedom of contract; therefore, the parties can choose *Shariah* principles as the governing law of the contract. They can also choose the jurisdiction of the courts of a designated country as the forum for resolving disputes between the contracting parties. However, the application of Islamic principles by the selected forum depends on the laws of the country in which the enforcement is sought.[48]

This is why the countries which adopted the English Contract Act to apply to contract disputes have written into their legislation that no law is applicable which is against the injunctions of the Qur'ān and Sunnah.

It is important to note here that the limitations on making contracts and in doing other business activities imposed by the Islamic law of contract are all for the benefit of the parties only. The things which are forbidden are physically, psychologically and spiritually damaging for human beings. For example, Islamic contract law allowed trade and contracts only based on mutual consent and disabled all deceptive business transactions. Islamic laws looked at everything from the perspective of human welfare. What is harmful is removed and what is beneficial is allowed.

Allah says in Qur'ān:

ٱلَّذِينَ يَتَّبِعُونَ ٱلرَّسُولَ ٱلنَّبِيَّ ٱلْأُمِّيَّ ٱلَّذِي يَجِدُونَهُۥ مَكْتُوبًا عِندَهُمْ فِي ٱلتَّوْرَىٰةِ وَٱلْإِنجِيلِ يَأْمُرُهُم
بِٱلْمَعْرُوفِ وَيَنْهَىٰهُمْ عَنِ ٱلْمُنكَرِ وَيُحِلُّ لَهُمُ ٱلطَّيِّبَٰتِ وَيُحَرِّمُ عَلَيْهِمُ ٱلْخَبَٰٓئِثَ وَيَضَعُ عَنْهُمْ إِصْرَهُمْ
وَٱلْأَغْلَٰلَ ٱلَّتِي كَانَتْ عَلَيْهِمْ فَٱلَّذِينَ ءَامَنُوا۟ بِهِۦ وَعَزَّرُوهُ وَنَصَرُوهُ وَٱتَّبَعُوا۟ ٱلنُّورَ ٱلَّذِيٓ أُنزِلَ مَعَهُۥٓ أُو۟لَٰٓئِكَ
هُمُ ٱلْمُفْلِحُونَ

> "(They are the people) who follow the Messenger, the Prophet (titled as) al-Ummi (who imparts to the people from Allah the news of the unseen and knowledge and secrets of socio-economic disciplines of life without himself being taught by any human in the world); whose (eminent attributes and exquisite powers) these people find written in the Torah and the Injil (Gospel); who enjoins on them virtues and forbids them vices, declares

> wholesome things lawful and impure ones unlawful for them and removes from them their heavy burdens and yokes (i.e., shackles) weighing upon them (due to their acts of disobedience and blesses them with freedom). So those who will believe in this (most exalted Messenger [blessings and peace be upon him]) and venerate and revere him and serve and support him (in his Din [Religion]) and follow this light (the Qur'an) that has been sent down with him, it is they who will flourish and prosper'."[49]

3.4 The juristic person

Another allegation levelled is that there is a deficiency in Islamic law of contract regarding the existence of the concept of the juristic person as a separate legal entity.

There are two groups of jurists: one advocating the non-existence of the juristic person in Islamic law; and another advocating their very existence in Islamic law. Due to these diverging opinions among the jurists, some orientalists alleged that there are no existing express provisions in Islamic law resources regarding the concept of the separate legal entity of the juristic person.

The orientalist Joseph Schacht has said: "Islamic law does not recognise juristic persons."[50] This view is based on the confusion caused by some sentences which have occurred in some books of Islamic jurisprudence.

For example, regarding *waqf*, it is stated that:

> The *waqf* has no obligation for itself, and its loans are primarily the responsibility of its trustee. These can be paid out of his property or estate if dead. Later on, the trustee or his legal heirs can get it out of the *waqf* property.[51]

From this, it has been wrongly inferred that as the *waqf* itself is not liable, its loans are paid by its trustee. Hence *waqf* is not a juristic person, and the obligations are essentially attributed to the natural persons only. The true meaning and interpretation of the above reference are that the liability of *waqf* is limited to its property, and its loans should be satisfied, firstly, from the trustee who is supposed to be vigilant. He will then adjust his payments or loan from the *waqf* property afterwards. There is no room for inference from this reference that *waqf* is not liable for its debts. The above reference is followed by the sentence:

> "The proof of loan against the *waqf* stands without the intervention of the responsibility of the trustee."

This has also been wrongly inferred from the viewpoint of some jurists who have held that a "Will" or a bequest of property cannot be made in favour of a "Mosque". From this, they infer that as the mosque cannot own property, so it is not a juristic person.

However, the exact position is that the concept of the juristic person does exist in the Islamic concept of law. Even the dissenting jurists on the acceptance of separate legal entities in *Shariah* law (based on *dhimunah*, *baitul mal*, *waqf*, etc.)

acknowledged the importance of justifying and accommodating the legal validity of a fictitious legal personality or separate legal entity under *Shariah* law.

According to the Islamic concept of law, persons are of two kinds: (1) a natural person; (2) a legal person or a juristic person. In the eyes of the law, a person whether real or juristic is the one who possesses some legal rights and liabilities and sometimes even a natural person is not considered to be a person possessed of legal rights and liabilities. At times, a person who is not a human being is treated as being a person by law having some legal rights and liabilities. Even a deceased person has rights and obligations on his/her estate. He/she is entitled to have his/her funeral expenses, debt and other obligations discharged out of his/her estate.

The Muslim jurists have been writing on the concept of 'juristic person' and have been vehemently asserting that the concept of juristic person exists in Islamic law and is always recognised. From a very early Islamic perspective, the concept of legal personality is clear regarding three institutions, i.e. *baitul mal*, *waqf* and *masjid*, which were developed in early Islamic states through the ages. Abdul Qadir 'Audah says:

> Islamic law has, since its dawn, recognised the existence of juristic persons. The jurists have discussed the state treasury and *waqf* as juristic persons. Similarly, they have considered the schools, orphanages, hospitals, etc. as the juristic persons and competent to hold and exercise the rights.[52]

Mustafa Zarqa states:

> When we referred to the original texts and sources of the *Shariah*, we found in it legal provisions which in substance propound the concept of the juristic person and its legal status. Moreover, also we found the legal provisions which personify the juristic person with all its principles and characteristics which are attributed to it by the latest (Western) law.[53]

He further states:

> On the same pattern of the latest (Western) legal position of the juristic person, it is found in the *Shariah* in the perfect form in the shape of the treasury, *waqf* and the state in which the head of the state personifies the entire Muslim community.[54]

It appears from the above quotations that the concept of the juristic person in Islamic law has existed in the most developed form since its inception. The jurists have developed the following essential characteristics of a juristic person:

i. It can perpetuate its legal status independent of the natural persons.
ii. It has legal rights and can acquire and own property in any capacity such as owner, leaser, pawnee and mortgagee, etc.
iii. It is responsible for legal obligations, can sue and be sued on its name.

According to the jurists who advocated the existence of the concept of a juristic person, although the legal person might be an artificial juristic person it can own property, run its business like a natural person. To sum up:

1. The word "person" is usually used to refer to an individual human being, but in law it has a technical meaning in the sense of right and duties. The Muslim jurists principally declared inanimate entities or artificial entities as having some of the rights and duties of legal or juristic persons. Zuhairah Ariff Abd Ghadas noted that some of the modern jurists of Fiqh like Mustafa Ahmad al-Zarka, Muhammad Abu Zuhrah, etc. justify the existence of a legal entity other than a human being as a legal person based on the theory of Fiqh known as *al-Dhimma'*. *Al-Dhimma* means guaranty or accountable.[55]

   According to Al-Kabashi (1989), some jurists view the terms *al-dhimmah* and *al-ahliyyah* (capacity) as being synonymous, both of which represent the entity that has rights, bear responsibilities, and obligations. Thus, if an entity (*al-dhimmah*) is recognised to be in existence, either artificial or real, it will have a certain capacity (*al-ahliyyah*) and therefore, will be subjected to specific obligations (*iltizamat*).[56]
2. Muslim jurists have declared *waqf* to be a separate legal entity and have ascribed to it some characteristics similar to those of a natural person. When a person dedicates his property for charitable purposes, such property, after being declared as a *waqf*, no longer remains in the ownership of the donor. The beneficiaries of the *waqf* can only enjoy the benefits and proceeds of the *waqf* rather than becoming its owners. Muslim jurists have treated *waqf* as a separate legal entity that may own property.
3. Jurists have also declared *baitul mal* i.e. state treasury as a juristic person. Imam al-Sarakhsi, a well-known Hanafi jurist, in his work "*al-Mabsut*" stated that *bait-ul-mal* has some rights and obligations.
4. The Muslim jurists have also declared "companies" as separate legal entities. A company is a modern form of partnership business which is permitted by Islamic law. The partnership is a contract in which a few individuals join together for the purpose of doing business with property, skills and goodwill. The main three kinds of partnerships, i.e. *Shirkat-ul-Amwal*, *Shirkat-ul-Mal* and *Shirkat-ul-Wujuh* respectively, are similar to modern forms of corporate activities. The joint-stock company business is also regarded as akin to the contract of *Shirkat*. A joint-stock company is a juristic person, no less than a real human being. Similarly, a municipal corporation is treated as a juristic person even though in reality it is not a person. So there are two types of juristic persons: corporation sole and corporation aggregate. A corporation sole comprises a series of successive persons occupying the office in succession. The corporation aggregate, on the other hand, consists of a group of persons who are sometimes said to be members or the shareholders of such corporations. A corporation aggregate is joint-stock companies (comprising many shareholders), municipal corporation consisting of the members representing the city, insurance companies, etc.

5. The Muslim jurists also declared that when a deceased person leaves liabilities exceeding his property, this property is neither owned by the deceased nor is it owned by his legal heirs. Being property of nobody, it has its existence, and it can be termed a legal entity. Debts on the deceased have preferential rights over the property as compared to the rights of the heirs.
6. According to the Muslim jurists, the mosque is also regarded as equal to the *waqf* because it also has the capability to own property and leaves rights and obligations. It is also considered a juristic person, although some jurists considered this not to be the case, as they have held that "will" of property cannot be made in favour of the mosque. The actual position is that this view has been rejected by the majority of Hanafi jurists. Muhammad Shaibani is for the validity of this will. Ibn 'Abidin Shami in Raad al-Muhtar has also emphasised the lawfulness of such a will. 'Allama Ramli says:

    > "The will in favour of a mosque is lawful, although the intention is to make it the owner of the property. The mosque is like a free natural person and can hold property."[57] Jurists also allowed the making of gifts directly in favour of the mosque.

7. The Muslim jurists also declared some other institutions such as hospitals, orphanages, educational institutions and banks, etc. to be juristic persons. All these are competent to hold and exercise rights. Similarly, a university or any other corporate body is also a legal person in the eye of the law no less than a real human being is. The law has devised a device by introducing a fiction whereby an imaginary person is considered to be a real person in the eyes of the law, and such a person is said to be a juristic person. They built their argument on the well-settled principle of Islamic jurisprudence that an action, deed or thing which is not explicitly prohibited by injunctions of the Qur'ān and Sunnah is considered to be permitted. As no prohibition exists in Islamic law, hence these are permitted. Any other form of business or association which are not prohibited is also permissible on the same footing.

It is worth noting that if we accept that there is no concept of the juristic person in Islamic law, then it will shatter the whole structure of Islamic commercial law and particularly the law of contract. All the above-mentioned forms of juristic person have become the most critical business and commercial institutions of the modern world, along with their religious and charitable status.

Notes

1 J. Schacht, Introduction to Islamic law, Clarendon Press (1964), p. 144.
2 J. Schacht, Introduction to Islamic law, Clarendon Press (1964), p. 144.
3 Dr. S.E. Rayner, The theory of contracts in Islamic law, p. 86.
4 Dr. S.E. Rayner, The theory of contracts in Islamic law, p. 100.
5 L. Milliot, La pensee juridique de I'Islam, Revue Internationale de droit compare, 1954, p. 441.
6 Dr. S.E. Rayner, The theory of contracts in Islamic law, p. 101.

7 Sanhuri, al-Wasit fi Sharh al-Qanun al-Madani (Beirut, n.d.), vol. 4, part.1, p. 1.
8 De Bellefonds Y. Linant, Traite de droit musulman compare, vol. 3, p. 57.
9 Dr. S.E. Rayner, The theory of contracts in Islamic law, p. 86.
10 Qur'ān 5:1 (Eng. trans. from 'Glorious Qur'ān' by Shaykh-ul-Islam Dr. Muhammad Tahir-ul-Qadri).
11 Imam Bukhari, *Sahih al-Bukhari*, vol. 1–3, pp. 251–252, (Beirut, nd: Dar al-Jil).
12 Seyed Hadi Hosseini, Restrictions on contractual liberty, p. 61.
13 See UCC, the current US commercial code, which mainly regulates the sale contract. English Rent Act 1977; or, Sale of Goods Act 1923 (New South Wales), (1990).
14 Dr. Hussain Hamid Hassan, An introduction to the study of Islamic law, p. 249.
15 Muhammad Bukhari, Sahih al-Bukhari, vol. 1–3, pp. 251–252, (Beriut, nd: Dar al-Jil).
16 Ahmad Ibn Taymiyah, Majmu al Fatawa, vol. 3, p. 333, Saudi Arabia King Fahad printing complex, 2006.
17 Ahmad Ibn Taymiyah, Majmu al Fatawa, vol. 3, p. 323, Saudi Arabia King Fahad printing complex, 2006.
18 Majid Rahmanian Koshkaki, An Islamic approach to contract management and financing in infrastructure projects, p. 36.
19 Dr. S.E. Rayner, The theory of contracts in Islamic law, p. 90.
20 Frustration of performance of contracts: A comparative and analytic study in Islamic law and English law, Ibrahim Saad Alhowaimil, 2013, p. 72.
21 Frustration of performance of contracts: A comparative and analytic study in Islamic law and English law, Ibrahim Saad Alhowaimil, 2013, p. 72.
22 Oussama Arabi, Contract stipulation in Islamic law the Ottoman Medjelle and Ibn Taymiyya 1998 30 International Journal of Middle East studies. Cambridge University press p. 29, 50.
23 Ahmad Ibn Taymiyah, Majmu al Fatawa, vol. 29, Saudi Arabia King Fahad printing complex, 2006, p. 127.
24 Ahmad Ibn Taymiyah, Majmu al Fatawa, vol. 29, Saudi Arabia King Fahad printing complex, 2006, p. 127.
25 Ibrahim Saad Alhowaimil, Frustration of performance of contract, A comparative and analytic study in Islamic law and English law, p. 73.
26 'Abd al-Razzaq as-Sanhuri, *Masadir al-Haqq fi al-Fiqh al-Islami*, p. 46 and Yusuf Musa, *al-Amwal wa Nazariyat al-'Aqd*, (Cairo, 1953) p. 44 as quoted by Dr. S.E. Rayner, The theory of contracts in Islamic law, p. 90.
27 Dr. S.E. Rayner, The theory of contracts in Islamic law, p. 91.
28 Al-Kasani, *Kitab al-Badai al-Sanai* (Cairo, 1909–1910; Ibn Abidin, *al-Raad al-Muhtar*, (Cairo, 1324) as quoted by Dr. S.E. Rayner, The theory of contracts in Islamic law, p. 91.
29 Ibrahim Saad Alhowaimil, Frustration of performance of contract, A comparative and analytic study in Islamic law and English law, p. 73.
30 Dr. S.E.Rayner. Theory of contract in Islamic law 1991, pp. 91–92.
31 Qur'ān, 2:229 (English translation from 'Glorious Qur'ān' by Shaykh-ul-Islam Dr. Muhammad Tahir-ul-Qadri).
32 Qur'ān, 4:14 (Eng. trans. from 'Glorious Qur'ān' by Shaykh-ul-Islam Dr. Muhammad Tahir-ul-Qadri).
33 Sahih Bukhari, Hadith No.2579.
34 Sunan Abu Dawud, Hadith No.1419.
35 Vogel Frank and Hayes Samuel, Islamic law of finance (Boston BRILL 2006) p. 98.
36 Qur'ān, 5:1 (Eng. trans. from 'Glorious Qur'ān' by Shaykh-ul-Islam Dr. Muhammad Tahir-ul-Qadri).
37 Qur'ān, 6:153 (Eng. trans. from 'Glorious Qur'ān' by Shaykh-ul-Islam Dr. Muhammad Tahir-ul-Qadri).
38 Qur'ān, 17:34 (Eng. trans. from 'Glorious Qur'ān' by Shaykh-ul-Islam Dr. Muhammad Tahir-ul-Qadri).

39 As quoted by Dr. S.E. Rayner, The theory of contract in Islamic law, p. 93.
40 Ibn Hazm, al-Ihkam fi Usul al-Ahkam, vol. 5, p. 305.
41 Ahmad Ibn Taymiyah, Majmu al Fatawa, vol. 3, p. 333; al-Shatibi, al-Muwafaqat, vol. 5, pp. 305–307.
42 Qur'ān, 4:29 (Eng. trans. from 'Glorious Qur'ān' by Shaykh-ul-Islam Dr. Muhammad Tahir-ul-Qadri).
43 Ibn Hazm, al-Ihkam fi Usul al-Ahkam, vol. 5, pp. 2-49; Ahmad Ibn Taymiyah, Majmu al Fatawa, vol. 3, p. 323.
44 'Abd al-Jalil al-Rawi, 'Principles on the Islamic law of contracts'. The George Washington law review, XXII, (1953-54) p. 38.
45 Ibn Qayyim al-Jawziyyah, Ilam al-Muwaqqiin An Rab al-Alamin, (Cairo, n.d) vol. 1, p. 299.
46 N. Shaeh, Freedom of contract: What does it mean in the context of Arab laws? (2001) 16 Arab law quarterly 4, 346, 357.
47 Qur'ān, 2:185 (Eng. trans. from 'Glorious Qur'ān' by Shaykh-ul-Islam Dr. Muhammad Tahir-ul-Qadri).
48 Ardeshir Atai, 'Overview of Islamic financial investments' (Atai Associates, n.d.) 9-0 [Online] http://www.ataiassociates .com/pdf/overview_of islamic_ financial_investment.pdf (accessed 2nd May 2011).
49 Qur'ān, 7:157 (Eng. trans. from 'Glorious Qur'ān' by Shaykh-ul-Islam Dr. Muhammad Tahir-ul-Qadri).
50 Joseph Schacht, An Introduction to Islamic law, p. 125.
51 Tanqih al-Hamidiya, vol.1, p. 206.
52 'Abd al-Qdir 'Audah: al-Tashri' al-Jinai, vol. 1, p. 292.
53 Mustafa Zarqa, *al-Madkhal al Fiqhi al-Aam*, vol. 3, p. 257.
54 Mustafa Zarqa, *al-Madkhal al Fiqhi al-Aam*, vol. 3, p. 285.
55 Zuhairah Ariff Abd Ghadas, *The myth of corporate personality: An overview from the common law and the Islamic law perspective*. Paper presented at the International conference on harmonization of shariah and civil law, International Islamic University, Malaysia.
56 Al-Kabashi, *al-Makashifi Taha, al-Dzimmah wa al-haq wa tathiruha bi al-mawt fi al-fiqh al-Islami*: *Dirasah muqaranah*, Riyadh: Maktabah al-Haramayn, p. 7.
57 Allama Ihayat al-Muhtaj Ramli, (Halb, Egypt) vol. 3, p. 116.

4 Key features of business and guiding principles of Islamic contract law

In this chapter we shall discuss two topics: key features of business and commercial transactions, along with very important guiding principles of Islamic contract law.

4.1 Key features of business

Following are the key features of trade and business under Islamic law of contract.

4.2 Earning a living

Islamic law does not require humans to deprive themselves of the need for well-being and development. However, it appreciates that it is necessary to work for these things. The very act of making a living is service to the Almighty. Making physical and mental efforts at work is a must. Allah says:

وَجَعَلْنَا ٱلَّيْلَ وَٱلنَّهَارَ ءَايَتَيْنِ ۖ فَمَحَوْنَآ ءَايَةَ ٱلَّيْلِ وَجَعَلْنَآ ءَايَةَ ٱلنَّهَارِ مُبْصِرَةً لِّتَبْتَغُوا۟ فَضْلًا مِّن رَّبِّكُمْ

> "And We have made the night and the day two signs (of Our might). Then We made the Sign of the night dark and We made the sign of the day bright so that you might look for your Lord's bounty (provision)."[1]

Even Friday is not a day for relaxing, as is generally understood by the masses. The Qur'ān enjoins the faithful to disperse in the land when the congregational worship is ended.

فَإِذَا قُضِيَتِ ٱلصَّلَوٰةُ فَٱنتَشِرُوا۟ فِى ٱلْأَرْضِ وَٱبْتَغُوا۟ مِن فَضْلِ ٱللَّهِ

> "Then after the Prayer is offered, disperse in the land and (then) look for Allah's bounty (i.e. sustenance)."[2]

There is a deep relation between input and output at work. This universal law is stated in the Most Sacred Book of Islam: "And that man (according to justice) will get only that for which he strives."[3]

The following *ahadiths* of the Prophet (PBUH) highlight the significance of earning one's keep. There is nothing wrong with doing manual labour in order to earn a living. Al-Miqdām (R.A) reported Prophet (PBUH) said:

مَا أَكَلَ أَحَدٌ طَعَامًا قَطُّ خَيْرًا مِنْ أَنْ يَأْكُلَ مِنْ عَمَلِ يَدِهِ وَإِنَّ نَبِيَّ اللَّهِ دَاوُدَ عَلَيْهِ السَّلَام كَانَ يَأْكُلُ مِنْ عَمَلِ يَدِهِ

> "No one eats any better food than someone who eats from what he earns by the work of his own hands. Allah's Prophet, Dāwūd (peace be upon him), used to eat from what he earned by the work of his own hands."[4]

According to Hazrat 'Aāisha (R.A), the mother of the faithful, the associates of the Prophet (PBUH) won their bread with the sweat of their brow:

كَانَ أَصْحَابُ رَسُولِ اللهِ صَلَّى الله عَلَيْهِ وَسَلَّمَ عُمَّالَ أَنْفُسِهِمْ

> "The Companions of Prophet (R.A) used to work doing manual labour."[5]

According to Islamic law, making efforts to gain a lawful living is an act of worship. According to Abd Allah (R.A), the Prophet (PBUH) said:

طَلَبُ الْحَلَالِ فَرِيضَةٌ بَعْدَ الْفَرِيضَةِ

> "Trying to gain a lawful livelihood is (the most important) obligation after obligatory worship."[6]

According to a *hadith*, the blessed are the labourers who work diligently and sincerely.

خير الكسب كسب العامل إذا نصح

> "A labourer's wage is best of all wages provided that he works sincerely."[7]

The Prophet (PBUH) gave glad tidings to the folks who engage in doing manual labour until they tire themselves out and smell."

من امسى كالا من عمل يديه أمسى مغفورا له

> "If someone got tired working manually until evening, he entered evening forgiven and pardoned."[8]

None of you must lag behind in the matter of seeking livelihood and (just) pray: "Allah, grant me with provisions," and he should know that the sky rains neither gold nor silver.[9]

It goes without saying that earning one's keep obligates one to shun begging. Islam made the breadwinners the productive members of the community.

4.3 Moderation in earning

As stated earlier, seeking a livelihood is essential for mankind. The Prophetic statement again affirms, "Trying to gain a lawful livelihood is (the most important) obligation after obligatory worship".[10] It does not entail, however, that work should occupy one for all one's waking hours. By maintaining a balance in life, the faithful may fulfil their duties towards the Lord and His creatures. On moderation in seeking a living, according to Jabir b. 'Abd Allah (R.A), the Prophet (PBUH) said:

أَيُّهَا النَّاسُ اتَّقُوا اللَّهَ وَأَجْمِلُوا فِي الطَّلَبِ فَإِنَّ نَفْسًا لَنْ تَمُوتَ حَتَّى تَسْتَوْفِيَ رِزْقَهَا وَإِنْ أَبْطَأَ عَنْهَا فَاتَّقُوا اللهَ وَأَجْمِلُوا فِي الطَّلَبِ خُذُوا مَا حَلَّ وَدَعُوا مَا حَرُمَ

> "People, fear Allah and be moderate in seeking a living, for no soul will die until it has received all its provision even if it is slow in coming. So fear Allah and be moderate in seeking provision; take what is permissible and leave what is prohibited."[11]

أَعْظَمُ النَّاسِ هَمًّا ، الْمُؤْمِنُ الَّذِي يَهُمُّ بِأَمْرِ دُنْيَاهُ وَأَمْرِ آخِرَتِهِ.

> "The one who has the most concerns is the believer, who is concerned about both his, worldly affairs and his Hereafter."[12]

Believers keep to a just balance in all matters, including spending. Sticking to the essence of the Divine inspiration cited below, they eschew the twin extremes of wastefulness and stinginess:

وَٱلَّذِينَ إِذَآ أَنفَقُواْ لَمۡ يُسۡرِفُواْ وَلَمۡ يَقۡتُرُواْ وَكَانَ بَيۡنَ ذَٰلِكَ قَوَامًا

> "And (these) are the people who are neither extravagant nor miserly when they spend. And their spending is (based on) a balance between the two extremes (of extravagance and miserliness)."[13]

The following traditions also urge economising, which is a solution to economic ills.

Ibn 'Umar (R.A) related that the Holy Prophet (PBUH) said:

الاقْتِصَادُ فِي النَّفَقَةِ نِصْفُ الْمَعِيشَةِ

> "Moderation in spending is a half of economy."[14]

'Abd Allāh b. Mas'ūd (R.A) reported that Prophet (PBUH) said: ما عَالَ مَنِ اقْتَصَدَ

> "If someone maintains a balance, he will not suffer poverty."[15]

However, moderation in using one's resources does not mean stinginess, shabbiness and avoidance of Divine bounties, as the following traditions establish. The faithful ought to put on good clothes and consume quality food if they can afford to, and give thanks to Allah, the Exalted.

'Umar b. al-Khattāb (R.A) narrated that he heard Prophet (PBUH):

مَنْ لَبِسَ ثَوْبًا جَدِيدًا فَقَالَ الْحَمْدُ لِلَّهِ الَّذِي كَسَانِي مَا أُوَارِي بِهِ عَوْرَتِي وَأَتَجَمَّلُ بِهِ فِي حَيَاتِي ثُمَّ عَمَدَ إِلَى الثَّوْبِ الَّذِي أَخْلَقَ فَتَصَدَّقَ بِهِ كَانَ فِي كَنَفِ اللهِ وَفِي حِفْظِ اللهِ وَفِي سَتْرِ اللهِ حَيًّا وَمَيِّتًا

> Whoever wears a new garment and then says: "All praise is due to Allah who clothed me with what I may cover my nakedness, and what I may beautify myself with in my life and then he takes the garment that has worn out and gives it in charity, he shall be under Allah's guard, Allah's protection, and Allah's covering, alive and dead."[16]

According to S ā lim:

عَنْ ابْنِ عُمَرَ أَنَّ رَسُولَ اللهِ صَلَّى اللهُ عَلَيْهِ وَسَلَّمَ رَأَى عَلَى عُمَرَ قَمِيصًا أَبْيَضَ فَقَالَ ثَوْبُكَ هَذَا غَسِيلٌ أَمْ جَدِيدٌ قَالَ لَا بَلْ غَسِيلٌ قَالَ الْبَسْ جَدِيدًا وَعِشْ حَمِيدًا وَمُتْ شَهِيدًا

> "Ibn ¢Umar (R.A) reported that Prophet (PBUH) saw ¢Umar wearing a white shirt and said: 'Is this garment of yours washed or a new one?' ¢Umar said: 'Rather it has been washed.' Holy Prophet (PBUH) said: 'Wear new clothes, live a good life and die and martyr.'"[17]

4.4 Freedom to work

Everyone has the right to seek employment, to take a job or to pursue a profession of his or her choice. None may be denied this inalienable right on the grounds of colour, caste, ethnicity or religious orientation. Allah says اوَبَرِّلٱ مَرَّحَوَ عَيۡبَلۡٱ ُهَّللٱ َّلَحَأَو

> "Whereas Allah has declared trade (i.e., buying and selling) lawful and usury unlawful."[18]

4.5 Creation of wealth

Humans are in need of the means of sustenance in order to survive, hence the obligation of earning and amassing wealth. Allah says:

رَّبُّكُمُ ٱلَّذِي يُزۡجِي لَكُمُ ٱلۡفُلۡكَ فِي ٱلۡبَحۡرِ لِتَبۡتَغُواْ مِن فَضۡلِهِۦٓۚ إِنَّهُۥ كَانَ بِكُمۡ رَحِيمٗا

> "Your Lord is He Who makes (the ships and) vessels sail in the sea (and rivers) for you so that you may look for His bounty (i.e., sustenance through internal and external trade). Indeed, He is Ever-Merciful towards you."[19]

فَإِذَا قُضِيَتِ ٱلصَّلَوٰةُ فَٱنتَشِرُواْ فِي ٱلۡأَرۡضِ وَٱبۡتَغُواْ مِن فَضۡلِ ٱللَّهِ

"Then after the Prayer is offered, disperse in the land and (then) look for Allah's bounty (i.e., sustenance)."[20]

4.6 Sharing personal resources

The Holy Prophet (PBUH) built a social fabric in which individuals considered themselves trustees of their possessions. The Holy Prophet (PBUH) urged on charitable donations to the poor and needy so that they might benefit from the sustenance from the people of substance:

طَعَامُ الْوَاحِدِ يَكْفِي الِاثْنَيْنِ وَطَعَامُ الِاثْنَيْنِ يَكْفِي الْأَرْبَعَةَ وَطَعَامُ الْأَرْبَعَةِ يَكْفِي الثَّمَانِيَةَ

"The food of one is sufficient for two, the food of two is sufficient for four, and the food of four is sufficient for eight."[21]

According to Abū Sa'īd al-Khudrī (R.A), the Holy Prophet (PBUH) said to his associates:

مَنْ كَانَ مَعَهُ فَضْلُ ظَهْرٍ فَلْيَعُدْ بِهِ عَلَى مَنْ لَا ظَهْرَ لَهُ وَمَنْ كَانَ لَهُ فَضْلٌ مِنْ زَادٍ فَلْيَعُدْ بِهِ عَلَى مَنْ لَا زَادَ لَهُ قَالَ فَذَكَرَ مِنْ أَصْنَافِ الْمَالِ مَا ذَكَرَ حَتَّى رَأَيْنَا أَنَّهُ لَا حَقَّ لِأَحَدٍ مِنَّا فِي فَضْلٍ

"'Whoever has a surplus travelling animal should return it to one who does not possess any and whoever possesses surplus baggage should return it to one who does not have any.' Then He mentioned various kinds of wealth and we started feeling as if we did not have any right to what is surplus to us."[22]

4.7 Timely payment of wages

Employees must be paid for their work as soon as they complete their work. Withholding wages or employing delaying tactics are irksome to a worker, which Islam treats as a form of oppression. Entrepreneurs must not delay in the payment of the wages of workers. ¢Abd Allāh b. ¢Umar (R.A) related that Holy Prophet (PBUH) said: أَعْطُوا الْأَجِيرَ أَجْرَهُ قَبْلَ أَنْ يَجِفَّ عَرَقُهُ

"Give the worker his wages before his sweat dries."[23]

"The command in the *hadith* to pay the worker before his perspiration dries signifies making prompt payment immediately after the completion of the assignment even if he does not sweat."[24]

If the people of means do not pay hired workers or employees in a timely way, then they are oppressors in the sight of the Holy Prophet (PBUH). He said: مَطْلُ الْغَنِيِّ ظُلْمٌ

"Delay in payment on the part of a rich man is injustice."[25]

Also, the Prophet (PBUH) warned against the exploitation of workers.

قَالَ اللَّهُ تَعَالَى ثَلَاثَةٌ أَنَا خَصْمُهُمْ يَوْمَ الْقِيَامَةِ رَجُلٌ أَعْطَى بِي ثُمَّ غَدَرَ وَرَجُلٌ بَاعَ حُرًّا فَأَكَلَ ثَمَنَهُ وَرَجُلٌ اسْتَأْجَرَ أَجِيرًا فَاسْتَوْفَى مِنْهُ وَلَمْ يُعْطِهِ أَجْرَهُ

"Allah Almighty says: I will be an adversary against three people on the Day of Rising: (one of them will be) a man who hires an employee and gets full work from him and then does not pay him his wages."[26]

Rendering one's services to someone against an agreed payment is a contract. The Muslim law enjoins both employers and employees to fulfil their respective duties. Allah pithily charges the faithful, "O believers! Fulfil (your) promises."[27] Elsewhere Allah depicts the character of ardent faithful, "And when they make a promise, they fulfil it."[28]

4.8 Social welfare

People who are able are under an obligation to support the less privileged so that none go without the necessities of life. For this purpose, they pay obligatory charity on their capital. However, this is not enough. Besides prescribing alms, Allah assigned a due share in our abundance to support such people who suffer and are destitute. Allah says وَفِيٓ أَمۡوَٰلِهِمۡ حَقّٞ لِّلسَّآئِلِ وَٱلۡمَحۡرُومِ

"And in their wealth was appointed a due share for the beggars and the destitute (i.e., all the needy)."[29]

وَٱلَّذِينَ فِيٓ أَمۡوَٰلِهِمۡ حَقّٞ مَّعۡلُومٞ ٢٤ لِّلسَّآئِلِ وَٱلۡمَحۡرُومِ

"And those (who are committed to sacrifice and) in whose wealth there is a fixed share, of one who begs and of one who is needy but does not beg."[30]

Prophetic Traditions also reinforce this theme of meeting the needs of the downtrodden so that they may live with dignity and honour.

When asked about Zakāt, the Prophet (PBUH) said:

إِنَّ فِي الْمَالِ لَحَقًّا سِوَى الزَّكَاةِ

"Indeed there is a duty on wealth aside from Zakāt (the Alms-due)."[31]

When Allah, the Exalted, granted the Prophet (PBUH) victories, He said:

أَنَا أَوْلَى بِالْمُؤْمِنِينَ مِنْ أَنْفُسِهِمْ فَمَنْ تُوُفِّيَ مِنَ الْمُؤْمِنِينَ فَتَرَكَ دَيْنًا فَعَلَيَّ قَضَاؤُهُ وَمَنْ تَرَكَ مَالًا فَلِوَرَثَتِهِ

"I have more right to be the protector of the believers than themselves. If any believer dies leaving a debt, I will pay it. If anyone leaves property, it goes to his heirs."[32]

The caliph ʻA lī (R.A) stressed the obligatory nature of alms: Allah has prescribed for the affluent Muslims to spend so much money (by way of charity) to eliminate the poverty of the destitute.[33]

4.9 Justice and benevolence

According to Imam al-Rāghib al-A|fahānī, ʻ*adl* (justice) denotes that whatever is obligatory for individuals to give must be given, and whatever they have the right to take should take. However, *iḥsān* means to give more than is due and to receive less than is one's right. Believers may practise either of them, taking the situation into account.

The Qur'ān emphasises justice and fairness when dealing in trade. Heeding this Scriptural directive, the believers engaged in business must shun cheating when selling a commodity. Allah says:

لَا تَظْلِمُونَ وَلَا تُظْلَمُونَ

"Deal not unjustly, and you shall not be dealt with unjustly."[34]

يَٰٓأَيُّهَا ٱلَّذِينَ ءَامَنُوا۟ لَا تَأْكُلُوٓا۟ أَمْوَٰلَكُم بَيْنَكُم بِٱلْبَٰطِلِ إِلَّآ أَن تَكُونَ تِجَٰرَةً عَن تَرَاضٍ مِّنكُمْ

"O believers! Do not devour one another's wealth unlawfully amongst yourselves unless it is a trade by your mutual agreement."[35]

The faithful are enjoined to give people their due without diminishing their rights. The Prophet Shuʻayb (peace be upon him) commanded his people:

وَيَٰقَوْمِ أَوْفُوا۟ ٱلْمِكْيَالَ وَٱلْمِيزَانَ بِٱلْقِسْطِ ۖ وَلَا تَبْخَسُوا۟ ٱلنَّاسَ أَشْيَآءَهُمْ

"And, O my people, give full measure and full weight with justice, and do not give people their things less than their due."[36]

According to Qur'ānic injunctions, *iḥ sān*, meaning beauty, balance, betterment, benevolence, piety and goodness, takes believers towards a higher moral plane. It points to beauty in utterance and performance and general behaviour. It requires the faithful to interact with others cordially and sincerely, and with benign well-wishing and kind words. Allah commands the believers to adopt a benevolent attitude towards parents.

وَوَصَّيْنَا ٱلْإِنسَٰنَ بِوَٰلِدَيْهِ حُسْنًا

"And We have enjoined man to behave benevolently towards his parents."[37]

The following verses emphasise benevolence while dealing with others: هَلْ جَزَآءُ ٱلْإِحْسَٰنِ إِلَّا ٱلْإِحْسَٰنُ

"And is the reward of good anything but good?"[38]

And,

لِّلَّذِينَ أَحْسَنُوا۟ ٱلْحُسْنَىٰ وَزِيَادَةٌ

"For those who do pious works there is good recompense and more (added to it)."[39]

Allah loves benevolent actions and the people who internalise this virtue: إِنَّ ٱللَّهَ لَمَعَ ٱلْمُحْسِنِينَ

"Certainly, Allah is with the the doers of good."[40]

And,

إِنَّ ٱللَّه يُحِبُّ ٱلْمُحْسِنِينَ

"Certainly, Allah loves the doers of good."[41]

And Allah Almighty says,

وَأَنفِقُوا۟ فِى سَبِيلِ ٱللَّه وَلَا تُلْقُوا۟ بِأَيْدِيكُمْ إِلَى ٱلتَّهْلُكَةِ وَأَحْسِنُوٓا۟ إِنَّ ٱللَّه يُحِبُّ ٱلْمُحْسِنِينَ

"And spend in the cause of Allah and do not cast yourselves into destruction with your own hands—and adopt spiritual excellence. Verily, Allah loves the spiritually excellent."[42]

An ardent believer is the only individual who selflessly interacts with all. Abū Dharr (R.A) narrated that Prophet (PBUH) said,

اِتَّقِ اَلله حَيْثُمَا كُنْتَ، وَأَتْبِعِ السَّيِّئَةَ الْحَسَنَةَ تَمْحُهَا، وَخَالِقِ النَّاسَ بِخُلُقٍ حَسَنٍ

"Fear Allah wherever you may be, follow-up a bad deed with a good deed and it will efface it, and deal with people with good character."[43]

Allah conjoins justice and benevolence:

إِنَّ ٱللَّهَ يَأْمُرُ بِٱلْعَدْلِ وَٱلْإِحْسَٰنِ وَإِيتَآيِٕ ذِي ٱلْقُرْبَىٰ وَيَنْهَىٰ عَنِ ٱلْفَحْشَآءِ وَٱلْمُنكَرِ وَٱلْبَغْيِۚ يَعِظُكُمْ لَعَلَّكُمْ تَذَكَّرُونَ

"Indeed, Allah enjoins justice and benevolence (towards everyone), and giving away to the kindred, and forbids indecency, evil deeds, defiance and disobedience. He admonishes you so that you may remember with concern."[44]

The word *al-'adl* in the preceding verse shows concern for justness, fair play and equity in the sphere of social domain and ethical matters. Justice is the universal law around the axis of which the entire system of the cosmos runs in harmony. In the real sense of the word, it denotes that everything takes its proper place.

Therefore, all deviation, excess, defect, extremism and violation of other people's rights run contrary to the fundamental principle of justice.

4.10 Guiding principles of Islamic contract law

Basic fundamental and guiding principles and rules for governing the business transaction and contract have been provided in the Qur'ān and Sunnah substantively. This is the unique feature of the Islamic law of contract, which is lacking in all other legal systems and contract laws of the world, which are not based on divine guidance. It is the beauty of Islamic contract law which differentiates it from other contract law of the world. The following are the guiding principles and also the bases of the general theory of Islamic contract law.

4.11 God-made laws

Islam is a rules-based religion.[45] The Islamic system of law is known as "God-made laws" and not only "man-made laws" (here the word man means human being). It is a hard fact that despite all his foresightedness and intelligence, man is unable to cover all the laws for every walk of life. As we know that the inventor of anything better knows the invention as compared to all others, God is the creator, He knows best how to deal with His creation, human beings. The safest course for man is to accept God-made laws. The Qur'ān says وَمَن لَّمْ يَحْكُم بِمَآ أَنزَلَ ٱللَّهُ فَأُو۟لَٰٓئِكَ هُمُ ٱلْكَٰفِرُونَ

> "Who does not judge (and rule) according to the injunctions sent down by Allah, it is they who are the disbelievers."[46]

It is part of Muslim belief that Islam as *Din* covers all aspects of human life through the divine principles contained in the Qur'ān and Sunnah, hence the obedience of all these principles is obligatory upon Muslims. The Islamic law of contract cannot be isolated from the rest of the legal and religious portion, so it must be followed as a part of the Muslim belief. The fundamental general principle for the law of Islamic contract is "obedience to God" and Divine commandments, i.e. entailing the respect and following of the principles of contract ordained in the Qur'ān and Sunnah. It means that the nature and function of all contracts under Islamic law of contract must be in line with the divine guiding principles of the Qur'ān and Sunnah, and should not be contrary to it. From this principle of "obedience of God", one should not infer that Islamic law or contract law of Islam is of a purely religious type. Islamic legislation is a balanced combination of spiritual and material or mundane elements. It provides spiritual direction along with legal safeguards. Thus, Islam is not merely a religion in the sense in which this term is understood in the West. It is rather a comprehensive mixture of the spiritual and material or secular way of life, which expresses itself in the conscience of the individual as well as in the behaviour of society. It provides principles for social rights and obligations in all dealings whether they pertain to economics, politics or international relations.[47]

4.12 Mutual consent is necessary

The mutual consent of the contracting parties is the basic requirement to conclude any valid contract. This concept is narrated in the following Qur'ānic verse and *hadith* of Prophet (PBUH):

يَٰٓأَيُّهَا ٱلَّذِينَ ءَامَنُوا۟ لَا تَأْكُلُوٓا۟ أَمْوَٰلَكُم بَيْنَكُم بِٱلْبَٰطِلِ إِلَّآ أَن تَكُونَ تِجَٰرَةً عَن تَرَاضٍ مِّنكُمْ

> "O believers! Do not devour one another's wealth unlawfully amongst yourselves unless it is a trade by your mutual agreement."[48]

According to this verse "the trade should be concluded by mutual consent: and is unlawful for a person to take his brother's property unless by the pleasure of his soul."[49]

This principle of mutual consent of parties is a general principle to be followed in all types of contracts and not only innominate contracts. The contract concluded without the mutual consent of the parties is not a valid contract in the eyes of the law. We shall discuss this as an ingredient of control separately.

4.13 Sanctity of contracts

According to Islamic law, all types of obligations must be fulfilled, especially obligations regarding financial, commercial and business matters that are meant to be honoured and fulfilled. Islamic commercial law is based on the sanctity of contracts.

The Islamic doctrines of the contract are based on the divine sanctions of Allah u as contained in the Holy Qur'ān and tradition of the Holy Prophet (PBUH).[50] Hence all contracts are considered sacred and, therefore, must be adhered to. The Qur'ān says يَٰٓأَيُّهَا ٱلَّذِينَ ءَامَنُوٓا۟ أَوْفُوا۟ بِٱلْعُقُودِ

> "O believers! Fulfill (your) promises."[51]

This principle is a general principle to be followed in all types of contract and business transactions and not only for nominate contracts, as the word "*uqud*" in this verse is used in a general sense. This looks very much like "*pacta sunt servanda*", the principle of Western law of contract.

4.14 Awareness of rights and duties

The Islamic principles and doctrines of the contract are comprised of rights and duties. Before the parties enter into a contract, they must be fully aware of their respective obligations to fulfil their promises. In the case of any breach of contractual promise, the party which breaches the contract is under the obligation to pay remedies while the other party has the right to claim for remedies or damages accordingly.[52]

4.15 Principle of general permissibility

The fundamental law for things is that they are permitted unless there is clear proof that establishes prohibition.

A beautiful principle that widened the concept of contracts beyond the scope of the nominated contract is the principle of general permissibility, which means that all things are permissible and allowed which are not forbidden in texts. This principle of the permissibility of all things is also applicable to sale, trade and business and commercial activities.

The things which have been forbidden are quite a few and listed; the rest are permitted. The method of the Qur'ān and Sunnah by which it deals with prohibition and permission upon which the whole Islamic legal system depends and developed is worth noting. In describing prohibitions, things are named and listed, while in describing permissions, general permission is given due to the large numbers of things included in it. Furthermore, in cases of emergency, need and enforced circumstances, Allah granted the concession and even lifted the prohibitions. Under these circumstances, unlawful becomes lawful. We discussed these under the heading of "Removal of difficulties".

In *mumamalt* the general rule is that everything that is not specifically prohibited is permissible. This rule has been emphasised in several Qur'ānic verses. For example,

قُلْ مَنْ حَرَّمَ زِينَةَ ٱللَّهِ ٱلَّتِيٓ أَخْرَجَ لِعِبَادِهِۦ وَٱلطَّيِّبَٰتِ مِنَ ٱلرِّزْقِۚ قُلْ هِيَ لِلَّذِينَ ءَامَنُواْ فِي ٱلْحَيَوٰةِ ٱلدُّنْيَا
خَالِصَةً يَوْمَ ٱلْقِيَٰمَةِۗ كَذَٰلِكَ نُفَصِّلُ ٱلْأٓيَٰتِ لِقَوْمٍ يَعْلَمُونَ

> "Say: Who has forbidden the adornment (and beautification) of Allah that He has produced for His servants and (who has also forbidden) the pure and clean food?' Say: '(All these bounties) that are (available generally) for the believers in the life of this world will be exclusively (for them) on the Day of Resurrection. This way, We elucidate Our Revelations for those who have knowledge."[53]

4.16 Justice, equity and equality

The general principles of Islamic legal systems such as justice, equity and equality are also considered very important and fundamental in the functional area of Islamic contract law. One of the essential contributions of the Islamic law of contract is the requirement to establish justice and fairness in all transactions.[54]

In this regard, the Qur'ān says إِنَّ ٱللَّهَ يَأۡمُرُ بِٱلۡعَدۡلِ وَٱلۡإِحۡسَٰنِ

> "Allah has enjoined justice and righteousness."[55]

The Qur'ān further provides:

إِنَّ ٱللَّهَ يَأۡمُرُكُمۡ أَن تُؤَدُّواْ ٱلۡأَمَٰنَٰتِ إِلَىٰٓ أَهۡلِهَا وَإِذَا حَكَمۡتُم بَيۡنَ ٱلنَّاسِ أَن تَحۡكُمُواْ بِٱلۡعَدۡلِ

> "Allah doth command you to render back your Trusts to those to whom they are due; and when ye judge between man and man that ye judge with justice."[56]

A well-known tradition of the Holy Prophet (PBUH) states: "There shall be no unfair loss nor the causing of such loss (*la darar wa la dirar*)."[57] According to Imam Razi: "Take recourse to just balance and weight. Tell the truth in selling commodities and do not conceal anything."[58] It is worth noting here that this concept of justice is superior to the distributive and remedial justice of its counterpart.

4.17 Prevention of violence and excessive gains

While concluding contracts, the parties ensure that violence and excessive gains should not occur. All contractual dealings and business transactions must be free from any violent action as well as from the means of excessive gain.

The Qur'ān and Sunnah prohibit violence and unlawful gain in strong terms. It permits only lawful acquisition of property; any misappropriation of property belonging to another person or the state is considered violence and unlawful gain. This also includes excessive gain in business transactions and undue profits, which should be avoided in contractual dealings. Excessive commission and services charges by any service providers are also prohibited. The Qur'ān says:

وَلَا تَأۡكُلُوٓاْ أَمۡوَٰلَكُم بَيۡنَكُم بِٱلۡبَٰطِلِ وَتُدۡلُواْ بِهَآ إِلَى ٱلۡحُكَّامِ لِتَأۡكُلُواْ فَرِيقٗا مِّنۡ أَمۡوَٰلِ ٱلنَّاسِ بِٱلۡإِثۡمِ وَأَنتُمۡ تَعۡلَمُونَ

> "And do not eat up one another's wealth among yourselves through injustice, nor take wealth to the authorities (as a bribe) so that, this way, you may (also) swallow a portion of others' wealth unfairly, while you are aware (that this is a sin)."[59]

4.18 Removal of difficulty

Islamic laws in general, and in contract law in particular, are not meant to be a burden and create difficulties for men. Instead, they are designed for man's benefit to facilitate humanity's individual and societal needs. Islamic law of contract is based on the removal of unnecessary difficulties wherever possible. The following Qur'ānic verses are only a few examples in this regard:

لَا يُكَلِّفُ ٱللَّهُ نَفۡسًا إِلَّا وُسۡعَهَا

> "Allah does not put under stress any soul more than its endurance."[60]

يُرِيدُ ٱللَّهُ بِكُمُ ٱلۡيُسۡرَ وَلَا يُرِيدُ بِكُمُ ٱلۡعُسۡرَ

> "Allah desires ease for you and does not desire hardship for you."[61]
>
> وَمَا جَعَلَ عَلَيْكُمْ فِي ٱلدِّينِ مِنْ حَرَجٍ
>
> "And has not laid upon you any hardship or constriction (in the matter of) Din (Religion)."[62]
>
> يُرِيدُ ٱللَّهُ أَن يُخَفِّفَ عَنكُمْ وَخُلِقَ ٱلْإِنسَٰنُ ضَعِيفًا
>
> "Allah intends to lighten your burden. And man has been created weak (and infirm)."[63]

Allah has also granted a variety of legal concessions, like the permission to break fast, and shorten and join prayers during travel. Moreover, the consumption of prohibited substances (i.e. pork and alcohol) in cases of dire necessity and forced circumstances is also permitted.

فَمَنِ ٱضْطُرَّ فِي مَخْمَصَةٍ غَيْرَ مُتَجَانِفٍ لِّإِثْمٍ فَإِنَّ ٱللَّهَ غَفُورٌ رَّحِيمٌ

> "Then if someone gets into a survival situation (and is forced by) ravenous hunger (and intense thirst i.e., driven by dire necessity, provided) he is not prone to sinning (i.e., eats what is forbidden without being wilfully inclined to sin), then Allah is indeed Most Forgiving, Ever-Merciful."[64]

The Prophet (PBUH), who was the prime example of how Islamic law was to be implemented, was himself described as always choosing the easier path whenever a choice was given to him between two possible paths, as long as the easier path was not sinful.[65] He a was also reported to have said to some of his followers on the occasion of their being dispatched as governors of Yemen, "Make things easy (for the people) and do not make them difficult."[66]

Islamic legal scholars unanimously consider this concept an indisputable fundamental principle of God in the enactment of laws. Consequently, in their implementation of the divine laws, they have deduced many secondary laws on this basis.[67]

4.19 The prohibition of riba *(interest)*

The first thing that should be kept in mind is that Islam and the Islamic legal system looked at everything from the perspective of human benefit and welfare. Everything which is beneficial is confirmed and allowed and that which is harmful is removed and prohibited.

In the Arabic language, the term *riba* refers to interest. The Qur'ān and the tradition of Prophet Muhammad a have unequivocally declared it prohibited in all business transactions. The issue of *riba* is the most fundamental and most far-reaching aspect of the Islamic financial system and contracts. Its interpretation is the subject of many debates around the world. It can be simply "prohibited gain". All Islamic jurists agreed that the Holy Qur'ān prohibits the payment and taking of *riba*. *Riba* is very harmful to an individual's economic condition as well as for society's economic growth. It has an adverse impact on the financial aspect of the person and country benefiting from it in the long run. Contracts in Islamic law involving *riba* cannot be concluded. We shall discuss this concept of *riba* along with *gharar* and *maysir* etc. in a separate chapter.

4.20 The prohibition of gharar *(risk)*

Gharar means uncertainty, in its limited sense and in a broader sense it could also mean deceit, doubtfulness, fraud, risk or a potential hazard that might lead to destruction or loss. Therefore, all business transactions and contracts whose existence or description are not certain are forbidden under the Islamic jurisprudence of contracts. So contracts involving *gharar* cannot be concluded under the Islamic law of contract.

4.21 The prohibition of Maysir *(gambling)*

According to the Islamic legal system, all forms of *Maysir* are forbidden. *Maysir* includes gambling, any game of chance, lotteries, casino games, betting on the outcome of races. Hence all business transactions and contracts based on *Maysir* are not allowed, as being harmful.

4.22 The prohibition of fraud and cheating

Fraud and cheating have been stoutly condemned in all types of contracts and business dealings. Fraud may include several practices such as giving short measures and low weight, false bidding to raise the price of an item, false swearing, hiding defects in any business dealing.

4.23 The prohibition of two mutually inconsistent contracts

If there is more than one contract, they must be congruent with each other. The Prophet (PBUH) has prohibited two mutually inconsistent contracts, for example, the sale of two different articles for one price, the contingent sale, and the sale of a single object for two prices.[68]

4.24 A contract should not be contrary to Maqasid al-Shariah

The most important principle of the Islamic law of contracts is that all contracts should be concluded in conformity with objectives of *Shariah*, which are the preservation of religion, preservation of self, preservation of mind, preservation of offspring and preservation of property.

Any business transaction or contract that offends or jeopardises any of these objectives (*Maqasid*) of *Shariah* is automatically invalid. *Maqasid al-Shariah* is alternately referred to as *Huquq Allah* (Rights of Allah) in Islamic law.[69] The objectives of *Shariah* or *Huquq Allah* have been mentioned in several verses of the Qur'ān.

4.25 The prohibition of dealing in certain forbidden commodities

The Qur'ān forbids the consumption of prohibited things; their sale and trade are also illegal. Carrion, blood, swine, the animals over which Allah's name is not pronounced at the time of slaughtering are all prohibited, as well as the meat of animals that have been dedicated to idols. Allah says:

إِنَّمَا حَرَّمَ عَلَيْكُمُ ٱلْمَيْتَةَ وَٱلدَّمَ وَلَحْمَ ٱلْخِنزِيرِ وَمَآ أُهِلَّ بِهِۦ لِغَيْرِ ٱللَّهِ

> "He has made unlawful for you only the dead animals and blood and the flesh of swine and the animals over which, whilst sacrificing, the name of someone other than Allah has been invoked."[70]

If something is scripturally prohibited, the faithful are not allowed to consume it. Nor may they trade in it, as is evidenced from the following narrative.

> 'Abd al-Rahman b. Wa'la al-Saba'I, who was from Egypt, reported that he asked 'Abd Allah b. 'Abbas (R.A) about what is extracted from grapes. Ibn 'Abbas (R.A) said that a man gave Prophet (PBUH) a small water-skin full of wine, and Prophet (PBUH) asked him: "Do you know that the Almighty Allah, has forbidden it?" He said: "No," then he whispered to another man. Holy Prophet (PBUH) said: "What have you whispered about?" He said: "I told him to sell it." The Prophet (PBUH) said: "The One who has forbidden drinking it has also forbidden selling it." So he opened the skin until its contents drained away.[71]

Islamic law prohibits using or dealing with certain commodities and sinful activities such as alcohol and its products, other intoxicants, drugs, pork, etc. Thus, individuals or institutions cannot use or exchange or trade or finance such ventures which deal with such forbidden commodities. To ensure the sustenance of legality and to avoid prohibitory dealings in all transactions, Ayatollah S.M. Teleghani wrote: "Islamic ordinance has a control function of both injection and prohibition (positive and negative) towards every single contract (*aqd*) and transaction (*Mu'amalah*), so that they may prevent profit on nullity without beneficial work while upholding freedom."[72]

4.26 Prohibition of trickery in contracts

While entering into any commercial transaction and contract, parties should abstain from all kinds of trickery deception and dishonesty, etc. The following *hadith* is the basis of this:

> Narrated by *Abdullah bin Umar* (R.A) that a man mentioned to the Holy Prophet (PBUH) that he said: "When you enter a transaction say: "No trickery," so whenever that man entered a transaction, he would say, "No trickery."[73]

4.27 Encourage and development of business

The doctrines of the Islamic law of contract also encourage people to involve themselves in all kinds of commercial transactions and businesses with the view of gaining profit and developing their economic growth. Allah u also encouraged human beings to engage in any type of business transaction. Only in this way could people achieve economic independence. Allah u says, to this effect, in the Holy Qur'ān: وَأَحَلَّ ٱللَّهُ ٱلْبَيْعَ وَحَرَّمَ ٱلرِّبَوٰا

> "Allah has declared trade (i.e. buying and selling) lawful and usury unlawful."[74]

A relevant *hadith* is that:

> "A truthful and trustworthy trade will rise up with the Prophets, the righteous and martyrs."[75]

It is a prerequisite for a man to be involved in trade and business for survival and to sustain his life. At the same time, in order to be involved in trade, it is a prerequisite to apply the Islamic doctrines of contract for the sake of managing the businesses honestly and justly in a well-disciplined manner as enjoined by Allah u and His Prophet (PBUH).

The Islamic legal system has encouraged to do and develop the business, as anyone cannot disassociate himself from business activities and commercial transactions to sustain his life and earning his livelihood.

4.28 Principle of profits and loss sharing

Islamic commercial law promotes investment for business in an equitable and just manner. According to this principle, all parties of a contract of business should partake in both the profits and losses from their enterprise. The risk of business is also equally distributed between them consistent with their sharing as a percentage in the capital of a specific enterprise.

This principle provides that a party in a business or contract is entitled to profit only when it also bears the risk of loss. This principle operates in several contracts such as contracts of partnership, sale or hire. According to the Islamic legal maxim: "with profit comes liability or risk".

4.29 Public welfare and no exploitation

The laws of the Islamic legal system are primarily enacted for public welfare and the general good of all humanity. "Legislative consideration can also be found in the giving of precedence to the general welfare over individual benefit, and the prevention of greater harm over a smaller one."[76] *Shariah* also forbids any financial transaction or dealing which leads to the exploitation of any party to the contract.

> Islam forbids its followers to exploit other people or to use unjust methods in acquiring wealth, but it allows them to use all the good and fair means in the acquisition of wealth. It also admits the right of the individual to his property and works with freedom, but within certain limitations, for it cannot tolerate misuse or abuse of these rights. In other words, it does encourage people in earning wealth and getting rich through just and lawful means; what it does not like is the use of wrong and unfair means to earn wealth.[77]

Notes

1 Qur'ān, 17:12 (Eng. trans. from 'Glorious Qur'ān' by Shaykh-ul-Islam Dr. Muhammad Tahir-ul-Qadri).
2 Qur'ān, 62:10 (Eng. trans. from 'Glorious Qur'ān' by Shaykh-ul-Islam Dr. Muhammad Tahir-ul-Qadri).
3 Qur'ān, 53:39 (Eng. trans. from 'Glorious Qur'ān' by Shaykh-ul-Islam Dr. Muhammad Tahir-ul-Qadri).
4 Narrated by al-Bukh¥rÏ in *al-ßa^Ï^*, 2:730 #1966; al->abar¥nÏ in *al-Mu¢jam al-KabÏr*, 20:267 #631; and al-BayhaqÏ in *al-Sunan al-Kubr¥*, 6:127 #11471.
5 Narrated by al-Bukh¥rÏ in *al-ßa^Ï^*, 2:730 #1965.
6 Narrated by al->abar¥nÏ in *al-Mu¢jam al-KabÏr*, 10:74 #9993.
7 Narrated by al-DaylamÏ in *al-Firdaws bi-Ma√th%or al-Khi~¥b*, 2:180 #2910; al-MundhirÏ in *al-TarghÏb wa al-TarhÏb*, 1:315 #1161; and al-HaythamÏ in *Majma¢ al-Zaw¥√id*, 4:61 #6213.
8 Narrated by al->abar¥nÏ in *al-Mu¢jam al-Awsa~*, 7:289 #7520; and al-HaythamÏ in *Majma¢ al-Zaw¥√id*, 4:63 #6238.
9 Narrated by al-Kitt¥nÏ in *al-TartÏbal-id¥riyya*, 2:23.
10 Narrated by al-BayhaqÏ in *al-Sunan al-kubr¥*, 6:128 #11695 & in *Shu¢ab al-¬m¥n*, 6:420 #8741; al-Qu\¥¢Ï in *Musnad al-Shih¥b*, 1:104 #121; al-DaylamÏ in *al-Firdaws bi-Ma√th%or al-Khi~¥b*, 2:441 #3918; and Ab‰ Nu¢aym in *¤ilya al-Awliy¥√*, 7:126.
11 Narrated by Ibn M¥jah in *al-Sunan*, 2:725 #2144; Ibn al-J¥r‰d in *al-Muntaq¥*, 1:144 #556; and al-Qaysar¥nÏ in *Tadhkirat al-¤uff¥*[illegible], 3:1083.
12 Narrated by Ibn M¥jah in *al-Sunan*, 2:725 #2143; and al-Kin¥nÏ in *Mi|b¥^ al-Zuj¥ja*, 4:169 #1395.
13 Qur√¥n 25:67 (Eng. trans. from 'Glorious Qur'ān' by Shaykh-ul-Islam Dr. Muhammad Tahir-ul-Qadri).
14 Narrated by al->abar¥nÏ in *al-Mu¢jam al-Awsa~*, 7:25 #6744; and al-BayhaqÏ in *Shu¢ab al-¬m¥n*, 5:254 #6567.
15 Narrated by al->abar¥nÏ in *al-Mu¢jam al-KabÏr*, 10:108 #10118; and al-HaythamÏ in *Majma¢ al-Zaw¥√id*, 10:252.
16 Narrated by al-TirmidhÏ in *al-Sunan*, 5:558 #3560.
17 Narrated by Ibn M¥jah in *al-Sunan*, 2:1178 #3558.
18 Qur'ān, 2:275 (Eng. trans. from 'Glorious Qur'ān' by Shaykh-ul-Islam Dr. Muhammad Tahir-ul-Qadri).
19 Qur'ān, 17:66 (Eng. trans. from 'Glorious Qur'ān' by Shaykh-ul-Islam Dr. Muhammad Tahir-ul-Qadri).
20 Qur'ān, 62:10 (Eng. trans. from 'Glorious Qur'ān' by Shaykh-ul-Islam Dr. Muhammad Tahir-ul-Qadri).
21 Narrated by Muslim in *al-ßa^Ï^*, 3:1630 #2059.

22 Narrated by Muslim in *al-ßa^Ï^*, 3:1354 #1728; Ab‰ D¥w‰d in *al-Sunan*, 2:125 #1663.
23 Narrated by Ibn M¥jah in *al-Sunan*, 2:817 #2443; and al-BayhaqÏ in *al-Sunan al-kubr¥*, 6:120 #11434.
24 Al-Man¥wÏ, *al-TaysÏr bi-shar^ al-J¥mi¢ al-|aghÏr*, 1:171.
25 Narrated by al-Bukh¥rÏ in *al-ßa^Ï^*, 2:845 #2270; al-TirmidhÏ in *al-Sunan*, 3:600 #1308; and Ibn ¤ajar al-¢Asqal¥nÏ in *al-Dir¥ya fÏ TakhrÏj A^¥dÏth al-Hid¥ya*, 2/164 #812.
26 Narrated by al-Bukh¥rÏ in *al-ßa^Ï^*, 2:792 #2150; Ibn M¥jah in *al-Sunan*, 2:816 #2442; and al-K¥s¥nÏ in *Bad¥√i¢ al-|an¥√i¢*, 4:174.
27 Qur√¥n, 5:1 (Eng. trans. from 'Glorious Qur'ān' by Shaykh-ul-Islam Dr. Muhammad Tahir-ul-Qadri).
28 Qur'ān, 2:177 (Eng. trans. from 'Glorious Qur'ān' by Shaykh-ul-Islam Dr. Muhammad Tahir-ul-Qadri).
29 Qur'ān, 51:19 (Eng. trans. from 'Glorious Qur'ān' by Shaykh-ul-Islam Dr. Muhammad Tahir-ul-Qadri).
30 Qur'ān, 70:24–25 (Eng. trans. from 'Glorious Qur'ān' by Shaykh-ul-Islam Dr. Muhammad Tahir-ul-Qadri).
31 Narrated by al-TirmidhÏ in *al-Sunan*, 3:48 #660; al-D¥raqu~nÏ in *al-Sunan*, 2:125; and S¥¢Ïd b. Man|‰r in *al-Sunan*, 5:100 #926.
32 Narrated by al-Bukh¥rÏ in *al-ßa^Ï^*, 2:805 #2176; Muslim in *al-ßa^Ï^*, 3:1237 #1619; and al-BayhaqÏ in *al-Sunan al-Kubr¥*, 7:53 #13123.
33 Narrated by S¥¢Ïd b. Man|‰r in *al-Sunan*, 5:109 #3578; al-HaythamÏ in *Majma¢ al-zaw¥√id*, 3:62 #4324; and Ibn ¤azm in *al-Mu^all¥*, 6:158.
34 Qur√¥n, 2:279 (Eng. trans. from 'Glorious Qur'ān' by Shaykh-ul-Islam Dr. Muhammad Tahir-ul-Qadri).
35 Qur'ān, 4:29 (Eng. trans. from 'Glorious Qur'ān' by Shaykh-ul-Islam Dr. Muhammad Tahir-ul-Qadri).
36 Qur'ān, 11:85 (Eng. trans. from 'Glorious Qur'ān' by Shaykh-ul-Islam Dr. Muhammad Tahir-ul-Qadri).
37 Qur'ān, 29:8 (Eng. trans. from 'Glorious Qur'ān' by Shaykh-ul-Islam Dr. Muhammad Tahir-ul-Qadri).
38 Qur'ān, 55:60 (Eng. trans. from 'Glorious Qur'ān' by Shaykh-ul-Islam Dr. Muhammad Tahir-ul-Qadri).
39 Qur'ān, 10:26 (Eng. trans. from 'Glorious Qur'ān' by Shaykh-ul-Islam Dr. Muhammad Tahir-ul-Qadri).
40 Qur'ān, 29:69 (Eng. trans. from 'Glorious Qur'ān' by Shaykh-ul-Islam Dr. Muhammad Tahir-ul-Qadri).
41 Qur'ān, 2:195 (Eng. trans. from 'Glorious Qur'ān' by Shaykh-ul-Islam Dr. Muhammad Tahir-ul-Qadri).
42 Qur'ān, 2:195 (Eng. trans. from 'Glorious Qur'ān' by Shaykh-ul-Islam Dr. Muhammad Tahir-ul-Qadri).
43 Narrated by al-TirmidhÏ in *al-Sunan*, 4:355 #1987; al-D¥rimÏ in *al-Sunan*, 2:415 #2791; Ibn AbÏ Shayba in *al-Mu|annaf*, 5:211 #25324; and al-Bazz¥r in *al-Musnad*, 9:416 #4022.
44 Qur√¥n, 16:90 (Eng. trans. from 'Glorious Qur'ān' by Shaykh-ul-Islam Dr. Muhammad Tahir-ul-Qadri).
45 H. Askari, Z. Iqbal & A. Mirakhor, Introduction to Islamic economics: Theory and application (Singapore: Wiley, 2015).
46 Qur'ān, 5:44 (Eng. trans. from 'Glorious Qur'ān' by Shaykh-ul-Islam Dr. Muhammad Tahir-ul-Qadri).
47 Dr. Saeed Ramadan, Islam, doctrine and ways of life, vol. 1. p. 2.
48 Qur'ān, 4:29 (Eng. trans. from 'Glorious Qur'ān' by Shaykh-ul-Islam Dr. Muhammad Tahir-ul-Qadri).
49 M.T. Mansuri, Islamic law of contract and business transactions, p. 3.

50 Muhammad Ma'sum Billah, Shariah standard of business contract, p. 41.
51 Qur'ān: 5:1 (Eng. trans. from 'Glorious Qur'ān' by Shaykh-ul-Islam Dr. Muhammad Tahir-ul-Qadri).
52 Muhammad Ma'sum Billah, Shariah standard of business contract, p. 42.
53 Qur'ān, 7:32 (Eng. trans. from 'Glorious Qur'ān' by Shaykh-ul-Islam Dr. Muhammad Tahir-ul-Qadri).
54 Afzal al-Rahman, Economics doctrines of Islam, Vol.1, 1974, p. 48.
55 Qur'ān: 16:90 (Eng. trans. from 'Glorious Qur'ān' by Shaykh-ul-Islam Dr. Muhammad Tahir-ul-Qadri).
56 Qur'ān: 4:58 (Eng. trans. from 'Glorious Qur'ān' by Shaykh-ul-Islam Dr. Muhammad Tahir-ul-Qadri).
57 Muhammad Wahidul Islam, Dissolution of contract in Islamic law, (1998) (13) *Arab law quarterly* 336, p. 340.
58 As quoted by Dr. Liaqat Ali Khan Niazi in his book, Islamic law of contract (1991), p. 3.
59 Qur'ān 2:188 (Eng. trans. from 'Glorious Qur'ān' by Shaykh-ul-Islam Dr. Muhammad Tahir-ul-Qadri).
60 Qur'ān, 2:286 (Eng. trans. from 'Glorious Qur'ān' by Shaykh-ul-Islam Dr. Muhammad Tahir-ul-Qadri).
61 Qur'ān, 2:185 (Eng. trans. from 'Glorious Qur'ān' by Shaykh-ul-Islam Dr. Muhammad Tahir-ul-Qadri).
62 Qur'ān, 22:78 (Eng. trans. from 'Glorious Qur'ān' by Shaykh-ul-Islam Dr. Muhammad Tahir-ul-Qadri).
63 Qur'ān, 4:28 (Eng. trans. from 'Glorious Qur'ān' by Shaykh-ul-Islam Dr. Muhammad Tahir-ul-Qadri).
64 Qur'ān, 5:3 (Eng. trans. from 'Glorious Qur'ān' by Shaykh-ul-Islam Dr. Muhammad Tahir-ul-Qadri).
65 Reported by Hazrat Ayesha in Sahih al-Bukhari (Arabic-English), vol. 4, p. 491, No. 760, Muslim (Sahih Muslim English trans.), vol. 4, p. 1246, No.5752.
66 Reported by Abu Burdah in Sahih al-Bukhari (Arabic-English), vol. 5, pp. 441–443, No. 630, Muslim (Sahih Muslim English trans.), vol. 3, p. 944, No. 4298.
67 Taarekh at-Tashree' al-Islami, pp. 19–20 and al-Madkhal, pp. 85–89.
68 R.H. Nawawi, Islamic law on commercial transactions, p. 59 (Kuala Lumpur CERT Publication, 2009).
69 Liaquat Ali Khan Niazi, Islamic law of contract (Lahore: Dyal Singh Trust Library, 1990), p. 1.
70 Qur'ān, 2:173 (Eng. trans. from 'Glorious Qur'ān' by Shaykh-ul-Islam Dr. Muhammad Tahir-ul-Qadri).
71 Narrated by Imam Muslim in al-Sahih, 3:1206 #1579.
72 Ayatullah Sayyid Mahmud Teleghani, Society and economics in Islam, (trans. From Persian) by R. Cambell (1982), p. 31 as quoted in Dr. Liaqat Ali Khan.
73 Imam Malik Ibn Anas, Al-Muwatta (trans. Eng), Aisha Abd Al-Rahman Bewley, 1989, No. 98 at 278.
74 Qur'ān, 2:275 (Eng. trans. from 'Glorious Qur'ān' by Shaykh-ul-Islam Dr. Muhammad Tahir-ul-Qadri).
75 Al-Hamimand al-Tarmizi, as quoted in Abdur Rahman, Doi, Shariah, The Islamic law, p. 350.
76 Shalabe Muhammad Mustafa, al-Madkhal fee at-Tareef bil fiqh Islami, 1969, p. 93.
77 Muhammad Ma'sum Billah, Shariah standard of business contract, p. 39.

5 Meaning and definition of contract in Islamic law

Before we proceed, it is pertinent to mention here that the Arabic language is a very vast language as compared to other languages. On the whole, one word in Arabic is used to describe more than dozens of meanings. The word *aqd* is also one of them. Generally speaking, the word *aqd* (contract) covers a wide range of meanings. It describes the obligations related to religious or spiritual, social or personal and commercial aspects of humans. For example, in the religious aspect, it consists of an obligation toward Allāh u; similarly, for the social aspect, it covers all obligations arising from ties of social relations such as marriage and adoption, etc. Moreover, for commercial aspects, it covers the whole spectrum of obligations of parties regarding their respective undertakings and commitment to contractual dealings.

5.1 Literal and lexiconic meaning

Aqd is an *Arabic* word which lexically means conjunction or to tie and is used to connote the corresponding word "contract" in Islamic law of contract. In the dictionary of lisan al Arab we read that they say that "*aqd al ahd*" means "make a covenant" and "*aqad al yamin*" means to give an oath.[1]

"The word *aqd* literally means to tie between two ends of something either physically or morally."[2]

"The a*qd* (contract) in the *Arabic* language originally means tying tightly, as in tying a rope or to bind the two ends of something and thereby forming a secure connection."[3]

"The corresponding *Arabic* word for the contract is '*aqd*' which means tie or bond."[4] "In *Arabic*, the word for contact is *al-aqd*, which literally means a 'tension' or 'tug'."[5] "In *Arabic* Philology, the term '*aqd*', has a number of meanings including.

i. To tie between two ends
ii. To fasten
iii. To link".[6]

5.2 Legal and juristic meaning

Generally, *aqd* covers everything a person commits himself to do, which includes unilateral and bilateral actions. The term *aqad*, in general, refers to a legal transaction that involves a bilateral declaration, namely the offer and acceptance. "The *aqd* is a legal transaction that creates a new legal situation."[7] "*Al-aqd* also signifies guaranteed and covenant.[8] Formally, a contract was defined as a joining through the utterances of two parties."[9]

In the legal sense *aqd* means:

i. The union of the declaration of one of the contracting parties with that of the other in a legal manner, the result of which is reflected in their subject matter.
ii. A contract or *aqd* is a statement or words that have the effect of legally binding a person to fulfill an obligation or to perform a duty.

Hence, we can conclude that *aqd* means

i. An agreement.
ii. Commercial arrangement.
iii. Legal transaction.
iv. Document.
v. Deed.

5.3 Technical and jurisprudential definition of aqd

After understanding the literal and lexical, legal and juristic meaning of the word *aqd* (contract), we now explain its definitions in its technical and jurisprudential aspects. Etymologically "Islamic contract" has many definitions, as there is no borderline for its definition. Actually, in early academic literature, we did not find any "single" definition of the word *aqd* or contract. The reason for this is that in that era, the jurists defined the "contract of sale" in detail. However, some legal experts (jurists) defined the term *aqd* independently from the contract of sale, which we have already explained in the previous section, i.e. to tie between two things, etc. In the commercial and business aspects the generic word *aqd* or contract deals with obligation and liabilities arising from temporal business transactions. The jurists defined "contract" as follows:

1. Imam Mohammad Abu Zahrah defines *aqd* as:

> "*Aqd* is the conjunction between two sayings from which an order of the *Shariah* is deduced, which is applicable to one party or both of them. This supported by the definition of the word, *Aqd*, offered by jurists that are a collation between two points of view, creating an obligation or its transfer or its termination."[10]

2. Al-Zuhayli defines *aqd* as the meeting of offer and acceptance in conformity with the formality prescribed by *Shariah*.[11]
3. "The word contract in Islamic jurisprudential usage means engagement and agreement between two persons in legally accepted, impactful and binding manners."[12]
4. Al-Shanhuri defines it as "the agreement of two wills to initiate an event with a legal impact, be it originating, transferring, modifying or ending a commitment."[13]
5. It is also defined as "an expression of the matching between a positive proposal made by one of the parties and the acceptance of the other party in a way which has an impact on the subject matter of the contract."[14] The same jurist defined it as "A conjunction of the offer emanating from one of the two contracting parties with the acceptance of the other in a manner that it may affect the subject matter of the contract."
6. Sir Abdul Rahim stated that

   > "a contract requires that there should be two parties to it, that one party should make a proposal and the other should accept it, that the minds of both must agree, that is, their declarations must relate to the same matter, and the object of the contract must be to produce a legal result."[15]

7. Syed Riaz-ul-Hassan Ghilani explains: "The bilateral lawful acts (contracts) are a source of obligation. A contract is entered into with the intention of creating legal consequences."[16]
8. In the *Medjelle aqd* (contract) is defined as: "The agreement of both parties to the fulfilment of a certain thing, arising from the agreement and concurrence of the offer and acceptance."[17]

   He further defines the conclusion of the contract as: "this is the legal tie which unites together (the offer and the acceptance in such a manner that there appears a sign of their dealing with a thing which was their subject matter."[18]
9. Dr. Hussain Hamid Hassan defined a contract as: "The legal relationship created by the promise of one of the contracting parties (promisor) with the promise of the other (promisee) as a result of which flow consequences in respect of the subject matter of the contract."[19]
10. A modern author, "M. Kabir Hassan", defined the word *aqd* as follows:

    > "A contract (*aqd*) can be defined as an agreement among contacting parties that is concluded through an offer and acceptance with the consequences of binding legal obligation.[20] An *aqd* contract is an agreement between two or more parties on a particular subject matter identified by them that is to be concluded through offer acceptance and triggers an obligation upon them."[21]

11. Scholars of different schools of *fiqh* defined *aqd* as the Hanafis define it, as "the correspondence of the offer of any of the contracting parties with| the acceptance of the other."[22]

The Shafis define a contract as a forceful link between the offer and acceptance.[23] The Hanbalis emphasise the specific meaning of a contract as "an agreement between two or more promises to initiate or transfer obligations."[24]

5.4 "Contract" as defined in different codes of Islamic countries

After giving the definition described by different jurists, it would be interesting to reproduce the definitions adopted and described in different civil codes of some Islamic countries.[25]

5.4.1 Iraq's civil code

"A connection of an offer emanating from one of the contracting parties, with the acceptance of the other party in a manner, which marks its effect on the object of the contract."[26]

5.4.2 Egypt's civil code

"A contract is concluded, subject to any special formality that may be required by law for its conclusion, merely from the moment when two parties have exchanged two concordant wills."[27]

5.4.3 Kuwait's civil code

"The connection of an offer with acceptance in view of producing an effect organised by law."[28] The language used in Kuwait's civil code of 1980 for the definition of a contract is somewhat different from languages used by the scholars in their definitions. However, the general idea of a contract remains the same.

5.4.4 Jordan's civil code

> "Connection and concurrence of an offer emanating from one of the contracting parties with an acceptance of the other party in a manner, which affects the subject of the contract and results in obligating each of the contracting parties with what was undertaken towards the other."[29]

5.4.5 UAE federal civil code

It gives a similar definition of the contract to that of the one given by Article 87 of the Jordan Civil Code of 1976.[30]

5.4.6 Bahrain's contract law

"All agreements are contracts if they are made by the free consent of the parties competent to contract for a lawful consideration and with a lawful object, and are not hereby (i.e. in the law) expressly declared to be void."[31]

5.4.7 Qatar's civil and commercial law

It gives a similar definition to the one given by article 73 of Iraq's civil code of 1951 that a contract is acknowledged as a source of obligation.[32]

5.4.8 North Yemen civil code

> "An offer, or what stands for an offer, made by one of the two contracting parties, of the other contracting party in a manner which affects the object of the contract (subject matter). A contract result is obligated to each of the parties with what was undertaken towards the others. No special form is required for contracting; the only requirement is mutual consent."[33]

5.5 Some similar terms to *aqd*

After explaining the meanings and definition of the term *aqd,* i.e. contract, it is the right place to explain some other terms which are considered similar or allied terms and are used concerning the doctrine of contract.[34]

5.5.1 Mithaq

Mithaq is a contract that signifies earnestness and firm determination on the part of parties to fulfil the contractual obligation. In other words, *mithaq* is a contract, which is considered to be sacred by the contracting parties, and has more sanctity than ordinary contracts. It is also defined as a covenant. A covenant is a form of agreement entered into by two or more persons on a particular subject matter in respect of carrying out a certain duty.

5.5.2 'Ahd

'Ahd means a unilateral promise or undertaking, although it also includes a bilateral obligation. It is a treaty in the form of a covenant agreement or covenant between two or more persons, nations or groups on certain obligations or responsibilities to be carried out.

5.5.3 Wa'ad

Wa'ad is an Arabic word that connotes the word "promise", which means an expression on a particular subject matter made by any single person or a group. In academic literature, its use is twofold i.e. one is as "an expression to do something in future" and secondly "an expression of intent to deliver something in the future".

Similarly, *wa'ad* in business or commercial dealings has twofold usage i.e. one is *wa'ad* as unilateral, in which someone declares that they will do something or perform a specific action in future for someone else on a voluntary basis. This type of offer is called *wa'ad.* Secondly, it may be bilateral, in which, when the offer is accepted by the offeree, this acceptance is also known as *wa'ad.*

"According to Islamic law, *al-Wa'ad* means promise. It is a promise which connotes an expression of willingness of a person or a group of persons on a particular subject matter. In a commercial transaction, a promise has a dual meaning. This is because, in a unilateral contract, the offer of the offeror is known as a promise, while in a bilateral contract, the acceptance of the offeree is known as promise as well."[35]

5.5.4 *Muwa'adah*

Muwa'adah is a term that needs further clarification when one studies *wa'ad*, as both of them originate from the same Arabic root of *wa'ada* and thus have a very close relationship.[36]

Muwa'adah is derived from the word *wa'ada*; it means mutual promise.[37] It is a verbal form that connotes a mutual relationship between the two parties involved. The difference between *wa'ad* and *muwa'adah* is that the former comes from one party while the latter comes from two parties on a mutual basis.[38]

Technically, in a jurisprudential sense, *muwa'adah* is a bilateral promise or undertaking by two parties to do something for each other in the future, either with or without any condition.[39] Some contemporary scholars define *muwa'adah* as "declaration by two persons on their interest to make a contract in the future whose consequences will fall on to them."[40]

Based on the above definitions, the main features of *muwa'adah* can be summarised as follows:

(i) There are two reciprocal promises given by two parties to each other; hence, they are bilateral. In other words, if there is a promise (from A) to sell and the promisee (i.e. B) also makes a counter promise to purchase, then each of them is a promisor as well as promisee.[41]
(ii) Both promises are on the same subject matter and based on the same condition if any. Thus, they are interdependent and interrelated.
(iii) The delivery of both promises will occur in the future.

Therefore, *muwa'adah* is different from *wa'ad* in terms of the parties giving the promise; in the former, both parties give promises to each other while in the latter only one party gives the promise.

5.6 Distinction between contracts and some other terms

For more understanding of the subject, we explain some more terms which are distinguished from the contract.[42]

5.6.1 *Contract and disposition*

Disposition means the action (including speech) of a discerning and free-willed person carrying legal consequences irrespective of whether these consequences are in the person's interest or not.[43]

Disposition is general while the contract is particular, and we can say that every contract is a disposition, but the opposite is not true; that is we cannot say that every act of disposition is a contract. The relationship between the two is that between the general and the particular is the absolute.[44] Sheikh Ahmad Ibrahim, in his article *"Al Okud wa al Shorut wa al Khiyarat"*, said that the relationship between contract and disposition can be one of difference, one of equality or one of the kinds between the general and the particular. Dr al Sanhuri was of the opinion that disposition is of a more general nature than contract.[45]

5.6.2 Contract and commitment

As for commitment, it is defined by al Sanhuri as "a judicial condition in which a person is bound to transfer a specific right, perform an act or refrain from performing an act."[46]

Since disposition may or may not include commitment, it can be said that disposition is more general than commitment and that each commitment is an act of disposition, but the opposite is not true.

5.6.3 Contract and conduct

Contract is sometimes referred to as a conductor, so it is worth examining the legal meaning of conduct. It can be defined as personal behaviour arising from one's own volition and may be performed orally or inferred from an action. As an action, conduct is that behaviour that results in tangible consequences, such as material harm.[47] Oral conduct, however, is manifested only by an utterance, as in a verbal agreement or a criticism. For conduct to be legally considered requires that a reasonable adult perform it.

Conduct may be unilateral conduct, which consists of a single utterance uttered by one person out of a single volition. This type of oral conduct originates or terminates an obligation merely by a single act of will, without the acceptance of another party. Examples of this are the conduct of making a trust or the initiation of proceedings for divorce.

It may be bilateral conduct, which consists of utterances that come from both contracting parties. This type establishes its obligation from the absolute agreement of the parties, as in the conduct of entering into a marriage or the conduct of a sales transaction.

It may also be conduct which neither involves an obligation to bind two parties nor the obligation of a single person, although it may be a part of legal proceedings. An example of this would be the testimony of a witness.[48]

Thus, there is a clear relationship between conduct and contract, conduct containing the general sense of the contract. Every contract is conducted, but conduct is not necessarily a contract.

5.6.4 Contract and obligation

In Islamic law, the term "obligation" is a reference to the belief that human beings have a responsibility to behave according to a specific code, as a result of general and particular commitments made by the society in which they live. For example, parents have an obligation to bring up their children in a positive and responsible way. Other obligations may be created by a particular agreement between two parties. The resulting contract may result in a special liability for persons to do, or avoid doing, a particular thing, according to what has been specified in the agreement.[49] Thus, a contract is a source of obligation. It may initiate an obligation, or an obligation may be the consequence of a contract.

5.6.5 Qur'ānic basis of contract

Above, we discuss in detail the meanings and definition of the term *aqd* (contract) by quoting different legal experts. It is pertinent to point out here that there are hundreds of Qur'ānic verses which deal with the legal matters of human beings, out of which more than a hundred verses deal with matters such as sale, purchase, lease, mortgage, pledge, partnership, properties and other matters related to business and commercial dealings and contracts, etc. The remainder are verses which deal with personal laws, family laws, penal laws, civil laws, constitutional law, administrative laws and international laws.[50] There are many Qur'ānic verses and Sunnah of the Holy Prophet (PBUH) which provide the basis of the principles of contract and contractual relationships.[51] All these verses emphasise the importance of fulfilling contractual agreements whether they are in the form of treaties, commercial contracts or social obligations.

The following are the Qur'ānic verses which provide the basis of the contract law and fundamental principles and guidelines regarding business and commercial activities.

يَٰٓأَيُّهَا ٱلَّذِينَ ءَامَنُوٓاْ أَوۡفُواْ بِٱلۡعُقُودِ

1. "O believers! Fulfil (your) promises."[52]

This verse provides the basis for the fulfilment of contracts. This is the primary verse that is general in nature and which embraces the entire area of a person's religious, moral, social and economic obligations. This verse provides a general and fundamental principle, governing the sanctity of all undertakings regarding contracts.

The following verses also provide the basis for the fulfilment of the contract:

وَلَا تَقۡرَبُواْ مَالَ ٱلۡيَتِيمِ إِلَّا بِٱلَّتِي هِيَ أَحۡسَنُ حَتَّىٰ يَبۡلُغَ أَشُدَّهُۥۚ وَأَوۡفُواْ بِٱلۡعَهۡدِۖ إِنَّ ٱلۡعَهۡدَ كَانَ مَسۡـُٔولٗا

2. "And (also) do not go near the orphan's property, but in a way that is beneficial (to the orphan), until he reaches his maturity. And always fulfil the promise. No doubt, the promise will be questioned about."[53]

يَٰبَنِيٓ إِسۡرَٰٓءِيلَ ٱذۡكُرُواْ نِعۡمَتِيَ ٱلَّتِيٓ أَنۡعَمۡتُ عَلَيۡكُمۡ وَأَوۡفُواْ بِعَهۡدِيٓ أُوفِ بِعَهۡدِكُمۡ وَإِيَّٰيَ فَٱرۡهَبُونِ

3. "O Children of Ya'qub (Jacob)! Recall My favours which I bestowed upon you and fulfil the promise (made) to Me; I shall fulfil the promise (made) to you. And always fear Me alone."[54]

ٱلَّذِينَ يُوفُونَ بِعَهْدِ ٱللَّهِ وَلَا يَنقُضُونَ ٱلْمِيثَٰقَ

4. "Those who fulfil their pledge to Allah and do not breach their covenant."[55]

إِنَّ ٱلَّذِينَ يُبَايِعُونَكَ إِنَّمَا يُبَايِعُونَ ٱللَّهَ يَدُ ٱللَّهِ فَوْقَ أَيْدِيهِمْ ۚ فَمَن نَّكَثَ فَإِنَّمَا يَنكُثُ عَلَىٰ نَفْسِهِۦ ۖ وَمَنْ أَوْفَىٰ
بِمَا عَٰهَدَ عَلَيْهُ ٱللَّهَ فَسَيُؤْتِيهِ أَجْرًا عَظِيمًا

5. "(O Beloved!) Indeed, those who pledge allegiance to you in fact pledge allegiance to Allah alone. Allah's hand is over their hands (in the form of your hand). Then whoever breaks his pledge breaks it only to his own harm. But he who fulfils what he has promised to Allah, He will bless him with immense reward."[56]

The above verses all provide the basis with which to sustain contractual covenants. The following are other verses that describe the importance of the fulfilment of contracts.

ٱلَّذِينَ هُمْ لِأَمَٰنَٰتِهِمْ وَعَهْدِهِمْ رَٰعُونَ

6. "And those who are watchful of their trusts and their pledges."[57]

إِلَّا ٱلَّذِينَ يَصِلُونَ إِلَىٰ قَوْمٍۭ بَيْنَكُمْ وَبَيْنَهُم مِّيثَٰقٌ

7. "But (do not fight) those who have allied with a people that between you and them there is a (peace) treaty."[58]

بَلَىٰ مَنْ أَوْفَىٰ بِعَهْدِهِۦ وَٱتَّقَىٰ فَإِنَّ ٱللَّهَ يُحِبُّ ٱلْمُتَّقِينَ

8. "Yes, he who fulfils his promise and adopts God fearingness (will indeed face no accountability); so Allah surely loves the pious."[59]

وَلَا تَعْزِمُوا۟ عُقْدَةَ ٱلنِّكَاحِ حَتَّىٰ يَبْلُغَ ٱلْكِتَٰبُ أَجَلَهُۥ

9. "And do not resolve firmly on wedlock (during this time) until the prescribed waiting term is over."[60]

   In the above verse, the fulfilment of the contract of marriage is emphasised.

يَٰٓأَيُّهَا ٱلَّذِينَ ءَامَنُوا۟ لَا تَأْكُلُوٓا۟ أَمْوَٰلَكُم بَيْنَكُم بِٱلْبَٰطِلِ إِلَّآ أَن تَكُونَ تِجَٰرَةً عَن تَرَاضٍ مِّنكُمْ ۚ وَلَا تَقْتُلُوٓا۟
أَنفُسَكُمْ ۚ إِنَّ ٱللَّهَ كَانَ بِكُمْ رَحِيمًا

10. "O believers! Do not devour one another's wealth unlawfully amongst yourselves unless it is a trade by your mutual agreement and do not kill yourselves. Surely, Allah is Kind to you."[61]

فَبِمَا نَقْضِهِم مِّيثَٰقَهُمْ لَعَنَّٰهُمْ وَجَعَلْنَا قُلُوبَهُمْ قَٰسِيَةً

11. "Then We laid Our curse on them because of their breach of promise (i.e., they were deprived of Our mercy)."[62]

فَبِمَا نَقْضِهِم مِّيثَٰقَهُمْ

12. "So (they were afflicted with punishments) because of their breaking the promise."[63]

ٱلَّذِينَ يَنقُضُونَ عَهْدَ ٱللَّهِ مِنۢ بَعْدِ مِيثَٰقِهِۦ وَيَقْطَعُونَ مَآ أَمَرَ ٱللَّهُ بِهِۦٓ أَن يُوصَلَ وَيُفْسِدُونَ فِي ٱلْأَرْضِۚ
أُو۟لَٰٓئِكَ هُمُ ٱلْخَٰسِرُونَ

13. "(These disobedient people are those) who break the promise of Allah after having confirmed it, and break that (relationship) which Allah has ordered to be joined, and create disorder in the land. It is they who are the losers."[64]

وَأَوْفُوا۟ بِعَهْدِ ٱللَّهِ إِذَا عَٰهَدتُّمْ وَلَا تَنقُضُوا۟ ٱلْأَيْمَٰنَ بَعْدَ تَوْكِيدِهَا وَقَدْ جَعَلْتُمُ ٱللَّهَ عَلَيْكُمْ كَفِيلًاۚ إِنَّ ٱللَّهَ يَعْلَمُ
مَا تَفْعَلُونَ

14. "And always fulfil the promise of Allah when you promise, and do not break oaths after making them firm, whilst you have already made Allah a surety over you. Surely, Allah knows well whatever you do."[65]

إِلَّا ٱلَّذِينَ عَٰهَدتُّم مِّنَ ٱلْمُشْرِكِينَ ثُمَّ لَمْ يَنقُصُوكُمْ شَيْـًٔا وَلَمْ يُظَٰهِرُوا۟ عَلَيْكُمْ أَحَدًا فَأَتِمُّوٓا۟ إِلَيْهِمْ عَهْدَهُمْ
إِلَىٰ مُدَّتِهِمْۚ إِنَّ ٱللَّهَ يُحِبُّ ٱلْمُتَّقِينَ

15. "Except those idolaters with whom you made an agreement, who then did not show any latitude (in executing the treaty) and who did not support (or reinforce) anyone against you. So fulfil the treaty with them till the end of the term. Surely, Allah loves those who fear Him."[66]

The above verse and the following verses provide basic principles and guidelines regarding business and commercial activities.

وَأَقِيمُوا۟ ٱلْوَزْنَ بِٱلْقِسْطِ وَلَا تُخْسِرُوا۟ ٱلْمِيزَانَ

16. "And keep weighing justly and do not make the balance fall short."[67]

وَأَوْفُوا۟ ٱلْكَيْلَ وَٱلْمِيزَانَ بِٱلْقِسْطِ

17. "And always give full measure and weight with justice."[68]

وَأَوْفُوا۟ ٱلْكَيْلَ إِذَا كِلْتُمْ وَزِنُوا۟ بِٱلْقِسْطَاسِ ٱلْمُسْتَقِيمِۚ ذَٰلِكَ خَيْرٌ وَأَحْسَنُ تَأْوِيلًا

18. "And measure in full whenever you measure out (anything), and (when you weigh anything) weigh with a straight balance. This (honesty) is better, and much better with regard to its consequence (as well)."[69]

In the following verses the consequences of those who break the covenant are prescribed in detail. These verses prohibited people from involving themselves in any transactions which are based on acts of fraud, unjust, interest or *riba*, monopolising, bribery and gambling, etc.

وَيْلٌ لِّلْمُطَفِّفِينَ ١ ٱلَّذِينَ إِذَا ٱكْتَالُوا۟ عَلَى ٱلنَّاسِ يَسْتَوْفُونَ ٢ وَإِذَا كَالُوهُمْ أَو وَّزَنُوهُمْ يُخْسِرُونَ ٣ أَلَا يَظُنُّ
أُو۟لَٰٓئِكَ أَنَّهُم مَّبْعُوثُونَ

19. "Woe to those who give less in measure or weight. When (they) take by measure from others, they take (from them) full. And when they (themselves)

give by measure or weigh to others, they give them less. Do they not believe that they will be raised up (again after death)"[70]

وَأَحَلَّ ٱللَّهُ ٱلْبَيْعَ وَحَرَّمَ ٱلرِّبَوٰا

20. "*Allah* has declared trade (i.e., buying and selling) lawful and usury unlawful."[71]

وَمَآ ءَاتَيْتُم مِّن رِّبًا لِّيَرْبُوَا۟ فِيٓ أَمْوَٰلِ ٱلنَّاسِ فَلَا يَرْبُوا۟ عِندَ ٱللَّهِۖ وَمَآ ءَاتَيْتُم مِّن زَكَوٰةٍ تُرِيدُونَ وَجْهَ ٱللَّهِ
فَأُو۟لَٰٓئِكَ هُمُ ٱلْمُضْعِفُونَ

21. "And the money that you lend as usury so that (your wealth) may increase through mingling with other people's money will not increase with Allah, but the money that you give as Zakat ([the obligatory Alms-due] and charity donations), seeking (solely) Allah's pleasure—so it is they who multiply (their money with Allah) manifold."[72]

وَلَا تَأْكُلُوٓا۟ أَمْوَٰلَكُم بَيْنَكُم بِٱلْبَٰطِلِ وَتُدْلُوا۟ بِهَآ إِلَى ٱلْحُكَّامِ لِتَأْكُلُوا۟ فَرِيقًا مِّنْ أَمْوَٰلِ ٱلنَّاسِ بِٱلْإِثْمِ وَأَنتُمْ
تَعْلَمُونَ

22. "And do not eat up one another's wealth amongst yourselves through injustice, nor take wealth to the authorities (as a bribe) so that, this way, you may (also) swallow a portion of others' wealth unfairly, whilst you are aware (that this is a sin)."[73]

وَيْلٌ لِّكُلِّ هُمَزَةٍ لُّمَزَةٍ ١ ٱلَّذِي جَمَعَ مَالًا وَعَدَّدَهُۥ ٢ يَحْسَبُ أَنَّ مَالَهُۥٓ أَخْلَدَهُۥ ٣ كَلَّاۖ لَيُنۢبَذَنَّ فِي ٱلْحُطَمَةِ

23. "Woe to everyone who slanders (face to face) and finds fault (in absence). (Woe to him) who accumulates wealth and keeps counting it. He thinks that his riches will keep him alive forever. By no means! He will certainly be cast into al-Hutama (the crushing up Fire)."[74]

يَٰٓأَيُّهَا ٱلَّذِينَ ءَامَنُوٓا۟ إِنَّمَا ٱلْخَمْرُ وَٱلْمَيْسِرُ وَٱلْأَنصَابُ وَٱلْأَزْلَٰمُ رِجْسٌ مِّنْ عَمَلِ ٱلشَّيْطَٰنِ فَٱجْتَنِبُوهُ لَعَلَّكُمْ
تُفْلِحُونَ ٩٠ إِنَّمَا يُرِيدُ ٱلشَّيْطَٰنُ أَن يُوقِعَ بَيْنَكُمُ ٱلْعَدَٰوَةَ وَٱلْبَغْضَآءَ فِي ٱلْخَمْرِ وَٱلْمَيْسِرِ وَيَصُدَّكُمْ عَن
ذِكْرِ ٱللَّهِ وَعَنِ ٱلصَّلَوٰةِۖ فَهَلْ أَنتُم مُّنتَهُونَ

24. "O believers! Wine and gambling and idols mounted (for worship) and divining arrows (for seeking luck—all) are filthy works of Satan. So turn away from them (completely) so that you may prosper. Satan seeks only to breed enmity and spite amongst you by means of wine and gambling, and hinder you from remembering Allah and observing Prayer. Will you abstain (from these evil-generating temptations)?"[75]

5.7 Sunnah basis of contract

There are several *hadith* of the Holy Prophet (PBUH) which provide the very basis of contracts and commercial transactions. "The development of the contract, trade, and commerce from the Islamic legal point of view could well be noticed from the number of verses of the Holy Qur'ān and *hadith* of the Holy Prophet (PBUH)."[76] The Holy Prophet (PBUH) himself did the business. "The Holy Prophet (PBUH) was a member of the attested trading clan of *Quraish*."[77]

Following are some *ahadith* of the Holy Prophet (PBUH). For the purpose of brevity, we are omitting the Arabic text of the *ahadith.*

1. Abu Hurairah (R.A) reported: "Holy Prophet (PBUH) was saying, there are three signs of a hypocrite: When he speaks he lies, when he makes a promise he breaks it, and when he is trusted he breaches his trust."[78]
2. Abdullah b. Amr (R.A) reported: Holy Prophet (PBUH) says:

> "Four characteristics constitute anyone who possesses them a confirmed hypocrite, and anyone who possesses one of them possesses a characteristic of hypocrisy till he abandons it: when he is trusted he breaches it, and when he talks he lies, when he makes a covenant or promise he acts treacherously, and when he quarrels he deviates from the truth."[79]

In the above *ahadith*, the Prophet (PBUH) declared a contract breacher to be a "hypocrite".

3. "A trustworthy and honest and truthful businessman will rise up with martyrs on the day of judgment."[80]
4. "A truthful and trustworthy trader will rise with the prophets, the righteous men and martyrs."[81]
5. "Nine parts out of ten of one's recommended livelihood lies in trade and commerce."[82]
6. Narrated by Jabir b. Abd. Allāh (R.A): The Holy Prophet (PBUH) said: "May Allāh's mercy be on who is lenient in his buying, selling and in demanding back his money."[83]
7. Muhammad b. Al-Muktadir said, "Allāh u loves his servant who is generous when he sells and when he buys, generous when he repays and generous when he is repaid."[84]

In the following *ahadith*, some basic and fundamental guidelines on the ethics of entering from commercial and business transactions are laid down.

8. Narrated by Abdullah bin Umar (R.A) that a man mentioned to the Holy Prophet (PBUH) that he said: "When you enter a transaction say: 'No trickery,' so whenever that man entered a transaction, he would say, 'No trickery.'[85]
9. Narrated by Said b. Al-Musayyab (R.A): "When you come to a land where they give full measure and full weight, stay there. When you come to a land where they shorten the measure and weight, then do not stay there very long."[86]
10. Ibn Abbas (R.A) narrated, the Holy Prophet (PBUH) said: "He who buys foodgrain should not sell it until he has taken possessions of it."[87]
11. Narrated by Abu Qatada Al-Ansari (R.A); the Holy Prophet (PBUH) said: "Beware of swearing; it produces a ready sale for a commodity but bolds out the blessings."[88]

12. Rafi' bin Khadij (R.A) narrated the Holy Prophet (PBUH) said: "The worst earning is the earning of a prostitute, the price of a dog and the earning of a cupper."[89]
13. Abu Zubair (R.A) said: "I asked Jabir (R.A) about the price of a dog and a cat; he said: 'The Holy Prophet (PBUH) disapproved of that'."[90]

Beside these Qur'ānic and Sunnah doctrines, there are also practices of the companions of the Holy Prophet (PBUH), related to contract, trade and business transactions. For instance, once Abd Al-Rahman b. 'Auf (R.A) said: "Brother I do not need all this (the property was given to him). Show me if there exist any market place (where) I can do my business." That brother informed him that there was a big market of Bani Qaynuqa'. The next day, Abd Al-Rahman b. 'Auf (R.A) went to the market with cheese and butter and later became a very successful businessman and used his property for the cause of Islam.[91]

5.8 Purposes of the *Shariah* doctrines of contract

There are many purposes of the *Shariah* doctrines of contracts and business transactions, some of which are listed below:

i. To encourage human beings to participate actively in a commercial transaction which eventually may make them financially independent and self-reliant. The Prophet (PBUH) says, to the effect:

> "Nine parts out of ten of one's recommended livelihood lies in trade and commerce."[92]

ii. To upgrade the status of mankind to a respectable position as *"Ashraf al-Makhluqath"* (the respectable creatures of Allāh u) through faith and discipline. Islamic law has always stressed how to discipline one's heart, mind and action and the Islamic law of the contract is no exception. It regulates and disciplines the parties involved in a contract so that honesty, justice and commitments are upheld. Allāh u has, in fact, despised those who transgress the limits of Islamic principles and neglect discipline, in their transactions.

وَلَا تَعۡتَدُوٓاْۚ إِنَّ ٱللَّهَ لَا يُحِبُّ ٱلۡمُعۡتَدِينَ

"And do not transgress limits; for Allāh loveth not transgressors."[93]

iii. To save the parties to that contract from any fraud and mischief, Islamic law of contract lays the basic principles, which if obeyed, will shelter the parties from any violence, misappropriation, dishonesty and fraud. Allāh u has indicated in the Holy Qur'ān that He disfavours and hates those who do mischief on earth.

وَيَسۡعَوۡنَ فِي ٱلۡأَرۡضِ فَسَادٗاۚ وَٱللَّهُ لَا يُحِبُّ ٱلۡمُفۡسِدِينَ

"*But they (ever) strive to do mischief on earth. And Allāh loveth not those who do mischief.*"[94]

iv. To emphasise on fulfilment and identify the contracts and agreements which are legally binding upon the parties and enforceable by the operation of law.[95] This is because an agreement or contract is binding upon all parties involved and this could be justified by a verse of the Holy Qur'ān when Allāh u says to the effect:

وَلَا تَقْرَبُوا۟ مَالَ ٱلْيَتِيمِ إِلَّا بِٱلَّتِي هِيَ أَحْسَنُ حَتَّىٰ يَبْلُغَ أَشُدَّهُۥ وَأَوْفُوا۟ بِٱلْعَهْدِ إِنَّ ٱلْعَهْدَ كَانَ مَسْـُٔولًا

"And be true to every promise to verify on the Day of Judgment for you will be called to account for every promise which ye had made."[96]

v. To maintain justice, morality and harmony in the area of trade and commerce. Imam Razi says: "Take recourse to just balance and weight. Tell the truth in selling commodities and do not conceal anything."[97]

Allāh u has always emphasised establishing justice in all transactions as He says:

وَأَوْفُوا۟ ٱلْكَيْلَ إِذَا كِلْتُمْ وَزِنُوا۟ بِٱلْقِسْطَاسِ ٱلْمُسْتَقِيمِ ذَٰلِكَ خَيْرٌ وَأَحْسَنُ تَأْوِيلًا

"And give full measure who ye measure, and weight with a balance that is straight. That is the most fitting and most advantageous in the final determination."[98]

vi. To ensure the sustenance of legality and to avoid prohibitory dealings in all transactions.

vii. To ascertain and enforce the rights and duties of the contracting parties. In a binding contract, both parties must perform their respective duties, which are legally recognised. As regards the rights of the contracting parties, if a party breaches the term or condition of the contract, then the other party has the legal right to bring an action against him.

viii. To save the parties from difficulties, Allah does not want human beings to suffer any difficulties. Allāh u wants His creatures to have a comfortable life.

He says, to this effect: يُرِيدُ ٱللَّهُ بِكُمُ ٱلْيُسْرَ وَلَا يُرِيدُ بِكُمُ ٱلْعُسْرَ

"Allāh intends every facility for you; He does not want you to put to difficulties."[99]

ix. To establish the spirit of brotherhood and understanding between the contracting parties based on mutual goodwill.

يَٰٓأَيُّهَا ٱلَّذِينَ ءَامَنُوا۟ لَا تَأْكُلُوٓا۟ أَمْوَٰلَكُم بَيْنَكُم بِٱلْبَٰطِلِ إِلَّآ أَن تَكُونَ تِجَٰرَةً عَن تَرَاضٍ مِّنكُمْ وَلَا تَقْتُلُوٓا۟ أَنفُسَكُمْ
إِنَّ ٱللَّهَ كَانَ بِكُمْ رَحِيمًا

"Eat not each other's property in an illegal way but let there be amongst you trade and business through mutual goodwill."[100]

This spirit of brotherhood and understanding in the transaction arises from the mutual consent of two or more parties to deal with each other in respect to their certain rights and the duties.[101]

وَتَعَاوَنُوا۟ عَلَى ٱلْبِرِّ وَٱلتَّقْوَىٰ

"And help ye one another in righteousness and piety."[102]

Such cooperation among all human beings may, in turn, strengthen the brotherhood.

إِنَّمَا ٱلْمُؤْمِنُونَ إِخْوَةٌ

"The believers are but a single brotherhood."[103]

The Prophet (PBUH) further said, to the effect that:

"All members are like one body. If one of its parts is ill, the whole body suffers from sleeplessness and fever."

x. To ensure security and peace in society and the whole world, such as the covenants between different nations and governments, as seen in the Treaty of *Hudaibiyah* between the Holy Prophet (PBUH) and the *Quraish*.
xi. To protect society's moral values, which can be seen generally in all contracts which observe Islamic principles and ethics, specifically in the contract of marriage, which aims to protect society from illegal and immoral sexual activities.

Notes

1 Tajal 'Arus min Jawaher al Nafus, vol. 2 the entry of "a*qd*".
2 Dr. Siti Salwani Razali, The concept of wa'ad in Islamic financial contract, p. 2.
3 Dr. Ala'eddin Kharofa, Transaction in Islamic Law, p. 1–2.
4 Philosophy of Islamic law of contract, Hideyuki shimizee, p. 8.
5 Rayner, S, *The theory of contracts in Islamic law*: A comparative analysis with particular reference to modern legislation in Kuwait, Bahrain and the UAE, London, Kluwer Law International, 1991, p. 114.
6 M. Kabir Hassan, Rasem N. Kayed & Umar A. Oseni, Introduction to Islamic banking and finance, principles and practice, p. 47.
7 Siti Salwani Razali, *Islamic law of contract*, (Singapore: Cengage Leaning Asia, 2010): 2.
8 Al-Faiumi, Ahmed, *Almuneer F Ghareb Alrafai Alkabeer*, Cairo; Alamiriah Press, 1922, item *Aqada*, p. 132.
9 Zedan, *Abdulkareem*, *Al-Madkhal Lederasat Al-Islamiah*, Beirut: Muasasat Aresalah, 1990, p. 239.
10 Imam Abu Zahrah, *Al-Milkiyyah wa Nazariyyat-al Uqud fi'l shari at al-Islamiyah*, p. 179, Dar al-Fikr al-'Arabi, Cairo, 1396 AH/1976 AC.
11 W. Al-Zuhayli, *Financial transactions in Islamic jurisprudence* (E.G. M.A. Trans. Vol. 2). (Damascus: Dar al-Fikr: 2003).

12 *Imam Akmal al Din Muhammad ibn Mahmud al Baberti, Sharh al 'Enayah 'ala al Hedaydh, on the margin of Sharh al Qadir*, vol. 5, p. 74.
13 Razaq Al-Sanhuri, *Al Wajizfi Sharh at Qanun at Madani*, vol. 1, p. 27 (1969 ed.).
14 *Murshed al Hainan, entry 262.*
15 Sir Abdur Rahim, Muhammadan Jurisprudence, pp. 282–283.
16 Syed Riaz ul Hassan Ghilani, Re-construction of legal thought in Islam, p. 203.
17 Article No.103 *Medjelle al-Ahkam-ul-Adalia* English translated by W.E. Grigsby, London.
18 Article No.104 *Medjelle al-Ahkam-ul-Adalia* English translated by W.E. Grigsby, London.
19 Dr. Hussain Hamid Hassan, *Al-Madkhal*, Li-Dirasat-il-Fiqh-al-Islami, Maktabah al-Mutanabi, Cairo, 1979, p. 235.
20 M. Kabir Hassan, Rasem N. Kayed & Umar A. Oseni, Introduction to Islamic banking and finance, principles and practice, p. 47.
21 M. Kabir Hassan, Rasem N. Kayed & Umar A. Oseni, Introduction to Islamic banking and finance, principles and practice, p. 49.
22 Kamal al-Din, Ibn Muhammad, Sharh fath al-Qadir, vol. 3, p. 187, Deirut: Dar al-Fikr.
23 Al-Zarkashi, Badr al-Din, al-Manthur fi al-Qawaid al-Fiqhiyyah, Kuwait: Wizarat al-Awqaf wa al-Shun al-Islamiyyah.
24 Zayn al-Din, ‘Abd al-Rahman ibn Rajab, al-Qawaid, Dar al-Kutub al-Ilmiyyah.
25 As quoted by Muhammad Ma’sum Billah in Shariah standard of business contract.
26 Article 73 of Iraq’s civil code of 1952.
27 Article 89 of the Egypt’s civil code of 1948.
28 Article 31 of the code of Kuwait’s civil code.
29 Article 87 of Jordan’s civil code of 1976.
30 Article 125 of UAE federal civil code 1985.
31 Article 12.1 of Bahrain’s Contract Law of 1969.
32 Article 7 of Qatar’s Civil and Commercial Law of 1971.
33 Article 137 of North Yemen civil code 1979.
34 As quoted by Dr. Muhammad Tahir Mansuri in Modern applications in Islamic finance
35 Muhammad Ma’sum Billah, Shariah standard of business contract.
36 OS – Article Dr. Mairan, p. 22.
37 Abdullah, M.F. and Ab Rahman, A. (2015), "Is Wa’dan any different to Muwa’adah? Empirical evidence from Malaysia", International Journal of Islamic and Middle Eastern Finance and Management, Vol. 8 No. 3, pp. 310–328. https://doi.org/10.1108/IMEFM-11-2014-0113.
38 Ibn Manzur, Lisan al-‘Arab, 3:462.
39 Hasan, 2008 Marjan, p. 84.
40 Nazih Kamal Hammad, al-Wafa bi al-Wad p. 730. (OS MD Faruk p. 115, Ref.7).
41 Abu Ghuddah Abd al-Sattar, Tijarah an taradin: Mabadi’ wa mumarasat, (2010).
42 As quoted by Dr. Ala’eddin Kharofa in Transaction in Islamic law p. 7–9.
43 Shalabi, p. 365. See also Dia Sit Khattab, *“Al Tasarruf al Qanuni wa al Waqi’a al Qanuniya”*, in Majallat al Qada’, Year 13, 1955, Issue 2, p. 40.
44 Majallat al Eqtesad wa al Qanun, year 4, issue 6, pp. 645–646.
45 Al Wajiz, vol. 1, p. 49.
46 Al-Sanhuri, Al Wasit, vol. 1, p. 125.
47 Al-Zarqa, Mustafa, *almadkhal Alfiqhi Alaam*, Damascus: University press, 1965, p. 194–195.
48 Ayatullah al-Uzma S.M., *Islamic laws of worship and contracts*, U.S, Az-Zahra Islamic foundation, 1993, p. 142.
49 Almuzafar, M And Umran, M, *Al-Madkhal Lederasat Alanzemah, Jaddah; Dar ala-faq*, 1993, p. 310.
50 Abdul Wahab Khallaf, *Ilm-e-usul-e-fiqh*, pp. 32–33.

51 M. Kabir Hassan, Rasem N. Kayed & Umar A. Oseni, Introduction to Islamic banking and finance, principles and practice, p. 51.
52 Qur'ān: 5:1 (Eng. trans. from 'Glorious Qur'ān' by Shaykh-ul-Islam Dr. Muhammad Tahir-ul-Qadri).
53 Qur'ān: 17:34 (Eng. trans. from 'Glorious Qur'ān' by Shaykh-ul-Islam Dr. Muhammad Tahir-ul-Qadri).
54 Qur'ān: 2:40 (Eng. trans. from 'Glorious Qur'ān' by Shaykh-ul-Islam Dr. Muhammad Tahir-ul-Qadri).
55 Qur'ān: 13:20 (Eng. trans. from 'Glorious Qur'ān' by Shaykh-ul-Islam Dr. Muhammad Tahir-ul-Qadri).
56 Qur'ān: 48:10 (Eng. trans. from 'Glorious Qur'ān' by Shaykh-ul-Islam Dr. Muhammad Tahir-ul-Qadri).
57 Qur'ān: 23:8 (Eng. trans. from 'Glorious Qur'ān' by Shaykh-ul-Islam Dr. Muhammad Tahir-ul-Qadri).
58 Qur'ān 4:90 (Eng. trans. from 'Glorious Qur'ān' by Shaykh-ul-Islam Dr. Muhammad Tahir-ul-Qadri).
59 Qur'ān 3:76 (Eng. trans. from 'Glorious Qur'ān' by Shaykh-ul-Islam Dr. Muhammad Tahir-ul-Qadri).
60 Qur'ān: 2:235 (Eng. trans. from 'Glorious Qur'ān' by Shaykh-ul-Islam Dr. Muhammad Tahir-ul-Qadri).
61 Qur'ān 4:29 (Eng. trans. from 'Glorious Qur'ān' by Shaykh-ul-Islam Dr. Muhammad Tahir-ul-Qadri).
62 Qur'ān 5:13 (Eng. trans. from 'Glorious Qur'ān' by Shaykh-ul-Islam Dr. Muhammad Tahir-ul-Qadri).
63 Qur'ān 4:155 (Eng. trans. from 'Glorious Qur'ān' by Shaykh-ul-Islam Dr. Muhammad Tahir-ul-Qadri).
64 Qur'ān: 2:27 (Eng. trans. from 'Glorious Qur'ān' by Shaykh-ul-Islam Dr. Muhammad Tahir-ul-Qadri).
65 Qur'ān 16:91 (Eng. trans. from 'Glorious Qur'ān' by Shaykh-ul-Islam Dr. Muhammad Tahir-ul-Qadri)
66 Qur'ān 9:4 (Eng. trans. from 'Glorious Qur'ān' by Shaykh-ul-Islam Dr. Muhammad Tahir-ul-Qadri).
67 Qur'ān 55:9 (Eng. trans. from 'Glorious Qur'ān' by Shaykh-ul-Islam Dr. Muhammad Tahir-ul-Qadri).
68 Qur'ān 6:152 (Eng. trans. from 'Glorious Qur'ān' by Shaykh-ul-Islam Dr. Muhammad Tahir-ul-Qadri).
69 Qur'ān 17:35 (Eng. trans. from 'Glorious Qur'ān' by Shaykh-ul-Islam Dr. Muhammad Tahir-ul-Qadri).
70 Qur'ān 83:1-4 (Eng. trans. from 'Glorious Qur'ān' by Shaykh-ul-Islam Dr. Muhammad Tahir-ul-Qadri).
71 Qur'ān 2:275 (Eng. trans. from 'Glorious Qur'ān' by Shaykh-ul-Islam Dr. Muhammad Tahir-ul-Qadri).
72 Qur'ān 30:39 (Eng. trans. from 'Glorious Qur'ān' by Shaykh-ul-Islam Dr. Muhammad Tahir-ul-Qadri).
73 Qur'ān 2:188 (Eng. trans. from 'Glorious Qur'ān' by Shaykh-ul-Islam Dr. Muhammad Tahir-ul-Qadri).
74 Qur'ān 104:1-4 (Eng. trans. from 'Glorious Qur'ān' by Shaykh-ul-Islam Dr. Muhammad Tahir-ul-Qadri).
75 Qur'ān 5:90-91 (Eng. trans. from 'Glorious Qur'ān' by Shaykh-ul-Islam Dr. Muhammad Tahir-ul-Qadri).
76 Muhammad Ma'sum Billah, Shariah standard of business contract, p. 17.
77 Watt. *Mohammad at Macca*, p. 33, as cited in Dr. S. E. Rayner, p. 77.
78 Bukhari, Muslim, as cited in *Mishkat al-Masabih* (*Arabic*), published by Qadhi Kutub Khana, Arambag, Karachi, Pakistan (1368H), p. 17.

79 Bukhari, Muslim, as cited in *Mishkat al-Masabih* (*Arabic*), published by Qadhi Kutub Khana, Arambag, Karachi, Pakistan (1368H), p. 17.
80 Ibn Maja and al-Hakim as quoted in Abd Al-Rahman, Doi, Shariah: The Islamic law, 1990 p. 350.
81 Tirmidhi as quoted in Abd Al-Rahman, Doi, Shariah: The Islamic law, 1990.
82 Abd Al-Rahman, Doi, Shariah: The Islamic law, 1990 p. 354.
83 Sahih al-Bukhari (Trans Eng) Dr. Muhammad Muhsin Khan. The translation of the meaning of Sahih al-Bukhari, Vol. 3, 1979, No. 290 at 164.
84 Imam Malik, Al-Muwatta, p. 279.
85 Al-Muwatta of Imam Malik Ibn Anas, (Trans. Eng), Aisha Abd Al-Rahman Bewley, 1989, No.98 at 278.
86 Al-Muwatta of Imam Malik Ibn Anas, (Trans. Eng), Aisha Abd Al-Rahman Bewley, 1989, No.99 at 278.
87 Sahih Muslim (Tran Eng) Abd. Al-Hamid Siddiqi, Vol. 3, No. 3640 at 801.
88 Sahih Muslim (Tran Eng) Abd. Al-Hamid Siddiqi, Vol. 3, No. 3914 at 845.
89 Sahih Muslim (Tran Eng) Abd. Al-Hamid Siddiqi, Vol. 3, No. 3805 at 825.
90 Sahih Muslim (Tran Eng) Abd. Al-Hamid Siddiqi, Vol. 3, No. 3808 at 825.
91 Abd Al-Rahman, Doi, Shariah: The Islamic law, 1990 p. 355.
92 As quoted by Abd Al-Rahman, Doi, Shariah: The Islamic law, 1990, p. 354.
93 Qur'ān 2:190 (Eng. trans. from 'Glorious Qur'ān' by Shaykh-ul-Islam Dr. Muhammad Tahir-ul-Qadri).
94 Qur'ān 5:64 (Eng. trans. from 'Glorious Qur'ān' by Shaykh-ul-Islam Dr. Muhammad Tahir-ul-Qadri).
95 Helana McFaquhar, *General Principles of Law* (1987), p. 141.
96 Qur'ān 17:34 (Eng. trans. from 'Glorious Qur'ān' by Shaykh-ul-Islam Dr. Muhammad Tahir-ul-Qadri).
97 As quoted in Dr. Liaquat Ali Khan Niazi, Islamic law of contract, p. 3.
98 Qur'ān 17:35 (Eng. trans. from 'Glorious Qur'ān' by Shaykh-ul-Islam Dr. Muhammad Tahir-ul-Qadri).
99 Qur'ān 2:185 (Eng. trans. from 'Glorious Qur'ān' by Shaykh-ul-Islam Dr. Muhammad Tahir-ul-Qadri).
100 Qur'ān 4:29 (Eng. trans. from 'Glorious Qur'ān' by Shaykh-ul-Islam Dr. Muhammad Tahir-ul-Qadri).
101 A.B.M. Hossain, *Commercial Laws in Islam*, (1983), p. 1.
102 Qur'ān 5:2 (Eng. trans. from 'Glorious Qur'ān' by Shaykh-ul-Islam Dr. Muhammad Tahir-ul-Qadri).
103 Qur'ān 49:10 (Eng. trans. from 'Glorious Qur'ān' by Shaykh-ul-Islam Dr. Muhammad Tahir-ul-Qadri).

6 Constitution or formation of a valid contract

After explaining the meanings and definitions of Islamic contracts, now we explain how a valid contract is formed and what necessary elements or conditions are required for the formation of a valid contract in the Islamic law of contract.

While reviewing the academic literature on the subject, it revealed that different authors and scholars described the constituent elements of an Islamic contract under different headings such as "pillars" or "main parts," "salient features" or "main components" and "primary cornerstone" of a valid contract. Similarly, the number of these *arkan* vary with author or jurist; some authors opine that the number of these elements is three, whereas others say they are five in number. For example, Dr. Wahbah al-Zuhayli while explaining cornerstones of a sale contract describes how:

> For the majority of *fuqaha'*, there are four cornerstones (*arkan*) for a sale: the seller, the buyer, the language of the contract and its object. Those are also parallel to the cornerstones of all contracts. For the majority of jurists other than the Hanafis, the cornerstones of sale are either three or four:[1] parties to the contract (buyer and seller), the object of the contract (price and what is priced), and language of the contract (offer and acceptance).

We will not delve into this difference of opinion and will try to sum up all these and describe them in our own style. We shall discuss this under the heading of "essential elements of a contract.".

6.1 Essential elements of a contract

Essential elements of a valid contract, as we explained earlier, are also known as components or pillars of a contract. In Arabic terminology, the word *rukn* is used for element or pillar. "The Arabic word *rukn* means pillar or supporter of something."[2] The plural of *rukn* is "*Arkan.*". Hence elements of a contract are called "*Arkan al-Aqd.*" All the *arkan* together constitute a valid contract. The Arabic term "*Takwin al-Aqd*" is used to explain the formation or constitution of a valid contract under the Islamic law of contract.

The essential elements are those primary and irreducible elements that constitute the fundamental structure of a contract, and the absence of either of these elements renders a contract null and void.

A contract is said to be valid if all essential elements are present while constituting it. Dr. Hussain Hamid Hassan explains the formation and essential elements of a contract as:

> The contract is created when its essential elements (*arkan*) and conditions (*shurut*), which the Lawgiver requires in these essential elements are found. An essential element (*rukn*), according to the generality of jurists, is that on which the existence of a thing depends regardless whether it is a part of its essence or lies outside it.[3]

No contract can be validly constituted without all these elements. Now we discuss these elements one by one.

6.1.2 **Sigha** *or form*

Sigha is an Arabic term, which means "form." It is the procedure by which a contract is created. The instrument or the means which make a valid contract is called *sigha* or "*sighat al-aqd*" and is considered as external proof of the contract. In a legal sense the term is used and applied both for *ijab* and *qabul* or offer and acceptance, i.e. from one side there should some terms making an offer, and from another side, there should be the acceptance of the same without variance. Jurists call it "expression of intent or will." Dr. M. Kabir Hassan explains it as "Form (*sigha*) of a contract in Islamic law is offer and acceptance (*ijab* and *qabul*). For a contract to be valid there should be an offer followed by its acceptance."[4] "An offer is a promise uttered to initiate a negotiation … An acceptance, what the promise utters in reply to confirm the offer."[5]

Now we discuss offer and acceptance in detail. We begin with the topic of the offer.

*6.1.3 Offer (*ijab*)*

In Islamic law, a valid contract is the result of the combination, connecting or tying of an offer (proposal) from one side and acceptance from the other side in a legal manner in accordance with *Shariah* principles. Mostly the formation or constitution of a valid contract is initiated by an offer hence an offer is considered an essential component of a valid contract.

6.1.4 Meanings of an offer

In the Arabic terminology word *Ijab* is used for the offer or proposal. "*Ijab* is the first proposal made by one of the parties in negotiating or concluding a bargain."[6]

According to the *Shorter Encyclopedia of Islam*:

In all legal transactions including marriage the observation of the prescribed legal form is most necessary and the mutual declarations, known in the *fiqh* books as *ijab* and *kabul* (i.e. offer and acceptance), are as a rule indispensable.[7]

6.1.5 Definitions of an offer

The definitions of the term offer prescribed by different authorities and writers are, as Article 101 of the *Medjelle* states: "*Ijab* (proposal) is the word first spoken by one of the contracting parties, from which comes the transference of property."[8]

An offer is an expression of willingness of a party to become bound by doing or not doing something. Quoting here Dr. Wahbah al-Zuhayli:

> The Hanafis view an offer, as an act of one of the two parties indicating a willingness to engage in a transaction. The offer thus may originate from the buyer or the seller, and acceptance is indicated by the second party. Thus, the offer is defined as the first action, and the acceptance as the secondary one, regardless of whether these originate with the buyer or the seller.

The person or a party who makes the offer is called "offeror."

6.1.6 Kinds of offer/modes of offer

To initiate the formation of a contract, an offer is made and conveyed to the other party. This offer may be made or conveyed expressly or impliedly in different ways, modes and manners.

"Islamic contract law recognised both express contracts as well as what has been described in common law as to contract by conduct. It presupposes the making of an offer either orally or by writing or by conduct."[9]

The general rule is that contracts can be made informally. "Generally speaking, there are no special formalities required for contracting parties."[10] Interestingly, the same is the case with the common law of contract. Following are the kinds or modes of the offer.

*6.1.6.1 Verbal offer (*kalam*)*

Offers may be made verbally. The utterance of words in forming a contract is considered the most effective way to perceive the meanings and a party's volition. The reason for this is that words are recognised as the basis of all kinds of expression. It should be kept in mind that meanings of the words used have the primary importance. "Basic rule in the context of Islamic law, however, is that the basis to be considered in the contract is the meaning, and not words and forms."[11] Words used by the offeror should be so clear that the offeree can easily grasp and understand them. Accordingly, any comprehensible phrase referring to the meaning of the formation of a contract can be considered. Also, any language, whether standard, local or even slang, understood by all parties, is permitted. If in the case that one of the parties speaks in a language not understood by another party, it must be interpreted.[12]

In the case of a verbal offer, expression in the past tense is preferred by the majority of Muslim jurisprudents. Present tense can also be used, but indicative or the imperative should be avoided if possible but scholars believe they could be used if there is an indication of the intent barring any other possibility of intending a different contract; meaning the intention of the parties is quite clear.[13] "The Hanafis agree that the language of request such as 'sell to me' or 'buy from me' does not constitute an offer or an acceptance; while language in the present or past tense such as 'I sold you' or 'I sell you', etc. would constitute an offer or an acceptance."[14]

*6.1.6.2 Offer by writing (*kitabah*)*

When parties are not contracting in the presence of each other, they can generate a contract by writing a letter sent by the offeror to the offeree.

Writing is the second means by which a contract can be created. It can be executed in any understandable language and via any means, such as a letter or electronic mail. When an email is sent offering a specific object for sale for a specific price, this amounts to a valid offer. Writing is also considered as a substitute for spoken words as in the case of a verbal offer, but the writing should be clear, readable and understandable. In fact, contact can be concluded in writing even if the two parties are capable of speaking.[15]

Abdur Rehman I. Doi opines in this regard that the offer "can be made in writing (*Bil Kitabah*). This form of an offer becomes effective as soon as the letter leaves the person offering and will remain valid until received by the recipient. The offer must be replied to immediately."[16]

Some Shafi jurists have the opinion that the party who is capable of contracting through verbal communication must not make the offer in writing. According to them, a contract in writing is permitted only for the person who is not capable of speaking.[17] But Hanafi and Maliki jurists and particularly modern scholars have the opinion that the offer can be made in writing even when parties are capable of verbal communication. It is worth mentioning here that in the case of a contract of loan the Qur'ānic verse requires it to be reduced in writing.

يَٰٓأَيُّهَا ٱلَّذِينَ ءَامَنُوٓاْ إِذَا تَدَايَنتُم بِدَيۡنٍ إِلَىٰٓ أَجَلٖ مُّسَمّٗى فَٱكۡتُبُوهُۚ

> "O believers! Whenever you strike deals with one another for a fixed period, reduce the transaction to writing ..."[18]

6.1.6.3 Offer by gesture or signs

All jurists are of the opinion to allow a party who cannot speak and listen, e.g. deaf and/or dumb persons, to make a contract through sign or by gesture because verbal expression for them is impossible as they are naturally unable to speak and listen.

The generality of jurists is of the view that a person who is able to speak or write is not allowed to make a contract by allusion. However, a person who is unable to speak and write, such as a dumb person who does not know how to write, the contract by allusion will be valid because this is possible.[19]

A party who is able to speak is not permitted to use a sign to interpret his intentions as spoken words and writing serves a more powerful form of expression of willingness than signs.[20] Signs must be clear and understood by the contracting parties.

Maliki and Hanbali schools permit the usage of signs, even if parties are able to speak or write, simply because they consider this to be a valid form of contract, which has the capacity to fully reflect the consent and intention of parties involved in the transaction as instrumental to expressing the will of contracting parties. However, there is an argument among scholars regarding a person who cannot speak, but who can write. In view of the full availability of new types of graphic representation through modern technology, writing is undoubtedly more acceptable and unambiguous than making signs, when a party is able to read and write. As has been mentioned, only in the exception of the marriage contract are both signs and writing required of a disabled person.[21]

Siti Salwani writes that Article 70 of the *Medjelle* stipulates that for dumb people, a sign or gesture is equal to speech. This, however, will be irrelevant in the context of the online contract.[22] Furthermore, regardless of whether someone has the capacity to speak or not, the internet allows him or her to access electronic commerce as long as he or she has the capability of utilising the keyboard, cyber pen or mouse.[23]

6.1.6.4 By acts or by conduct

This is termed as the principle of *almuatah* in Islamic law, which occurs by taking certain goods and giving the required money. This simply refers to the conduct of a seller displaying commodities for sale and attaching to them the prices and a simple statement such as first come, first served. Likewise in the conduct of a buyer who takes the commodity and pays its price and, in return, the seller delivers the commodity to the buyer without any expression of words. In Islamic law, the majority of jurists allow this form of concluding a contract; some of them are of the view that, in order to form a contract through conduct or act, it is necessary that the subject matter must be of a small value—not expensive, such as a house, land, or gold;[24] nevertheless, Maliki and Hanbali jurists, even in the case of expensive subject matter, permit this. Shafi jurists do not allow the formation of contracts by actions. The aim of the formation of contract in Islamic law is the form indicating the intention of the parties to conclude the contract; thus, the exchange of goods between two parties without any written document or signature, or the exchange of spoken words of offer and acceptance, are considered adequate for formation. Moreover, silence can be considered a valid tool of expression of the parties' will if the circumstances of the case reflect that the silence of the party receiving an offer or goods can refer to acceptance of the deal.[25]

6.1.6.5 By agent/representative

An offer for entering into a contract can either be made by the offeror himself or by his agent or representative. According to Article 1449 of the *Medjelle*: the agent is someone who stands in someone's place in respect of that business.[26] Thus an agent is fully entrusted with all kinds of business transactions,[27] which can be done by the representative of the principal, such as entering, concluding or rescinding a contract.[28]

According to Prof. Abdul Rahman I. Doi, "An offer can be made through a message sent through some person whose honesty is not doubted and the offer is accepted."[29]

An agent is responsible when he intends to make an offer on behalf of the principal to a third party to declare clearly "I have been sent by Mr. R as an agent to offer you his house for Rs.30 lac." The agent is also responsible for complying with all the instructions given by the principal, and the principal is also equally responsible for notifying the sale or purchase made by the agent.[30]

6.1.7 Counter offer

For concluding a valid contract, it is required that the offer made by the offeror must be accepted by the offeree in the same manner and the same sense as it was made. In the case where one party makes an offer and the other party instead of accepting it as it is, alters it and does not agree in the same manner as it is offered, then it is not an acceptance but a counter offer in the eyes of the law.

> The interconnection between the offer and acceptance is possible only if the offer is accepted as it is. If however, some change is made in the offer or some clarification is added by the person to whom the offer is made, it will not be taken to be an acceptance but only a counteroffer, which would revoke the actual offer. It would be the counter offer which would require to be accepted.[31]

6.1.8 Offer and invitation to treat

In common law of contract, an offer is an expression of the willingness of a party (offeror) to become bound to doing or not doing something. Hence the offer must be distinguished from an invitation to treat which is not intended to result in any binding obligation. An invitation to treat is not an offer but is merely a statement for inviting others to a treat etc. An invitation to treat can be defined as a "declaration which does not contain all the elements of an offer." The difference of the legal effects of both is that an offer once accepted binds the offeror to act according to the offer. On the other hand, in the case of an invitation to treat, there is no such binding. Similarly, where any party inquires for specific goods or seeking to initiate negotiations with another party, such inquiry, investigation or negotiation also does not amount to an offer in the legal sense. Such statements are termed an invitation to treat which is simply an expression of willingness to enter into negotiations which may lead to the conclusion of an offer at a later stage.

Under Islamic law of contract, some jurists relate the concept of invitation to treat under common law to the principle of *Al-mu'atah* (display of goods). *Mu'atah* is a kind of spot sale in which the counter values are presented, exchanged or about to be exchanged without any verbal communication in terms of offer and acceptance. According to Islamic jurists, before the agreement can be concluded in such conduct, it is necessary to determine the intention of the person displaying the goods by reference to the circumstances, nature of the goods involved or whether such practice is already known to trade usage. This is especially true in the context of the concept that it is not the wording but the intention of the party that has to be taken into consideration in commercial matters. This needs more explanation so we discuss it under the following heading separately.

6.1.8.1 Principle of mu'atah *(display of goods)*

Islamic jurists regarding the application of the principle of *mu'atah* are divided into three opinions.

1. According to Hanafi and Hanbali, there is a valid contract when the buyer takes any commodity displayed on the shelf then pays the price as stated if standard trade usage views that this may affect the legal transfer of such commodities. Similarly, in modern times when the display of goods is made on interest i.e. on websites, it may constitute a valid offer if the trade usage recognises the display as an offer. However, it will only be valid if the price is satisfactorily described in it. According to them, it may be applicable if it has become the customary practice of the community and it may be made not only in contracts involving cheap items but also expensive items.

   They support their argument that Allāh u has permitted the sale but does not mention the specific express words *(lafz)* for it; therefore there is a need to refer back to *'urf* (custom) or the trade practice of the community.
2. Some jurists say that *mu'atah* may give effect to a valid contract if there is a definite indication of consent. According to them a virtual display of goods with simple words such as "for sale, while stocks last" or "offer for sale" may constitute an offer. This is because such words indicate the seller's intention to make an offer, thus signifying his consent.

According to them, *mu'atah* may also be applicable not only in the contract of sale but also in hire purchase, partnerships and other types of transactions. In their view, the presence or the display of goods represents the consent of the parties to enter into the contract.

They based their views on the practice of the Prophet (PBUH) who did not stress that the contract is neither only *ijab* and *qabul* nor prohibit expressly the principle of *mu'atah,* therefore, in this case, he suggested that *mu'atah* or sale through conduct or display of goods is strong *qarinah* (inference), sufficient to constitute consent.[32]

3. The third view is contrary to the above two views. According to this view the contract of *mu'atah* is not valid on the grounds that mere conduct does not imply any intention to contract. From this view, we can understand that unless there are specific words, written words or gestures asserting an indication of an intention to enter into the contract, a mere display of goods does not imply an offer.

To them, in the contract, consent is essential and it can only be construed from the express indication of express words, written, etc. They based their argument upon the verse in which Allāh u says;

يَٰٓأَيُّهَا ٱلَّذِينَ ءَامَنُواْ لَا تَأۡكُلُوٓاْ أَمۡوَٰلَكُم بَيۡنَكُم بِٱلۡبَٰطِلِ إِلَّآ أَن تَكُونَ تِجَٰرَةً عَن تَرَاضٖ مِّنكُمۡۚ وَلَا تَقۡتُلُوٓاْ أَنفُسَكُمۡۚ
إِنَّ ٱللَّهَ كَانَ بِكُمۡ رَحِيمٗا

> "O believers! Do not devour one another's wealth unlawfully amongst yourselves unless it is a trade by your mutual agreement and does not kill yourselves. Surely, Allāh is Kind to you."[33]

They further quote the famous *hadith* of the Prophet (PBUH): "Verily trade is based on mutual consent."[34]

According to their views, the consent can only be achieved by the words spoken or expressly written words or gestures. Therefore, a mere display of goods or *mu'atalt* may not constitute an offer.

This is supported by As-Sharbini, who is of the view that merely weighing or measuring and taking away the subject matter without any *ijab* and *qabul* will not constitute a valid contract. Such ambiguous conduct will not constitute a valid offer or acceptance unless there is a clear indication to that effect.[35]

This group has adopted the strict view of rejecting the principle *of mu'atah*. By rejecting *mu'atah* a mere display of goods may become an invitation to treat only and is not a valid offer. Even under the Islamic law of contract, to be valid, an offer must be addressed.[36] When it is not clear to whom the offer is addressed, it is unreasonable to infer that the seller indeed intends to make an offer. It only implies the seller's intention to invite a person to make an offer. Advocates of this view hold that a mere display of goods or principle of *mu'atah* does not constitute an offer; on this an analogy can be made that *mu'atah* is only similar to an invitation to treat.

6.1.9 Communication of offer

The offer has no legal effect unless and until it is communicated to the offeree. In this regard, Baillie says:

> A letter or message may be substituted for verbal and personal communication in the contract of sale, the place of receipt of the letter and delivery of the message being accounted for the meeting. An offer sent by letter or message may be retracted before its receipt and acceptance, and the retraction is valid,

> whether known to the party addressed or not; so that, if acceptance is declared after an offer has been actually retracted, the sale is not completed.[37]

The contract may be made by instantaneous methods of long-distance communication, such as telex or the telephone. Zakhaili has said that according to him, *fuqaha'* recognises such a type of contract.[38]

6.1.10 Termination of offer

The offer may be terminated or extinguished under the following ways or causes:

6.1.10.1 By revocation

The revocation means abrogation. An offer may be revoked at any time, before communication. In *fiqh*, *'Ikalah* means to annul and to put an end. According to the *Medjelle Ahkam-ul-Adaliyyah*. "Ikale, dissolution, nullification; that is the dissolving and making void the contract of sale."[39]

The offeror can revoke his offer before its acceptance by the offeree. According to juristic opinion, it is not necessary that the offeree should accept the offer as soon as it is made to him nor that the offer is revoked merely by the separation of the parties if the offer is not accepted.

6.1.10.2 By lapse of time

Where the offeror fixed a time for acceptance, the offer will stand revoked on the expiry of the time so fixed. It will also not be permissible that in case the time is not fixed the offer should remain open indefinitely without any response from the person to whom the offer is made. If there is any custom or rule of business to govern this matter, it will be the customary rule which will govern it. Otherwise, the offer can be said to be open only for a reasonable time.

6.1.10.3 By withdrawal of the offer

The offer is extinguished by its withdrawal, express or implied, on the part of the party which makes it before its acceptance by the other party. The express withdrawal is one when the party which makes the offer shows its reluctance to making the contract, and the implied withdrawal is one when there proceeds something implying a reluctance to the offer by the party which makes it.

The jurists in general hold that the party making an offer is entitled to withdraw it any time it wishes as long as this offer does not coincide with the acceptance by the other party.

6.1.10.4 The death of a contracting party or it's losing the capacity of making a contract

The offer is likewise extinguished by the death of either of the parties before the acceptance. If the party which made an offer died before its acceptance by the other party, this offer would be extinguished, and the contract would not exist by the acceptance which proceeded afterward. Like the death of either party in a contract is the rule about losing the capacity of making a contract by either party or interdiction imposed on either of them prohibiting it from the disposition.[40] If a party dies or it loses its legal capacity, there will be no more offer.

What has been said with respect to the party which makes an offer the same is said with respect to the party to which the offer has been directed. If that party dies or loses its legal capacity or interdicted before accepting the offer, the offer will be extinguished, because the right of acceptance or the option of acceptance will not be inherited by its heirs.

6.1.10.5 The refusal of an offer

In the same manner, the offer is extinguished when the party to which it is directed refuses to accept it, regardless of whether this refusal is explicit. If an acceptance comes forth after this refusal, the contract will not be completed by it, but it will be considered to be a new offer requiring fresh acceptance by the first party which made the offer.

6.1.10.6 The destruction of the subject matter of the contract

The offer becomes invalid by the destruction of the subject matter of the contract before its acceptance, regardless of whether this destruction is total or partial. The change in the subject matter also will be considered partial destruction putatively. The status quo of the subject matter as it was at the time of making the offer is a condition for the survival of the offer so that it may result in producing the effects and fit for connection of the acceptance with it.[41]

*6.1.11 Acceptance (*qabul*)*

In the Islamic law of contract, the Arabic word *qabul* is used for acceptance. The *qabul* or acceptance is a statement by the offeree, giving his/her assent to the offer made by the offeror. When an offer made by offeror and offeree is agreed to that it is said that acceptance has been made. As a result of effective acceptance, a valid *aqd* between the parties becomes legally binding. Generally, acceptance means an act whereby a party agrees to an offer made to him. If unqualified, a binding contract is thereupon concluded.

6.1.12 Meaning of an acceptance

According to Patrick Hughes:

> *Qabul* means consent. It is a term in the Muhammadan Law of marriage, contracts, etc.[42]

6.1.13 Definition of acceptance

According to Article 102 of the *Medjelle*:

> *Qabul* (acceptance) is the word spoken in the second place for the making of a disposition of property, and the agreement (*aqd*) becomes complete by it.[43]

6.1.14 Modes of an acceptance

As we explained, an acceptance of an offer constitutes a valid contract. Acceptance can be verbal, by conduct or in writing, as stated earlier.[44] When an offer is made and conveyed to the offeree then the offeree has to convey the acceptance to the offeror. This acceptance may be made or conveyed in the following different ways, modes and manners.

6.1.14.1 Verbal acceptance

Acceptance may be made verbally in response to the verbal offer. There is no dispute amongst jurists regarding the conclusion of the contract verbally. Hence utterance of words in forming a contract is considered the most effective way to perceive the meanings and a party's volition. The reason for this is that words are recognised as the basis of all kinds of expression. As a result of oral acceptance, the contract becomes binding. There is no specific proclamation or utterance that needs to be used to signify acceptance. Except in contract for marriage where the jurists have differed in opinion, generally, there are no specific words or terms required to constitute acceptance.[45] The wording used by the offeree while making acceptance should be so precise that the offeror can easily understand them. Also, any language, whether standard, local or even slang, understood by all parties is permitted. If in the case that one of the parties speaks in a language not understood by another party, it must be interpreted.[46]

6.1.14.2 Written acceptance

Writing is the second means by which a contract can be created. It can be executed in any understandable language and via any mean, such as a letter or electronic mail. A written acceptance shall be made against a written offer. Writing is also considered as a substitute for spoken words as in the case of verbal acceptance, but the writing should be clear, readable and understandable. When an email is sent offering a specific object for sale for a specific price, upon its acceptance by the offeree via an email, it becomes a binding contract.

16.1.14.3 Acceptance by gesture or signs

All jurists are of the opinion to allow a party who cannot speak and listen, e.g. deaf and/or dumb persons to make a contract through signs or by gesture because verbal expression for them is impossible. So when an offer is made by gesture or signs, an acceptance shall also be made by gesture or signs. Signs must be clear and understood by both parties.

According to the *Medjelle* in Article 70, "The known signs of a dumb man are equal to words spoken."[47] This, however, will be irrelevant in the context of the online contract. Furthermore, regardless of whether someone can speak or not, the internet allows him or her to access electronic commerce as long as he or she has the capability of utilising the keyboard, cyber pen or mouse.[48]

16.1.14.4 Acceptance by acts or by conduct

When an offer is made by conduct, its acceptance should also be made by conduct only. An offer or acceptance may be expressed by an act or conduct. This simply refers to the conduct of a purchaser in response to the conduct of a seller displaying commodities for sale and attaching to them the prices and a simple statement such as first come, first served. Likewise, in the conduct of a buyer who takes the commodity and pays its price and, in return, the seller delivers the commodity to the buyer without any expression of words. For example, a seller may say to a buyer, "I sold you this food for Rs.200"; the buyer puts the money on the desk and picks up the food. This is called acceptance by conduct or act. In Islamic law, the majority of jurists allow this form of concluding a contract; some of them are of the view that, in order to form a contract through conduct or act, it is necessary that the subject matter must be of a small value—not expensive, such as a house, land, or gold;[49] nevertheless, Maliki and Hanbali jurists, even in the case of expensive subject matter, permit this. Shafi jurists do not allow the formation of contracts by actions. The aim of the formation of contract in Islamic law is the form indicative of the intention of the parties to conclude the contract; thus, the exchange of goods between two parties without any written document or signature, or only by act or conduct, is considered adequate for formation.

Other examples of sale are: a trader says, "Take this garment for a hundred rupees" and the offeree takes it. A person tenders two hundred rupees to a shopkeeper and takes two melons from the shop; the shopkeeper takes the money and remains silent. A person asks a butcher to cut him five hundred rupees worth of lamb chops and the butcher cuts and weights the meat. In all these cases the acceptance is made by conduct.

16.1.14.5 Acceptance by agent/representative

When the offer for entering into a contract is not made directly by the offeror, but it is made by his agent or representative, then an acceptance can also be made by the agent or representative of the offeree. According to the *Medjelle*: "*Wakalet* (agent) is for someone to make someone stand in his place in respect of that business.[50] Thus an agent is entirely entrusted with all kinds of business transactions and contracts.

16.1.15 Rules of acceptance

Following may be some rules of acceptance:

1. **Acceptance should correspond to the offer (proposal):** The acceptance must correspond to the proposal by the purchaser accepting the thing proposed and for the consideration proposed by the seller. If there is any variance in these, there is no contract.[51] When the acceptance is made verbally or in writing, it is necessary that it does correspond to each element of the offer without any condition, limitation or modification.[52] Otherwise, it will not be considered as acceptance.
2. **Acceptance should be either from seller or buyer:** Muslim jurists take two different approaches while interpreting the term *qabul* in the case of a sale contract. The majority view is that *qabul* is made by the buyer or the person to whom the subject matter of the contract is addressed regardless of whether this comes first or later; whereas the Hanafi school holds a more flexible approach when *qabul* is defined as the word uttered later corresponding to the terms which already exist.
3. Moreover, it may be expressed by either the seller or the buyer. This is somewhat similar to common law.
4. **Acceptance must be made before the offer lapses:** According to Shafi's jurists acceptance must be made immediately after an offer is made, and there should be no gap between offer and acceptance. Under Islamic law, in order to effect a contract, the offer must be accepted by the offeree, and the acceptance must be in the same meeting (*majlis*) not later.[53] Traditionally it was said that acceptance must be made before the offer lapses. This refers to the need for a contemporaneous response. When an offer is made verbally, it is impossible to take a literal interpretation of this as an offer immediately lapses once the offer is spoken entirely. Therefore, it has been constructively construed to the effect that the offer persists so long as the meeting continues unless it is withdrawn.

The majority of schools of jurists emphasise that so long as the meeting for bargaining exists, the acceptance may be made at any time before the *majlis* breaks up.[54] This is to enable the offeree to think carefully before accepting the offer.[55] The reason for allowing the delay is simply because the unity of place affixes the two separate things, i.e. the offer and the acceptance and connects the gap between the utterance of offer and acceptance.[56] Furthermore, to require an immediate response will disrupt the smooth flow of commercial activities without any justification for requiring such. This is contrary to the views from Shafi which requires that acceptance must be made immediately.

However, it seems that such a requirement of immediate acceptance of an offer in the same meeting between the offeror and offeree may not be plausible in the modern business world as business people need time to think about the possibility and viability of making a contract and to finally decide positively.

5. **Acceptance must be communicated:** Under Islamic law, when an offer is made by one party, and is accepted by the other party, it must be communicated to the person from whom the offer comes. The communication of

> acceptance is complete the moment it comes to the knowledge of the offeror.[57] If the acceptance does not come to the knowledge of the offeror, it would not be an effective acceptance, and no contract will be formed. This is the majority view of the classical Muslim jurists.[58] The majority of Islamic jurists hold the view that it is necessary that acceptance shall be actually communicated to the offeror. Shafi jurists hold different views that so long as the acceptance is shouted loud enough in an ordinary situation to be heard, such acceptance is effective.[59]

For example, B accepts the offer by sending a letter through the post office to the offeror A. Here, the acceptance is complete against B, when A receives the letter and acceptance comes to the knowledge of A when he receives the letter and the agreement is complete and enforceable. This topic needs some more detail, as follows.

The classical Muslim jurists did not distinguish as to whether the means of communication adopted by the *inter absentee* is instantaneous or otherwise. It is merely suggested that where the contract is formed *inter absentee* the notion of *majlis* is extended to the time when the offeree receives the offer. While the common law in England views that when the instantaneous communication is used, the parties are presumed to be in each other's presence, this is still considered as *inter absentees* communication by Muslim jurists.

However, in the case of telephone conversations, the meeting place will remain so long as the line is open or the contract is uninterrupted.[60] There is still the requirement that the acceptance must be communicated. Hence, the contract will still be concluded at the place where the offeror hears the acceptance, and this is similar to the common law principle. In a telephone conversation, the session starts at the moment when the conversation starts and ends when the parties enter into another discussion or when the conversation is cut off.

By analogy, we can say that to apply the principle applicable to the contract *inter absentee* to the telephone conversation in the online contract is more appropriate than the postal rule. This is because even though the contracting parties are not present physically, the communication through the telephone is instantaneous and similar to the online contract.

The general rule that the acceptance must be communicated shall be given recognition for contracts formed in cyberspace. Due to its unique features, any data message communication should be deemed to have been received when it has reached the information system of its intended recipient. It does not matter that the receipt is affected by a machinery system as opposed to a human being.

If we agree with this proposition, then it is suggested that in the case of the online contract the instantaneous rule should be applied. This is because in Islamic law there is no vast difference with the common law principle of communication of acceptance. However, in Islamic law, we still have the unique feature of the notion of *majlis 'aqad.*

The majority view of Muslim jurists is that when an offer is made to a person who is not present near the offeror, the *majlis* (meeting) will continue until the offeree receives the offer. For example, if the offer is sent by letter through the post office, the *majlis* will continue until the offeree receives the letter and he will be given some time to accept the offer, but not for long.[61]

However, in English law, A (offeror) needs not to receive the acceptance letter. A contract is concluded the moment when the offeree (B) posts the acceptance letter, no matter whether the offeror (A) receives the letter or not. This is known as 'postal rule' which is an exception to the general rule that the offeror (A) must receive the acceptance to conclude a binding contract. It is to be noted that the general rule of acceptance is applicable only in the instantaneous mode of communication of acceptance such as face-to-face acceptance, acceptance by telephone, fax, email, etc.[62]

If the acceptance is communicated by email, it is complete the moment the acceptance in the email enters the designated email account of A. Therefore, if B wants to revoke the acceptance, he must have to revoke it before it enters the designated email of A and not afterwards. As email is an instantaneous way of communication, B will not have sufficient time to revoke the offer in which case he has to think twice before he accepts the offer.[63]

When a contract is made *inter absentee* the offer and acceptance can be communicated by using modern systems of communication, such as telex, fax, email, etc., and the offer and acceptance would be considered valid.[64] Islam does not prohibit people adopting the latest technology if it is beneficial for them and not contradictory to the basic *Shariah* principle *al-maslaha al-mursalah* (public interest consideration) which is also a source of law in *Shariah* which allows the adoption of a modern technology by the people to maximise human resources and convenience for human benefit.

Notes

1 *Sharh Al-Minhaj for Shaykh Zakariyya Al-Ansari* (vol.2, p. 180 onwards), and Al-Buhuti (3rd printing (*Hanbali*), vol.2, p. 3.
2 Al-Sarakhsi, al-Osul, vol. 2, p. 12.
3 Dr. Hussain Hamid Hassan, An introduction to the study of Islamic law, p. 255.
4 M. Kabir Hassan, Rasem N. Kayed & Umar A. Oseni, Introduction to Islamic banking and finance, principles and practice, p. 58.
5 Saleh, N., "Definition and Formation of Contract under Islamic and Arab Laws," (1990), *Arab Law Quarterly*, 5(2): 101.
6 Hughes, Dictionary of Islam, p. 197.
7 H.A.R. Gibb & J.H. Kramers, *Shorter Encyclopedia of Islam*, p. 157.
8 Article No.101, *Medjelle al-Ahkam-ul-Adalia* English translated by W.E. Grigsby, London.
9 H. Ramadan, Understanding Islamic law: from classical to contemporary (USA, Rowman Altimira Publishing 2006) 105.
10 S.H Amin, *Remedies for breach of contract in Islamic anand Iranian law* (London, Royston Publishing, 1984) 13.
11 Abd a-Karim Zaydan, *al-Madkhal li Dirasat al-Shari'ah al-Islamiyyah*, Bughdad: Maktaba al-Quds, 1982, p. 92.
12 Alaeddin Kharofa, *The loan contract in Islamic Shariah* (Leeds Publication, 2002) 11.
13 Kasani Abu Baker, Badai al-Sanai (Vol.1 Cario Sharikh Almtbuat alilniyyah 1910) 133.

14 Wahbah Az-Zuhayli, "Al-Fiqh al-Islami wa 'adillatuh," vol.1, p. 9.
15 Ala Eddin Kharofa, *Transactions in Islamic Law*, p. 17.
16 Abdur Rehman I. Doi, Shariah the Islamic law, p. 356, published by A.S. Noor Deen Kuala Lumpur Malaysia 4th print 2015.
17 Jaber Al-Shafiy, *Majlis al-Aqd fi al-Fiqh al-Eslamy wa al-Qanoon al-Wadhe* (Dar al-Jamea'a al-Jadeedah 2001) 154.
18 Qur'ān 2:282 (Eng. trans. from 'Glorious Qur'ān' by Shaykh-ul-Islam Dr. Muhammad Tahir-ul-Qadri).
19 Dr. Hussain Hamid Hassan, An introduction to the study of Islamic law, p. 263.
20 Ibn Nujaymn Z.Ibrahim, *Alsashbah wa alnazair* (Damascus. Dar Alfiker, 2005) 197.
21 Abdullah, Hassan, *Sales and contracts*: In Early Islamic Commercial Law, Pakistan, Islamic Research Institute, 1994, p. 9.
22 Siti Salwani Razali, Islamic Law of Contract (2010), United Kingdom: Cengage Learning, p. 5.
23 Hurriyyah El-Islamy, *Business on the Internet, The Islamic Perspective*, p 17.
24 Ibn Qudamah M *Al-Sharh al_Kabir* vol.3 (Beirut Dar al-Fkr 1995) 3.
25 Ibn Taimiah Ahmed. *Alfatawi* vol 29 (Riyadh Ministry of Islamic Affairs 1997) p. 546.
26 Article No.1449, *Medjelle al-Ahkam-ul-Adalia* English translated by W.E. Grigsby, London.
27 Dr. Liaquat Ali Khan Niazi, Islamic law of contract, p. 157.
28 Abdur Rehman I. Doi, Shariah the Islamic law, p. 368.
29 Abdur Rehman I. Doi, Shariah the Islamic law, p. 356.
30 Abdur Rehman I. Doi, Shariah the Islamic law, p. 368.
31 Dr. Liaquat Ali Khan Niazi, Islamic law of contract, p. 68.
32 Wahbah Az-Zuhayli, *Al-Fiqh al-Islami wa'adillatuh*, vol. 4, p. 2939.
33 Qur'ān 4:29 (Eng. trans. from 'Glorious Qur'ān' by Shaykh-ul-Islam Dr. Muhammad Tahir-ul-Qadri).
34 As-Sharbini, Mughni al-Muhtaj 2:325 (1994).
35 Al-Sharbiny, Mughni al-Muhtaj, vol. 2, p. 324.
36 Al-Sharbiny, Mughni al-Muhtaj, vol. 2, p. 324.
37 Neil B.E. Baillie, The Moohummudan law of sale, (1850) p. 14.
38 Dr. Wahab al-zakhaili, al-Fiqh al-Islami wa Adillatuhu, ed.1, p. 108 Dar al-Fikr Damascus.
39 Article No.163, *Medjelle al-Ahkam-ul-Adalia* English translated by W.E. Grigsby, London.
40 *al-Anwar li A'mal al-Akbar*, 1:306 as quoted by Dr. Hussain Hamid Hassan in *An introduction to the study of Islamic law*, p. 272.
41 Badran Abul Aynayn, *Tarikh al-Fiqh al-Islami*, p. 377.
42 Hughes, *Dictionary of Islam*, p. 477.
43 Article No.102, *Medjelle al-Ahkam-ul-Adalia* English translated by W.E. Grigsby, London.
44 Abbas, Amanat, *Islamic law in the contemporary context*. Stanford: Stanford University Press, 2007.
45 Article No.3, *Medjelle al-Ahkam-ul-Adalia* English translated by W.E. Grigsby, London.
46 Dr. Ala'eddin Kharofa, *The loan contract in Islamic Shariah* (Leeds Publication, 2002) p. 11.
47 Article No.70, *Medjelle al-Ahkam-ul-Adalia* English translated by W.E. Grigsby, London.
48 Hurriyyah El-Islamy, *Business on the Internet, The Islamic Perspective*, p. 17.
49 Ibn Qudamah M *Al-Sharh al_Kabir* Vol. 3 (Beirut Dar al-Fkr 1995) p. 3.
50 Article No.1449, *Medjelle al-Ahkam-ul-Adalia* English translated by W.E. Grigsby, London.
51 Neil B. Baille, Muhammadan Law of Sale, Delhi Law House, p. 2.

52 Article No.177, *Medjelle al-Ahkam-ul-Adalia* English translated by W.E. Grigsby, London.
53 Zuhaily, W. 1997. *Al-fiqh al-Islami wa adillatuhu*, Damascus: dar al-Fikr.
54 S.E. Rayner, *Theory of Contracts in Islamic Law*.
55 Wahbah Az-Zuhaily, Al-Fiqhul Islamiy wa Adillatuh, vol. 4, p. 107.
56 Al-Rushdan, *al-Hidayah Sharh Bidayah al-Mubtada*, vol. 3 p. 21.
57 Dr. Liaquat Ali Khan Niazi, 1990, Islamic law of contract, p. 67.
58 Dr. Liaquat Ali Khan Niazi, Islamic law of contract p. 67; S.E Rayner. Theory of contracts under Islamic law, p. 100.
59 S.E Rayner, *Theory of Contracts under Islamic Law*, p. 100.
60 Owsia, P., Formation of Contract, p. 575.
61 Owsia P., Formation of contract, p. 575.
62 Hill, S.W.B.H.M. 2001, Email contract: When is contract formed. Journal of law and information science, 12(1): 47–56; Munir, A.B. 1999, Cyber law policies and challenges, Singapore: Butterworth; Suri, R.K. 2001, Information technology laws, Malaysia: ILBS.
63 Electronic commerce Act 2006 (Malaysia), section 5.
64 Bakar, Mohd Daud. 2000. Contracts in Islamic commercial transactions and their application in modern Islamic financial system, p. 5.

7 Parties and their legal capacities

7.1 Introduction

Parties and their legal capacities is the second most essential element of a valid contract after *sigha* (offer and acceptance). In Islamic law of contract, the parties to a contract are those involved in an agreement reached through the making of an offer and an acceptance. There must be more than one party to make a valid bilateral contract. An essential requirement for the conclusion of a valid contract is the necessity that the contracting parties should be qualified to enter a contract. Thus, such parties are required to possess legal capacity (*Ahliyyah*). Ahliyyah means the capacity of competence. Technically it refers to the ability or competence of a person to establish rights for himself or to undertake responsibility. The right to contract and the obligations can only exist where there is the legal capacity to contract.

Capacity, according to jurisprudents, is a quality that makes a person qualified for acquiring rights and undertaking duties and responsibilities.[1] A person who has the ability in a specific area is capable of performing a particular act.[2]

Legally capable persons who are technically termed as *mukallaf* and the fitness of a person for the application of the law to his actions are called legal capacity or *zimmah*. According to Sadr-ush-Shariah, *zimmah* or legal capacity is defined as "the quality by which man becomes fit for what he is entitled to and what he is subject to."[3]

The right to which a person is entitled is known as *Ma Lahu,* and the obligation to which a person is subject is known as *Ma Alayh.* The capacity constituted by combining both the qualities is known as *Taklif-i-Shari'i* or *zimmah* or *ah'liyyat*; the person fulfilling the requirements of the legal capacity is known as *ah'l* or *mukallaf*, and he alone is the addressee of the divine commandments. Hence, he is the subject of the law of *Shariah.*

Muslim jurists have defined a legally capable person as: "A living free human being of mature age and under-standing possessing Islamic faith, not suffering from any factor which fully or partly affects his legal capacity."

7.2 Classification of Ahliyyah or different aspects of Ahliyyah

The Islamic jurists divided *Ahliyyah* into two kinds.[4] Shaykh-ul-Islam Prof. Dr. Muhammad Tahir-ul-Qadri describes "legal capacity" or ah'liyyat as divided into two aspects:

1. Receptive capacity (*Ahliyyah al-wujub*).
2. Active or executive capacity (*Ahliyyah al-ada'*).[5]

7.3 Ahliyyah al-Wujub

This relates to the capacity for inheriting rights and obligations, i.e. to receive rights and obligations. A person in this category can acquire rights and be imposed with obligations in accordance with *zimmah*.[6]

"*Ahliyyah al-Wujub* is the completeness of an individual which enables him to acquire rights and be imposed with obligations as provided by law."[7]

A more modern approach is that an individual is deemed from a legal view irrespective of his physical aspects or his mental state that is; merely his ability to acquire legal rights. Without these unique features of ability in law, he is not deserving of those rights. Even so, every human being can meet the conditions of *al-Wujub* because these are inherent from birth.[8]

7.4 Types of Ahliyyah al-Wajub

Ahliyyah al-Wujub may be further classified into three categories, and they are:

7.4.1 Complete capacity

A perfect or complete receptive capacity relates to the capacity through which a person receives rights and obligations. A person acquires this capacity or ability after his birth until his death. This makes him able to enter into contracts. A child, although he has obtained a full capacity to receive rights and obligations, still cannot undertake contractual obligations except through guardian.

7.4.2 Incomplete capacity

This is a type of capacity that enables a person to receive only limited legal rights but no obligations. For example, a fetus is entitled to the right to be attributed to its parents and also has the right to get a share of inheritance only when it is born alive.

7.4.3 Totally devoid of the ability

A person in this category has no rights whatsoever. He is like an embryo which is dead upon delivery.

7.5 Ahliyyah al-Ada'

Unlike the Ahliyyah al-wajub, which deals with acquiring rights and obligations etc., this capacity deals with actions, deeds, performance and execution, etc.

> Ahliyyah-al-Ada' literally means the capacity of performance. It is the most essential element for making a valid contract. It is also known as the capacity

> for execution which is defined as the "capacity of a human being for the issuance of words and performance of deeds to which the lawgiver has assigned certain legal effects."[9]

This is the ability of a person to start or to perform an action. The capacity of performance is that a person is qualified to take action which is legally valid. This kind of capacity does not exist before a person acquires proper mental awareness and becomes discerning. When a child reaches the age of discernment, he acquires the capacity of performance, but this capacity is considered deficient until the person reaches the age of maturity of reason; then he is considered fully capable of performing and taking legally valid action, and he will be asked to undertake all legal responsibilities—bodily, financial and otherwise—and he will be entitled to all his legal dues. The ability to act thus is a whole requisite which enables a person to acquire rights and means that they have obligations imposed on them.[10]

7.6 Types of Ahliyyah al-Ada

There is a very lengthy discussion on the difference of opinion on types of *Ahliyyah al-Ada* which is outside the scope of this study. However, we shall explain it very briefly. Jurists divided *Ahliyyah al-Ada* into mainly two categories.

7.6.1 Incomplete or deficient capacity

A person in this category can take part in some actions and not in others. He can participate in specific actions that are of particular importance to him but only under the care and supervision of some other person. A person between the age of seven years and the onset of puberty falls into this category.

It is assigned to a non-pubert who possesses some discretion and to the *ma'tuh* (lunatic) who has attained puberty yet lacks complete mental development. A person who possesses an insufficient capacity is not capable of entering into any contract and also cannot be held criminally liable. They do not understand the meaning of the contract and cannot mean it. Deficient aptitude includes the discerning child and the idiot. The list is sometimes extended to include the indebted, the foolish and the forgetful. The discerning boy and the idiot can be placed under interdiction.[11]

7.6.2 Complete capacity

Complete capacity is established for a human being when he attains full mental development and acquires the ability to discriminate. Thus, the requirement of this capacity is reason (*aql*) and discretion. This type of *ahlivyah (capacity)* allows a person to act according to the laws of *Shariah*. He has attained puberty and is becoming mature *(bulugh arrashidy)*. He has the right to enter into the contract on his own accord. One who has attained puberty is deemed to have the ability to complete *ada*' and is, therefore, able to conduct himself in accordance with *Shariah* law. This means that he can enter into a contract and the contract is valid and in all his other dealings he is subjected to *Shariah* law.[12] The sign of puberty is ejaculation in a male, and menstruation in a female: in the absence of these signs, puberty is presumed to have occurred by the age of 15 years in both male and female according to the majority of the jurists and at 18 years for a male and 17 years for a female according to Imam Abu Hanifah.

7.7 The stages of capacity under Islamic law

Under Islamic law the capacity or *Ahliyyah* of a person starts from the embryo stage and continues until he becomes a complete person during which he goes through five stages.[13]

7.7.1 The Embryo (janin) Stage

This starts from conception until the birth of the child. This is the stage of *Ahliyyah al-Wujub* that is not complete. He/she has only four rights endowed upon him/her, provided that he/she is born alive.

1. The right to descend from both parents.
2. The right to receive property from them or those nearest in kinship to him.
3. The right to receive property that is willed to him (if any).
4. The right to benefit from the rents of premises (if any).

7.7.2 The childhood stage

This stage is from birth to seven years of age, a period during which the child is said to have the *Ahliyyah al-Wujub* that is complete. He has the right to receive his rights and usually does so through his guardian on matters relating to *tasarrufat.* Where something is bought for him, or he is given something to own, it is necessary for the guardian to see that the deal is properly done. However, the child at this stage does not have the *Ahliyyah al-Ada'.* Therefore he cannot be held responsible for his promises, and his contracts are void. He may do so if the contract is made by his guardian on his behalf in accordance with Islamic law.[14]

7.7.3 The mumayyiz stage

Mumayyiz is the stage reached where a person (minor) realises the difference between good and evil, between something beneficial and harmful. He knows how to negotiate and understand a sale and purchase agreement for example of relinquishing property and acquiring ownership of a property. This period of one's life is from seven years of age to the onset of puberty. At this stage, he can buy and sell, but only with his guardian's consent. Any contract is illegal if the activities bring suffering to him especially one which involves his property moving to another.[15]

*7.7.4 The puberty (***baligh***) stage*

This period covers the time from puberty up to such a stage that the person has acquired necessary worldly knowledge.

Such a person is deemed *mukallaf* (responsible for his act) and falls into the category of the capacity of complete *ada'*. Legally he is considered a mature person and wise enough to understand commercial dealing and send or receive money and property.

7.7.5 The prudence stage

According to Maliki and Hanbali cleverness is perceived as the presence of mind to enable a person to manage one's financial affairs or regarding one's religious attitude.[16] Jurists defined cleverness or intelligence as the capability to manage one's financial affairs; however, it is not limited to any particular age group as it may not develop simultaneously with one's physical age. Intelligence can even precede puberty.[17] Hence the principal elements for the capacity of performance are puberty and prudence, and these refer to actual physical and mental growth.

Some jurists are of the view that one who can distinguish between admittance and denial is deemed as having reached this stage. More than this he must be a thinking person, able to understand what he says,[18] and one who is capable of distinguishing between useful and harmful, profitable and unprofitable things or transactions and able to understand the consequences of his actions.

7.8 How to determine the capacity

We explained that legal capacity is required by a person to enter into a legally binding contract. The question may arise how this capacity can be determined? There is no specific provision in Qurān and Sunnah which fixes a particular age of majority.

Following Qur'ānic verse provides the guideline to determine the capacity:

وَٱبْتَلُوا۟ ٱلْيَتَٰمَىٰ حَتَّىٰٓ إِذَا بَلَغُوا۟ ٱلنِّكَاحَ فَإِنْ ءَانَسْتُم مِّنْهُمْ رُشْدًا فَٱدْفَعُوٓا۟ إِلَيْهِمْ أَمْوَٰلَهُمْ ۖ وَلَا تَأْكُلُوهَآ إِسْرَافًا
وَبِدَارًا أَن يَكْبَرُوا۟ ۚ وَمَن كَانَ غَنِيًّا فَلْيَسْتَعْفِفْ ۖ وَمَن كَانَ فَقِيرًا فَلْيَأْكُلْ بِٱلْمَعْرُوفِ ۚ فَإِذَا دَفَعْتُمْ إِلَيْهِمْ أَمْوَٰلَهُمْ
فَأَشْهِدُوا۟ عَلَيْهِمْ ۚ وَكَفَىٰ بِٱللَّهِ حَسِيبًا

> "And evaluate and test the orphans (for the sake of their training) till they attain to (the age of) marriage. Then if you discern in them ingenuity (and the knack of planning), hand over their assets to them. And devour not their wealth spending it wastefully and in haste (fearing that after) they grow mature (they will take it back). The one who is affluent must absolutely abstain (from the orphan's property), but he who is indigent (himself) should consume but a fair portion of it (only). And when you return to them their assets, take witnesses over them. And Sufficient is Allah at reckoning."[19]

The following *ahadith* of the Prophet (PBUH) are quoted by the jurists as guidelines to determine legal capacity.

> It is not recorded (the acceptance of their religious practice) upon three categories namely those who are asleep until they awake, children until they have the dream and the lunatic until he is sane.[20]

For a woman, the onset of menstruation will determine their age of majority, according to the following *hadith*:

> Where a female believer has been visited with menstruation, it is incumbent on her whatever is incumbent on her mother.[21]

It is worth mentioning here that in the above-quoted verse, the age of maturity i.e. *rushed* is declared the criteria for the legal capacity. The word *rushed* has been differently interpreted by the jurists. Some jurist described it as the age of prudence or puberty or the age of majority and others related it to either the discovery of one's natural emission or calculation of the calendar years. *Fuqaha'* (jurists) have different views regarding this. According to the majority of fuqaha such as Abu Hanifah, As-Shaibani, Abu Yusof, Ibn Qudama, Imam Nawawi and also the compilers of the *Medjelle,* who share the same view, the age of *rushed* occurs only when a minor reaches the age of 15 years.[22]

There are some *fuqaha'* which claim that the age of *rushed* for a male person is 19 or 18 or 17 years for the female.[23] Mahmasani claimed that a minor below the age of *rushed* or 15 years is not able to be a party to the contract unless the contract is proven to be for his/her advantage and ratified by the guardian.[24]

Imam Abu Hanifah declared the age of 18 for a male and 17 for a female as the age of majority.[25]

7.9 Division of capacity for the purpose of transactions

Jurists also divided the capacity to enter into a contract by keeping in view the nature of transactions. By keeping in view that whether the transactions are beneficial or not for the capacity-lacking person, Hanafies divided the validity of the dealings into three kinds:

i) **Beneficial transactions:** If the transactions are purely for the benefits of the non-pubert then it is permissible. These are like the acceptance of a gift or of *sadaqah* etc. These are allowed to a non-pubert, who can discriminate and has been permitted to do so by his guardian.
ii) **Harmful transactions:** If the transactions are harmful, then they are not permitted. Granting of divorce, manumission and *qard,* etc., which are not beneficial, are not permitted to be entered into, by the non-pubert or *sabi mumayyaz* (minor possessed with discretion).

iii) **Transactions equally likely to result in benefit or harm:** These are sale, hire and partnership. They are considered valid if the permission of the guardian is granted.

Some jurists disagree with the above view, and they refuse to acknowledge any capacity for the Sabi Mumayyaz. According to them; it makes no difference whether the transactions are beneficial or harmful.[26]

7.10 Circumstances or factors which prevent the legal capacity of a person

There are certain circumstances and factors, which impair the legal capacity of a person and prevent him from concluding contracts and making dispositions in his property. The contracts concluded by persons having impaired legal capacity such as being insane, a drunkard, sleeping or unconscious are called "artificial contracts," i.e. *Al-aqud-al-sowri*. Following are factors which prevent the legal capacity of a person.

1. **Insanity:** Insanity, in Arabic known as *Junun*, refers to an abnormal mental state of a person that affects his or her capability or ability to make rational decisions. An insane person cannot distinguish between good and evil, and is destitute of intelligence; hence insanity eliminates the legal capacity of a person.

   Jurists divided insanity into two kinds:

   i. *Asli* (regular): when a person attains puberty during his lunacy.
   ii. *Tari* (casual): which appears after a person has attained puberty and developed sanity together with mature understanding.[27]

   As regards the legal effects of the utterances and dispositions of the insane, he/she is like a minor without discretion, which does not produce any effect. Contracts entered into by the insane are void.
2. **Lunacy or idiocy *('Atah)*:** *'Atah* is defined as "the mental derangement of a person who is confused in his speech and who sometimes speaks like a sensible person and sometimes like lunatics."[28] They are called an idiot or imbecile and *Ma'tuh* in Arabic.

   It refers to an inborn weakness. It is an incapable state of mind where a person is inconsistent in his decisions and behaviours. *Ma'tuh* is the partial or temporarily insane person who sometimes acts like a sane person and sometimes like an insane person. *Ma'tuh* is treated like a minor; thus, he is not allowed to enter into valid contracts, which are disadvantageous for him. However, *Ma'tuh* is allowed to conclude a beneficial transaction.
3. **Forgetfulness:** Forgetfulness is defined as: "A circumstance that befalls a man without his volition causing loss of remembrance of something."[29]

The majority of jurists think that a contract concluded through forgetfulness is not a contract at all. They rely on the following *hadith* of the Holy Prophet (PBUH):

"My Ummah is forgiven for that which they have done through mistake or forgetfulness or under coercion."[30]

Some jurists declare that statements made by mistake or forgetfulness are valid for the formation of contracts in certain circumstances. They maintain that the door will otherwise swing open for setting up false defences.

4. **Prodigality:** *Safah* or prodigality refers to the following two situations.

Firstly, where a person is not capable of acting correctly and of taking a right financial decision for his benefits. In this regard, it is defined as: "*Safah* is that weakness of intellect which urges a person to act concerning his property contrary to the dictates of intellect with the non-existence of mental disorder."[31]

Secondly, *safah* or prodigality refers to a situation where a person is not capable of spending his or her wealth appropriately but wastes and spends his wealth improperly. In this regard, it has been defined as: "*Safah* is the disposition of one's property contrary to the dictates of the intellect and the *Shariah* by spending it without righteous purpose, squandering and using of more of it than necessary despite the persistence of one's intellect in reality."[32] *Safah* is the opposite of the word *rushed* which signifies the handling of financial matters in accordance with the dictates of reason and accordingly to preserve one's wealth properly. The situation of prodigality adversely affects the legal capacity of such a person.

5. **Death-illness:** Death-illness has been defined as follows:

> Death-illness is that form of illness from which death is to be apprehended in most cases, and illness which disables the patient from looking after affairs outside his house if he is a male, and the affairs within her home if she is female, provided the patient dies in such condition before a year has passed.[33] This usually happens when the disease gets worse from day to day until death ensues.

To constitute this malady of death-illness there must be (a) proximate danger of death, so that there is a preponderance of apprehension of death; (b) some degree of subjective apprehension of death in the mind of the sick person; and (c) some external indication, chief among which would be inability to attend to ordinary avocations.[34] In this condition, the person is supposed to make individual decisions under strong emotions regarding dispositions of his/her property which may cause injustice to his/her legal heirs and creditors, etc. This is why such a person is not considered competent to enter into a valid contract.

6. **A drunk or one intoxicated:** The drunken person is one who is in a state of intoxication due to the consumption of liquor or intoxicants and does not know what he is saying. Intoxication is a condition which overtakes a man

on account of taking an intoxicant, and along with it, his intelligence remains suspended, being neither lost nor diminished.[35] The following two situations may arise in a case of intoxication:

(i) **Voluntarily:** This situation arises by willfully taking intoxicants. A person becomes intoxicated out of his own choice, and he intentionally took intoxicants. The Malikis and Hanbali jurists declared the contracts entered into by such persons not valid as intoxication takes away a person's rational power to make a proper decision, and it prevents a person from distinguishing what is right and evil or beneficial and harmful.

However, some jurists declared the contracts entered into by such persons valid ones. They argued that the person intoxicated intentionally, knowing that it is prohibited and a crime. This could serve as a sort of punishment to such a person as a crime should not absolve a person from the duties acquired by him.

(ii) **Involuntarily:** Involuntarily intoxication, on the other hand, could be caused by some lawful means. These may be the following cases:

- (i) When it is caused by drugs taken as medicine or anaesthetic (anaesthesia).
- (ii) When he is about to die of thirst and no other drink is available.
- (iii) When a person drinks intoxicating liquor without knowing that it is forbidden liquor.
- (iv) When he is forced to do so under duress.

The majority of jurists have the view that contracts entered into by a person intoxicated involuntarily are not valid.

7. **Insolvency or bankruptcy**: According to jurists, an insolvent or a bankrupt person cannot enter into a valid contract regarding alienation or disposition of his property.

   A person is considered bankrupt when his debts are equal to or exceed his assets. The court, on the demand of his creditors, passes a prohibitory order restraining him to alienate his property or dispose of it and directs the sale of his property for the benefit of his creditors. The purpose of this order is to safeguard and protect the right of creditors.

   The precedent for such regulation was set by the Prophet Muhammad a. It is narrated that Mu'adh ibn Jabal was a generous man and always gave his possessions away. He was always in debt. His debts were more than his property. So, he came to the Prophet (PBUH) and requested him to ask his creditors to withdraw their claims on the debts. They, however, refused. The Prophet (PBUH) later sold all Mu'adh's property to pay the debts, to the extent that he had nothing left. Hence a bankrupt person loses his capacity to enter into a valid contract.

8. **Coercion:** Coercion is to compel a person without having such a right, to do a thing without his consent or through fear. It is also defined as "an action directed against a person who suppresses his valid consent." Contracts and

dispositions made under coercion are not valid according to the majority of Muslim jurists. Hanafis, however, maintain the contract of the person coerced is valid but is suspended, on the extinction of coercion. The *mukrah* (coerced person) has the right to ratify it or revoke it. They also hold that the contracts of marriage, divorce, manumission are valid even with coercion.

Notes

1 Sheikh Ahmad Ibrahim, "Al Ahliyya wa Awaredoha," in the journal of Al Qanun wa al Eqtesad, year 1, p. 352.
2 Abdul Karim Zaydan, *Al-Madakhil Lil Dirasah as-Shariah Islamiyyah*, p. 312.
3 Tauzih, p. 419 as quoted by Shaykh-ul-Islam Prof. Dr. Muhammad Tahir-ul-Qadri in "Islamic concept of law," p. 21.
4 Dr. Hussain Hamid Hassan, *Al-Madkhil lil dirasah al-Fiqh Islami*, 1970, p. 320.
5 Shaykh-ul-Islam, Prof. Dr. Muhammad Tahir-ul-Qadri, Islamic concept of law, p. 21.
6 Sanhnrr, *Sharh al-qanun MadanT, an-nazariyyah al-'Ammah Lil Iltizam Nazartyyat al-'aqdi*, p. 77.
7 Anuar Sultan, *An-nazariyyah al-Ammah Lil Iltizam Masadir al-Iltizam*, p. 77.
8 Abdul Razak Ahmad Al-Sanhuri, *Syarh Qanun al-Madaniy*, p. 315.
9 Dr. Hussain Hamid Hassan, al-Madkhal, p. 320.
10 Abdul Razak Ahmad Al-Sanhuri, Syarh Qanun al-Madaniy, p. 285.
11 Ahmad Abu al-Fath, Al Moamalat, p. 143.
12 Wahbah Az-Zuhayli. *Al-fiqhu! Islamiy Waadillatuhu*, p. 122.
13 Wahbah Az-Zuhayli, *Al-fiqhul Islamiy Waadillatuhu*, p. 122.
14 Wahbah Az-Zuhayli, *Al-fiqhul lslamiy Waadillatuhu*, p. 124.
15 Wahbah Az-Zuhayli, *Al-fiqltul Islamiy Waadillatuhu*, p. 124.
16 Wahbah Az-Zuhayli, *Al-fiqhu! lslamiy Waadillatuhu*, p. 124.
17 Abdul Karim Zaydan, *al-Madkhal*, p 316.
18 Syeikh Muhd Isa, Hamish, *As-Sharb Al-Kabtr*, Cairo, Ch.4, p. 126.
19 Qur'ān, 4:6 (Eng. trans. from 'Glorious Qur'ān' by Shaykh-ul-Islam Dr. Muhammad Tahir-ul-Qadri).
20 Al-Bayhaqi, *Sunan al-Kubra*, Ch.6, p. 57.
21 Al-Bayhaqi, *Sunan al-Kubra*, Ch.6, p. 58.
22 Ibn Qudama, Al-Mughnr Muhtaj, Cairo 1367 AH, Vol 4, p. 460.
23 Hamilton, *The Hedaya*, Premier Book House Lahore, 1982, p. 530.
24 S.Mahmassani. Al-Nazrtyyah al-'ammah lil mujibat wal 'uqud ftl-Shari'ah Islamtyyah, Beirut, 1948, Vol 2, p 104.
25 Zakariya al-Barry, *Hukum Anak-anak da/am Islam*, Jakarta, 1977, p 118.
26 Ahmad Ibrahim Bik, *al-Iltazamat fi al-Shar al-Islami*, Cairo: Dar al-Ansar, 1944, pp. 120–121.
27 Abdul Karim Zaydan, *al-Madkhal*, p. 317.
28 'Ubaid Allāh ibn Mass'ud, Sadr al-Shariah, al-Tawdih, al-Maktabah al-Khayriyyah, 1322 H, vol. 2, p. 168.
29 Hassan, *al-Hukm al-Shar'I inda al-Usuliyyin, Dar al-Nahdah al-'Arabiyyah*, 1972, p. 186.
30 Haythami, *Majma al-Zawaid*, vol. 6, p. 250.
31 Amir Badshah, Taysir al-Tahrir, Cairo: Mustafa al-Babi al-Halabi, 1351 AH, vol. 2, p. 300.
32 Hassan, *al-Hukm al-Shar'I inda al-Usuliyyiyn*, p. 210.
33 Ahmad Hassan, *Principles of Islamic jurisprudence*, Islamabad: Islamic Research Institute, 1993, p. 323.
34 D.F. Mulla, *Mahomedan law*, p. 148.
35 Hassan, *al-Hukm al-Shar'i*, p. 204.

8 Subject matter

Subject matter is the essential and vital element of a valid contract, without which no contract can be made and performed. When we review the academic literature on Islamic contracts, we see that the "considerations object" and the "subject matter" are more or less discussed in the same way in a contract made. Consideration is "a permissible exchange of contractual obligations" by contracting parties. A contractual obligation of one party may be the consideration of the contractual obligation of the other party. It may be a number of things like a commodity, cash or price, a usufruct, and the performance of an act, according to the nature of a contract. For example, in the case of a contract of sale of the property, it might be valuable land or building, etc. and in the case of commodity, it may be price; in the case of a contract of hire it might be usufruct, etc.

Similarly, in the case of a contract of employment or maintenance, consideration might be to do some work or to provide some service, etc. In this way, consideration may be the subject matter of a contract. The object of a contract for which a contract is made may also be the consideration. Hence the subject matter of a contract depends upon the purpose or object of making the contract. Some authors discuss the object of a contract under a separate heading.

8.1 Conditions for a valid subject matter

The traditional Muslim jurists described some qualifications, attributes and requisites for a subject matter of a contract to be a valid one and suitable for dealing. According to them, the subject matter of a contract should exist, possibly be of value, free from ambiguity, i.e. an adequately defined and legal one, etc. The Muslim jurists more or less described the following conditions for the subject matter of a contract that should be fulfilled when a contract is concluded.

8.2 Subject matter should be fit for transaction

In the Islamic law of contract, the subject matter of a contract should be fit for the transaction. It should be a thing which can be transacted, otherwise the contract will be invalid. Things that are incompatible for transactions cannot be the subject matter. These are things that cannot be acquired, such as the sun and air etc., and these are natural things, common to all humanity. Under the fitness of the subject matter or object of a contract, Dr. Hussain Hamid Hassan explained a general rule, i.e. "it should be a property having some value which is owned by someone and free from any legally binding right."[1] We explain it further in a little detail as follows.

8.3 It should be a "property" or "usufruct"

The subject matter of the contract should be a valuable property in the eyes of Islamic law. If a subject matter is not a "property" its transaction is not allowed and is inadmissible in Islamic law of contract. Similarly, a contract related to dirty things and useless or harmful things is also not allowed. According to Prof. Dr. Ala' Eddin Kharofa, "According to Islamic jurisprudent, the subject matter of a contract could be physical property, as in granting, sale and mortgage,[2] privilege or benefit,[3] as in rent."

8.4 It should have some value

Subject matter must have some clear material value. Goods, a commodity or any other thing without real value cannot be the subject matter of the contract. Hence, "the subject matter must be a property which has commercial value because of the *Shariah* and owned by the contractor."[4] Thus any transaction or contract regarding a property without value is null and void.

The price of the subject matter in the case of a contract of sale and purchase must be definite and specific. "If the price is uncertain, the sale is void."[5]

> It should involve real or corporeal money or property in possession of someone. If it was not money, or if it was money or property but not real or corporeal, or if it was real but not in possession of anybody, then the contract is nugatory.[6]

8.5 It should be ownable

The subject matter of a contract should be the type of property or thing which is ownable by any individual or contractor. The contracts and transaction in the property which is not ownable are not allowed, and also things before being owned are not fit for transactions.

Regarding the property which might have commercial value but is without an owner,[7] in Islamic law it is not allowed to transact such articles, but once acquired, they can become a subject of the transaction.

Similarly, public properties, which are used by the public at large, such as rivers and roads etc., are also excluded and cannot be the subject matter of the contract of an individual. Likewise, a contract involving the sale of a mosque is also invalid.[8]

8.6 No charge should be attached

According to Islamic law, the subject matter of the contract should be free from any legal charge or encumbrance. It is not legal to make a transaction of the subject matter when any charge or encumbrance is attached to it.

Similarly, when the right of a man (other than the owner) is attached to the property, transaction in this property is prohibited, for it violates this right.[9]

8.7 Existence of subject matter

The condition regarding subject matter is that it must actually exist at the time of entering into a contract. For the contract to be correct, the subject of the contract has to exist.[10] It should be kept in mind that the existence of subject matter should be actual, i.e. it must exist in reality. It is not sufficient that it exists in the eyes, or in the opinion, of the contracting parties. It is also not sufficient that the existence of subject matter is potentially possible, but it must be physical and actual.

If in any transaction, the subject matter has not yet come into existence or its acquisition is not possible, such a contract is not valid in the eyes of Islamic laws of contract. The wisdom behind this prohibition of the contract in the non-existing matter is the fear of *gharar* or risk which may affect the consent which is an essential element of contact;[11] likewise this may involve deceit and lead to conflict and dispute. Classic jurists quoted examples such as the sale of fruits on a tree at the beginning of the season; fish still in the water; milk in the udders of an animal; standing crops; the fetus still in the womb of an animal.

The Muslim jurists went to great lengths and had different opinions regarding this matter. Wahbah Zuhayli explains the viewpoint of the *fuqaha'* on this issue in the following words:

> The object of a contract must be present during the contracting session. Contracting over a non-existent object is invalid, like selling crop before it is visible, on the assumption that the crop might not appear. Equally prohibited are cases involving what is known as "the fear of non-existence" (*khatar al-adam*) like the assumption that a fetus might not survive upon birth. This requirement is mandatory in the Hanafi and Shafi schools, regardless of whether the transaction involves commutative (*mu'awadat*) or gratuitous (*tabarru'at*) contracts.[12] Any transaction involving *ma'dum* is void whether the case is sale (*bay*), gift (*hibah*) or pledge (*rahn*). This view is based on a tradition of the Prophet (PBUH) wherein he is reported to have prohibited the sale of the fetus of an animal (*bay habal al-hablah*)[13] as well as the sale of an embryo (*al-madamin*)[14] and sperm (*al-malaqih*).[15] He is also reported to have prohibited people from dealing in transactions where the seller did not possess the object. This is because the object was treated as *madum* during the contract. They have established an exception to this general rule, i.e. the prohibition of *bay al-madum* in cases about the sale by advance (*salam*), contract of manufacturing (*istisna*). These transactions are approved, despite the absence of the object of the contract, by way of *istihsan* (juristic preference) in order to cater to the needs of mankind.[16]

However, Ibn al-Qayyim, an eminent Hanbali jurist, has differed from this opinion. He is of the view that the non-existence of an object does not constitute a reason for prohibition. He tries to denounce the confusion between uncertainty and non-existence. He says:

> There is nothing in the Qur'ān nor in the Sunnah that asserts the view that contracting over a *madum* (non-existing object) is disallowed. What is available in the Sunnah regarding transactions involving existent commodities is contained in the *hadith*: "do not sell what is not with you (i.e. not in your possession)." The *hadith* indicates that the *'illah* (legal effective cause) here is not *'adam* or non-existence but *gharar* (uncertainty). The uncertainty is due to the inability to deliver the subject matter of the contract, for instance, a runaway camel (*al-bair al-sharid*). Whenever the *'illah* is removed the *hukm* too stands removed, for are you not aware that the Lawgiver has permitted *'ijaara* and *al-musaqah* because of the absence of uncertainty? The Lawgiver, instead, disallowed the sale of a runaway camel because of the element of *gharar* inherent in it even though it is in existence. Similarly, the lawgiver has disapproved of the hire of a camel in cases where the owner of the camel cannot deliver the animal for use. Above all, this principle applies to all forms of commutative contract in contrast with *al-wasiyyah* (bequests). Al-Wasiyyah is a pure gratuitous contract to which *gharar* does not apply. Thus a contract concerning a will created over an absent subject matter is a valid contract.[17]

8.8 Possession and deliverability of subject matter

The subject matter should be in the possession of its owner and deliverable to another party at the time of entering into a contract. If it is not in the possession of a contracting party and not deliverable to another contracting party, the contract is void. This condition applies to property transaction contracts such as sale, mortgages and pledges, etc. Possession means either physical or constructive possession at the time of concluding the contract. The Muslim jurists, therefore, prohibit the sale of a stray animal, whose whereabouts are not known, or fish in the sea or birds in the air.[18] Imam Malik, however, allowed the gratuitous transactions on the non-existent subject matter because they are voluntary.[19]

Similarly, besides possession, the ability to deliver the subject matter of a contract at the time of entering it is also the condition for the validity of the contract. Hence the owner of the subject matter should have the power to hand it over to another party. The inability to deliver renders the contract inadmissible in the eyes of the Islamic law of contract. Dr. Hamid Hassan Hassan described this inability to deliver as follows:

> Jurists have distinguished between the two forms among the forms of inability to deliver the object. The first form is that the inability to deliver the object is absolute. By absoluteness, they mean that everyone is unable to deliver the object of the contract, and not the party to the contract alone, and in all cases in general, and not in one case to the exclusion of others. They illustrate it by

the example of a stray camel which does not know its place, and a bird in the air and fish in the water. The rule of this form is that the contract is invalid.

The second form is that the inability to deliver the object (subject matter) is relative, that is, absolute. By that, they mean that delivery is impossible by the seller without the interference by the ruling authorities. This means that if the debtor is left alone, he is unable to pay the debt. Delivery of the object by the debtor is impossible, but it is possible with the help of others, namely with the help of the ruler. The jurists have illustrated this form by the example of selling the usurped goods to their usurper because the seller is unable to deliver the goods to him in this situation without the intervention of the ruler.[20]

8.9 Knowledge of the subject matter

The subject matter of the contract must be well known to the contracting parties at the time of entering into the contract; otherwise the contract will be invalid. It means the contracting parties must precisely know the details of the particulars of the subject matter. They must be accurately known, identified and defined to prevent any ambiguity.

The general principle in Islamic law of contract is that in the case of the property-related contract the subject matter must be precisely specified, determined and ascertained as regards its essence, quantity and value, etc., and in the case of another contract, its attributes, like an obligation or performance, etc. If the subject matter is not known or unspecified, the contract is void as there are chances that the subject matter may differ from the subject matter agreed, which may amount to cheating and gambling, which may lead to conflict or dispute.[21]

Knowing, ascertaining and determining the subject matter may be attained in two ways, i.e. by inspection or examining the subject matter and by the description of the subject matter.

8.10 By inspection or examining

The subject matter becomes known when the parties to a contract inspect or examine it at the time of concluding the contract. If the subject matter is present at the time of making the contract, then the majority of jurists opine that its inspection or examination is necessary. Failure of the parties to examine the subject matter invalidates the contract. The examination is the sole medium through which sale is possible, according to these jurists.[22]

If the subject matter is present at the time of the meeting of the contracting parties the Hanafis and Hanbalis hold that knowledge of the subject matter is attained by pointing out where the subject matter is, even if it is in a hidden place.[23] Maliki is of the opinion that no valid contract can take place unless the parties have laid eyes on it, except when it is impracticable to see the subject matter, and that it can be attained by description;[24] whereas Shafi states that as a general rule the knowledge is attained only by seeing the subject matter whether or not it is present at the meeting of the contracting parties.[25]

8.11 By description

The second way of knowing the subject matter is by description. When the subject matter is not present at the time of the conclusion of the contract, then knowledge may be ascertained by a description of it. Such description must be detailed in such a way that there should not remain any vagueness and uncertainty about the subject matter. If the goods or property to be sold is already known, like the house or horse of a seller who has only one house or horse, a description highlighting its specification or characteristics would be deemed to be sufficient. However, if the sale is of fungible (*mithli*) goods, then genus, kind and quantity must be described.

8.12 Legality or suitability of subject matter

The subject matter of a contract should be a licit one. That is, it should in principle be something legal and must be such that transactions are legally permissible within it. If it is not legal according to *Shariah* rules, then the contract is nugatory. Legality is related to the subject matter itself and the purpose of the transactions. Thus, a contract whose subject matter is within the list of things prohibited by the Qur'ān and Sunnah, such as alcoholic drink, intoxicants, blood, drugs, pork, dead animals, the flesh of swine, etc., is void. Similarly, a contract made for the commission of any offence such as the perpetration of unlawful killing or a robbery, etc. is also unlawful.

The subject matter should be legally clean and permissible, and it should not be contrary to the objectives of *Shariah* but must be aligned with it. Likewise, it must not oppose the will and intention of the lawgiver. Legality also requires that it should be beneficial and that it should not be harmful to the contracting parties or the public at large. It should not be against the public interest, public order or morality.

> The proofs and rules of the *Shariah* indicate that intentions are taken into account in contract, that affects their validity and invalidity, and lawfulness and unlawfulness of a contract, but more seriously than it affects the action which is not a contract with respect to making it lawful and unlawful. The same item becomes lawful sometimes and unlawful at other times depending on the variation of intention and intended objectives.[26]

8.13 The object of a contract

The object is part and parcel of a contract in Islamic law. Every contract is made to achieve some particular objective. It refers to the primary purpose for which the contract is concluded. For example, the purpose of a contract of sale is to transfer the ownership of the property or any commodity from one party (seller) to the other party (buyer) against some consideration agreed upon by both parties. Similarly in the contract of the buyer, the purpose is to own the usufruct against a consideration or compensation.

Actually, "object" is one of the essential ingredients of law in the Islamic concept of law. "The objects of law indicate the purpose of the revolution of the divine law. They embody the motives and intentions that necessitated the specific manifestation of divine legal guidance."[27]

Notes

1 Dr. Hussain Hamid Hassan, An introduction to the study of Islamic law, p. 302.
2 Badran, 412 as quoted by Dr. Ala'eddin Kharofa in Transactions in Islamic law, p. 19.
3 Ahmad abu al Fath, vol. 1, p. 185.
4 Al-Sharbini, *Mughni al-Muhtaj*, vol. 2, p. 11.
5 Muhammad Ayub, *Understanding Islamic finance*, 2007, p. 99–27.
6 Al-Sanhuri, *Masader al-Haq*, vol. 3, p. 103.
7 Dr. Siti Salwani Razali, The concept of wa'ad in Islamic financial contract, p. 75.
8 Al-Sanhuri, *Masader al-Haq*, vol. 3, p. 103
9 Dr. Hussain Hamid Hassan, An introduction to the study of Islamic law, p. 310.
10 Al-Kasani, *Badae al-Sanae*, vol. 5 p. 138.
11 Al-Kasani, *Badai al-Sanai*, vol. 5, p. 171.
12 Al-Kasani, *Badai al-Sanai*, vol. 5 p. 187, Shiribini, *Mughni al-Muhtaj*, vol. 2, p. 20.
13 Shawkani, *Nayl al-Awtar*, Lahore; Ansar al-Sunnah al-Muhammadiyyah, vol. 5, p. 156.
14 Haythami, *Majma al-Zawaid*, vol. 4, p. 104.
15 Haythami, *Majma al-Zawaid*, vol. 4, p. 104.
16 Wahbah Az-Zuhaily, *Al-Fiqhul Islamiy wa Adillatuh*, vol. 4, pp. 173–174.
17 Ibn al-Qayyim, *Ilam al-Muwaqiin* Cairo Maktaba al-Mulliyah al-Azhariyyah, 1968, vol.1, p. 358.
18 Al-Kasani, *Badai al-Sanai*, vol. 5, p. 147.
19 Al-Dardir, *al-Sharh Saghir*, vol. 4, p. 142.
20 Dr. Hussain Hamid Hassan, An introduction to the study of Islamic law, pp. 330–333.
21 Dr. Hussain Hamid Hassan *al-Madkhal*, p. 311.
22 Shirazi, *al-Muhadhdhab*, vol. 1, p. 263.
23 Al-Kasani, *Badai Sanai*, vol. 5, p. 171.
24 Al-Battab, *Mawahib al-Jalil*, vol. 4, p. 285.
25 Al-Sharbini, *Mughni al-Muhtaj*, vol. 2, p. 3.
26 Ibn al-Qayyim, Ilam *al-Muwaqqiin*, vol. 3, p. 96.
27 Shykh ul Islam Prof. Dr. Muhammad Tahir ul Qadri, Islamic concept of law, p. 12.

9 Mutual consent and intention to create legal relationship

In this chapter, we shall discuss the topic of free mutual consent of the parties and intention to create legal relationship, as both are interlinked.

9.1 Free mutual consent

The word "consent" in Islamic law is qualified or limited by using the word mutual with it, that is, "mutual consent"; then it is further qualified by using the word "free" with it, which is "free mutual consent." Hence a free mutual consent of the contracting parties is required to conclude a binding contract. When both parties exert their free mutual consent while concluding a contract, it is considered a valid contract.

When a party offers something to the other party for the purpose of making a contract, it is assumed that the party is doing this with his/her free consent. Similarly, when another party accepts the offer for finalising the contract, it is presumed that another party is doing this with his/her free consent. It becomes the free mutual consent of both parties. Further, for free mutual consent, one should do something voluntarily, and consent should be made without one being compelled, forced or coerced into the act. It should be free from any other factor which could render the consent "not free." A valid contract should be concluded willingly and with mutual consent.

9.2 Literal meanings

The Arabic words *rida* and *taradi* etc. are used for mutual consent which means the pleasure of heart and soul (opposite of discontent), will (*ikhtiyar*), consent (*muwafaqah*) and so forth.[1] So, when consent happens between two or more persons, it is called *taradi*, i.e. mutual agreement, as it is based on *tafa'ul*, which requires the participation of more than one party since usually trade and commerce are concluded between two and more parties. Therefore, the mutual consent of both parties is required for the conclusion of the contract.[2] It is also called *consensus ad idem* (meeting of the minds).

It is important that the contracting parties agree on the same issues in the same manner in order that their consent be deemed undivided and absolute.[3]

9.3 Definition

Muslim jurists have undertaken two approaches in the definition of consent. The Hanafi school defines it as contentment which reaches its end in a way that its effect is apparent, such as a smile on the face and the like. In other words: *rida* is to like something and to have a preference for that.[4] On the other hand, other schools define consent *(rida)* as the intention of doing something without being vitiated by coercion.[5] So, the consent according to the Hanafi school is more specific than that of the other schools. Thus, although the choice does not peak at its end and the pleasure does not actualise, the mere intention to attain the effect in the subject matter is named as consent according to the majority, while for the Hanafi school it is not called consent unless, at least, the preference is fulfilled and the pleasure is actualised.[6]

Sanhuri stresses the importance of two elements in a contract, i.e. freedom to choose (*hak al-khiyar*) and consent (*rida*).[7] The term *rida* here implies the need to perform an act with the feeling of ease, purity and good faith. The majority of scholars describe *rida* as an intention to do something without any force or compulsion.[8]

9.4 Consent under Islamic law of contract

Islamic law of contract regards mutual consent as an important element of any contract. Consent of the parties in any commercial and non-commercial transaction has been regarded as one of the essential ingredients to render such transactions as valid. Where consent is absent, the contract may become either void or can be invalidated depending on the extent to which such consent is vitiated. Islamic law of contract has a broader application as compared to the civil law of contract. In Islamic law of contract, like civil law of contract, there must exist elements of offer and acceptance—which connotes the idea of consent between both parties before they entered into a contract. A party cannot conclude a contract with another party without his free will, and similarly, a person cannot be said to have accepted an offer if he has not consented to the terms of the contract.

Jurists have clearly explained the importance of free mutual consent for concluding a contract. The contract must be based on free consent from both parties.[9] The free consent of parties is essential in the discharge and execution of the Islamic contract law.[10] It is a fundamental principle in the Islamic law of contract that both parties must demonstrate free consent while conducting a transaction. The proof of free consent between the offeror and the offeree is very significant and highly required as the essence of Islamic contract law.[11]

Offer and acceptance are based on consent or *rida*. The demonstration of the consent of the seller is known as *ijab* (offer), and the demonstration of the consent of the buyer is known as *qabul* (acceptance).[12]

9.5 Qur'ānic and Sunnah basis of mutual consent

The concept of free mutual consent has been narrated in the Qur'ān and the *Ahadith* of the Holy Prophet (PBUH). Qur'ān says that:

يَٰٓأَيُّهَا ٱلَّذِينَ ءَامَنُواْ لَا تَأۡكُلُوٓاْ أَمۡوَٰلَكُم بَيۡنَكُم بِٱلۡبَٰطِلِ إِلَّآ أَن تَكُونَ تِجَٰرَةً عَن تَرَاضٖ مِّنكُمۡ

"O believers! Do not devour one another's wealth unlawfully amongst yourselves unless it is a trade by your mutual agreement."[13]

إِنِّيٓ أُرِيدُ أَن تَبُوٓأَ بِإِثۡمِي وَإِثۡمِكَ فَتَكُونَ مِنۡ أَصۡحَٰبِ ٱلنَّارِۚ وَذَٰلِكَ جَزَٰٓؤُاْ ٱلظَّٰلِمِينَ

"I want (I commit no offence and) you take my sin (i.e. the sin of killing me), and also your own sin (the preceding one on account of which your offering has been rejected all) on you. You will then become one of the inmates of Hell. And that is but the punishment of the wrongdoers."[14]

These verses very clearly indicate that under Islamic law the mutual consent of the parties is the base for the formation of the contract. Thus, any transaction must be carried out by the free will of the contracting parties.

The Holy Prophet (PBUH) said: "The contract of sale is valid only by mutual consent."[15] Moreover, "It is unlawful for a person to take his brother's property unless he offers it willingly."[16] In another *hadith*, the Prophet (PBUH) said: "Verily trade is based on mutual consent."[17] An Islamic legal maxim says: "none is allowed to deal with another's property without his/her permission," and another maxim says: "any order given for dealing with the property of others is void."[18]

According to these verses and *ahadith*, the fundamental base of civil transactions is the mutual agreement of the proprietors.[19]

9.6 Ways/modes to express the consent

Islamic law emphasises that the consent of the contracting parties should be the central pillar in any contract. Thus, mutual agreement is the basis of a contract. The Prophet (PBUH) says: as mentioned earlier, "It is unlawful for a person to take his brother's property unless he offers it willingly."[20] However, since the consent is a hidden and internal matter of the mind, jurists have agreed that such consent does not have any effect on the contract unless it is expressed externally. So there must be some action to express this consent, and such expression is indicated by the formation of the contract which is called *sighah.* Muslim jurists mention several ways to express consent, such as by using the verbal expression, by writing, by signs and by conduct or by the agent. The contracting parties may make offer and acceptance by using any of these tools. However, nowadays they can make it also by using other media such as talking over the phone, sending messages, using icons that denote approval or otherwise, chatting on social networks, etc.

As we know, acceptance of an offer constitutes a valid contract. Hence, to initiate the formation of the contract, consent by one party is conveyed to the other party. This consent may be conveyed in different ways, modes and manners, mentioned below. For a valid consent, no specific mode is required, it may be express or implied; only clarity is sufficient for conveying it.

9.6.1 By oral declaration

The utterance of words or oral declaration in forming a contract is considered the most effective way to perceive the meanings and a party's volition and consent. This oral declaration would be the expression of offer and acceptance between the contracting parties. It means that a contract cannot exist unless one party makes an offer to enter into a legal relationship and the other party responds to it. An offer states what the offeror wishes to do and expects in exchange, while an acceptance shows an offeree's willingness to be bound by the terms of the offer. Hence, without the offeree's assent to the terms of an offer the parties have not agreed upon, so there can be no contract.[21]

9.6.2 By writing

Writing is the second means or way by which consent of a party is conveyed to the other party in written format.

When parties are not contracting in the presence of each other, they can generate a contract through writing letters and sending these to each other. In this way, consent can be conveyed by writing. The most explicit is an expression of *sighah* in writing, as reducing the contract into a piece of an agreement is encouraged in the Qurān; i.e. an agreement should be in writing.[22]

9.6.3 By signs

All jurists think and allow a party who cannot speak and listen, e.g. deaf and/or dumb persons to make a contract and convey their consent through signings or by gesture. Signs must be clear and understood by the contracting parties. "The expression of *sighah* through signs made by a dumb person is equal to verbal *sighah* in time of emergency."[23]

9.6.4 By action/delivery

With regard to *sighah* through action, both Hanafi and Hambali jurists accept its validity.[24]

Since mutual consent is the basis for a contract, a sale contract is concluded by an actual exchange carried out in a way that demonstrates the consent of the parties on the contract, and such an arrangement is called *bay' al-ta'ati*, i.e. sale by delivery. This is also considered proof of mutual consent.

9.6.5 By agent/representative

As a valid contract can be concluded by others apart from the parties themselves, consent of one contracting party may be conveyed to the other contracting party by agent or representative.

9.6.6 By silence

Silence carries both the consent and otherwise. So, mere silence should not be paid attention to because what carries more than one possibility cannot be used as evidence for the argument. However, if silence associates with something which indicates the consent, in that case, it will be considered. The silent person is in a situation where he must talk, yet he remains silent instead. In this case, such silence and refusal to talk is considered as an indication of his consent.

9.7 Factors which vitiate the mutual consent

Free mutual consent of parties is a prerequisite for a valid contract. There should not be any compulsion, pressure, oppression and constraint from either side for concluding a contract. There are some factors that vitiate consent. If consent is obtained by coercion, fraud, cheating, mistake and misrepresentation or by some other illegal means, the contract shall be invalid. So a contract entered into freely is binding, but if it is found that the consent has been impaired by certain factors that cause defect and weaken the free choice of the parties, it could be said that consent has been prejudiced. We have also discussed these factors in a separate chapter. Some of these factors are discussed below to make the concept clearer:

1. **Coercion (*ikrah*):** According to Mu'jam Lughah al-Fuqaha', *ikrah* can be defined as an act of forcing someone to do or abstain from doing something against his own free will.[25] It is also defined that to force someone to do something which he does not want to do with the frightening from a person who can execute what he has threatened.[26] Coercion is one of the impediments and defects of mutual consent.[27] In *hadith*, the Holy Prophet (PBUH) said: "My people are forgiven for that which they have done through mistake, forgetfulness and under coercion."[28]
2. **Mistake:** Mistake constitutes an impediment to consent. One of the contracting parties, for example, thinks that the subject matter is from a certain genus, but it is not so, for example if a person buys a piece of jewellery which is supposed to be gold or diamond but it is copper or glass. In such a transaction, there is no contract simply because the supposed subject matter of the contract has not been properly ascertained.[29]
3. **Fraud and cheating:** *Taghrir* refers to the fraudulent act by one party either by words or through conduct to induce someone to enter into a contract.[30] Fraud and cheating also affect free consent. This means that some people may try intentionally to deceive other people so that they enter into a contract. It occurs whenever a party knowingly makes a false representation of a material fact with the intention of causing the other party to enter into a contract, and the other party justifiably relies on the representation and suffers damages. This happened in the assent of consent.
4. ***Ghabn***: *Ghabn* means *al-Naqs* (reduction) or the difference in the sale and actual market price.[31] It is also one of the blemishes that affect consent. It means to deceive and refers to *naqs* or decrease. It is defined by jurists as

being one of subject matters not being equivalent to one another, such as where items are sold for less than their market price or more.[32]

5. **Misrepresentation:** This is also a vitiating factor that affects the free consent of the parties to conclude a valid contract. Some jurists discuss misrepresentation as a separate factor that vitiates consent. Some jurists such as Wahbah al-Zuhayli have discussed fraud and misrepresentation under the topics of *Ghabn* and *al-Taghrir*.
6. **Ignorance (*jahalah*):** Ignorance is also one of the blemishes that affect the consent and intention of the contracting parties. Extreme ignorance is considered one of the defects that make the contract invalid. The rationale behind this is that in the presence of ignorance the mutual consent is not available, and it leads to dispute among the parties. The Prophet said: "when you sell anything on credit the measure, weight, and maturity date shall be known and defined."[33]
7. **The non-existence of the subject matter:** As earlier explained, selling off the non-existent item, whether it is not existent in fact or it is not available because in the custody of the seller, is prohibited. Parties cannot agree and cannot give their consent when the subject matter is absent and not available. The principle of free consent requires that the contracting parties have a certain and definite knowledge of the subject matter.

In the opinion of Muslim jurists, consent derived in this manner is defective since if the victims know that they will be cheated or defrauded, they will surely not agree to sign the contract.[34]

9.8 Intention to create legal relation

Our heading of the topic is "mutual consent and intention to create a legal relationship." Both "consent" and "intention" are hidden and internal things and related to the mind of a person. These are interlinked with each other.

Intention is the fundamental principle of all general acts and particularly of juridical acts. One cannot complete an act if there is no intention in the mind. The importance of intention has been emphasised by the Prophet (PBUH) through one famous *hadith* which states as "Verily, the acts are judged by the intentions."[35]

Under the Islamic law of contract, an intention to create legal relations is significant. If there is a lack of intention to create a legal relationship, the agreement may not, in all probabilities, be enforceable by law.[36]

Imam Ibn al-Qayyim writes:

> The evidences and rules of the *Shariah* reveal that intentions are taken into consideration in the contract. These intentions affect validity, and invalidity, and lawfulness and unlawfulness, of a contract, but more seriously, that they affect the action, which is not a contract, with respect to making it lawful, or unlawful. The same item becomes lawful, sometimes, and unlawful, at other times, depending on the variation of intentions and intended objectives.[37]

Imam Ibn Hazm also emphasised the significance of intention by illustrating that "if a person sells grapes, or dates, to a person about whom he is knowing that buyer will use them against them Muslim public, such a sale is invalid."[38]

Allah says:

> "Help one another in the righteousness and piety, but help not one another in sin and rancour."[39]

Imam Shatibi writes:

> Deeds are to be judged by intentions, and objectives are taken into account in dispositions, such as rituals and dealings. Roots of that are innumerable. Objective and motivating cause differentiates between a ritual and dealing—that is, contracts and dispositions. They also determine the validity, or invalidity, of these acts. Thus, when an ultimate objective of an act is unlawful, the act is also unlawful. For instance, when a sale is intended to be a means for riba, such sale is invalid.[40]

Legal maxims also describe the importance of intention:

> Matters are determined according to intentions.[41]
>
> In contracts, the effect is given to intention and meaning and neither words nor forms.[42]

The intention, as defined by the above jurists and other scholars, means the purpose of doing something in which the ultimate aim is to obey Allah u and to be close to Him. The expression of the heart to have such intention is fundamentally to manifest benefits and to suppress the harms whether immediate or deferred. In *Shariah*, intention is regarded as the will to do something in search of the pleasure of Allah u.[43]

There is no disagreement among Muslim jurists that the intention of the contracting party making a contract should be in harmony with the intention of the lawgiver. If the intention of the contracting party is inconsistent with the intention of the lawgiver, such a contract will become invalid.[44]

Usually, the agreement which has a consideration is regarded as having an intention to create a legal relationship between the parties. Business contracts are usually considered as having the intention to create a legal relationship in one way or another. Some social agreements may lack the intention to create a legal relationship and it depends on the case-by-case basis and circumstances of the agreement; for example, if a friend of anyone promises to give *qard al-hasan* (interest-free loan) to him, B, for any amount, but later on refuses to conclude the deal. Here the contract may not be enforceable due to a lack of consideration. This is an example of a social contract where there is a lack of intention to create a legal relationship between the parties.[45] In all commercial contracts, the intention to create legal relations is presumed to be therein. However, the party that claims that there is a lack of intention to create the legal relationship has to prove, beyond a shadow of a doubt, its tangible existence.

Now we explain some other factors or elements to constitute a legally valid consent backed by intention to create a legal relationship.

9.9 Offer and acceptance

In order to ensure the existence of mutual consent, Muslim scholars observe that there are three conditions that are necessary in order to constitute a valid contract, i.e. offer and acceptance must be clear and definite (clarity), the agreement between offer and acceptance (conformity) and the connection of acceptance to the offer (continuity). The clarity of offer and acceptance means that there must be clear and definite manifestation to show the consent of the contracting parties. The conformity between the offer and acceptance means that the acceptance should agree with the offer in all its details whether this agreement is explicit or implicit. The continuity of the offer and acceptance means the connectedness of the two in the meeting, i.e. *majlis al-'aqd* if both parties present in the meeting.[46]

9.10 Free will (*iradah*)

Free will is also part of mutual consent and called *iradah*. When one has the intention to perform an act, then he has the power of doing and executing the acts. Free will is a subcomponent of intention in which its prerequisite is that there should be an intention. In simpler words, no intention, no will. Al-Asfahani said that a will is a force composed of desire, need and hope to commit such acts. It is an inclination of one's soul to do something with the ability to execute it. In other words, when one has the *iradah*, he makes an effort in pursuit of his intention.[47]

9.11 Choice (*khiyar*)

Choice is the preference made when one encounters more than one option. Choice can also be meant as a decision. There was a lengthy discussion on choice by Muslim jurists. The first is by al-Bazdawi where he says that *ikhtiyar* signifies intending an undecided matter which is between existence and non-existence and within the capacity of a person to perform it and later he made his choice by giving preference to one decision over the other. Ibn Abidin has given a straightforward meaning, that is, to intend something and want it. The majority of jurists defined *ikhtiyar* as to intend to do something over anything else with "pure will." Pure will is the opposite of coercion. Coercion is inherently incompatible with the word consent. Generally, consent cannot be materialised without one's choice.[48]

The Hanafi jurist, on the other hand, holds a different view about it. According to Hanafi jurists, consent and choice are two different things; consent is *rida* while choice is *ikhtiyar*.

Notes

1 Ahmad ibn Muhammad ibn Ali Al-Fayyumi, al-Misbah al-Munir fi Gharib al-Sharh al-Kabir, (1323 AH), Egypt
2 Al-Qurtubi, al-Jami li Ahkam al-Qur'ān, 5/153 (1984) Beirut.
3 S.S. Razali, Islamic law of contract, p.17 (2010) Singapore.
4 Ala al-Din al-Bukhari, Kashf al-Asrar an Usul Fakhr al-Islam al-Bazdawi, 4/536 (1997) Beirut.
5 Ala al-Din al-Mardawi, al-Insaf fi Ma'rifat al-Rijih min al-Khilaf ala Madhhab al-Imam Ahmad ibn Hanbal, 4/253 (1997) Beirut.
6 Al-Mawsu'ah al-Fiqhiyyah, 22/228 (1992).
7 A.S. Nabil, Unlawful gain and legitimate profit in Islamic law, p.108 (2nd ed.), (1986) UK.
8 Abu Abdullah Ibn Majah, Sunan Ibn Majah, vol. 2, p. 737.
9 Vohrah, B & Aun, W.M. The commercial law of Malaysia (2010)
10 H.H.A Rehman, Offer and acceptance in Islamic law of contract, Journal of Shariah 8(2) 2000; S.E Rayner, The theory of contract in Islamic law, (1999) London.
11 Ala'eddin Kharofa, Transactions in Islamic law, (2000) Kuala Lumpur.
12 Al-Zuhaili, Al-Fiqh al-Islami wa adillatuhu, vol. 7, p. 5040.
13 Qur'ān 4:29 (Eng. trans. from 'Glorious Qur'ān' by Shaykh-ul-Islam Dr. Muhammad Tahir-ul-Qadri).
14 Qur'ān 5:29 (Eng. trans. from 'Glorious Qur'ān' by Shaykh-ul-Islam Dr. Muhammad Tahir-ul-Qadri).
15 Abu Abdullah Ibn Majah, Sunan Ibn Majah, Hadith No. 2185, Istanbul.
16 Ahmad al-Dardir, al-Sharh al-Kabir with Hashiyat al-Dasuqi 15569 (1995) Beirut.
17 As-Sharbini, Mughni al-Muhtaj 2:325 (1994).
18 Azman Ismail & Habibur Rahman, Islamic legal maxims, essentials and applications, Kuala Lumpur, 217 (2013).
19 Abu Ghuddah Abd al-Sattar, Tijarah an taradin: Mabadi' wa mumarasat, 6, (1993).
20 Ahmad al-Dardir, al-Sharh al-Kabir with Hashiyat al-Dasuqi 15569 (1995) Beirut.
21 Abdur Rahman Haqqi, The philosophy of Islamic law of transactions, Kuala Lumpur, 75 (2009).
22 Qur'ān 2:282 (Eng. trans. from 'Glorious Qur'ān' by Shaykh-ul-Islam Dr. Muhammad Tahir-ul-Qadri).
23 Imam al-Khatib al-Syarbini, Mughni al-Muhtajla ma'rifah al-Manhaj, vol. 2, p. 17, Beirut.
24 A.M al-Kasani, Badai al-Sanai fi tartib al-Syarai, vol. 5, p. 177 Beirut.
25 Article 948, *Medjelle al-Ahkam-ul-Adalia* English translated by W.E. Grigsby, London.
26 Abd al-Karim Zaydan, al-Wajiz fi sharh al-Qawaid al-Fiqhiyyah fi al-Shariah al-Islamiyyah, 58 (2003) Beirut.
27 Nash'at Ibrahim Al-Darini, al-Taradi fi Uqud al-Mubadalat al-Maliyyah, 362 (1982) Jeddah.
28 Nur al-Din 'Ali Haythami, Majma al-Zawaid, vol. 6, p. 250 (1982) Beirut.
29 Abdur Rahman Haqqi, The philosophy of Islamic law of transactions, Kuala Lumpur, 101 (2009).
30 M.A al-Zarqa, al-Mudkhal al-Fiqhi al-'Am, p.4 63 Damsyiq.
31 M.A al-Zarqa, al-Mudkhal al-Fiqhi al-'Am, p. 463 Damsyiq.
32 Abdur Rahman Haqqi, The philosophy of Islamic law of transactions, Kuala Lumpur, 108 (2009).
33 Abd al-Sattar Abu Ghuddah, Tijarah an taradin: Mabadi' wa mumarasat, 12 (1993).
34 S.E. Rayner, The Theory of Contracts in Islamic law, Arab and Islamic laws series, Graham and Trotman, 1991, London.
35 ImamBukhari, al-Sahih, Hadith No. 1.
36 R.H. Nawawi, Islamic law of commercial transaction, (1999) Malaysia.

37 Ibn al-Qayyim, Ilam al-Muwaqqin, vol. 3, p. 96.
38 Ibn Hazm, al-Muhalla, vol. 9, p. 29.
39 Qur'ān, 5:2.
40 Al-Shatibi, al-Muwafaqat, vol. 2, p. 324..
41 Ahmad al-Zarqa, Syarh al-Qawaid al-Fiqhiyyah, p.47 (1989).
42 Ali Ahmad al-Nadwi, Jamharah al-Qawid al-Fiqhiyyah fi al-Muamalat al-Maliyyah, Syarikah al-Rajhi al-Masrafiyyah li al-Istithmar, vol. 1, p. 550 (2000).
43 Dr. Muhammad Abdul Jalil, Islamic law of contract is getting momentum, p. 185.
44 Dr. Muhammad Tahir Mansoori, Shariah Maxims: modern applications in Islamic finance, p. 18.
45 S.A. Alsagoff, Principles of the law of contract in Malaysia (2003).
46 Muhammad Naim bin Omar, The implications of ghubn in Islamic contracts: An analysis of current practices, p. 2178.
47 Dr.Muhammad Abdul Jalil, Islamic law of contract is getting momentum, p. 185–186.
48 Dr. Muhammad Abdul Jalil, Islamic law of contract is getting momentum, p. 185–186.

10 Vitiating factors

As we explained earlier, when all essential elements are present in a contract-making process, a valid contract is said to be concluded. Sometimes there may be certain defects or obstacles which affect the performance of a contract. These "defects" or obstacles may be called "vitiating factors" which render a contract void or voidable depending on the nature or type of vitiating element involved, e.g. mistake, undue influence, misrepresentation, coercion, duress, etc.

In this chapter, we shall discuss these major vitiating elements in a little bit of detail. We now discuss these one by one.

10.1 Mistakes

A mistake as a defect or vitiating element in a contract is a state of misunderstanding. The mistake is an erroneous belief as to some matter relevant to legal liability. It is akin to ignorance.

As for concluding a valid contract, the free consent of the parties is an essential element. The Qur'ānic verse reads as: "O believers! Do not devour one another's wealth unlawfully amongst yourselves unless it is a trade by your mutual agreement."[1] Similarly, the Prophet (PBUH) is reported to have said: "Acts are dependent on intentions (consent)'',[2] which means that any contract or declaration is stipulated by intention (consent) to render it legally valid. The essence of the contract is the full consent of the parties.

In the *Medjelle*: "In contracts, the effect is given to intention and meaning and not to words and phrases. Consequently, a contract for sale subject of redemption has the force of a pledge."[3]

10.2 Literal meaning

In the Arabic language, as in the Qur'ān, the word is extended to include both meanings: an unintentional and deliberate mistake.[4] So a linguistic definition could be: "Mistake" is the antithesis of correctness.[5]

10.3 Definitions of mistake

Subsequently, Islamic Jurisprudence, *fiqh,* and the principles of jurisprudence, *Us-l al-fiqh,* used this word as a technical term with two unintentional meanings:

> 1. Error in logic (opposite of *sawab*), synonymous with *batil* the invalid..., 2. Unintentional action, it may be more accurately defined as an act contrary to law, in which the intention of committing an illegal act is lacking, while the action itself may be deliberate ...'.[6]

This definition indicates that *fuqaha'* consider a mistake to be an inner perception in the mind of the perceiver, which is not right. This is of value not only to the lawyer who seeks the precise definition but also because it indicates the subjective nature of the mistake, while Shariah mostly adopts the objective standpoint.[7]

Two terms are used for mistake: i.e. *khata'* and *ghalat.* It is well worth noting that the word *ghalat* is used more frequently in civil matters while the word *khata'* is used more in criminal law.[8]

10.4 Qur'ānic and Sunnah basis of mistake

The Qur'ān mentions *khata'* in several places with the meaning of a deliberate mistake or unintentional act.[9] The traditions, *hadiths*, mostly supported the latter meaning.[10] The reason for that might be that the meaning was left to be derived from the applications of texts of the Qur'ān and the Sunnah by the efforts, *ijtihad*, of the jurists to clarify the meaning precisely.

10.5 Classification of mistake

A mistake may concern the subject matter of a contract or may relate to the description of the subject matter or its type. Hence it could be classified as to the nature of the transaction, the nature of the sold object, the identity of the party, the value, the quality and the quantity.

10.6 Legal effects of the contractual mistake

Under Islamic law of contract, there are two legal effects of the contract entered into by mistake. Firstly, *void ab initio* and secondly voidable. It means that when a mistake relates to the nature of the subject matter its effect is to render the contract void, and when it relates to the quality, its effect is to render the contract voidable. Now we explain these effects a little further.

10.7 Rendering the contract void

Therefore, the majority of jurists, *fuqaha*, agree that there is no legal effect if a person makes an unintentional slip of the tongue; making a mistake in a commercial transaction, not knowing a statement or action made during the transaction, imposes a transfer of ownership.[11] The contract is void.

Their position is similar when the "mistake" occurs as to the nature of the sold object so that one of the parties believes it to be other than it is. For example: when one of the parties believes the commodity to be wheat when, in fact, it is barley. Article 208 of the *Medjelle* reads:

> If the species of the thing sold has been stated, and the thing sold turns out to be of another species, the sale is void. Example: the vendor sells a piece of glass stating that is a diamond. The sale is void.[12]

However, the contract will be void if the mistake here is concerning the substance (*jins*) or even the quality of the goods (a mistake as to meaning). As has been previously discussed, a mistake about the substance (*jins*) of the object of contract constitutes a just cause for voiding the contract *ab initio*. If the object is declared in kind (*jins*) and the object proves to be of another kind the sale is invalid (*batil*).[13] The reasoning followed for rendering such contracts of mistake as void (*batil*) is based on the concept of the object as a pillar of the contract, and the maxim that "what was intended has not happened and what has happened was not intended." If the purpose of the obligation has been subject to mistake and is not that which the parties initially intended, then the object of the contract is non-existent, and the contract itself becomes void for want of an essential condition.[14]

When the contract is void, the parties to the contract have another solution besides terminating the contract, that is, exercising *Khiyar al-Ayb* (option of the defect); for example, in the case where the species is the same but an appreciable difference exists between the object which was contracted for (which renders the contract as void). For instance, if cloth is sold in a different colour or pattern than the one intended, it is not in accordance with the purpose of the contractor; it may be arguable here that such a mistake of meaning may be actionable under the option of description (*Khiyar al-Ayb*).[15]

The contract becomes void though on the limited grounds that the destruction of the property, which is the subject matter of the contract, before acceptance, frustrates the contract. It has been laid down in Article 914 of the *Medjelle*:

> "If someone destroys the property of another under the impression that it is his own property, he is responsible."[16]

10.8 Rendering the contract voidable

If the mistake concerns a *wasf* (quality), of a thing which is not substantial, then the contract is voidable, but the purchaser has an option (*khiyar al-wasf*) to ratify the contract or to repudiate it.[17]

Similarly, if there is a mistake relating to the quantity again the contract is voidable, as stated in the *Medjelle*:

> The sale of things estimated by measure of capacity, or by enumeration and which closely resemble each other and things estimated by weight ... if it is found to short; however, the purchaser has the option of cancelling the sale, or of purchasing the amount actually delivered for the proportionate part of the price.[18]

The contract will be voidable if the consequences of such sales or contract are of a more limited nature. Another example of this kind of effect is that if a seller represents the object as a ruby, and it is later found to be yellow, the sale is *prima facie* valid because the mistake is not as to the substance of the object and is not deemed to have affected the usufruct intended by the purchaser and the true sale.[19] The object of such a contract is extant and thereby fulfils the essential contractual condition. However, the representation made by the seller as to its quality is at fault and therefore renders the contract voidable.[20]

Broadly speaking, an avoidable contract becomes executory on taking delivery while a void contract does not affect taking delivery.[21]

10.9 Misrepresentation

The parties to a contract or business people, before concluding a particular contract often make some statements during the negotiations to induce each other to make the contract. If these statements are false statements of fact and are not honest statements then these fall under the heading of "misrepresentation," and it shall vitiate the contract.

Misrepresentation is an incorrect statement of fact, or mixed fact and law, made by one party to another with the object, and having the result, of inducing the other to enter into a contract. It may be made by a statement or other acts or by concealment but not by mere omission, silence or inaction. Misrepresentation is a sort of adulteration designed to prompt the offeree into entering a contract in the belief that it will benefit him. This can arise from an act such as hiding defects in goods in order to sell them more easily. It can also result from the offeror, or a third party colluding with the offeror, advertising untrue features in the consideration in order to prompt the offeree to finalise the contract.

10.10 Qur'ānic verses regarding misrepresentation

Allāh u has also reminded humanity of the danger of one doing an act, which is contrary to what one preaches. Allāh u says the following: كَبُرَ مَقْتًا عِندَ ٱللَّهِ أَن تَقُولُواْ مَا لَا تَفْعَلُونَ

> "It is most hateful in the sight of Allāh that you should say what you do not do."[22]

10.11 Kinds of misrepresentation

Misrepresentation in a contract may include the following situation:

i. In a contract whereby a party gives information about any aspect of the contract which is not valid, but the other party to whom the information has been given believes it.
ii. If a party misleads the other in any manner to enter into the contract, but this was later found out by the other party.

10.12 Legal effect of misrepresentation

A misrepresentation, having the result of inducing the representee to enter into a contract with the representor, renders the contract void, or at least voidable by the representee, so that he is not bound thereby and may recover any money or property transferred in pursuance of the contract. He may further recover damages if the representation were made fraudulently or probably, negligently, but not if made innocently, though in this case, the representee may recover an indemnity against any consequence of the obligation set aside.[23]

Articles 310 to 334 of the *Medjelle* deal with the option for misrepresentation.

Therefore, the legal consequence of a contract which is entered into by misrepresentation is that it is deemed to be voidable[24] and the party will have the opinion of either continuing or terminating that contract. If the victimised party chooses to continue, the contract will become valid, but if he chooses to rescind it, the contract will become void.

There are two consequences of misrepresentation in a contract: either it can be revoked, or it is resolvable. This is according to the Hanbali school of law. However, the Hanafi school considers a contract only to be remediable by claiming compensation.[25] In a contract of sale, a proven misrepresentation can lead to two choices for the party suffering damages. He can agree to property compensation (*Arsh*), being the difference in value between the property with defects and the property in good condition,[26] or he can revoke the contract and return the property.[27]

10.13 Coercion (*ikrah*)

Different jurists discussed misrepresentation under different headings like coercion, duress and undue influence, etc. The Arabic term used in Islamic law of contract is *ikrah*. We shall discuss it under the heading of coercion (*ikrah*). If a contract is entered into by a party whose consent is obtained by another party, who is in a position to dominate the will of the actual party, the contract is said to be made under coercion, i.e. *ikrah*.

10.14 Literal meaning

Literally, *ikrah* is derived from the root word *ka a ha* which is constructed as *akrahahu* meaning "to force someone to do something against his wishes." The word *kurh* is also the antonym of the *hub* (love);[28] as such, these two terms are used in the opposite sense.

10.15 Definitions

The following are the different definitions of coercion, defined by different jurists.

1. "By coercion, one designates the action of one person against another suppressing the consent of this latter person or vitiating his consent."[29]
2. "An action directed against a person, which suppresses his true consent."[30]
3. "Forcing a person to perform an act against his wishes by way of any threat of which the person exerting coercion is capable so that the coerced person is intimidated and deprived of free consent."[31]
4. "Coercion is to force another person to do what he does not wish."[32]
5. "Coercion is a physical or moral constraint directed against a person in order to compel him to ratify or not ratify a juridical act."[33]
6. "Duress is an order from one person to another to commit an act of utter words under threat of the infliction of evil in the case of non-compliance."[34]
7. "Force a person to do something, be it verbal or indeed without his consent other than by way of the Shariah."[35]
8. "Duress should be defined as the exercise of an unlawful pressure on a person to create in him the kind of fear which causes him to enter into a contract."[36]

Medjelle-al-Ahkam al-Addliyya defines it as: *"Ikrah* is to compel without right, a person to do a thing without his consent or by fear."[37]

Coercion involves an action performed through illegal pressure of enforcement and threat. Attempting to make a contract under coercion means forcing a party to enter into an obligation against his will. Consequently, the element of volition is missing and the agreement justly negated. Some examples of persons who can be coerced or influenced by someone other persons who are physically weak, old, sick and unconscious or have any fiduciary relationship with the person nominating them.

10.16 Qur'ānic verses regarding coercion

لَآ إِكۡرَاهَ فِي ٱلدِّينِ

"There is no compulsion in *Din* (religion)."[38]

ذَٰلِكَ بِأَنَّهُمُ ٱسۡتَحَبُّواْ ٱلۡحَيَوٰةَ ٱلدُّنۡيَا عَلَى ٱلۡأٓخِرَةِ وَأَنَّ ٱللَّهَ لَا يَهۡدِي ٱلۡقَوۡمَ ٱلۡكَٰفِرِينَ

"That is because they loved and preferred the life of this world to the Hereafter and because Allāh does not guide the disbelieving folk."[39]

وَلَا تُكۡرِهُواْ فَتَيَٰتِكُمۡ عَلَى ٱلۡبِغَآءِ إِنۡ أَرَدۡنَ تَحَصُّنٗا لِّتَبۡتَغُواْ عَرَضَ ٱلۡحَيَوٰةِ ٱلدُّنۡيَاۚ وَمَن يُكۡرِههُّنَّ فَإِنَّ ٱللَّهَ مِنۢ
بَعۡدِ إِكۡرَٰهِهِنَّ غَفُورٞ رَّحِيمٞ

"And do not force your maids into prostitution to obtain the benefit of the worldly life if they desire to keep themselves chaste (or wish to safeguard their chastity through marriage). And whoever will compel them, then (even) after they are compelled, Allāh is Most Forgiving, Ever-Merciful."[40]

10.17 *Ahadith* regarding coercion

Ibn Majah narrated that the Prophet (PBUH) says:

> "Liability is exempted from a duressed person."

The Prophet (PBUH) says to the effect that:

> "Allāh u has lifted away from my people the responsibility of acts done by mistake, in forgetfulness, and under coercion."[41]

Dr. Liaqat Ali Niazi quoted the words of Joseph Schacht as follows:

> "Some maxims acquired the full status of a tradition from the Prophet (PBUH) rather late. The rhyming maxim 'there is no divorce and no manumission under duress' (*la talaq wa-la alaq fi ighlaq*) appears as a tradition from the Prophet only in Ibn Hanbal and some of the classical collections; Malik (Muwatta' iii.69)."[42]

10.18 Conditions for the presence of coercion in a contract

According to Syed Ameer 'Ali:

> The doctrine, that in order to avoid a contract entered into by a free, sane and adult person, on the ground of *ikrah* or compulsion, it must be shown that the "compeller" was in a position to carry out any threat held out by him, and that the threat itself was such as would influence the conduct of a reasonable person, only represents in another form the rule of equity, that the coercion was such as would give rise to the presumption, that it might be *bona fide* stop the exercise of free volition on the part of the person affected thereby.[43]

There are some conditions to be fulfilled for the presence of forceful coercion in a contract, and these are as follows:

i. There should be actual coercion before concluding a contract, and it should be legally unjustified with all respect.
ii. The compeller must be capable of carrying out the threatened harm and has the power or authority to execute what he threatened against the other party.
iii. The compelled person must believe that if he does not comply with the compeller's demands, the threat promised by the compeller will be inflicted upon him and the threat would constitute damage or harm to his life, person or property.

iv. The threat must be of such a nature as to intimidate the victim, i.e. it must be of significant and imminent danger, and the contract has been entered into as a result of the pressure from this threat.
v. The coercion does not look to the violation of property or other legal rights such as the selling or damaging of one's property or the damaging of someone else's property or accusing him falsely, or drinking alcohol, or committing adultery, etc.
vi. What the person is being compelled to do must injure one's self or unlawfully induce a sense of fear.[44]

10.19 Kinds of *ikrah*

The jurists classified the coercion in the following kinds:

1. **Maljian:** It is also called *Ikrah Tamm* and in English termed as perfect coercion. It leads to the destruction of life or loss of a limb. It is the compulsion that is by a hard blow. It annuls the juridical act done under constraint.
2. **Ghair maljian:** It is also called *Ikrah Naqis* and in English is termed as imperfect coercion. This causes only grief and pain. It is compulsion which is by things like a blow or imprisonment. Imperfect or minor coercion also annuls consent but supposes that the contracting party who suffered this coercion could still exercise his free will. Such would be the case if he was threatened with blows not liable to cause his death or to cripple him.[45]

Some jurists have also classified the coercion into "unjust coercion" (*ikrah bi ghayr haq*) and "just coercion" (*ikrah bi haq*). They describe above said two kinds, i.e. *Maljian* and *Ghair maljian*, under the heading of unjust coercion. They also further explain the just coercion as an action taken by the authorities to force a person to carry out a valid act relating either to another person or to public interest, such as forcing a debtor to repay his debt.[46] The condition for the coercion to be justified is that the acts to be done under coercion must conform with *Shariah* rules. However, some jurists so not agree that this kind of coercion is justified.

10.20 Effects of a contract under coercion

Jurists have different opinions regarding the validity of a contract concluded under coercion. According to the majority of jurists, if a party enters into a contract under the state of duress or coercion, that contract will become voidable, and the party who has been inducted into the contract has the free option of either continuing or terminating, i.e. annulling it.[47] They maintain that the coercion does not render the correct void but merely voidable; they consider such a contract suspended subject to ratification. However, some jurists have the opinion that contracts concluded under coercion are void because they regard the act under coercion non-existent since the essential condition of the juridical act, i.e. the will, is vitiated.[48] Accordingly, a contract or conduct leading to an obligation under proven duress is not binding.[49]

Notes

1 Qur'an 4:29 (Eng. trans. from 'Glorious Qur'ān' by Shaykh-ul-Islam Dr. Muhammad Tahir-ul-Qadri).
2 Al-Bukhari Muhammad, Sahih Al-Bukhari, vol. 1, p. 110, para1.
3 Article No.3, *Medjelle al-Ahkam-ul-Adalia* English translated by W.E. Grigsby, London.
4 The Encyclopaedia of Islam, vol. 3, p. 1100, New Edition, 1965, Brill, Leidn, Netherlands.
5 *Al-Maws'a al-Fiqhiyya*, vol. 19 p. 129, *khata'* entry.
6 The Encyclopedia of Islam, vol. 3, p.1100.
7 Salama Muhammad, *Nazariyyat Al-Aqd fi Al-Figh Al-Islami*, p. 439.
8 Compare this with ''The theory of contracts in Islamic law"p.177 by Dr. S.E. Rayner.
9 Qur'ān: 2:286, 4:92 and 33:5 (Eng. trans. from 'Glorious Qur'ān' by Shaykh-ul-Islam Dr. Muhammad Tahir-ul-Qadri).
10 Ibn Hajar Ahmed, *Bulugh al-Maram*, (First Edition), Dar –us-Slam Publications, Riyadh, para. 922, p. 380.
11 *Al-Maws-'a al-Fiqhiyya*, vol. 19 pp.156–157.
12 Article No.208, *Medjelle al-Ahkam-ul-Adalia* English translated by W.E. Grigsby, London.
13 See Article 208, *Medjelle* which provides that; M.E. Hamid, "Does the Islamic law of contract recognize a doctrine of Mistake" in Journal of Islamic and comparative law, vol. 4, 1972, pp.1–16.
14 Al-Kasani I.A.b.A.B.bM.u., 1997, Badi'u Sanai fi Tartibi al-Shara, vol. 6, Bairut: Dar'ul Kutub al-Ilmiah.
15 Sanhuri, Masadir al-Haqq, vol. 2, p. 114.
16 Article No. 914, *Medjelle al-Ahkam-ul-Adalia* English translated by W.E. Grigsby, London.
17 Al-Zarqa Mustafa, "'*Al-Madkhal Al-Fiqhi Al-amm*" vol. 1, p. 395, para. 191/4.
18 Article No. 223, *Medjelle al-Ahkam-ul-Adalia* English translated by W.E. Grigsby, London.
19 Al-Kassani, bada'I al-Sana'i, vol. 5, p. 140.
20 S.E. Rayner, The theory of contracts in Islamic law, p. 182.
21 Article No.366 *Medjelle al-Ahkam-ul-Adalia* English translated by W.E. Grigsby, London.
22 Qur'ān 61:3 (Eng. trans. from 'Glorious Qur'ān' by Shaykh-ul-Islam Dr. Muhammad Tahir-ul-Qadri).
23 David M. Walker, The Oxford Companion to Law. New York: Oxford University Press (1980), p. 844.
24 Wu Min Aun, Business law in Singapore, (1984) p. 64.
25 Albuti, M. Tawfeeq, The common sales: The effect of the sale restrictions on their legality, Damascuse: Dar Alfikr, 1998, pp.128–131.
26 M.E. Hamid, "Does the Islamic law of contract recognize a doctrine of mistake?" (1969), Journal of Islamic and comparative law, 4, pp. 1–16.
27 M.E. Hamid, "Does the Islamic law of contract recognize a doctrine of mistake?" (1969), Journal of Islamic and comparative law, 4, pp. 1–16.
28 Bardisi, Zakaria, 1960 al-Ikrah baina al-Shariah wa al-Qanun, in Cairo. In MajAllāh al-Qanun wa al-Iqtisad. Cairo: Cairo University.
29 Sarakhsi, al-Mabsut, vol. 14, p. 39.
30 Fakhr al-Din Uthman ibn Ali Zaylai, Tabyan al-Haqaiq, Bulaq: al-Maktabah al-Kubra al-Amiriyyah, 1313–1315, vol. 5, p. 181.

31 Bukhari, Abd Aziz, (1995). Kasful Asrar, Cairo: Faruq hadithah.
32 Ibn Hajar Asqalani, (1407 H). Fathul Bari, Cairo: Salafiyyah.
33 Zarqa', Mustafa (1968). Al-Madkhal al-Fiqh al-Am, Damascus: Darul Fikr.
34 Abu Zahrah, Muhammad (1977), al-Milkiyyah wa Nazariyatul Aqd, Cairo: Darul Fikr Arabi.
35 Madkur, Muhammad Salam (n.d.) Nazariyatul Aqd. Cairo: Darul Nahdah.
36 El-Hasan, A.W. Ahmad 91986) The Doctrine of Duress in Shariah, Sudan and English Law Arab Law quarterly.
37 Article No.7, *Medjelle al-Ahkam-ul-Adalia* English translated by W.E. Grigsby, London.
38 Qur'ān 2:256 (Eng. trans. from 'Glorious Qur'ān' by Shaykh-ul-Islam Dr. Muhammad Tahir-ul-Qadri).
39 Qur'ān 16:107 (Eng. trans. from 'Glorious Qur'ān' by Shaykh-ul-Islam Dr. Muhammad Tahir-ul-Qadri).
40 Qur'ān 24:33 (Eng. trans. from 'Glorious Qur'ān' by Shaykh-ul-Islam Dr. Muhammad Tahir-ul-Qadri).
41 As cited in Mir Maliullah, Muslim Jurisprudence and the Qur'ānic law of crime, (1982), p. 32.
42 Schacht, *Origins of Muhammadan Jurisprudence*, p. 180.
43 Syed Ameer 'Ali, Muhammadan law, p.47.
44 Cherif Bassiouni, The Islamic criminal justice system, Oceana publications Ltd. New York, 982, p.190 & Mansuri, p. 151–152.
45 Zaydan, al-Madkhal, p. 361.
46 Muhammad Shaqrah (1986), *al-Ikrah waatharuhu fi tasaarufat*, Kuwait: Manar Islami.
47 Zarka, al-Madkhal, vol. 1, p. 371.
48 Zahayli, al-Faqh al-Islami, vol. 4, p. 216.
49 Nabil A. Saleh, "Remedies for breach of contract under Islamic and Arab law," 91989), legal journals Arab law quarterly, Sweet & Maxwell Ltd. ALQ 4 (4), pp. 269–290.

11 Forbidden elements

11.1 Introduction

Islam, as already explained, provides guidance for all aspects of human behaviour including economic and business activities. It has made the vast resources of this earth available to humanity, and everyone is free to make use, mould and transform them according to his needs. It also imposed a few limits and prohibitions for the benefit of human beings.

Some critics of Islamic law of contract describe these limits and prohibitions as a deficiency in Islamic law of contract. However, the truth and reality are that these are a vital factor of Islamic contract jurisprudence alone, that distinguishes it from other counterparts of world contract jurisprudence. It is the beauty of Islamic law of contract in particular and Islamic law in general which has the inherent quality to protect human beings from losses, hard-heartedness, selfishness, exploiting, devastation, unfairness and other adverse consequences of all types of dealing between people. This is why Islamic law of contract has described some limits and prohibited elements which are unjust and may damage, demean and diminish the human personality due to their harmfulness. As Allah is the Creator of all human beings, hence He is the only one who knows better where to grant freedom to what extent and where to impose some limitations and prohibitions for what and why. "Indeed Allah will not prohibit of something unless it is not good for people," in the meaning of a *hadith*, so it forbids the matters in man's best interest.

11.2 The relation between purposes and prohibitions in Islamic law of contract

The purpose of Islamic law is to establish a balanced and stable society through equity and justice, instead of creating rift and faction in society. Hence it forbids all those factors which may cause imbalance, instability, rift or faction in society. This is narrated in the following Qur'ānic verse:

وَٱلسَّمَآءَ رَفَعَهَا وَوَضَعَ ٱلْمِيزَانَ٧ أَلَّا تَطْغَوْاْ فِي ٱلْمِيزَانِ٨ وَأَقِيمُواْ ٱلْوَزْنَ بِٱلْقِسْطِ وَلَا تُخْسِرُواْ
ٱلْمِيزَانَ٩

> "And He is the One Who has maintained the sky raised high and (He is the One) Who has set up the balance (for justice). So that you violate not the balance whilst weighing. And keep weighing justly and do not make the balance fall short."[1]

The basic rationale behind the prohibition of some elements is to protect human beings from their folly and extravagance in their financial dealings to each other. It is not uncommon in commercial transactions, for one of the parties to be stronger than the other, or perhaps more intelligent or more experienced; so the disadvantaged party needs some protection and guidance before an agreement or contract is concluded.

This idea of protecting the weak against exploitation by the strong led to the elaboration of a rule of general application, commanding that any transaction should be devoid of *riba*, uncertainty, fraud, cheating and gambling, etc.

Islamic law wants people to work hard to create sustenance in their lives and not to get easy money without physical activities or by burdening the other to make themselves wealthier. Hence it forbids interest on the loan. Islamic law also wants to save a person from all forms of economic as well as social exploitation; hence, it forbids the elements which may cause exploitation, such as *riba*/interest, fraud and cheating etc.

Islam wants to save the people from extreme hardship and to prevent the rich from growing more affluent and the poor becoming more miserable as the result of unfair dealings in business or social activities; this is why *riba*, fraud, cheating and gambling etc. are forbidden in all commercial dealings to prevent the creation of enmity and hatred of one another.

By imposing limitations and forbidding some idler, cruel and blood-sucking elements for making contracts, Islamic law wants to achieve the purpose of establishing a wise economic system where all kinds of injustice and inequality are eliminated and all forms of exploitation and oppression are controlled.

In the previous chapter, we explained the vitiating factors, namely mistakes, misrepresentation and coercion, etc. This chapter is chiefly concerned with prohibitory elements or forbidden factors in Islamic law of contract unanimously acknowledged by all Muslim jurists. The most prominent are those forbidding interest-bearing transactions (*ribawi*), risky or uncertain transactions (*gharar*) and transactions involving gambling or games of chance (*Qimar* or *Maysiar*). Islamic law puts a blanket prohibition on these elements in commercial transactions.[2] Now we discuss these one by one in detail.

*11.3 Usury/*riba

Riba and its prohibition is the most distinctive and eminent topic in Islamic law of contract, as it is the major forbidden element in making contracts, although much academic literature is available on *riba* and this is an intensively discussed issue in Islamic law of contract. However, surprisingly, its unanimous meanings and a comprehensive definition have not been crystal clear to date, and there are many different definitions of *riba* which are described by different jurists. Hence the topic requires further probing and research. There are too many and too detailed material interpretations, and jurists' opinions on *riba* cannot be covered in this small chapter.

11.3.1 Literal meanings

Riba is an Arabic word, which stands for excess, increase, addition, expansion or growth. A well-known scholar explained the *riba* of Arabs in the pre-Islam period as follows:

> In the pre-Islam period, a person used to owe a debt to his creditor then he would say to his creditor "I offer you such and such amount and you give me more time to pay."[3]

Another renowned scholar has explained *riba* in the following words:

> Riba, that was known and practised by the Arabs, was that they used to advance loan in the form of Dirhams or Dinars (silver and gold coins) for a certain period with an agreed increase in the amount of the principal advanced.[4]

Riba is derived from the derivative word *raba-wa*. The literal meaning of the word *riba*, in Arabic, is to increase, to grow, expansion and addition, mount up and rise. In the specific sense, *riba* is generally translated into English as usury or interest, but in fact, it has a much broader sense under *Shariah*.[5]

11.3.2 Technical meaning/definition

"*Riba* is the act of taking advantage of those people who need money to meet their basic needs/necessities through the act of renting them money at a price called "interest."[6] Technically, *riba* refers to an increase in the principal amount in the case of a loan transaction. Accordingly, anything chargeable, in addition to the principal amount as a contractual obligation, falls within the purview of *riba*. Hence, in Islamic law of contract, it is generally considered as a contractual increase on loaned money or commodity. *Riba* is defined as "an increase that has no corresponding consideration in an exchange of property for property."[7] "*Riba* is an increase without any corresponding consideration which has been stipulated in favour of one of the two parties, in a contract of exchange."[8]

It is pertinent to note that *riba* should be understood as an addition or interest charged on a loan, regardless of the willingness of the borrower to enter into a contract by which he will have to repay an addition or interest as well as the principal amount.

It should be kept in mind that "profit" is also a kind of increase and gain, but it must be distinguished from *riba*. Any profit gained from lawful trade is not prohibited. Not all types of increases, growth or gains are prohibited. The term *riba* refers to unjust and exploitative gains made in the trade of business.

11.3.3 Qur'ān basis of prohibition of riba

The Qur'ān has explicitly dealt with the issue of *riba*. The wording of the Qur'ānic prohibition developed gradually; during the Makah period, there was merely a strong recommendation against taking interest. The outright condemnation came later, in the Medina period, i.e. the prohibition of *riba* first came into being during the Makah period but was not plainly stated until the Medina period, when the Islamic community flourished. [9]

It should be kept in mind that the Qur'ān is also very much concerned to differentiate between *riba* and lawful commercial transactions, as shown by the verse: "Allah has declared trade (i.e., buying and selling) lawful and usury unlawful."[10] So *riba* was forbidden, and at the same time, investors and labourers are encouraged to do business to earn their livelihood. This verse is general which permits all kinds of business and trades which are valid according to the Islamic law of contract and prohibits all kinds of *riba*.

The Qur'ānic references regarding the prohibition of *riba* are to be found in four Qur'ānic surahs i.e. al-Baqarah, al-Imran, al-Nisa and al-Rum as explained below.

11.3.3.1 First revelation (five years before Hijrah*)*

وَمَآ ءَاتَيۡتُم مِّن رِّبٗا لِّيَرۡبُوَاْ فِيٓ أَمۡوَٰلِ ٱلنَّاسِ فَلَا يَرۡبُواْ عِندَ ٱللَّهِۖ وَمَآ ءَاتَيۡتُم مِّن زَكَوٰةٖ تُرِيدُونَ وَجۡهَ ٱللَّهِ
فَأُوْلَٰٓئِكَ هُمُ ٱلۡمُضۡعِفُونَ

> "And the money that you lend as usury so that (your wealth) may increase through mingling with other people's money will not increase with Allah, but the money that you give as Zakat ([the obligatory Alms-due] and charity donations), seeking (solely) Allah's pleasure—so it is they who multiply (their money with Allah) manifold." [11]

In this verse Allāh as expressed His disapproval of *riba* (and stated that a person taking *riba* thinks that his wealth is increasing, but in the sight of Allāh from an overall perspective, it is not increasing. On the other hand, when someone gives something to charity, then his wealth is increasing in the sight of Allāh.)

11.3.3.2 Second revelation (early Madinan period)

oوَأَخۡذِهِمُ ٱلرِّبَوٰاْ وَقَدۡ نُهُواْ عَنۡهُ وَأَكۡلِهِمۡ أَمۡوَٰلَ ٱلنَّاسِ بِٱلۡبَٰطِلِۚ وَأَعۡتَدۡنَا لِلۡكَٰفِرِينَ مِنۡهُمۡ عَذَابًا أَلِيمٗا

> "And (also) because of their taking riba, despite that they were forbidden to do it, and because of their usurping others' wealth wrongfully (they were punished). And We have prepared a torturous torment for those of them who disbelieve." [12]

In this verse, the Qur'ān tells us that *riba* was also prohibited for Jews and that they incurred the grievous punishment wrath of Allāh for taking *riba*.

11.3.3.3 Third revelation (after Ghazwah Uhud)

يَٰٓأَيُّهَا ٱلَّذِينَ ءَامَنُواْ لَا تَأۡكُلُواْ ٱلرِّبَوٰٓاْ أَضۡعَٰفٗا مُّضَٰعَفَةٗۖ وَٱتَّقُواْ ٱللَّهَ لَعَلَّكُمۡ تُفۡلِحُونَ

> "O believers! Do not live on usury doubled and redoubled, and keep fearing Allah so that you may prosper." [13]

In this verse, the Qur'ān has pointed out the cruel practice of taking *riba* on top of *riba* prevalent amongst Arabs. The believers have been enjoined to refrain from such acts.

11.3.3.4 Fourth revelation (shortly after al-Imran)

ٱلَّذِينَ يَأۡكُلُونَ ٱلرِّبَوٰاْ لَا يَقُومُونَ إِلَّا كَمَا يَقُومُ ٱلَّذِي يَتَخَبَّطُهُ ٱلشَّيۡطَٰنُ مِنَ ٱلۡمَسِّۚ ذَٰلِكَ بِأَنَّهُمۡ قَالُوٓاْ إِنَّمَا ٱلۡبَيۡعُ
مِثۡلُ ٱلرِّبَوٰاْۗ وَأَحَلَّ ٱللَّهُ ٱلۡبَيۡعَ وَحَرَّمَ ٱلرِّبَوٰاْۚ فَمَن جَآءَهُۥ مَوۡعِظَةٞ مِّن رَّبِّهِۦ فَٱنتَهَىٰ فَلَهُۥ مَا سَلَفَ وَأَمۡرُهُۥٓ إِلَى ٱللَّهِۖ
يَمۡحَقُ ٱللَّهُ ٱلرِّبَوٰاْ وَيُرۡبِي ٱلصَّدَقَٰتِۗ وَٱللَّهُ لَا يُحِبُّ كُلَّ oوَمَنۡ عَادَ فَأُوْلَٰٓئِكَ أَصۡحَٰبُ ٱلنَّارِۖ هُمۡ فِيهَا خَٰلِدُونَ
oكَفَّارٍ أَثِيمٍ

> "Those who live on usury will not be able to stand (on the Day of Judgment), but like the one whom Satan has made insane with his touch (i.e., damnation). This is because they used to say that trade (i.e., buying and selling) is similar to usury, whereas Allah has declared trade (i.e., buying and selling) lawful and usury unlawful. So, if someone refrains (from usury) on receiving admonition from his Lord, then he can keep whatever he took in the past and his case is with Allah. But those who continued with usury (despite the admonition) would be the inmates of Hell. They will abide there permanently. Allah eliminates usury (i.e., deprives usurious profits of prosperous growth) and multiplies alms gifts (i.e., increases blessings of clean wealth manifold through charity donations). And Allah does not like anyone who is ungrateful and disobedient." [14]

This revelation severely censured those who took *riba* and mixed it with trading and business. These verses also established a clear distinction between trade and *riba* by declaring the trade as permitted.

11.3.3.5 Fifth revelation (nine or ten ah *before farewell pilgrimage)*

فَإِن لَّمۡ تَفۡعَلُواْ فَأۡذَنُواْ بِحَرۡبٖ مِّنَ oيَٰٓأَيُّهَا ٱلَّذِينَ ءَامَنُواْ ٱتَّقُواْ ٱللَّهَ وَذَرُواْ مَا بَقِيَ مِنَ ٱلرِّبَوٰٓاْ إِن كُنتُم مُّؤۡمِنِينَ
وَإِن كَانَ ذُو عُسۡرَةٖ فَنَظِرَةٌ إِلَىٰ oٱللَّهِ وَرَسُولِهِۦۖ وَإِن تُبۡتُمۡ فَلَكُمۡ رُءُوسُ أَمۡوَٰلِكُمۡ لَا تَظۡلِمُونَ وَلَا تُظۡلَمُونَ
oمَيۡسَرَةٖۚ وَأَن تَصَدَّقُواْ خَيۡرٞ لَّكُمۡ إِن كُنتُمۡ تَعۡلَمُونَ

> "O believers! Fear Allāh and write off whatever balance remains of usury if you are believers (true to the core of your hearts). But if you do not do so,

then be warned of the declaration of war from Allāh and His Holy Messenger a. And if you repent, then your principal amounts are (lawfully) yours. (In this case) you will neither do any wrong nor be wronged. And if a debtor is under financial stress, he should be given respite till he feels at ease to pay. And your forgiving (the loan) is better for you if you know (what significance it has in the sight of Allāh to console the poor)."[15]

11.3.4 Sunnah basis of prohibition of riba

The *riba* is also prohibited by ahadith and Sunnah of Prophet Muhammad a. There are detailed varieties of usurious transactions regarding paying, taking and charging of *riba* which are categorically forbidden.

There is a significant number of ahadith.[16] Here a selection of commonly quoted ahadith is reproduced.

1. The Prophet (PBUH) said: "There is no *riba* except in loaning."[17]
2. The Prophet (PBUH) said: "Verily *riba* is in loaning."[18]
3. The Prophet (PBUH) said:

   "While exchanging gold for gold, silver for silver, wheat for wheat, barley for barley, dates for dates and salt for salt, an exchange like for like (in equal measure). Whosoever gave more or took more; verily he made a *riba* deal. However, you are permitted to exchange gold for silver, wheat for dates or barley for dates as you wish (in equal or unequal measures) provided that; such an exchange is a spot."[19]

4. The Holy Prophet (PBUH) on his last pilgrimage said that

   "Every form of interest '*riba*' is cancelled, capital indeed is yours which you should have. Wrong not, and you shall not be wronged. God has given his injunctions that interest is forbidden. I first start with (the amount of) interest (which people owe) to Abbas and declare it all cancelled."[20]

5. The Holy Prophet (PBUH) on his last pilgrimage, also said that "Beware, all *riba* outstanding from the *riba* prevalent during the pre-Islamic era is void. You are entitled to your principal money. Neither shall you oppress nor shall you be oppressed."[21]
6. From Jabir, who said: "The Prophet (PBUH) cursed the one who charges *riba*; he who gives it; the one who record it; and the two witnesses; saying that "they are all equal."[22]
7. From 'Ubadah Ibn Samit who said:

   The Prophet (PBUH) said: '"Gold for gold, silver for silver, wheat for wheat, barley for barley, dates for dates, salt for salt, like for like, in equal weights from hand to hand. If those species differ, then sell as you like as long as it is from hand to hand."[23]

8. According to Abu Huraira (R.A) the Prophet (PBUH) said: "Avoid seven great destructive sins." Then (the people) asked: O Allah's Apostle, what are they." He mentioned the worst seven things, and one of them was to eat up usury (*riba*)."[24]
9. There are roughly 70 grades of usury with suchlike grades of polytheism.[25]
10. 'Abd Allah b. Hanzala (R.A), narrated the Prophetic tradition:
    "A man's knowingly consuming one dirham of usury is worse than thirty-six incestuous acts."[26]
11. Ibn Mas'ud (R.A) reported that Allah's Prophet (PBUH) said:
    "There is no one who deals in usury a great deal but he will end up with little (i.e., his wealth will decrease since there will be no blessing in it)."[27]
12. Do not sell one dinar for two dinars, or one dirham for two dirhams.[28]
13. The Prophet (PBUH) said: "As soon as a society deeply indulges in *riba* and adultery, the wrath of God becomes due for it."[29]
14. The Prophet (PBUH) said: "In any society when *riba* becomes common, it causes hunger and poverty in it. And in any society, when bribery becomes common, it makes it depressed (as compared to other nations)."[30]

It is pertinent to note here that an explicit prohibition of *riba* is there in the above-mentioned Qur'ānic verses and Ahadith. Hence there is no question about it. All jurists are unanimous on the prohibition of *riba*.

11.3.5 The kinds of riba

Traditionally there are two main kinds of *riba*: *riba al-duyun* (interest earned on lending money to another party) and *riba al-buyu* (a sale transaction in which a commodity is exchanged for an unequal amount of the same commodity and supply is postponed). *Riba al-buyu* is further divided into two types: *riba al-Fadl* (riba in excess) and *riba al-Nasia* (*riba* in losses).

The word *nasia* means to postpone, defer or wait and the word *fadl* means to increase, add or exceed.

Now we explain these kinds *riba an-Nasia* and *riba al-Fadl* in a little bit more detail.

11.3.5.1 Riba an-Nasia (excess of delay)[31]

Riba al-Nasia is derived from the Arabic root *nasi'a*, which means to "delay," "postpone" or "defer." *Riba al-Nasia* refers to the time that is allowed to the borrower to pay off the loan, in return for the "addition" or the "premium." Hence it is equal to the interest charged on loans.

Riba in loans is defined as a contractual increase, be it standard or executive, on loaned capital that could be either in money form or in kind. All Qur'ānic verses unanimously imply only this kind of interest. *Riba an-Nasia* is also called *riba al-Qurudh* or *riba al-Quran*, but Islamic scholars and jurists prefer to use the term *riba al-Nasia*.[32] This kind of *riba* was practised in the pre-Islamic period in the Arabian Peninsula when it was known as *Riba al-Jahiliyyah*. It was widespread during the time of Prophet Muhammad a. This kind of *riba* strictly prohibits any loans or debts in which an increase accrues to the creditor, and also the charging of excessive fees for late payments.[33] *Riba al-Nasia* applies to loan transactions. It is a type of usury that arises due to exchange not being immediate, with or without excess in one of the counter-values. It refers to an increase in the amount of debt owing, due to a delay in payment of the debtor with the passage of time. *Riba al-Nasia* includes interest-based lending; compensation for lending; selling money for profit; or a predetermined payment for a loan, which may be a loan of money or a load of goods, which in modern times is known as money lending.[34] An example of *riba al-Nasia* is where a creditor lends money to a debtor for a fixed period at a determined rate of interest to be paid monthly; usually, this interest occurs through interest-bearing loans in everyday financial transactions.[35] Contracts which pay or receive interest are forbidden under the Islamic law of contract. Hence for a contract to be valid, it is necessary for it to be free from *riba*.

The following are some ahadith which define and prohibit *riba al-Nasia*:

1. Sulayman b. 'Amr narrated that his father said: "I heard Prophet (PBUH), during his Farewell pilgrimage, say: 'All riba of the Era of Ignorance is abolished; you will have your capital sums. Do not deal unjustly, and you will not be dealt with unjustly…"[36]
2. 'Abd Allah b. Salam (R.A) said to Abu Burda (R.A):

   > "You are in a land where usury is widespread. If a man owes you something and gives you a load of straw or a load of barley or a load of fodder, do not take it from him. It is usury."[37]

3. Yahya b. Abu Ishaq al-Huna'I narrated that he asked Anas b. Malik (R.A): "What if a man gives his brother a loan, then (the borrower) gives him a gift?" Anas b. Malik (R.A) said in answer that Prophet (PBUH) said:

   > "If anyone of you borrows something then he gives (the lender) a gift or gives him a ride on his riding-beast, he should not accept the gift or the ride unless they used to treat each other in that manner beforehand."[38]

4. Abu al-Minhal related that he asked al-Bara b. Azib and Zayd b. Arqam about money-changing and they said:

   > We used to be merchants during the time of Prophet (PBUH), and we asked Prophet (PBUH) about money-changing, and he said: "There is no harm if it is hand to hand. If there is a delay, then it is not proper."[39]

11.3.5.2 Riba al-Fadl *(excess of surplus)* [40]

This type of *riba* occurs with the payment of an addition by the debtor to the creditor in exchange for commodities of the same kind, or the exchange of low-quality for better-quality commodities.[41] The Prophet Muhammad a prohibited *riba al-Fadl* when he said: "Gold for gold, silver for silver, wheat for wheat, barley for barley, dates for dates, equal for equal, and hand to hand; if the commodities differ, then you may sell as you wish."[42]

Riba al-Fadl was prohibited because it could be used as a subterfuge for *riba al-Nasia*, and the prohibition prevents circumvention of the *Shariah* as well as risk and uncertainty. Thus, in order to avoid this type of *riba*, the exchange of goods from both sides must be equal and instant.[43]

Riba al-Fadl is the selling of one commodity for another of the same kind on the spot and in excess. An example of this is exchanging one kilo of a fine type of dates for two kilos of low-quality dates.

The Qur'ān categorically denounced and disallowed *riba* but did not characterise it. The definition of this *riba* has come from Prophetic traditions. The following traditions define and interdict *riba al-Fadl* (surplus interest).

Abu Sa'id al-Khudri and Abu Hurayra (R.A) reported:

> Holy Prophet (PBUH) appointed a man as an agent in Khaybar who brought him some dates of a excellent kind. Holy Prophet (PBUH) said: "Are all the dates of Khaybar like this?" He said: "No, Holy Prophet (PBUH). We take one sa' of this kind for two sa's and two sa's for three sa's." Holy Prophet (PBUH) said: "Do not do that. Sell the worse ones for dirhams and then buy the good ones with those dirhams."[44]

According to Abu Sa'id al-Khudri (R.A), Prophet (PBUH) said:

> "Do not sell gold for gold except like for like, and do not give more of one and less of the other. Do not sell silver except like for like, and do not give more of one and less of the other. And do not exchange something to be given later for something to be given now."[45]

According to 'Uthman b. 'Affan (R.A), Prophet (PBUH) said:

> "Do not sell one dinar for two dinars, or one dirham for two dirhams."[46]

According to Abu Sa'id al-Khudri (R.A), Prophet (PBUH) said:

> "Gold for gold, silver for silver, wheat for wheat, barley for barley, dates for dates, salt for salt, like for like, hand to hand. Whoever gives more or asks for more, he has engaged in riba, and the taker and the giver are the same."[47]

In business transactions, if gold is sold for gold and silver for silver, their quantities must be equivalent and the transaction must take place on the spot; otherwise, this will be a usurious deal.

> Ma'mar b. 'Abd Allah narrated that he sent his slave with a sa' of wheat and he said: "Sell it, then buy barley." The slave went and took a sa' and part of a sa' more. When he came to Ma'mar he told him about that, and Ma'mar said to him: "Why did you do that? Go and give it back, and do not take anything

> but like for like, for I used to hear Prophet (PBUH) says: 'Food for food, like for like.' And our food at that time was barley." It was said to him: "It is not like it." He said: "I am afraid that it may be similar."[48]

Fadala b. 'Ubayd (R.A) narrated:

> On the Day of Khaybar, I bought a necklace for twelve dinars, in which there were gold and pearls. I separated them and I found (it worth) more than twelve dinars in it. I mentioned that to the Prophet (PBUH) and he said: "It should not be sold until they are separated."[49]

To sum up, we can say that by reaffirming the type of *riba* mentioned in the Qur'ān, the Holy Prophet (PBUH) introduced new two forms of *ribā*, i.e. *riba al-Fadl* and *riba al-Nasia. Riba al-Fadl* takes place in a homogeneous exchange with an increase from one side in terms of weight or measurement. *Riba al-Nasia* takes place when articles of the same genera or different genera are exchanged with a deferment from one party. The prohibition of *riba al-Fadl* and *riba al-Nasia* seeks to forestall the entry of real *riba* through the back door.

Overall, there is not a great distance between *riba al-Nasia* and *riba al-Fadl*; in fact, they are almost identical except that *riba al-Nasia* relates to loan transactions and *riba al-Fadl* relates to exchange transactions.

11.3.6 The contracts should be free from riba

One of the fundamental principles that govern transactions in the Islamic law of contract is that the contracts should be free from *riba*. It is unanimously agreed by all jurists. It is to note that as the *riba* is excess in return of which no reward or equivalent counter value is paid, hence it may be concluded that all unjust enrichment due to this kind of transactions or business is considered as *riba*.

11.4 *Gharar*

Gharar is also one of the significant prohibited factors or elements of contracts in Islamic law of contract and is one of the causes of invalidity of a contract. *Gharar* refers to uncertainty and lack of knowledge about the concluding of a contract, which makes it speculative.

11.4.1 Literal meanings

The word *gharar* derives from the root verb *gharara/gharar*, which means risk, uncertainty and lack of knowledge. The word *gharar* in the Arabic language covers a variety of harmful elements such as deceit, cheating, danger, peril and risk, which might lead to destruction and loss.[50]

In broad concept, its literal meanings include uncertainty or hazard, delusion, doubt, suspicion, indeterminacy and speculation, etc.

11.4.2 Definitions of gharar

One thing that must be kept in mind is that while defining *gharar*, the early jurists explained it in the context of sale contract as a practical example or hypothetical. By keeping in view this fact, several definitions have been formulated by jurists. These are as follows:

1. Sarakhsi defined it as "*gharar* takes place where the consequences (of the transaction) remain unknown."[51]
2. Ibn Hazm defined it as "*gharar* in sales occurs when the purchaser does not know what he has bought, and the seller does not know what he has sold."[52]
3. Ibn Abidin defined it as "*gharar* is uncertainty about the existence of the subject matter of the sale."[53]
4. Ibn al-Qayyim defined it as "*gharar* as being the subject matter, the vendor is not in a position to hand over to the buyer whether the subject matter exists or not."[54]
5. Ibn Rushd defined it as "*gharar* is to be found in contracts of sale, when the seller suffers a disadvantage as a result of his ignorance, about the price of the article or the indispensable criteria, relating to the contract, or its object, quality, or time of delivery."[55]
6. The modern scholar Sanhuri sums up all the above definition and explained that *gharar* takes place in the following circumstances:
   (a) when it is not known whether the subject matter exists.
   (b) if it exists at all, whether it can be handed over to the buyer.
   (c) when the want of knowledge affects the identification of the genus or species of subject matter.
   (d) when it affects its quantum, identity or necessary conditions.
   (e) when it relates to the date of future performance.[56]
7. Ibn Taymiyyah, a classical jurist, explained the *gharar* in terms of types of sale. According to him, *gharar* is of three types. First, *bay' ma'dum*, that is, a sale of nonexisting; second, *bay' sinin*, that is the sale of something where the seller can never deliver; and third, *bay' majhul*, that is, the sale of an unknown object.[57]

From the above definitions, it is clear that as a technical term, it is applied to uncertainty about the outcome of a contract and undertaking anything blindly without sufficient knowledge. *Gharar* is a business contract of not knowing exactly what will be the outcome,[58] which may lead to dispute and litigation.

11.4.3 Gharar *and business risk*

The word "risk" is also used in the meanings of *gharar*. We know that risk is inherent in business: no one can predict whether there will be a profit or a loss in the future. All profit and risk-sharing business involve some element of risk and uncertainty. So not all types of risk are prohibited. Hence the risk in business and trade is not *gharar*. Similarly, there are also some contemporary financial transactions that involve risks and uncertainties. Here the question may arise as to what kind and to what extent the element of uncertainty and risk is *gharar*. The answer is

> lately, scholars have differentiated between *gharar-e-kathir* and *gharar-e-qalil* (too much and nominal uncertainty) and declared that only those transactions that involve too much or excessive uncertainty in respect of the subject matter and the price in a contract should be prohibited.[59]

11.4.4 Qur'ānic verses regarding gharar

There is not any direct Qur'ānic verse on the prohibition of *gharar*. However, the following verses are often quoted, which forbid all commercial transactions that involve injustice.

لَا تَأْكُلُوٓاْ أَمْوَٰلَكُم بَيْنَكُم بِٱلْبَٰطِلِ إِلَّآ أَن تَكُونَ تِجَٰرَةً عَن تَرَاضٍ مِّنكُمْ

> "Do not devour one another's wealth unlawfully amongst yourselves unless it is a trade by your mutual agreement."[60]

لَا تَأْكُلُوٓاْ أَمْوَٰلَكُم بَيْنَكُم بِٱلْبَٰطِلِ وَتُدْلُواْ بِهَآ إِلَى ٱلْحُكَّامِ لِتَأْكُلُواْ فَرِيقًا مِّنْ أَمْوَٰلِ ٱلنَّاسِ بِٱلْإِثْمِ وَأَنتُمْ تَعْلَمُونَ

> "Do not eat up one another's wealth amongst yourselves through injustice, nor take wealth to the authorities (as a bribe) so that, this way, you may (also) swallow a portion of others' wealth unfairly, whilst you are aware (that this is a sin)."[61]

11.4.5 Ahadith on the prohibition of gharar

There are several ahadith where the Prophet (PBUH) strictly prohibits transactions involving an element of *gharar*. For instance:

1. "O Prophet of Allāh! A man comes to me and asks me to sell him what is not with me, so I sell him (what he wants) and then buy the goods for him in the market (and deliver)." And Prophet (PBUH) said: "Sell not what is not with you."[62]
2. Abu Hurairah (R.A) narrated that the Holy Prophet (PBUH) forbade sale by pebbles and the *gharar* sale, i.e. indeterminate and speculative transactions.
3. It is narrated by Anas ibn Malik that Prophet (PBUH) forbade the sale of fruit till it was ripe. He a further said: "If Allāh spoiled the fruits what right would one party have to take the money of his brother?"
4. He a also said: "Do not buy fish in the sea, for it is *gharar*."
5. He a also forbade, the (sale of) the covering (copulation) of the stallion.
6. He a forbade sale of what is in the wombs, sale of the contents of the udders, sale of a slave when he is a runaway, and (sale of the) stroke of the divers (*darbat al-ghais*, sale in advance of the yield of a diver's dive, whatever it was).

11.4.6 The general principle to avoid gharar

The general principle to avoid *gharar* in business transactions can be inferred to be that a contract must not be doubtful or uncertain as far as the rights and obligations of the parties are concerned. The object of the contract and subject matter must be precisely determined and the terms of the contract must be clear and known, i.e. of measurable (*makil*), weighable (*mawzun*) or countable (*ma'dud*) objects.

It may be also inferred that the commodity must be defined and determined and known to the contracting parties. This rule applies to any commodity which can be weighed and measured. A sold commodity is deemed to be sufficiently known to the two parties if it is there and they have inspected it; a commodity that is not there cannot be sold unless both parties have previously seen it. The purchaser has the right of option to refuse to buy it after inspection.

11.4.7 Exceptions to the general principle

There are a few exceptions to this rule which are tolerated by Muslim jurists when, in the course of the transaction, a matter of necessity or need accidentally arises and which is essential to the contract.[63] Among these are the following.

11.4.7.1 Contract of salam

It is a contract where the sale of the object is not in existence or is not capable of being delivered at the time of the contract. The price must be paid during the session of the contract, and delivery of the sale object must take place at the future date.[64]

For the *salam* sale to be valid jurists laid down certain conditions to be fulfilled and they are;

i. The subject matter of the sale must be precisely specified.[65]
ii. The delivery of the goods should be postponed to a future date, and the subject matter must be available from the time of the conclusion of the contract to the time of the delivery. The contract of *salam* is void when the goods are not available or perish at any time between the time of the conclusion of the sale and the time of delivery.[66]
iii. The *salam* sale should be allowed on the non-existent subject matter. It is not essential whether or not it is available at the time of the conclusion of the sale. The sale is valid if it would be available at the time the delivery or it would come from a place known to have been capable of producing such goods because the possibility of *gharar* in such a situation is remote.[67]

11.4.7.2 Contract of istisna'

The second exception is the contract of *istisna'*. It is a contract whereby the sale of future goods is allowed in certain conditions. The *istisna'* contract allows for an order to be placed with a manufacturer to make a certain product answering a definite description at an agreed price to be paid either in advance or upon completion.[68]

It is required for a valid contract of *istisna'* that the subject matter should be well defined without ambiguity with respect to quality, quantity and other relevant characteristics.

11.4.7.3 Sale of debt

The third exception is the sale of debt, which per se, is not allowed even at face value, because the subject matter or the amount of debt is not there and if the debtor defaults in payment, the debt purchaser will lose. However, subjecting it to the rules of *hawalah* (assignment of debt) will validate the transaction, because, under the rules of *hawalah*, the purchaser of debt (if it is on the face value) will have recourse to the original debtor and *gharar* is removed.

However, speculation per se, which means sale-purchase, keeping in mind possible change in prices in the future, is not prohibited.

11.4.8 The purpose of the prohibition of gharar

The broad purpose behind all prohibited elements is that if they are allowed, they may bring about economic crisis in the long run and cause exploitation. It is the purpose of *gharar* to prevent monopoly, undue enrichment, and exploitation and to encourage fair trade. Islamic law of contract forbids forms of contracts that involve speculation, bribery, gambling and interest-bearing, etc. All these eventually lead to disputes between the parties and resultant harmful effects on the economy and community.

> Generally, the purpose of prohibiting *gharar* is to avoid disorder in society due to frustration or loss of property or the heavy burden of debts that would affect the smooth running of the family institutions or relations. This is compatible with the spirit of Islam that chooses to prevent harmful activities from occurring rather than merely curing them.[69]

11.4.9 Legal effect of gharar *on contracts*

It is an external prohibited attribute that invalidates the contracts, i.e. *gharar* is forbidden in Islamic finance contracts. Generally, jurists agree that *gharar* should be avoided in commercial transactions and contracts. All financial and business transactions must be based on transparency, accuracy and disclosure of all necessary information regarding the subject matter. There should not be any ambiguity that gives rise to speculation, and if there are any kinds of uncertainty, ambiguity or non-disclosure about a subject matter in a contract, the contract is void.[70] In Islamic law of contract, business transactions which cause injustice to the parties in the form of hazard leading to uncertainty, undue benefit and enrichment at the cost of another party are forbidden.

Depending on its scale and magnitude, *gharar* may render a contract null and void or it may constitute the basis of indemnity and compensation. A slight *gharar* may, on the other hand, be deemed to be tolerable in which case its presence would not affect the essential validity of a contract.[71]

Muslim jurists differ on the effects of *gharar* on gratuitous contracts. Some of the views are that *gharar* does not affect donations. However, the majority of jurists have the view that the subject matter of donation should be known and determined. As regards will, all the jurists are unanimous that it is valid even if the subject matter is non-existent, undetermined and outside the control of testator or beneficiary. It is also valid to make a bequest of an undetermined portion of the property. This testament is treated as valid, and it is the duty of the heirs to specify that portion.

11.5 *Qimar* and *maysir* (gambling)

Qimar (gambling) and *Maysir* (games of chance) are also two main forbidden elements in contracts. *Qimar* includes every form of a gain or money, the acquisition of which depends purely on chance. *Maysir* means getting something too quickly or getting a profit without working for it. All contracts involving *qimar* and *maysir* are prohibited. Dicing, lotteries and wagering are also included in the definition of gambling and *maysir*.

11.5.1 Literal meaning

Maysir means getting something too quickly or getting a profit without working for it, and *qimar* means an increase by chance. According to the shorter encyclopedia of Islam:

> *Maysir* means casting lots by arrows, a method by which a head of cattle was divided. This was the custom of the Arabs before Islam.

The word *maysir* is said to include all games of chance, such as dice, cards, etc.[72]

> The game was considered a pagan practice and the Qur'ān (2:219 and 5:93) forbade it along with wine and idols as a major sin.[73]

According to Imam Nawawi:

> On the other hand, the law forbids challenges to a game of mall on horseback, throwing the ball, swimming, chess or the game of rings; it forbids also challenges to certain bodily exercises, such as standing upon one foot; and challenges to certain games of chance, as for instance, guessing the number of the objects held closed in the hand.[74]

11.5.2 Definitions

Gambling can be defined as a contract among two or more persons involving the exchange of money or other valuables depending upon the uncertain outcome of a staged event.[75]

Muslim jurists have interpreted *maysir* to mean any form of a game of chance and gambling. Hassan and others defined *maysir* as "A game of chance or gambling that involves the acquisition of wealth by chance or winning the game or speculation without any form of consideration or compensation for such wealth."[76] Obaidullah,[77] De Lorenzo[78] and El-Gamal[79] have opined that options are a kind of *maysir* because the transaction has a zero–sum game nature. In options, they argue, buyers and sellers have diametrically opposite expectations. The gain of one party results from the loss of another party. Depending on the actual outcome, one party wins at the expense of others. Therefore, they argue, it is an example of *maysir*. *Maysir* is involved in a contract where the ownership of goods depends on the occurrence of a predetermined, uncertain event in the future. In other words, there will be a definitive gain for one party and definitive loss for the other party, but when a contract is concluded, it is not sure who will be the winner or the loser.

Franz Rosenthal says:

> "Gambling" is a term that appears to be of rather recent coinage in the English language. It seems to be a derivation from "game." Its range of meaning is broad and its use is by no means unambiguous. It can be stretched to include many other concepts such as betting and wagering, following hunches and daring others to do so. By preference, "gambling" is assumed to be restricted to contracts among two or more human beings which involve the exchange of money or other valuables depending upon the uncertain outcome of a staged event. "Staged" is the crucial word in this definition. It limits it to games of all kinds and sporting competitions of men and animals as well as all types of lotteries.[80]

The form most familiar to the Arabs was gambling by casting lots by means of arrows on the principle of the lottery. The arrows were marked and served the same purpose as a new lottery ticket. An item e.g. the carcass of a slaughtered animal, was divided into unequal parts. The marked arrows were then drawn from a bog. Those who drew blank arrows got nothing, while other arrows indicated prizes big or small. Whether one got a significant share, or a small share, or nothing, depended on pure luck. Dicing and wagering are rightly held to be within the definition of gambling and *maysir*.[81]

11.5.3 Prohibition of qimar *(gambling) and* maysir *(games of chance)*

Islamic law of contract forbids all forms of transactions in which gain and profit comes from mere chance or speculation and not from doing work. So all forms of *qimar* and *maysir* are categorically prohibited. A valid contract should not contain an attribute of *qimar* and *maysir*. So any arrangements between contracting parties, each of whom undertakes the risk of a loss where a loss for one means again for the other, is forbidden. So unjustified enrichment through games of chance is forbidden. So gambling, lottery, lucky draw, speculation and all games of chance in which anyone gains at the cost of the one losing, have been prohibited. There is no difference of opinion of almost all jurists regarding the prohibition of *qimar* and *maysir*. Hence, unlike *gharar*, which is sometimes accepted to a certain degree, *qimar* and *maysir* are not tolerated or allowed at all.

The Qur'ān has explicitly prohibited this practice. It says:

يَٰٓأَيُّهَا ٱلَّذِينَ ءَامَنُوٓاْ إِنَّمَا ٱلۡخَمۡرُ وَٱلۡمَيۡسِرُ وَٱلۡأَنصَابُ وَٱلۡأَزۡلَٰمُ رِجۡسٞ مِّنۡ عَمَلِ ٱلشَّيۡطَٰنِ فَٱجۡتَنِبُوهُ لَعَلَّكُمۡ
تُفۡلِحُونَ

> "O believers! Wine and gambling and idols mounted (for worship) and divining arrows (for seeking luck–all) are filthy works of Satan. So turn away from them (completely) so that you may prosper."[82]

11.5.3.1 The wisdom behind this prohibition

The wisdom behind the prohibition of *qimar* includes reliance on accidental gains or luck. Islam encourages people to earn their means of livelihood in a legitimate manner through hard work and due diligence. Besides, *qimar* destroys the source of families' livelihoods by impoverishing the losers and unfairly enriching the winners through prohibited means. Through this, enmity and hatred are generated among the players.

11.5.3.2 Qur'ānic basis of prohibition of qimar *and* maysir

Along with above-quoted Qur'ānic verse, following are also more Qur'ānic verses which are quoted for the prohibition of *qimar* and *maysir*:

يَسۡـَٔلُونَكَ عَنِ ٱلۡخَمۡرِ وَٱلۡمَيۡسِرِۖ قُلۡ فِيهِمَآ إِثۡمٞ كَبِيرٞ وَمَنَٰفِعُ لِلنَّاسِ وَإِثۡمُهُمَآ أَكۡبَرُ مِن نَّفۡعِهِمَا

> "They ask you about alcohol (i.e., intoxicants) and gambling. Say: 'Major sin lies in both of them and also some (worldly) profit for the people, but their sin is greater than their profit.'"[83]

Here gambling is forbidden by referring to its evils and it is pointed out that its evil was higher than its usefulness. Further, the Qur'ān disapproved of gambling as a social evil:

يَٰٓأَيُّهَا ٱلَّذِينَ ءَامَنُوٓاْ إِنَّمَا ٱلۡخَمۡرُ وَٱلۡمَيۡسِرُ وَٱلۡأَنصَابُ وَٱلۡأَزۡلَٰمُ رِجۡسٞ مِّنۡ عَمَلِ ٱلشَّيۡطَٰنِ فَٱجۡتَنِبُوهُ لَعَلَّكُمۡ
إِنَّمَا يُرِيدُ ٱلشَّيۡطَٰنُ أَن يُوقِعَ بَيۡنَكُمُ ٱلۡعَدَٰوَةَ وَٱلۡبَغۡضَآءَ فِي ٱلۡخَمۡرِ وَٱلۡمَيۡسِرِ وَيَصُدَّكُمۡ عَن ذِكۡرِ ٱللَّهِ oتُفۡلِحُونَ
oوَعَنِ ٱلصَّلَوٰةِۖ فَهَلۡ أَنتُم مُّنتَهُونَ

> "O believers! Wine and gambling and idols mounted (for worship) and divining arrows (for seeking luck–all) are filthy words of Satan. So turn away from them (completely) so that you may prosper. Satan seeks only to breed enmity and spite amongst you by means of wine and gambling, and hinder you from remembering Allāh and observing Prayer. Will you abstain (from these evil-generating temptations)?"[84]

All forms of gambling are prohibited:

حُرِّمَتۡ عَلَيۡكُمُ ٱلۡمَيۡتَةُ وَٱلدَّمُ وَلَحۡمُ ٱلۡخِنزِيرِ وَمَآ أُهِلَّ لِغَيۡرِ ٱللَّهِ بِهِۦ وَٱلۡمُنۡخَنِقَةُ وَٱلۡمَوۡقُوذَةُ وَٱلۡمُتَرَدِّيَةُ
وَٱلنَّطِيحَةُ وَمَآ أَكَلَ ٱلسَّبُعُ إِلَّا مَا ذَكَّيۡتُمۡ وَمَا ذُبِحَ عَلَى ٱلنُّصُبِ وَأَن تَسۡتَقۡسِمُواْ بِٱلۡأَزۡلَٰمِۚ ذَٰلِكُمۡ فِسۡقٌۗ ٱلۡيَوۡمَ
يَئِسَ ٱلَّذِينَ كَفَرُواْ مِن دِينِكُمۡ فَلَا تَخۡشَوۡهُمۡ وَٱخۡشَوۡنِۚ ٱلۡيَوۡمَ أَكۡمَلۡتُ لَكُمۡ دِينَكُمۡ وَأَتۡمَمۡتُ عَلَيۡكُمۡ نِعۡمَتِي
وَرَضِيتُ لَكُمُ ٱلۡإِسۡلَٰمَ دِينٗاۚ فَمَنِ ٱضۡطُرَّ فِي مَخۡمَصَةٍ غَيۡرَ مُتَجَانِفٖ لِّإِثۡمٖ فَإِنَّ ٱللَّهَ غَفُورٞ رَّحِيمٞ

> "Forbidden to you is carrion (the animal that dies and is not slaughtered according to Islamic law) and (the discharged) blood and pork and that (animal) on which the name of someone other than Allāh has been invoked whilst slaughtering and (the animal) that dies by strangling or by a violent blow (not by any sharp instrument) or by falling from a height or the one that has been gored to death or which has been ripped apart and gnawed by a wild beast, save the one which you slaughter (before it dies), and (that animal too is forbidden) which has been slaughtered on idolatrous altars (dedicated to false gods). And this (is also unlawful) that you learn our fortune through divining (with arrows or divide shares by such means). All these works are sins. This day, the disbelievers have lost all hopes of (their heinous designs because) your Din ([Religion] has prevailed). So, (O believers,) fear them not and always fear Me alone. Today I have perfected your Din (Religion) for you and have completed My Blessing upon you, and have chosen for you Islam (as) Din (a complete code of life). Then if someone gets into a survival situation (and is forced by) ravenous hunger (and intense thirst i.e., driven by dire necessity, provided) he is not prone to sinning (i.e., eats what is forbidden without being wilfully inclined to sin), then Allāh is indeed Most Forgiving, Ever-Merciful."[85]

All these Qur'ānic commandments finally made gambling in all its forms absolutely unlawful for Muslims and declared gambling and diving with arrows as infamy, wickedness and of Satan's handiwork.

11.5.4 Relationship between gharar *and* qimar

There is a relationship between *gharar* and *qimar* in terms of the uncertain outcome. Another term for a game of chance is *maysir*, as used in the Qur'ān. The references in the Qur'ān to games of chance may conveniently be cited to support the prohibition of risky or hazardous transactions. The wisdom behind the prohibition of these forms of transactions is the resultant injustice that flows from undue advantage, deceit and fraud.[86]

11.6 Fraud and cheating

11.6.1 Literal meanings and definitions of fraud

Fraud is the obtaining of a material advantage by unfair or wrongful means, and it involves a moral as well as a legal obligation.

Fraud refers to manoeuvre practised by one of the practices to induce a person to a contract without which he would not have entered it. It also refers to concealing the defects of and adulteration in merchandise.

Fraud includes a number of practices such as giving short measure and short weight (*tariff*), false bidding to raise the price of an item (*najash*), leaving an animal un-milked for a long time to give a false impression to the buyer about its milk yield (*tasriyah*), the practice of meeting villagers at the outskirts of the town in order to purchase their merchandise before they reach the market place (*talaqqi al-rukban*), false swearing and hiding defects in sale.

> The law in every case lays down definite rules, and in circumstances in which a party has not complied with the same, the suffered party is relieved. Thus, if in a sale of profit, the purchaser should discover that the seller had practised fraud in stating the price of the wares, in such a case, according to Abu Hanifa, the purchaser is at liberty either to adhere to or undo the bargain as he pleases and if such fraud should be practised in a sale of friendship, the purchaser is at liberty to deduct the amount of the fraud from the price.[87]

> In the light of the above principle, if any loss of property has been caused to the victim of a fraud, he is entitled to compensation from the wrongdoer. A person who commits or practices fraud is not to be allowed to derive any advantage from his own wrong on the principle of prohibition of unjust enrichment.[88]

> The prohibition of giving short measure and weight, the necessity of telling the truth and of giving true accounts, the prohibition of telling lies, of unfaithfulness and of cheating and observing that the (equitable) recompense of lending is to settle one's debt and to thank the lender.[89]

11.6.2 Fraud in a broader view

Sometimes a man's act may be induced by something said or done by another with a view to producing a specific effect. If what is so represented by words or conduct be untrue, that is, be not in accordance with facts, and the person making such representation knows of it, he is said to be guilty of fraud (*ghurur*). Fraud according to Islamic jurisprudence directly affects the judgement of its victim and his intention only indirectly and remotely. Therefore, such a man will be said to intend and consent to the doing of the act itself and also to its having legal effect. As regards the person who has practised deception, fraud would refer to his motive in performing the act and not to his intention, as already indicated. Sometimes the person performing an act may not be aware of its legal character or consequences, or he may perform an act or abstain from performing an act in misapprehension or ignorance of certain facts. The question which the law has to deal with in such cases is generally put in the form: How far is such ignorance (*jahl*) of the law in fact an excuse.[90]

11.6.3 Cheating: meanings and definition

Misconduct, trickery, falsehood and betrayal are forms of fraud and cheating. If individuals who take unfair advantage of others through these crooked means upset the social equilibrium, they are guilty of cheating and fraud. These forms of wrongs and practices damage society as well as businesses. Sellers who give in to the temptation to cheat are enemies of society. Allah, the Exalted, destroyed previous nations when they wronged people by not giving full measure and weight.

The wretched people of the Prophet Shu'ayb habitually cheated in trade in spite of the fact that the Lord had granted them goodly provisions. The Prophet enjoined them to resist:

قَدْ جَآءَتْكُم بَيِّنَةٌ مِّن رَّبِّكُمْۖ فَأَوْفُوا۟ ٱلْكَيْلَ وَٱلْمِيزَانَ وَلَا تَبْخَسُوا۟ ٱلنَّاسَ أَشْيَآءَهُمْ

> "Indeed, there has come to you from your Lord a clear sign. So give full measure and weight, and do not decrease whilst giving people their things."[91]

They, the champions of deception and corruption, did not heed his exhortations. Mocking their Prophet's call to observe the Divine regulations in conducting business, the dwellers of Madyan (Shu'ayb's nation) said:

قَدْ جَآءَتْكُم بَيِّنَةٌ مِّن رَّبِّكُمْۖ فَأَوْفُوا۟ ٱلْكَيْلَ وَٱلْمِيزَانَ وَلَا تَبْخَسُوا۟ ٱلنَّاسَ أَشْيَآءَهُمْ

> "O Shu'ayb, does your prayer only command you that we forsake those (gods) which our fathers have been worshipping, or that we refrain from doing with our wealth what we like? Surely, you (alone) must be the most tolerant and guided one!"[92]

The Prophet (PBUH) of the people of Madyan kept on exhorting them to mend their ways, and follow the divinely prescribed business practices, yet they did not take his counsel. Allah Almighty seized them for their inquiry and a mighty blast struck the wrongdoers from among them.

وَلَمَّا جَآءَ أَمْرُنَا نَجَّيْنَا شُعَيْبًا وَٱلَّذِينَ ءَامَنُوا۟ مَعَهُۥ بِرَحْمَةٍ مِّنَّا وَأَخَذَتِ ٱلَّذِينَ ظَلَمُوا۟ ٱلصَّيْحَةُ فَأَصْبَحُوا۟ فِي
دِيَٰرِهِمْ جَٰثِمِينَ ٩٤ كَأَن لَّمْ يَغْنَوْا۟ فِيهَآۗ أَلَا بُعْدًا لِّمَدْيَنَ كَمَا بَعِدَتْ ثَمُودُ ٩٥

> "And when Our command (of torment) came We saved Shu'aib and the believers with him through Our Mercy but a dreadful Blast seized the wrongdoers. So they reached the morning (as dead) lying prostrate in their homes—. As if they had never put up their. Listen! (The people of) Madyan are doomed as were doomed (the people of) Thamud."[93]

The extermination of the people of Shu'ayb cautions us against cheating and deceiving customers, employees, employers and anyone who confides in us.

The contractors and the businesspeople who swindle buyers may think that their wealth will immortalise them. However, on the contrary, the Qur'ān directs people to engage in fair dealings with their fellows and render them their due; what is left will be enough to meet their material needs. Traders must take into consideration the fact that the fruit of righteous dealings is right in the sight of the Sustainer.

بَقِيَّتُ ٱللَّهِ خَيْرٌ لَّكُمْ إِن كُنتُم مُّؤْمِنِينَ ۚ وَمَآ أَنَا۠ عَلَيْكُم بِحَفِيظٍ

> "That which is left over from Allah's provision (only that) is better for you if you have faith."[94]

11.6.4 Qur'ānic basis of prohibition of fraud and cheating, etc.

The Qur'ān has disapproved of fraud, cheating and deception in whatever form they might be. The words *khilabah, ghishsh* and *tatfif* have been used in the Qur'ān and the Sunnah to convey the meanings of fraud and cheating.

Fraud and cheating have been strongly condemned in the following texts of the Qur'ān.

وَيْلٌ لِّلْمُطَفِّفِينَ ٱلَّذِينَ إِذَا ٱكْتَالُوا۟ عَلَى ٱلنَّاسِ يَسْتَوْفُونَ وَإِذَا كَالُوهُمْ أَو وَّزَنُوهُمْ يُخْسِرُونَ أَلَا يَظُنُّ أُو۟لَٰٓئِكَ أَنَّهُم مَّبْعُوثُونَ لِيَوْمٍ عَظِيمٍ يَوْمَ يَقُومُ ٱلنَّاسُ لِرَبِّ ٱلْعَٰلَمِينَ

> "Woe to those who give less in measure or weight! When (they) take by measure from others, they take (from them) full. And when they (themselves) give by measure or weigh to others, they give them less. Do they not believe that they will be raised up (again after death). For a Terrible Day. The Day when all mankind will stand before the Lord of all the worlds?"[95]

It has been ordained in respect of defrauding people in the matter about wealth:
يَٰٓأَيُّهَا ٱلَّذِينَ ءَامَنُوا۟ لَا تَأْكُلُوٓا۟ أَمْوَٰلَكُم بَيْنَكُم بِٱلْبَٰطِلِ

> "O believers! Do not devour one another's wealth unlawfully amongst yourselves."[96]

Assisting falsehood or fraud has been ruled out:

وَٱلَّذِينَ لَا يَشْهَدُونَ ٱلزُّورَ وَإِذَا مَرُّوا۟ بِٱللَّغْوِ مَرُّوا۟ كِرَامًا

> "And these are the people who do not attend (both verbally and practically) the false and untruthful matters, and when they pass by evil activities, they pass on (observing caution) with utmost nobility and dignity."[97]

It means "nor do they knowingly take part in anything that is based on falsehood." This is the view of Razi.[98]

These injunctions pertain to deceit in commercial transactions which are unfortunately rampant in our society.

وَلَا تَنقُصُوا۟ ٱلْمِكْيَالَ وَٱلْمِيزَانَ

> "And do not give short measure and weight."[99]

These are also of a generally applicable rule of ethics touching upon every aspect of moral and social relation.

Defrauding in general in mutual relations of business has been prohibited: وَأَقِيمُوا۟ ٱلْوَزْنَ بِٱلْقِسْطِ وَلَا تُخْسِرُوا۟ ٱلْمِيزَانَ

> "And keep weighing justly and do not make the balance fall short."[100]

There are comprehensive injunctions against all sorts of dishonest dealings and every breach of trust comes within them.[101]

وَلَا تَأْكُلُوٓا۟ أَمْوَٰلَكُم بَيْنَكُم بِٱلْبَٰطِلِ وَتُدْلُوا۟ بِهَآ إِلَى ٱلْحُكَّامِ لِتَأْكُلُوا۟ فَرِيقًا مِّنْ أَمْوَٰلِ ٱلنَّاسِ بِٱلْإِثْمِ وَأَنتُمْ تَعْلَمُونَ

> "And do not eat up one another's wealth amongst yourselves through injustice, nor take wealth to the authorities (as a bribe) so that, this way, you may (also) swallow a portion of others' wealth unfairly, whilst you are aware (that this is a sin)."[102]

إِنَّ ٱلَّذِينَ يَكْتُمُونَ مَآ أَنزَلَ ٱللَّهُ مِنَ ٱلْكِتَٰبِ وَيَشْتَرُونَ بِهِۦ ثَمَنًا قَلِيلًا أُو۟لَٰٓئِكَ مَا يَأْكُلُونَ فِي بُطُونِهِمْ إِلَّا ٱلنَّارَ
وَلَا يُكَلِّمُهُمُ ٱللَّهُ يَوْمَ ٱلْقِيَٰمَةِ وَلَا يُزَكِّيهِمْ وَلَهُمْ عَذَابٌ أَلِيمٌ

> "Indeed, those who conceal (those verses of) the Book (Torah) which Allah has revealed, and take in exchange for that a small price, eat nothing but fill their bellies with Fire. And Allah will neither speak to them nor purify them on the Day of Resurrection. And for them is a painful torment."[103]

It is worth mentioning here that all these Qur'ānic verses and enunciation about deceit and cheating refer to business and commercial dealings.

11.6.5 Sunnah basis of prohibition of fraud and cheating, etc.

Fraud and cheating have been strongly condemned in the Sunnah. Some ahadith dealing with fraud and cheating and reinforcing the theme of above-mentioned Qur'ānic verses are as follows:

1. Cheating while buying and selling and deceiving in business is such an enormity that the Prophet (PBUH) dissociated himself from the people who deceive or cheat. ليس منا من غش

   > "He who cheats is not one of us."[104]

2. In another tradition, the Prophet (PBUH) condemned dishonesty and betrayal as the traits of the inmates of Hell. He said:

   > "And the people of the Fire are of five types: A weak man who lacks the wisdom (to avoid evil); those who are your followers that do not have any

care for family and wealth; one who is dishonest and is a miser even for a little; a man who will betray you morning and evening with regard to your family and your wealth"—and he mentioned miserliness or lying—"and the one whose language is obscene."[105]

3. In some other traditions, the Prophet (PBUH) condemns cheating. Hakim b. Hizam (R.A) reported that the Prophet (PBUH) said:

   "The seller and the buyer have the option (to revoke the sale) as long as they have not separated (or he said: "until they separate"). If they speak the truth and make things clear, they will be blessed in their sale. If they conceal and lie, the blessing of their transaction will be obliterated."[106]

4. 'Uqba b. Amir (R.A) narrated that Prophet (PBUH) said:

   "It is not lawful for a Muslim to sell goods knowing that there is a defect in them without mentioning it."[107]

5. Abu Hurayra (R.A) narrated that Prophet (PBUH), passing by a pile of foodstuff, put his hand (deep) in it and found that it had got wet. He said: "What is this, seller of the foodstuff?" He said: "It got rained on, Prophet (PBUH)." He said: "Why do you not put it on top of the food so that people can see it? Whoever deceives does not pertain to me."[108]

   In the aforementioned hadith, the words of the man, "it got rained on," indicate that the seller did not make the pile of foodstuff wet, but he was guilty of hiding the most part, hence the Prophet's expression of disapproval. In like manner, giving less measure in dim light and displaying good vegetables but selling stale vegetables are sneaky ways to make money.
6. According to 'Ali (R.A), the Blessed Prophet (PBUH) said:

   "Deceiving an al-mustarsal (an ignorant entrant into the market) is usury."[109]

   Here deceiving is being equated to usury.

   In Islamic law of contract, a contract must be free from fraud and cheating. In a case where one of the contracting parties cheats the other in whatever form or meanwhile concluding a contract, the harmed party has every right to invalidate the contract by exercising his or her legal right.
7. The Prophet (PBUH) is reported to have said: "If both the parties spoke the truth and described defects of the goods, then they would be blessed in their transactions, and if they told lies and hid something, then the blessing of their transaction would be lost."[110]
8. The Holy Prophet (PBUH) also said: "False swearing (by the seller) is beneficial to the trade, i.e. it may persuade the buyer to purchase the goods, but in that way, he will be deprived of God's blessing to the earnings."[111]
9. It is reported that a person came to Holy Prophet (PBUH) who was always defrauded in buying. The Holy Prophet (PBUH) instructed him to say at the

time of buying: "There should not be any attempt to deceive, and I have the right to cancel it within three days."[112]

10. "The truthful merchant will be on the day of resurrection together with the Prophets, the faithful ones, the martyrs and the pious people."[113]
11. The Holy Prophet (PBUH) once happened to pass by a heap of grain in a market place and on examination found that the grain beneath the surface was wet while that on the surface was dry. He chided the seller for resorting to such deceptive tactics and said: "he who deceives is not one of us."[114]

Following are practical examples of the prohibition of things due to fraud and deceit.

11.6.6 Sale of milk in the udder

The sale of milk in the udder is prohibited because there is the possibility of fraud. The Prophet (PBUH) says in this regard:

> "Do not tie up the udders of she-camel or sheep with its udders tied up, he has two options after milking it: either to retain it or to return it with a measure of dates."[115]

11.6.7 **Najsh** *is forbidden*

Najsh is a kind of fraud in which one would offer a high price for something without having the intention to buy but merely to cheat somebody else who wanted to buy. Such a person would agree with the seller to buy the thing at a high price in the presence of the actual buyer in order to cheat him. In this way the actual buyer is being trapped. Similarly, in another scenario the seller would falsely tell the buyer that he had previously bought the goods at a specific price which was in reality higher than the actual price. The Holy Prophet (PBUH) prohibited all bargains which contained an element of fraud and deceit or were transacted to defraud other people. The concept of hoarding can be related here.

11.6.8 False oath in commercial transactions

To earn good profits, some traders bear witness, using Allah's name, that their commodities are flawless. At times they wrongly assure customers very solemnly that they were offered a higher amount of money a few moments ago, yet they did not sell. Through such tricks, they might entrap customers. On realising the nature of such a trader, customers disregard his or her words. A great many oath-takers unwittingly damage their business and industry in this way.

Wild exaggerations, false oaths and gross misstatements are employed to deceive clients into buying articles. Though swearing oaths may win the confidence of some customers, yet the gains are denuded of Divine blessings. Such earnings, though much, seem paltry.

The Qur'ān warns the faithful of the penalty in the Hereafter for selling oaths.

إِنَّ ٱلَّذِينَ يَشْتَرُونَ بِعَهْدِ ٱللَّهِ وَأَيْمَٰنِهِمْ ثَمَنًا قَلِيلًا أُو۟لَٰٓئِكَ لَا خَلَٰقَ لَهُمْ فِي ٱلْأَخِرَةِ وَلَا يُكَلِّمُهُمُ ٱللَّهُ وَلَا يَنظُرُ
إِلَيْهِمْ يَوْمَ ٱلْقِيَٰمَةِ وَلَا يُزَكِّيهِمْ وَلَهُمْ عَذَابٌ أَلِيمٌ

> "Certainly, those who sell the promise of Allah and their own oaths for a small price, it is they who will not have any share in the Hereafter. And on the Day of Resurrection Allah will neither speak to nor look at them, nor will He purify them, and for them will be painful torment."[116]

In the following tradition, the Prophet (PBUH) warned the faithful to beware swearing oaths in business dealings.

Abu Hurayra (R.A) reported Prophet (PBUH) as saying:

> "Taking oaths hastens the sale of goods but eradicates the blessings."[117]

The theme of avoidance of taking oaths in business transactions and selling is echoed in another hadith. Abu Qatada al-Ansari (R.A) reported that he heard Prophet (PBUH) say:

> "Beware of swearing a great deal when selling, for it brings about a sale, then erases (the blessing of the profit)."[113]

Giving one's word in the Name of Allah when not lying is a minor offence, whereas employing His holy Name in order to deceive others is a significant offence.[119] Traders, therefore, must not swear falsely so that they may make a roaring trade. Swearing false oaths in the Name of Allah is as good as swindling.

It is narrated from Abu Dharr (R.A) that the Prophet (PBUH) said:

> "There are three to whom Allah will not speak on the Day of Resurrection, nor will He look at them nor sanctify them, and theirs will be a painful torment." Holy Prophet (PBUH) repeated it three times. Abu Dharr (R.A) said: "May they be lost and doomed! Who are they, Holy Prophet?" He said: "The one who lets his ower garment hang below his ankles, the one who reminds others (of his gifts), and the one who sells his product using a false oath."[120]

Enticing people to buy one's goods is normal in society, yet Islamic law thought to abhor this practice, as evidenced by the following Prophetic tradition.

> It is related from 'Abd Allah b. Abi Awfa (R.A) that a man set up some goods in the market and swore by Allah that he had been offered for them an amount that he had not been offered in order to entice a Muslim man into buying them. So it was revealed [Q. 3:77]: "Certainly, those who sell the promise of Allah and their own oaths for a small price."[121]

Another hadith also tells us what type of sinful conduct will ruin traders.

> Holy Prophet (PBUH) said, “Indeed, traders are wicked and sinful.” He was asked: “Prophet (PBUH), has Allah not permitted buying and selling?” The Prophet (PBUH) said: “Of course (Allah has made buying and selling lawful)! But when they speak, they (in order to sell their commodities) lie and swear, and thus become fall into error.”[122]

Swearing a false oath which leads to someone’s undeserved loss or one’s undue profit is not permitted under any circumstance; it is one of the cardinal offences in the sight of Allah.

According to ‘Abd Allah b. Unays al-Juhani (R.A), Prophet (PBUH) said:

> “Indeed among the worst of the major sins is shirk (believing in multiple gods as partners) with Allah, disobeying the parents and (swearing) the false oath. No one insists on taking an oath in which he swears, including the like of a wing of a mosquito (of falsehood) in it except that a spot is placed in his heart until the Day of Resurrection.”[123]

The atonement for false oaths is repenting to Allah in all sincerity and then mending one’s character.

Hence the making of false oaths is deceit, and false swearing in commercial transactions has been disallowed:

> Narrated Abu Huraira (R.A): I heard Allāh’s Apostle a saying, “The swearing (by the seller) may persuade the buyer to purchase the goods but that will be deprived of Allāh’s blessing.”[124]

There is another *hadith* of the Holy Prophet (PBUH):

> Narrated ‘Abdullah bin Abu Aufa: a man displayed some goods in the market and swore by Allāh u that he had been offered so much for that, that which was not offered and he said so, to cheat a Muslim. On that occasion that following verse was revealed:
>
> “Verily! Those who purchase a small gain at the cost of Allāh’s covenant and their oaths (they shall have no portion in the Hereafter … etc.).”[125]

11.6.9 Concealing defects of a commodity

Disclosing the defect of a tradable product is a duty of the seller. The primary sources of Islamic law have spelt out the necessity of keeping business transactions free from unlawful acts such as fraud, deception, forgery and concealment of flaws which might cause loss to individuals and society. Sellers who practise this Islamic ordinance reap the religious and material reward: such conscientious traders earn the trust of purchasers and merit the approval of the Highest. Bringing the defect of a product to light is an act of honesty, an essential quality of a Muslim trader's character.

Sellers, merchants and purveyors are under obligation to reveal the defects of the commodities they sell. 'Uqba b. 'Amir (R.A) narrated that he heard the Prophet (PBUH) say:

> "The Muslim is the brother of another Muslim; it is not permissible for a Muslim to sell his brother goods in which there is a defect, without pointing that out to him."[126]

If anyone sells a commodity with a defect without mentioning it, he or she earns the displeasure of Allah and is deprived of its blessing.

> It was narrated that Wathila b. al-Aqsa' (R.A) said: "I heard Prophet (PBUH) said: 'Whoever sells defective goods without pointing it out will remain subject to the wrath of Allah, and the angels will continue to curse him.'"[127]
>
> Abu Hurayra (R.A) narrated that Prophet (PBUH), passing by a pile of foodstuff, put his hand (deep) in it and found that it had got wet. He said: "What is this, the seller of the foodstuff?" He said: "It got rained on, Prophet (PBUH)." He said: "Why do you not put it on top of the food so that people can see it? Whoever deceives does not pertain to me."[128]

This event emphasises the importance of honesty in business. On one occasion, the Prophet (PBUH) said:

> "The seller and the buyer have the option (to revoke the sale) as long as they have not separated (or he said: "until they separate"). Should they speak the truth and make things clear, they will be blessed in their sale. Should they conceal and lie, the blessing of their transaction will be obliterated."[129]

Every Muslim should be a well-wisher of their fellows. Before selling a defective commodity, a trader must disclose its fault. All preceding Prophetic tradition reinforces this argument.

11.6.10 Hoarding is forbidden

Traders are not allowed to collect and keep large amounts of food, money and valuable objects secretly to create a shortage in the market which may cause the rise in price. Hoarding is illicit, to make more profit as it upsets market equilibrium.

On the prohibition of such hoarding resources, Allah says in the Qur'ān:

> وَلَا يَحۡسَبَنَّ ٱلَّذِينَ يَبۡخَلُونَ بِمَآ ءَاتَىٰهُمُ ٱللَّهُ مِن فَضۡلِهِۦ هُوَ خَيۡرًا لَّهُمۖ بَلۡ هُوَ شَرٌّ لَّهُمۡۖ سَيُطَوَّقُونَ مَا بَخِلُواْ بِهِۦ يَوۡمَ ٱلۡقِيَٰمَةِ

"And those who are niggardly in giving away (from the wealth) which Allah has bestowed upon them out of His bounty must never consider this miserliness of any benefit to themselves; it is rather injurious to them. Soon on the Day of Resurrection, this wealth they are niggardly about will be put around (their necks) like a neck-fetter."[130]

Greedy folk who live in the lap of luxury and close their eyes to the needs of the downtrodden are forewarned of adverse consequences:

ٱلَّذِي جَمَعَ مَالٗا وَعَدَّدَهُۥ ٢ يَحۡسَبُ أَنَّ مَالَهُۥٓ أَخۡلَدَهُۥ ٣ كَلَّاۖ لَيُنۢبَذَنَّ فِي ٱلۡحُطَمَةِ ٤ وَمَآ أَدۡرَىٰكَ مَا ٱلۡحُطَمَةُ ٥ نَارُ
ٱللَّهِ ٱلۡمُوقَدَةُ ٦ ٱلَّتِي تَطَّلِعُ عَلَى ٱلۡأَفۡـِٔدَةِ ٧ إِنَّهَا عَلَيۡهِم مُّؤۡصَدَةٞ ٨ فِي عَمَدٖ مُّمَدَّدَةِۭ ٩

"(Woe to him) who accumulates wealth and keeps counting it! He thinks that his riches will keep him alive forever. By no means! He will certainly be cast into al-hutama (the fire). And what will make you understand what al-hutama (the crushing up Fire) is? (It) is a fire kindled by Allah. That will rise over the hearts (with its torture). Indeed, that (fire) will be closed upon them all around, in towering columns (of fierce flames and they will not find any way to escape)."[131]

Islamic law instils a sense of fair play in people's minds and forbids them from hoarding:

وَٱلَّذِينَ يَكۡنِزُونَ ٱلذَّهَبَ وَٱلۡفِضَّةَ وَلَا يُنفِقُونَهَا فِي سَبِيلِ ٱللَّهِ فَبَشِّرۡهُم بِعَذَابٍ أَلِيمٖ ٣٤ يَوۡمَ يُحۡمَىٰ عَلَيۡهَا فِي
نَارِ جَهَنَّمَ فَتُكۡوَىٰ بِهَا جِبَاهُهُمۡ وَجُنُوبُهُمۡ وَظُهُورُهُمۡۖ هَٰذَا مَا كَنَزۡتُمۡ لِأَنفُسِكُمۡ فَذُوقُواْ مَا كُنتُمۡ تَكۡنِزُونَ

"And those who hoard silver and gold and do not spend it in the cause of Allah, warn them of a grievous torment. The Day when this (gold, silver and wealth) will be heated in the Fire of Hell, their foreheads sides and backs will be branded with this (heated material, and it will be said to them:) "This is the same (wealth) that you treasured for (the benefit of) your souls. So taste (this wealth) which you had been amassing."[132]

When traders or businesspeople store large amounts of things, they intend to sell goods at an inflated price so that they may overcharge. With a view to deterring his followers from hiding away commodities for public use, the Blessed Prophet (PBUH) said:

"Whoever hoards is a sinner."[133]

Ibn 'Umar (R.A) related that the Prophet (PBUH) said:

"If anyone withholds grain for forty nights (out of the desire for a high price), he is free from Allah's obligation and Allah will renounce him."[134]

Ma'mar b. 'Abd Allah (R.A) narrated that Prophet (PBUH) said:

> "No one but sinner hoards."[135]

Mua'dh b. Jabal (R.A) reported that Prophet (PBUH) said:

> "The man who hoards goods is evil. If Allah lowers prices, he is grieved, and if Allah raises prices, he is happy."[136]

In the other traditions, the Prophet (PBUH) denounced those individuals who, driven by sheer greed, acquire wealth at the expense of others by manipulating the prices of food items and other necessities of life.

The Prophet (PBUH) blessed traders but cursed hoarders.

> "He who brings goods to the market is blessed with the provision, but he who withholds them is cursed."[137]

Hoarding is an unproductive and antisocial habit. A scarcity of certain goods even during stable economic times can be a significant drain on customers' personal finances. By outlawing hoarding, Islam closed the door to greed, avarice and exploitation. Nothing is more destructive to a believer's faith than getting caught up in the hot pursuit of passion and base desires.

The remedy to the evil of cheating is bearing in mind that Allah, the Exalted, is watching over us and that the reckoning will examine even the minutest deeds, good and evil.

إِنَّ رَبَّكَ لَبِٱلْمِرْصَادِ

> "Indeed, your Lord is Ever-Watchful (over them)."[138]

Thus, in all transactions involving cheating, fraud or deceit the affected party has the right to cancel the contract within any reasonable time.

11.6.11 Legal effect of a contract under fraud or cheating

There is a circumstance whereby a contract is entered into by a person under fraud or cheating, which is to say that the consent of a party to the contract has been obtained by the fraudulent act of the other party. In this situation, such a contract is deemed to be voidable, and the party whose consent had been obtained fraudulently by another person has a choice of whether to continue with the contract or rescind it.

Imam Shafie, Malik, Hambali, Ibadin, Ibn mas'ud, Ibn Amr, Abu Hurairah, Abu Yousuf and others are of the view that a contract made under fraud is voidable and thus it is the option of the party (victim) to ratify or to cancel the contract.[139]

11.7 The contracts contrary to *maqasid al-Shariah*

The objects or *maqasid* of the *Shariah* regarding a human being are fivefold: to preserve his/her religion, life, progeny, intellect and property. All the injunctions/commandments of the *Shariah* are directed towards the realisation of these five objectives known as the *maqasid al-Shariah*. These are:

1. Preservation of *Din* (religion).
2. Preservation of *Nafs* (life).
3. Preservation of *Nasl* (progeny).
4. Preservation of *'Aql* (intellect).
5. Preservation of *Mal* (property).

11.7.1 A contract should not be contrary to maqasid al-Shariah

Any transaction or contract that offends or jeopardises any of these objectives is invalid in Islamic law, i.e. any contract or agreement that militates against any of the above-mentioned objectives is not valid. Hence conformity of contracts and agreements with *maqasid al-Shariah* is the legal requirement in Islamic jurisprudence of contract.

It is pertinent to note here that the *maqasid al-Shariah* is alternatively referred to as *Huquq Allāh* (rights of God). A right of God in Islamic law refers to everything that involves the benefit of the community at large and the welfare of humanity. Taftazani defines *Huquq Allāh* in the following words:

> By rights of God is meant that which comprehends a public benefit, not peculiar to any individual. It is referred to as God because of the greatness of its significance and generality of benefit.[140]

Thus, *Huquq Allāh* in this sense corresponds with public rights or public policy in modern law which is made for the benefit and the welfare of the community at large. The objectives of *Shariah* or *Huquq Allāh* have been emphasised in a large number of texts of the Qur'ān and the Sunnah, for example for the protection of life. The following verses on this topic can be cited.

مِنْ أَجْلِ ذَٰلِكَ كَتَبْنَا عَلَىٰ بَنِيٓ إِسْرَٰٓءِيلَ أَنَّهُۥ مَن قَتَلَ نَفْسًۢا بِغَيْرِ نَفْسٍ أَوْ فَسَادٍ فِي ٱلْأَرْضِ فَكَأَنَّمَا قَتَلَ ٱلنَّاسَ
جَمِيعًا وَمَنْ أَحْيَاهَا فَكَأَنَّمَآ أَحْيَا ٱلنَّاسَ جَمِيعًاۚ وَلَقَدْ جَآءَتْهُمْ رُسُلُنَا بِٱلْبَيِّنَٰتِ ثُمَّ إِنَّ كَثِيرًا مِّنْهُم بَعْدَ ذَٰلِكَ فِي
ٱلْأَرْضِ لَمُسْرِفُونَ

> "On account of this, We prescribed (this commandment in the Torah sent down) to the Children of Israel that whoever killed a person (unjustly), except as a punishment for murder or for (spreading) disorder in the land, it would be as if he killed all the people (of society); and whoever (saved him from

unjust murder and) made him survive, it would be as if he saved the lives of all the people (of society, i.e., he rescued the collective system of human life). And indeed, Our Messenger came to them with evident signs. Yet, even after that, the majority from amongst these people are certainly those who commit excesses in the land."[141]

وَلَكُمۡ فِي ٱلۡقِصَاصِ حَيَوٰةٞ يَٰٓأُوْلِي ٱلۡأَلۡبَٰبِ لَعَلَّكُمۡ تَتَّقُونَ

"And there is a (guarantee of) life for you in retribution (i.e., the vengeance of murder), O wise people, so that you may guard (against bloodshed and destruction)."[142]

Similarly, for the protection of wealth and property, the Qur'ān says:

يَٰٓأَيُّهَا ٱلَّذِينَ ءَامَنُواْ لَا تَأۡكُلُوٓاْ أَمۡوَٰلَكُم بَيۡنَكُم بِٱلۡبَٰطِلِ إِلَّآ أَن تَكُونَ تِجَٰرَةً عَن تَرَاضٖ مِّنكُمۡۚ وَلَا تَقۡتُلُوٓاْ أَنفُسَكُمۡۚ
إِنَّ ٱللَّهَ كَانَ بِكُمۡ رَحِيمٗا

"O believers! Do not devour one another's wealth unlawfully amongst yourselves unless it is a trade by your mutual agreement and does not kill yourselves. Surely, Allāh is Kind to you."[143]

The following hadith can also be cited in this regard.

In a hadith, the Holy Prophet (PBUH) said: "Allāh u has made the life and property and honour of each one of you unto the other sacred and inviolable like this day of this month in this territory."[144]

These kinds of protection are named "public policy" in the other laws of the world and all the contracts and agreements are required to be in align or conformity with public policy. The Islamic law of contract also requires conformity of contracts and agreements with *maqasid al-Shariah.*

The requirement of the conformity of contract with the objectives of the *Shariah* is similar to the requirement of modern law that an agreement should not be against public policy.

11.8 Two mutually inconsistent contracts or contingent contracts

In Islamic law of contract, it is necessary that where there is more than one contract at a time, they must be congruent with each other and should not be mutually inconsistent. Along with all prohibited contracts, two mutually inconsistent contracts are also prohibited in Islamic law of contract, for example, the sale of two articles for two prices, contingent sale and the sale of a single object for two prices.[145] In this regard following the *ahadith* of the Holy Prophet (PBUH) it is cited:

> It is narrated by Abu Hurayrah (R.A) that the Holy Prophet (PBUH) prohibited from two sales in one sale (*bay 'atan fi bay'*).[146]

The *hadith* of two sales in one sale has been interpreted in several ways.

11.8.1 Prohibition of two mutually contingent contracts

Two mutually contingent and inconsistent contracts are prohibited by the Holy Prophet (PBUH). This refers to:

1. The sale of two articles in such a way that one who intends to purchase an article is obliged to purchase the other also at any given price.
2. This occurs where one person says to other "I sell you this article at this price on the condition that you sell your house at this price."
3. The sale of a single article for two prices when one of the prices is not finally stipulated at the time of the execution of the sale.
4. This kind of sale has been understood in two ways: In the first way, one of the two prices is payable in cash, and the other is payable later. For example, A says to B: "I sell you this commodity for one hundred in cash and one hundred and fifty on credit." In the second way, one of the contracting parties says: "I sell this garment cash down for such and such a price on the condition that I will repurchase it after a certain delay at a certain another price."
5. Contingent sale: it occurs when a contract is made contingent upon another contract when both are mutually inconsistent, for example: A says to B, "I sell you my house if C sells his house to me." Here the completion of the first contract is contingent upon the second contract.
6. Combining sale and lending in one contract.

In order to avoid this prohibition, jurists consider it preferable that a contract of sale must relate to only one transaction, and different contracts should not be mixed in such a way that the reward and liability of contracting parties involved in a transaction are not fully defined. Therefore, rather than signing a single contract to cover more than one transaction, parties should enter into separate transactions under separate contracts.

Islamic banks may come across several transactions in which there could be interdependent agreements or stipulations that have to be avoided. The combination of some contracts is permissible subject to certain conditions:

- *Bai'* (sale) and *ijarah* (leasing) are two contracts of totally different impacts; while ownership and risk are transferred to the buyer in *Bai'*, neither ownership nor risk transfer from the lessor to the lessee. It is necessary, therefore, that lease and sale are kept as separate agreements. In Islamic banks' *Ijarah Muntahia-bi-Tamleek* (lease culminating in the transfer of ownership to the lessee), the relationship between the parties throughout the lease period remains that of the lessor and lessee, and the bank remains liable for the risks and expenses relating to ownership. Transferring ownership risk to the lessee during the lease period would render the transaction void. However, one of the parties can undertake a unilateral promise to sell, buy or gift the asset at the termination of the lease period. This will not be binding on the other party.

- *Shirkah* and *ijarah* can be combined, meaning that a partner can give his part of ownership in an asset on lease to any co-partners. Jurists are unanimous about the permissibility of leasing one's undivided share in a property to any other partner.[147] However, the sale of ownership units to the client in diminishing *musharakh* will have to be kept totally separate, requiring "offer and acceptance" for each unit.
- *Musharakah* and *mudarabah* can also be combined. For example, banks manage depositor's funds on the basis of *mudarabah*; they can also deploy their funds in the business with the condition that the ratio of profit for a sleeping partner cannot be more than the ratio that their capital has in the total capital.
- Contracts of agency (*wakalah*) and surety-ship (*kafalah*) can also be combined with sale or lease contracts, with the condition that the rights and liabilities arising from various contracts are taken as per their own rules. As per the present practice of Islamic banks, *wakalah* is an essential component of *mudarabah, salam* and *istisna* agreements.
- Islamic banks can structure products by combining different modes subject to the fulfilment of their respective conditions. For example, they can combine *salam* or *istisna* with *murabaha* for pre-shipment export financing. Diminishing *musharakah* is also a combination of *shirkah* and *ijarah*, added by an undertaking by one party to periodically sell/purchase the ownership to/from another partner.

Similarly, the exchange of two liabilities is prohibited. Transactions between two parties involve an exchange of any of the following types: physical property for corporeal property, physical property for a corresponding liability or a liability for another liability. Each one of these can be immediate for both parties or delayed for both or immediate for one party and delayed for the other. In these ways, Ibn Rushd has identified nine kinds of sales.[148] Out of the above categories of exchange, an exchange involving delay from both sides is not permitted as it amounts to the exchange of debt for a debt, which is prohibited. That is why full prepayment is necessary for valid contracts of *salam*.

11.8.2 The prohibition of dealing in certain forbidden commodities

The Qur'ān forbids the consumption of prohibited things; their sale and trade are also illegal. Carrion, blood, swine, the animals over which Allah's name is not pronounced at the time of slaughtering are all prohibited, as well as the meat of animals that have been dedicated to idols. Allah says:

إِنَّمَا حَرَّمَ عَلَيْكُمُ ٱلْمَيْتَةَ وَٱلدَّمَ وَلَحْمَ ٱلْخِنزِيرِ وَمَآ أُهِلَّ بِهِۦ لِغَيْرِ ٱللَّهِ

> "He has made unlawful for you only the dead animals and blood and the flesh of swine and the animals over which, whilst sacrificing, the name of someone other than Allah has been invoked."[149]

If something is scripturally prohibited, the faithful are not allowed to consume it. Nor may they trade it, as is evidenced from the following narrative.

> 'Abd al-Rahman b. Wa'la al-Saba'I, who was from Egypt, reported that he asked 'Abd Allah b. 'Abbas (R.A) about what is extracted from grapes. Ibn 'Abbas (R.A) said that a man gave Prophet (PBUH) a small water-skin full of wine, and Prophet (PBUH) asked him: "Do you know that the Almighty Allah, has forbidden it?" He said: "No," then he whispered to another man. Holy Prophet (PBUH) said: "What have you whispered about?" He said: "I told him to sell it." The Prophet (PBUH) said: "The One who has forbidden drinking it has also forbidden selling it." So he opened the skin until its contents drained away.[150]

Islamic law prohibits using or dealing with certain commodities and sinful activities such as alcohol and its products, other intoxicants, drugs, pork, etc. Thus, individuals or institutions cannot use or exchange or trade or finance such ventures which deal with such forbidden commodities. To ensure the sustenance of legality and to avoid prohibitory dealings in all transactions. Ayatollah S.M. Teleghani wrote: "Islamic ordinance has a control function of both injection and prohibition (positive and negative) towards every single contract (*'aqd*) and transaction (*Mu'amalah*), so that they may prevent profit on nullity without beneficial work while upholding freedom."[151]

11.8.3 Prohibition of trickery in contracts

While entering into any commercial transaction and contract, parties should abstain from all kinds of trickery deception and dishonesty, etc. The following *hadith* is the basis of this:

> Narrated by Abdullah bin Umar (R.A) that a man mentioned to the Holy Prophet (PBUH) that he said: "When you enter a transaction say: 'No trickery,' so whenever that man entered a transaction, he would say, 'No trickery.'"[152]

Notes

1 Qur'ān, 55:7–9 (Eng. trans. from 'Glorious Qur'ān' by Shaykh-ul-Islam Dr. Muhammad Tahir-ul-Qadri).
2 M. Kabir Hassan, Rasem N. Kayed & Umar A. Oseni, Introduction to Islamic banking and finance, principles and practice, p. 110.
3 Ibn Jarir al-Tabari, Tafseer Ibn Jarir, vol. 3, p. 101.
4 Abubakr al-Jassas, Ahkamul Quran, p. 465.
5 Haqqi, A.R.A (2009), *The philosophy of Islamic law of transactions*, CERT publications.
6 Yahia Abdul-Rahman, The art of Islamic banking and finance (2010), pp. 2, 105, 106.
7 Muhammad ibn Mahmud Babarti, *al-Inayah ala al-Hidayah*, Cairo: Mustafa al-Bibi al-Halabi, 1970, vol. 7, p. 3.
8 Muhammad Ala Thanwi, *Kashshaf Istilahat alfunum*, vol. 3, Beirut, Sharikat al-Khayyat le al-kutub, 1998, p. 592.

9 Nabil A. Saleh, Unlawful gain and legitimate profit in Islamic law, 2nd ed. pp. 13, 15.
10 Qur'ān 2:275 (Eng. trans. from 'Glorious Qur'ān' by Shaykh-ul-Islam Dr. Muhammad Tahir-ul-Qadri).
11 Qur'ān 30:39 (Eng. trans. from 'Glorious Qur'ān' by Shaykh-ul-Islam Dr. Muhammad Tahir-ul-Qadri).
12 Qur'ān 4:161 (Eng. trans. from 'Glorious Qur'ān' by Shaykh-ul-Islam Dr. Muhammad Tahir-ul-Qadri).
13 Qur'ān 3:130 (Eng. trans. from 'Glorious Qur'ān' by Shaykh-ul-Islam Dr. Muhammad Tahir-ul-Qadri).
14 Qur'ān 2:275-6 (Eng. trans. from 'Glorious Qur'ān' by Shaykh-ul-Islam Dr. Muhammad Tahir-ul-Qadri).
15 Qur'ān 2:278-80 (Eng. trans. from 'Glorious Qur'ān' by Shaykh-ul-Islam Dr. Muhammad Tahir-ul-Qadri).
16 As quoted by Mufti Muhammad Shafi, The issue of interest (in Urdu—1996), Idara Muarif, Karachi, p. 79.
17 Imam Nisai, Sunan Nisai, Hadith No.4504.
18 Imam Muslim, Sahih Muslim, Hadith No.2991.
19 Imam Tirmizi, Sunan Tirmizi, Hadith No.1161.
20 Abu Daud, *al-Sunan*, Hadith No.3334, (Al-Rushd Publication) 2003.
21 Imam Muslim, *Sahih*, Chapter of Hajj.
22 Imam Muslim *Sahih*, Hadith No.4093, Darussalam Publishers, 1999.
23 Imam Muslim *Sahih*, Hadith No.4064, Darussalam Publishers (1999), p. 953.
24 Muhammad al-Bukhari, Sahih Bukhari Hadith No.6857 (Darussalam Publishers, 1999) 572.
25 Narrated by al-Bazzar in al-Musnad, 5:318 #1935; al-Mundhiri, al-Targhibwa al-Tarhib, 3:5 #2846; and al-Haythami in Majma al-Zawaid, 4:117.
26 Narrated by Ahmad b. Hanbal in al-Musnad, 5:225 #22007; al-Tabarani in al-Mu'jam al-Awsat, 3:125 #2682; and al-Daraqutni in al-Sunan, 3:16 #48.
27 Narrated by Ibn Majah in al-Sunan, 2:765 #2279.
28 Narrated by Imam Muslim in al-Sahih, 3:1209 #1585.
29 As quoted by Mufti Muhammad Shafi, The issue of interest (in Urdu, 1996), Idara Muarif, Karachi, p. 79.
30 As quoted by Mufti Muhammad Shafi, The issue of interest (in Urdu, 1996), Idara Muarif, Karachi, p. 79.
31 Ali Saeed al-Shamrani, Islamic financial contracting forms in Saudi Arabia: Law and practice (A thesis submitted for the degree of PhD), p. 42–44.
32 Muhammad Ayub, Understanding Islamic finance (John Wiley & Sons Ltd 2007) 50.
33 Angelo Venardos, Islamic banking and finance in South-East Asia: Its development and future (world scientific publishing Co Ltd 2005) 73; Kabir Hassan and Mervyn Lewis, Handbook of Islamic banking (Edward Elgar publishing Ltd 2007) 43.
34 Angelo Venardos, Islamic banking and finance in South-East Asia: Its development and future (world scientific publishing Co Ltd 2005) 73; Hij Siti Faridah Abd Jabbar, Islamic finance: fundamental principles and key financial institutions, Company Lawyer (2009) 30 (1) 2.
35 Hij Siti Faridah Abd Jabbar, Islamic finance: fundamental principles and key financial institutions, Company Lawyer (2009) 30 (1) 2.
36 Narrated by Abu Dawud in al-Sunan, 3:244 #3334; and al-Bayhaqi in al-Sunan al-Kubra, 5:275 #10245.
37 Narrated by al-Bukhari in al-Sahih, 3:1388 #3603.
38 Narrated by Ibn Majah in al-Sunan, 2:813 #2432.
39 Narrated by al-Bukhari in al-Sahih, 2:726 #1955.
40 Ali Saeed al-Shamrani, Islamic financial contracting forms in Saudi Arabia: Law and practice (A thesis submitted for the degree of PhD), pp. 42–44.

41 Muhammad Ayub, Understanding Islamic finance (John Wiley & Sons Ltd 2007) 53; Hij Siti Faridah Abd Jabbar, Islamic finance: fundamental principles and key financial institutions, Company Lawyer (2009) 30 (1) 3.
42 Muslim ibn al-Hajjaj Nisaboori, Sihih Muslim; Hadith # 4063 (Darussalam Publishers 1999) 953.
43 Mahmoud El-Gamal, Islamic finance; law, economics and practice (Cambridge University Press 2006) 51.
44 Narrated by al-Bukhari in al-Sahih, 2:767 #2089.
45 Narrated by Imam Muslim in al-Sahih, 3:1211 #1584.
46 Narrated by Imam Muslim in al-Sahih, 3:1209 #1585.
47 Narrated by Imam Muslim in al-Sahih, 3:1211 #1584.
48 Narrated by Imam Muslim in al-Sahih, 3:1214 #1592.
49 Narrated by Abu Dawud in al-Sunan, 3:249 #3352.
50 Muhammad Darir, *al-Gharar fi al-uqud*, Beirut, Muassasat al-Rsalah, 1999, p. 35.
51 Sarakhasi, al-Mabsut, Beirut, Dir al-Maarif, 1978, vol. 13, p. 194.
52 Ibn Hazm, al-Muhalla, Dar al-Afaq al-Jadid, vol. 8, pp. 343-389.
53 Ibn Abidin, Radd al-Muhtar, vol. 4, p. 147.
54 Ibn al-Qayyim, I'lam al-Muqin, vol. 1, p. 357.
55 Ibn Rushd, Bidayat al-Mujtahid, vol. 2, p. 156.
56 Sanhuri, Masadir al-Haqq, vol. 3, pp. 31–41.
57 Ibn Taymiyyah, *Nazariyah al-Aqad*, Beirut, Dar al-ilm 1323H, p. 24.
58 Imam Malik, *Muwatta*, 5 Cairo, Matba'ah as-Saadah 1332 H, p. 42.
59 Muhammad Ayub, *Understanding Islamic finance*. England: John Wiley & sons Ltd: p. 58.
60 Qur'ān 4:29 (Eng. trans. from 'Glorious Qur'ān' by Shaykh-ul-Islam Dr. Muhammad Tahir-ul-Qadri).
61 Qur'ān 2:188 (Eng. trans. from 'Glorious Qur'ān' by Shaykh-ul-Islam Dr. Muhammad Tahir-ul-Qadri).
62 Abu Dawud, *al-Sunan*, Hadith No.3503, Muslim, Sahih Muslim, vol. 3, p. 56.
63 Ibn Rushd, *Bidayah al-Mujtahid*, vol. 2, p. 146–148.
64 Noel J. Coulson, *Commercial law in Gulf States*, p. 21.
65 Al-Sarakhsi. *Kitab al-Mabsut*, vol. 13, p. 124, see also ibn Juzay, *al-Qawanin Fiqhiyyah*, p. 269.
66 Al-Kasani, *Badai' al-Sanai'*, vol. 5, p. 211.
67 Sharbiny, Mughni Muhtaj, vol. 2, p. 106, see also Ibn Qudamah, *al-Mughni*, vol. 4, p. 293.
68 Al-Zuhayli, Wahbah, *al-Fiqhul Islamy wa Adillatuh*, vol. 4, p. 636.
69 Mohd Sahri Abd. Rahman, *The gharar in share trading*, 1994, monograph, p. 8.
70 Hij Siti Faridah Abd Jabbar, Islamic finance: fundamental principles and key financial institutions, Company Lawyer (2009) 30 (1) 3.
71 Hashim Kamali, Uncertainty and risk taking (Gharar) in Islamic law, IIUM Law Journal, 1999, vol. 7, # 2, p. 200.
72 Robert Roberts, *The social laws of the Qur'ān*, p. 116.
73 Gibb and Kramer, *Shorter encyclopaedia of Islam*, p. 315.
74 Al-Nawawi, op. cit, p. 483.
75 M. Kabir Hassan, Rasem N. Kayed & Umar A. Oseni, Introduction to Islamic banking and finance, principles and practice, p. 71.
76 M.K. Hassan, Et. Al, *Introduction to Islamic banking and finance* 71 (2013).
77 M. Obaidullah, *Financial engineering with Islamic options*, *Islamic economic studies* 6, No.1, 84 (1998).
78 Y.T.Delorenzo, *Covered options, scholars's answers*, http://musliminvestor.com/answers/covered-options.html. March 17, 2016.
79 M. El-Gamal, *Discussion forum: Islamic financial derivatives*, in international journal of Islamic financial services, 1 (1999).

80 Franz Rosenthan, *Gambling in Islam*, E.J. Brill, Leiden, Netherlands; 1975, pp. 1–2.
81 'Abdullah Yusuf 'Ali, The Holy Qur'ān, translation and commentary, al-Rajihi company, Saudi Arabia, (1983), p. 111.
82 Qur'ān 5:90 (Eng. trans. from 'Glorious Qur'ān' by Shaykh-ul-Islam Dr. Muhammad Tahir-ul-Qadri).
83 Qur'ān 2:219 (Eng. trans. from 'Glorious Qur'ān' by Shaykh-ul-Islam Dr. Muhammad Tahir-ul-Qadri).
84 Qur'ān 5:90-91 (Eng. trans. from 'Glorious Qur'ān' by Shaykh-ul-Islam Dr. Muhammad Tahir-ul-Qadri).
85 Qur'ān 5:3 (Eng. trans. from 'Glorious Qur'ān' by Shaykh-ul-Islam Dr. Muhammad Tahir-ul-Qadri).
86 M. Kabir Hassan, Rasem N. Kayed & Umar A. Oseni, Introduction to Islamic banking and finance, principles and practice, p. 71.
87 M.A. Mannan, *Islamic economics, theory and practice (A comparative study)*, p. 194.
88 Anwar Ahmad Qadri, *Islamic jurisprudence in the modern world*, p. 352.
89 Dr. Umar A. Farrukh, *Ibn Taimiyya on public and private law*, Beirut, p. 173.
90 Sir Abdul Rahim, Muhammadan law, pp. 223–224
91 Qur'ān, 7:85 (Eng. trans. from 'Glorious Qur'ān' by Shaykh-ul-Islam Dr. Muhammad Tahir-ul-Qadri).
92 Qur'ān, 11:87 (Eng. trans. from 'Glorious Qur'ān' by Shaykh-ul-Islam Dr. Muhammad Tahir-ul-Qadri).
93 Qur'ān, 11:94-95 (Eng. trans. from 'Glorious Qur'ān' by Shaykh-ul-Islam Dr. Muhammad Tahir-ul-Qadri).
94 Qur'ān 11:86 (Eng. trans. from 'Glorious Qur'ān' by Shaykh-ul-Islam Dr. Muhammad Tahir-ul-Qadri).
95 Qur'ān 83:1-6 (Eng. trans. from 'Glorious Qur'ān' by Shaykh-ul-Islam Dr. Muhammad Tahir-ul-Qadri).
96 Qur'ān 4:29 (Eng. trans. from 'Glorious Qur'ān' by Shaykh-ul-Islam Dr. Muhammad Tahir-ul-Qadri).
97 Qur'ān 25:72 (Eng. trans. from 'Glorious Qur'ān' by Shaykh-ul-Islam Dr. Muhammad Tahir-ul-Qadri).
98 Muhammad Afzal, *The Message of the Qur'ān*, p. 558.
99 Qur'ān 11:84 (Eng. trans. from 'Glorious Qur'ān' by Shaykh-ul-Islam Dr. Muhammad Tahir-ul-Qadri).
100 Qur'ān 55:9 (Eng. trans. from 'Glorious Qur'ān' by Shaykh-ul-Islam Dr. Muhammad Tahir-ul-Qadri).
101 Dr. Ahmad A. Galwash, *The religion of Islam*, vol. 2, Doha Printing Press, Doha, 1963, p. 30.
102 Qur'ān 2:188 (Eng. trans. from 'Glorious Qur'ān' by Shaykh-ul-Islam Dr. Muhammad Tahir-ul-Qadri).
103 Qur'ān 2:174 (Eng. trans. from 'Glorious Qur'ān' by Shaykh-ul-Islam Dr. Muhammad Tahir-ul-Qadri).
104 Narrated by Abu Dawud in al-Sunan, 3:272 #3452.
105 Narrated by Imam Muslim in al-Sahih, 4:2197 #2865.
106 Narrated by al-Bukhari in al-Sahih, 2:732 #1973.
107 Narrated by al-Bukhari in al-Sahih, 2:731 #1972.
108 Narrated by Imam Muslim in al-Sahih, 1:99 #102.
109 Narrated by al-Bayhaqi in al-Sunan, 5:348 #10707.
110 Muhammad ibn Ismail Bukhari, *Sahih*, Beriut: Dar al-Kitab al-Arabi, 1323AH, No.2079, p. 410.
111 Muhammad ibn Ismail Bukhari, *Sahih*, Beriut: Dar al-Kitab al-Arabi, 1323AH, No.2087, p. 412.
112 Ibn Majah, *Sunan*, No.2205, vol. 2, p. 743.
113 Ibn Majah, *Sunan*, No.2139, vol. 2, p. 724.

114 Muslim, *Sahih*, No.102, vol. 1, p. 99.
115 *Bukhari*, as quoted in Dr. S.E. Rayner, Theory of contract in Islamic law, 1991 p. 216.
116 Qur'ān, 3:77 (Eng. trans. from 'Glorious Qur'ān' by Shaykh-ul-Islam Dr. Muhammad Tahir-ul-Qadri).
117 Narrated by al-Bukhari in al-Sahih, 2:735 #1981.
118 Narrated by Imam Muslim in al-Sahih, 3:1228 #1607.
119 Al-'Asqalani, Fath al-bari, 4:100.
120 Narrated by Imam Muslim in al-Sahih,1:102 #106.
121 Narrated by al-Bukhari in al-Sahih, 2:735 #1982.
122 Narrated by Ahmad b. Hanbal in al-Musnad, 3:428 #15569.
123 Narrated by al-Tirmadhi in al-Sunan, 5:236 #3020.
124 *Sahih Bukhari*, English translation by Muhammad Muhsin Khan, Nadvi and Munawar Edition, p. 170.
125 *Sahih Bukhari*, English translation by Muhammad Muhsin Khan, Nadvi and Munawar Edition, p. 170.
126 Narrated by Ibn Majah in al-Sunan, 2:2246.
127 Narrated by Ibn Majah in al-Sunan, 2:755 #2247.
128 Narrated by Imam Muslim in al-Sahih, 1:99 #102.
129 Narrated by al-Bukhari in al-Sahih, 2:732 #1973.
130 Qur'ān, 3:180 (Eng. trans. from 'Glorious Qur'ān' by Shaykh-ul-Islam Dr. Muhammad Tahir-ul-Qadri).
131 Qur'ān, 104:2-9 (Eng. trans. from 'Glorious Qur'ān' by Shaykh-ul-Islam Dr. Muhammad Tahir-ul-Qadri).
132 Qur'ān, 9:34-5 (Eng. trans. from 'Glorious Qur'ān' by Shaykh-ul-Islam Dr. Muhammad Tahir-ul-Qadri).
133 Narrated by Imam Muslim in al-Sahih, 3:1227 #1605.
134 Narrated by Ahmad b. Hanbal in al-Musnad, 2:33 #4880.
135 Narrated by Imam Muslim in al-Sahih, 3:1228 #1605.
136 Narrated by al-Tabarani in al-Mujam al-Kabir, 20:95 #186.
137 Narrated by Ibn Majah in al-Sunan, 2:278 #2153.
138 Qur'ān, 89:14 (Eng. trans. from 'Glorious Qur'ān' by Shaykh-ul-Islam Dr. Muhammad Tahir-ul-Qadri).
139 Dr. S.E. Rayner, Theory of contract in Islamic law, 1991, p. 221.
140 Masud ibn Umar Taftazani, *al-Talwih*, Cairo: Maktabah Muhammad Ali Sabih, 1957, vol. 2, p. 151.
141 Qur'ān 5:32 (Eng. trans. from 'Glorious Qur'ān' by Shaykh-ul-Islam Dr. Muhammad Tahir-ul-Qadri).
142 Qur'ān 2:179 (Eng. trans. from 'Glorious Qur'ān' by Shaykh-ul-Islam Dr. Muhammad Tahir-ul-Qadri).
143 Qur'ān 4:29 (Eng. trans. from 'Glorious Qur'ān' by Shaykh-ul-Islam Dr. Muhammad Tahir-ul-Qadri).
144 Bukhari, *Sahih*, Hadith No.7447, p. 1562.
145 R.H. Nawawi, *Islamic law on commercial transactions*, (Kuala Lumpur CERT Publication Sdn. Bhd; 2009), pp. 59–100.
146 Abu Dawud, *Sunan*, Hadith No.3540, vol. 3, p. 769.
147 Usmani, 2000a p. 86.
148 Ibn Rushd, 1950, p. 125.
149 Qur'ān, 2:173 (Eng. trans. from 'Glorious Qur'ān' by Shaykh-ul-Islam Dr. Muhammad Tahir-ul-Qadri).
150 Narrated by Imam Muslim in al-Sahih, 3:1206 #1579.
151 Ayatullah Sayyid Mahmud Teleghani, Society and economics in Islam, (trans. From Persian) by R. Cambell (1982), p. 31 as quoted in Dr. Liaqat Ali Khan.
152 Imam Malik Ibn Anas, Al-Muwatta (trans. Eng), Aisha Abd Al-Rahman Bewley, 1989, No.98 at 278.

12 Classification of contract

Early jurists and legal experts classified the contracts concerning several perspectives and explained them by assigning them different terms and names. Much literature is available on these classifications of the contracts. While describing the categories, independent legal reasoning and the various perspectives of contracts were kept in view by the learned jurists.

A cursory review of the academic literature shows that the early as well as modern jurists, while discussing the various classification of contracts, classified a contract according to its nature, circumstances, legal consequences, functions, purposes and according to its time of completion, etc.

12.1 Classifications of the contract according to its nature

Most Muslim jurists have classified contracts according to their nature, including whether they are *Shariah*-compliant or contain some prohibited elements such as interest-bearing, deceptive, speculative or fortuitous elements. The nature of a contract is considered in line with explicit provisions in the texts used to assess the legality or otherwise of certain contractual transactions. This classification includes unilateral contracts (*'aqd infiradi*), bilateral contracts (*'aqd thuna'i*), quasi-contracts (*shibh al-'aqd*) and joint contracts or multilateral contracts.

12.2 Unilateral contract (*'aqd infiradi*)

A unilateral contract is defined as a transaction by one party only, or by which one party binds himself.[1]

According to another source, a unilateral contract is:

> One in which the offeror promises to pay for an act done by the other party, the acceptance takes the form of performing the act. The offer and resulting contract are unilateral, that is, one-sided because only one party makes a promise.[2]

Hence a unilateral contract is considered as a one-party transaction, i.e. which is made by a single person who intends to establish a form of legal relationship with another party through a promise. Such a promise is a self-imposed contract and becomes binding on the person who makes it. It only becomes binding on the person in whose favour it has been made once he or she accepts the promise. A typical example of a unilateral contract is a promise made by somebody in the form of a reward for whoever does something or finds a missing thing. Such reward (*ju'alah*) is usually open to anyone and whoever finds the thing becomes entitled to the reward and thus may be regarded as accepting the offer. The permissibility of a unilateral contract is approved by the majority of Muslim jurists based on the event narrated in the Qur'ān on what transpired between Prophet Yusuf (Joseph) and his brothers.

قَالُواْ نَفْقِدُ صُوَاعَ ٱلْمَلِكِ وَلِمَن جَآءَ بِهِۦ حِمْلُ بَعِيرٍ وَأَنَا۠ بِهِۦ زَعِيمٌ

> "They (the servants of the king's court) said: 'We are missing the royal goblet, and the man who brings it (after searching) will get a camel's load of grain as a reward and I pledge myself for it.'"[3]

The following two Qur'ānic verses are also quoted for unilateral contracts: وَأَوْفُواْ بِٱلْعَهْدِۖ إِنَّ ٱلْعَهْدَ كَانَ مَسْـُٔولًا

> "And always fulfil the promise. No doubt, the promise will be questioned about."[4]
>
> وَإِذْ أَخَذَ رَبُّكَ مِنۢ بَنِيٓ ءَادَمَ مِن ظُهُورِهِمْ ذُرِّيَّتَهُمْ وَأَشْهَدَهُمْ عَلَىٰٓ أَنفُسِهِمْ أَلَسْتُ بِرَبِّكُمْۖ قَالُواْ بَلَىٰ شَهِدْنَآ
>
> "And (call to mind) when your Lord brought forth the human race from the loins of the Children of Adam and made them bear testimony to their own souls (and said:) 'Am I not your Lord?' They (all) said: 'Why not! We bear witness (that You alone are our Lord.)'"[5]

The contracts mentioned in all the above Qur'ānic verses are unilateral in nature.

12.3 Bilateral contract (*'aqd thuna'i*)

A law dictionary defines a bilateral contract as "the one, in which the parties are under an obligation reciprocally towards each other whereby for instance one party, in a contract of sale and purchase, becomes bound to deliver the thing sold while the other to pay the price."[6]

"A bilateral contract is a contract in which of the two parties is bound to fulfil obligations towards the other."[7]

The *Medjelle* defines a bilateral contract as when "Two parties taking upon themselves an undertaking to do something. It is composed of the combination of an offer and an acceptance."[8]

From the above-mentioned definitions, it is clear that for bilateral contracts there should be at least two contracting parties One party makes an offer, the other accepts and the contract becomes binding on both parties providing the subject matter is ascertained, and it falls within the scope of items that are tradable. In this case, there must be a consensus among the parties, which is usually based on mutual consent. Once the offer has been accepted, a legal relationship is established between the parties and individual rights and obligations are also established.

The following Qur'ānic verses are quoted for bilateral contracts.

يَٰٓأَيُّهَا ٱلَّذِينَ ءَامَنُوٓاْ أَوۡفُواْ بِٱلۡعُقُودِ

> "O believers! Fulfil (your) promises."[9]

أَوۡفُواْ بِٱلۡعَهۡدِۖ إِنَّ ٱلۡعَهۡدَ كَانَ مَسۡـُٔولٗا

> "And always fulfil the promise. No doubt, the promise will be questioned about."[10]

Bilateral contracts are broadly divided into the following six kinds by Muslim jurists:

i. Contracts of exchange (*mu'awadah*).
ii. Contracts of security (*tawthiqat*).
iii. Contracts of the partnership (*shirkah*).
iv. Contracts of safe custody (*wadi'ah*).
v. Contracts relating to the use of an asset (*ijarah*).
vi. Contracts relating to the performance of a work or rendering of specific services (e.g. *wakalah* and *ju'alah*).

The above bilateral contracts are the most prevalent forms commonly practised of contracts in modern Islamic financial transactions. The above list is not final; any contract other than these if it fulfils the requirements of a bilateral contract may be added to this list.

12.4 Multilateral contracts

As above, we mentioned that unilateral contracts are those which are entered into by just one individual and in the case of bilateral contracts entered into by at least two parties. In some situations, they can even be entered into by a group of people. Those contracts are called multilateral contracts, in which a group of people can enter into a valid legal relationship that binds all of them in a joint contract. For example, in a case whereby property is jointly owned by a group of owners and these owners wish to sell it, these owners may sell that property with the condition that they are in complete agreement to do so.

Likewise, if a single owner of the land wishes to sell his land to a group of people which has common interests over that land the owner of that land may do so. In both examples, such contracts are known as joint contracts and are binding on all the parties involved in those contracts.

In the case of any breach of contract by any of the individuals of the joint party, all partners (joint parties) must share the responsibility of such a breach. In other words, if one of the several partners of the joint party breaches a condition of the contract, the other affected party may bring an action against every partner of the joint party in law.[11]

It is to be observed that in the application of a joint contract, none of the partners of the joint party has the right to do anything which might be injurious to the rights of the other fellow partners.[12]

12.5 Quasi-contract (*shibh al-'aqd*)

In the dictionary, a quasi-contract has been defined as:

> An act or event from which, though not a consensual contract, an obligation arises as if from a contract, for instance, an executor or administrator is bound to satisfy the liabilities of the decreased if he has contracted to do so.[13]

Basically, a quasi-contract is an arrangement that is not a contract in its real sense but resembles one. By its very nature, it is not a contract, but its legal implication establishes what may be likened to a contract. In essence, a quasi-contract is an obligation that originates from the operation of law and not by an agreement between parties. Some bilateral contracts can also be transformed into quasi-contracts depending on the manner in which they were created. For instance, when a buyer wrongly pays the price of a commodity to the wrong person due to a mistaken identity, such a relationship is a quasi-contract, as it is not originally based on mutual consent. As a result, the person receiving the money in error or wrongly must return it to the buyer for onward payment to the rightful seller.

The following Qur'ānic verse is quoted for quasi-contracts:

إِنَّ ٱللَّهَ يَأۡمُرُكُمۡ أَن تُؤَدُّواْ ٱلۡأَمَٰنَٰتِ إِلَىٰٓ أَهۡلِهَا

> "Surely, Allāh commands you to render the trusts to those who are worthy of them."[14]

12.6 Classification of a contract according to its legal consequences

The jurist and experts of Islamic law of contracts have also classified contracts based on their legal consequences into different kinds. Some authors like Dr. Hussain Hamid Hassan explained it concerning the validity and invalidity of a contract. This classification emphasises the extent of the validity or binding nature of a particular contract. Thus, the legal consequences of a contract may result in being declared as valid (*sahih*), invalid or deficient (*fasid*), void (*batil*) and binding (*lazim*). The classification according to the legal consequences is essential to establish enforceability and unenforceability of a contract. Now we discuss these kinds in a little bit more detail.

*12.6.1 Valid contract (*sahih*)*

"A valid contract is one whose essential elements are completed and whose conditions are fulfilled and which is not prohibited by the lawgiver."[15]

More specifically, when all elements or ingredients of a contract, such as its form, i.e. offer and acceptance, its subject matter, and contracting parties are there, in order for all conditions to have been met, and also free from vitiating and prohibited factors, the contract may be regarded as a valid one.

The *Medjelle* defines it as *al-Baiy*, which in its substance and attributes is according to the law.[16] If we elaborate this definition of *Medjelle* we may say that when a contract as regards both of its *asle* (essential elements, nature or essence) and *wasf* (external attributes) is in accordance with Islamic law of contract, it is said to be a "valid contract."

In other words, a valid contract under Islamic law of contract requires the following attributes:

i. The parties to the contract must possess legal capacity.
ii. The mode of contract must be in line with the *Shariah*.
iii. The objective of the contract must be valuable or recognised by the Islamic provisions.
iv. The consideration must also be valuable.
v. The consent of the parties must be obtained freely.
vi. Any aspect of the contract must not be contrary to public policy (i.e. the *Shariah*).
vii. No aspect of the contract shall involve fraud, misrepresentation, undue influence or illegality, etc.[17]

The following Qur'ānic verses are quoted for the fulfilment of a valid contract:
أَوْفُوا بِالْعَهْدِ إِنَّ الْعَهْدَ كَانَ مَسْئُولًا

> "And always fulfil the promise. No doubt, the promise will be questioned about."[18]

*12.6.2 Invalid or deficient contract (*fasid*)*

An invalid contract is an agreement between the parties whereby the foundation of the contract is valid but the attributes of the contract are unlawful.[19] It means that if a contract is lawful in its substance but unlawful in its description, it is invalid. The description in a contract may involve the specification of price or the quality of the subject matter. If either of these is missing in the contract, it will be declared deficient or invalid. If there is any defect in the price of the goods sold, that contract becomes an invalid contract.[20]

Hence from the above, it is clear that any form of contract short of critical elements or missing elements for a valid contract may be considered an invalid contract. It shall only be validated if the items that make it deficient are duly addressed and removed from it.

12.6.2.1 Legal effect of an invalid contract

An invalid contract is not enforceable under Islamic law. According to Imam Abu Hanifa, an invalid contract cannot be completed by possession. Once it is concluded, it has to be revoked by either party.[21]

In an invalid contract, some rights are available for the contracting parties. "Once the contract is concluded, either party or both, have the right to revoke the contract, regardless of whether the goods have been transferred or not, or whether the price has been paid or not."[22] It means that if the price has been paid by the buyer, the buyer has the right to recover it. The buyer has the right to keep the goods until the seller returns the price paid.[23] Similarly, if the goods sold have been transferred by the seller to the buyer, the seller has the right to claim the goods back. If the goods become perished in the hands of the buyer, the buyer is liable to compensate it.[24] Once the contract is concluded, the buyer has no right to claim the goods from the seller, nor the seller has the right to claim the price of the goods sold.

*12.6.3 Void contract (***batil***)*

A contract that does not fulfil the conditions relating to form, i.e. offer and acceptance, subject matter, consideration, etc. or involves any illegal external attribute is regarded as a void contract. *Medjelle* defines a void contract as "a contract which is not good in its foundation"[25] or we may say that when a contract with regard to its *asal* and *wasf* is not in accordance with Islamic law of contract, it is said to be a void contract. "A void contract is a sale that has a defect in its essential aspects, such as a sale by an insane person."[26]

Below are the circumstances whereby a contract is said to be void:

i. A contract made by a legally incapable party or parties.
ii. A contract made by either or both parties upon a mistake.
iii. A contract made without valid consideration.
iv. A contract which involves immorality or illegality.
v. A contract whose objectives are unlawful.
vi. A contract which is made against public policy.
vii. A contract to restrain a legal trade.
viii. A contract which involves impossibility or frustration of performance.
ix. If the foundation or substance of a contract is unlawful or illegal.
x. Any other contract or agreement which is directly or indirectly contrary to the divine sanctions is void *ab initio*.

Dr. Hussain Hamid Hassan suggests: "A void contract has no existence in the eyes of the law, it does not confer a right, does not become obligatory and does not transfer any property."[27]

12.6.3.1 Legal effect of a void contract

The legal effects of a void contract are as follows: a void contract cannot be validated by a consent.[28] A void contract cannot confer any beneficial consequences,[29] for it always results in a negative consequence, i.e. not enforceable in the eyes of the law.

12.6.4 Voidable contract

A voidable contract is: "One which may be either avoided or confirmed by matter arising exposes facts."[30] A voidable contract is one whose essential elements exist, and the conditions required are also fulfilled, but some vitiating factor or element is connected with it. It is a contract that is legally recognised by its essence (*asl*) and not by its circumstances (*wasf*).[31]

12.6.4.1 Legal effect of voidable contract

In a voidable contract, one of the parties has the free option and choice of either continuing with the contract or rescinding it. It must be remembered that from the moment when the contract is entered into, until the time when the party makes his choice, the voidable contract shall have the legal effect which it is intended to have. Such a voidable contract can, however, be disputed only by certain persons under certain conditions and the right of the recession may be bounded by the party entitled to exercise it. If a third person acquires rights under a voidable contract or other transaction without notice and for value, he cannot afterwards be put in a worse position by it being set aside.

Similarly, it must be kept in mind that, for the cancellation of a voidable contract, one contracting party does not require the consent of another party, but each of them has the right to cancel it independently, but by bringing it the other party's knowledge. However, when contracting parties execute the voidable contract and things sold are handed over to the purchaser by the seller, then it cannot be rescinded in such a way as before taking the possession.

*12.6.5 Binding contract/enforceable contract (***nafidh***)*

When a contract is a sound in its substance and description, it becomes binding on the parties and is enforceable under the law. A binding contract can either be revocable or irrevocable. A revocable contract is a binding contract where either of the parties is given an option to revoke the contract at any stage; for example, partnership contracts such as *musharakah* and *mudarabah* are revocable. An agency contract (*wakalah*) is also revocable at the instigation of either of the parties. Irrevocable binding contracts are those that cannot be revoked at any stage once they are concluded. For example, if a valid contract of sale is duly executed while its substance and description are both lawful, none of the parties can rescind the contract without reasonable grounds. A binding contract is enforceable under the law. An enforceable contract does not usually affect the rights of a third party. It only relates to the rights of the parties to the contract. Therefore, all binding contracts are enforceable.

12.6.6 Unenforceable or non-binding contract

An unenforceable contract is different from a void contract. The unenforceable contract is based on three circumstances which are as follows:

i. A contract which is unenforceable permanently.
ii. A contract which is unenforceable temporarily.
iii. A contract that is either unenforceable temporarily or permanently.

12.6.7 A contract which is unenforceable permanently

A contract, which cannot be enforced at all at any time and in any situation, is called an unenforceable permanently; such as a contract with an illegal foundation or substance or a contract whose subject matter according to the Islamic law of contract is illegal or unlawful. For example, a contract to sell pork is permanently unenforceable.

12.6.8 A contract which is temporarily unenforceable

A contract may sometime be unenforceable only for a particular time span. An easy example of such a contract is a contract whereby both parties verbally agree to conclude it by signing a formal written agreement; it remains unenforceable temporarily unless and until a formal written agreement is prepared and signed by both parties; on the signing of a formal written agreement in the future the contract becomes enforceable.

12.6.9 A contract which is either temporarily or permanently unenforceable

Actually, this is the form of contract which is called voidable; in which a party has the option either to terminate it or to rectify it.

12.7 Classification of contracts about the time of completion

Having regard to time of completion, the Muslim jurists have divided contracts into the following three kinds.[32]

1. **Contract immediately enforceable:** This is a contract which unconditionally becomes complete after the offer is accepted and its consequences in the form of obligation ensue immediately. Thus, a contract will be regarded immediately enforceable if:
   i. It is free from any option reserved for a party, like the option of the buyer to revoke a contract within some time/days.
   ii. It does not depend upon ratification by the party concerned.
   iii. It is not contingent upon a condition or the occurrence of an uncertain event in the future.

2. **Contract effective from future date:** Such a contract is not valid according to the majority of the jurists since they hold that the effects should ensue immediately without any delay.[33] They, however, allow the contracts made on usufructs to be effective from a future date like the contract of leasing, manufacturing, suretyship, and *hawalah*, i.e. assignment of debt. Similarly, agency, divorce and *wafq* contracts are also valid from a future date.
3. **Contingent contract:** This is also called a conditional contract. It is a contact which is contingent upon the occurrence of an uncertain event. Such a contract takes effect on the occurrence of the contingency. As a general rule, the contingent contract is not valid mainly when they belong to the class of commutative contracts. According to Hanafi jurists, even the gratuitous contracts are not permissible if made to take effect on the occurrence of the contingency. There are, however, some exceptions to this general rule and there are some contracts which are allowed to be made contingent upon an uncertain event such as agency, bequest, and suretyship, assignment of debt and divorce.[34]

12.8 Classification according to the purpose of contracts

Jurist also classified the contracts according to the purpose of a contract into the following seven kinds:

1. **The contract for ownership or alienation of property:** The contracts of ownership are those contracts whose purpose is to make a person owner of a property or its usufructs. They may be for consideration, such as contract of sale and hire. Other examples are money-changing, composition, manufacturing contract and assignment of debt, etc. They may be made without consideration as in will and donation etc.[35]
2. **Contracts extinguishing rights:** These are also called contracts of abandonment which refer to surrendering of rights to a person or property such as in discharging of debt. The object of such contracts is to extinguish established rights. They may also be with consideration and without consideration.
3. **Contracts of authorisation:** These are also called the contracts of replacement authority which refer to authorising any third party to act as replacement or substitute for a party. The purpose of these contracts is to delegate power or authority to a party to carry out a transaction as in proxy such as agency, permission to a person placed under an interdiction person for dispositions.
4. **Contracts limiting the rights of others:** These contracts are used to confine or restrict the liberty of a party's conduct and to prevent him/her from the right of disposal and use of the property. Examples are preventing insane, lunatic, minor and insolvent person from dispositions.
5. **Contracts of security:** These are also called contracts of guarantee which are used to secure a creditor's money against the debtor. The purpose of such a contract is to protect and secure the debt of creditors. Examples are a mortgage, suretyship, assignment of debt and pledge, etc.

6. **Contract of partnership:** The purpose of contracts falling in this category is to share the profit and risk of a business such as *musharakah, mudharabah, muzara'ah.*
7. **Contracts of deposits and bailments:** These are also called contracts of custody and are used to protect the possession of the property. These contracts aim at safeguarding the property of a person like deposit and bailment.[36]

Notes

1 A.N. Shah's legal and commercial dictionary, (1985) "Unilateral."
2 E.A. Lichtenstein, Contract of law, p. 9.
3 Qur'ān 12:72 (Eng. trans. from 'Glorious Qur'ān' by Shaykh-ul-Islam Dr. Muhammad Tahir-ul-Qadri).
4 Qur'ān 17:34 (Eng. trans. from 'Glorious Qur'ān' by Shaykh-ul-Islam Dr. Muhammad Tahir-ul-Qadri).
5 Qur'ān 7:172 (Eng. trans. from 'Glorious Qur'ān' by Shaykh-ul-Islam Dr. Muhammad Tahir-ul-Qadri).
6 E.R. Hards Ivany, Mozley and Whitley's law dictionary (1980) "Bilateral contract."
7 Daphne A.Dukelow and Betsy Nuse, The dictionary of Canadian law (1991), "Bilateral contract."
8 Article No. 103, *Medjelle al-Ahkam-ul-Adalia* English translated by W.E. Grigsby, London.
9 Qur'ān 5:1 (Eng. trans. from 'Glorious Qur'ān' by Shaykh-ul-Islam Dr. Muhammad Tahir-ul-Qadri).
10 Qur'ān 17:34 (Eng. trans. from 'Glorious Qur'ān' by Shaykh-ul-Islam Dr. Muhammad Tahir-ul-Qadri).
11 Sir Abd al-Rahim, Muhammadan law, p. 288, Dr. Liaquat Ali Khan Niazi, Islamic law of contract, p. 100.
12 Sir Abd al-Rahim, Muhammadan law, p. 288.
13 E.R. Hards Ivany, Mozley and Whitley's law dictionary (1980), "Quasi contract."
14 Qur'ān 4:58 (Eng. trans. from 'Glorious Qur'ān' by Shaykh-ul-Islam Dr. Muhammad Tahir-ul-Qadri).
15 Dr. Hussain Hamid Hassan, An introduction to the study of Islamic law, p. 458.
16 Article No.108, *Medjelle al-Ahkam-ul-Adalia* English translated by W.E. Grigsby, London.
17 As quoted by Muhammad Ma'sum Billah in Shariah standard of business contract, pp.109-10.
18 Qur'ān 17:34 (Eng. trans. from 'Glorious Qur'ān' by Shaykh-ul-Islam Dr. Muhammad Tahir-ul-Qadri).
19 Article No.109, *Medjelle al-Ahkam-ul-Adalia* English translated by W.E. Grigsby, London.
20 Article No.364, *Medjelle al-Ahkam-ul-Adalia* English translated by W.E. Grigsby, London.
21 Dr. Liaquat Ali Khan Niazi, Islamic law of contract, p. 78.
22 Article No.372, *Medjelle al-Ahkam-ul-Adalia* English translated by W.E. Grigsby, London.
23 Article No.374, *Medjelle al-Ahkam-ul-Adalia* English translated by W.E. Grigsby, London.
24 Article No.371, *Medjelle al-Ahkam-ul-Adalia* English translated by W.E. Grigsby, London.
25 Article No.110, *Medjelle al-Ahkam-ul-Adalia* English translated by W.E. Grigsby, London.

26 Article No.362, *Medjelle al-Ahkam-ul-Adalia* English translated by W.E. Grigsby, London.
27 As quoted in Dr. Liaquat Ali Khan Niazi, Islamic law of contract, p. 79.
28 Article No.370, *Medjelle al-Ahkam-ul-Adalia* English translated by W.E. Grigsby, London.
29 Noel J. Coulson, Commercial law in the Gulf states, p. 56.
30 E.R. Hards Ivany, Mozley and Whitley's law dictionary (1980), "voidable contract."
31 Dr. Hussain Hamid Hassan, An introduction to the study of Islamic law, p. 460.
32 Madhur, al-Madkhal, p. 611.
33 Darir, *al-Gharar fi al-'uqud*, pp. 4–5.
34 Ibn al-Qayyim, *I'lam al-Muwaqqi'in* vol.3, p.237 & Ibn Taymiyyah, *Nazariyyat al-'Aqd*, p. 227.
35 Al-Uzma Ayatullah, Islamic laws of worship and contracts, p. 142.
36 Dr. Wahbah Al-Zuhaili, *al-Fiqh al-Islami wa Adillatuhu*, vol. 4 (Damascus, Daral Fikr, 1984) pp. 244–245.

13 Cessation and dissolution of contract

13.1 Introduction

Islamic law of contract emphasises the sanctity of contracts, i.e. the parties must fulfil their contractual obligation. Besides this, the concept of dissolution of a contract is also deeply rooted in the Islamic law of contract. The doctrine of dissolution of contract in Islamic law of contract is the proof of the flexibility and avoidance of hardship in performing the contract. It is also to save the contracting parties from any harm and unfair loss, etc. A contracting party might sometimes not receive the performance which was due to him because of the failure of the other contracting party to honour his side when one of the contracting parties fails to perform his contractual obligation.

On the other hand, the fulfilment of a contractual undertaking may be disturbed or permanently frustrated as a result of events or occurrences for which none of the contracting parties are responsible. In any case, the obligations arising out of a contract cease to exist. Whatever the causes might be, the situation makes the performance of the contract either impossible or different from that which was initially contemplated by the parties. Sometimes the impact of the performance of the contract is wholly hindered, and the parties are, therefore, discharged from their obligations. Sometimes a contract only needs readjustment.

13.2 Dissolution of a contract

Reviewing academic literature in depth on the subject of dissolution of the contract, it reveals that different authors and scholars described it under different legal terms, such as discharge of a contract, dissolution of the contract, cessation of contractual obligation and termination of a contract, etc. They also used the terminology like modes or methods and grounds of dissolutions.

Similarly, there is also a difference of opinion regarding the categorisation of the discharge of the contract. Some authors opine that the number of these categories is three, whereas other says there are four, and some also made further subdivisions of these numbers, for example:

1. The renowned jurist Sobhi Mahmassani names it the cessation of contractual obligations and categorises it into the following three kinds and calls them the causes of cessation:[1]
   i. Rescission or dissolution by mutual agreement (*iqalah*) in binding contracts.
   ii. Termination revocation (*faskh*) in non-binding contracts due to their nature or on account of any of the options.
   iii. Nullity (*butlan*) or defect (*fasad*) in invalid contracts.
2. The modern jurist Dr. Abdal Razzaq Sanhuri names it the dissolution of contract and categorises it into the following three kinds:[2]
   i. Dissolution due to a non-binding (*ghayr lazim*) contract.
   ii. Dissolution by a termination (*faskh*).
   iii. Dissolution by mutual agreement (*iqalah*).
3. Dr. Liaqat Ali Khan Niazi the author of the book *Islamic Law of Contract* names it discharge of contract and categorises it into the following four kinds:
   i. By performance.
   ii. By express agreement.
   iii. By operation of the doctrine of frustration.
   iv. By breach.[3]

It is interesting to note that some Muslim jurists also distinguish between the dissolution of contract and the discharge of contract. There are very lengthy and detailed discussions on the "discharge" or "dissolution" or "termination" etc. However, we will not delve into diversions of opinions. We adopt the classification of those jurists and experts who mainly categorised into two classes by keeping in view the two Arabic terms *zawal* and *inhilal*, which have been translated as cessation and dissolution respectively. This is why we named this chapter "Cessation and dissolution of contract" instead of any other terms such as "discharge and termination of contract," etc. We shall discuss it under the following headings and subheadings, to ensure clarity for the readers.

1. Cessation of contract by performance.
2. Cessation of contract by assigning of debt.
3. Dissolution of contract by mutual agreement.
4. Dissolution of a contract automatically.
5. Dissolution of contract by revocation and termination, etc.
6. Dissolution of contract by the impossibility of performance, etc.

13.3 Cessation of contract by performance[4]

The main aim of a contract in Islamic law, as in other law, is a performance of contractual obligations. Performance is one of the categories of discharge of contract, and a contract usually ends upon the fulfilment of the obligation arising out of it. Islamic law is very strict about the performance of the contract. Mostly, the performance must be precise and exact according to the terms and conditions of the contract.

The parties must perform contractual obligations at the exact time if so required, otherwise within a reasonable time. Every type of contract in Islamic law has its own method of discharging the obligations, and it must be performed accordingly. For example, following are the methods of discharging the following three types of obligations:

*13.3.1 The delivery of a non-specific property (*dayn*)*

Dayan is a contractual obligation to pay a sum of money or deliver non-specific property, i.e. fungibles. The sources of debt, *dayn*, in Islamic jurisprudence, can be found in the contracts of sale, hire, settlement *sulh*, *salam* and loan (*qard*). In the sale contract, the price is to be paid in cash or fungibles; it is *dayn*, likewise, in the case of a hire contract. In a loan (*qard*) contract, the borrower is aligned to return its equivalent in amount, type and description at the end of the loan period.

*13.3.2 The delivery of a specific property (*ayan*)*

Ayan is a contractual obligation to pay a sum of money or deliver a specific property, i.e. corpus. The most common expression of the obligation to deliver in Islamic law appears in the contract of sale and the contract of hire, which are considered models for all bilateral contracts.

13.3.4 Obligation to perform an act

Unlike the above two methods of discharging an obligation, this form of discharging obligation concerns agreement to perform any act. This type of obligation is commonly used to define terms of employment and includes any work. The contract of work or employment in Islamic law is terminated if the employee did his job according to the agreement and the employer paid the money to the employee. The contract of employment can be further subdivided into two categories. The first covers the employees whose work affects the goods upon which he works. Examples of this category include the tailor, the dyer or the carpenter. The second category includes employees whose work has no apparent effect on the item given to him to work on, with such examples including the porter or the boatman.

13.4 Cessation of contract by assignment of debt (*hawalah*)

The word *hawalah* means transfer or shifting a thing from one place to another. Assignment or *hawalah* is an agreement to transfer debt from the liability of the original debtor to the liability of another person. The debtor is freed from a debt while another is responsible for it. Thus, the responsibility for payment shifts to another party. It also refers to the document by which the transfer or assignment takes place, such as a bill of exchange, promissory note, cheque or draft. The mechanism of *hawalah* is used for the settling of accounts by book transfers, without the need for physical transfer of cash. The debtor who transfers debt is referred to as a debtor-assignor (*muhil*), the creditor creditor-assignee is *muhal*, and the new debtor to whom transfer is made is the transferee (*muhal alayh*).[5]

13.5 Dissolution of contract by mutual agreement (*iqalah*)

Iqalah is an Arabic term which means removal or reversal. Al-Zuhaili defines *iqalah* as "termination of the contract by mutual consent of the parties in case one of them is regretful and wants to turn away from the contract."[6] According to Ibn Najim, "*iqalah* is the withdrawal of contract and its cancellation by the agreement of the parties in case of binding contracts."[7]

After the formation of a valid, enforceable and binding contract, the parties are under the obligation to perform it. If one of the parties regrets his actions and wants to revoke his part of the undertaking in the contract, he is not permitted to do so except with the consent and approval of the other party. This principle can be justified in the sense that a contract is formed by mutual consent and, therefore, cannot be dissolved except by the same mutual consent.[8] The *Shariah* considers it permissible if one or both of the contracting parties regret their actions for them to dissolve the contract with mutual satisfaction, and this procedure of dissolution is called *iqalah*).[9]

The two parties may agree that the contract should be considered dissolved when obligations are not met. A contract may be dissolved by agreement, with a court order or without a court order. As here the dissolution is made through a valid agreement or contract, hence all conditions to make this a valid contract should be met too. Some conditions have also been discussed in Articles 190 to 196 of the *Medjelle*. By this method of discharge, the parties return to their original status or situation like that of their pre-contract status as if the contract never took place; thus the contract is annulled, along with all its effects.[10]

13.6 Dissolution of a contract automatically

The fourth mode for dissolution of a valid contract is automatic dissolution. A contract can be dissolved automatically if, after making a valid contract, it becomes impossible to put it into execution due to an obvious reason outside the control of the parties. When it is impossible to fulfil one of the party's commitments, the commitments of the other party are automatically nullified, and the contract is automatically dissolved.[11]

The following are certain causes or situations where the contract is automatically dissolved:

13.6.1 Death

A contracting party is naturally exempted by his death from the liability arising out of the contract. (However, all contracts are not dissolved in general by the death of either of the contracting parties.) Al-Zuhaili has determined certain types of contract which may be dissolved by the death of one of the contracting parties as follows:[12]

i) Contract of the lease (*ijarah)*: The lease contract, despite being legally binding from both sides, is automatically dissolved by the death of one of the contracting parties.[13]
ii) Mortage (*Rahn)* and surety (*kafalah)*.
iii) Partnership (*sharikah)* and agency (*wakalah)*.
iv) Contracts of *muzara'ah* (a temporary sharecropping contract) and *musaqa* (a sharecropping contract over the lease of a plantation, limited to one crop period).

13.6.2 Expiry of a period of contract and achievement of the purpose

The contract would automatically be dissolved if the limited period of its effect expires or the purported object of the contract is achieved. This is like the expiry period in the case of a time-bound lease contract and the settlement of debt in the case of mortgage and surety contracts and execution of the agent of the tasks for which he was made the agent in the case of a contract of agency.[14]

13.6.3 Non-performance within the stipulated time

If a contract stipulates that non-performance of a party within a fixed period would entitle the other party to repudiate the contract, such repudiation gives rise to the automatic dissolution of the contract. It can be illustrated by reference to a rent contract, where if there is a condition for the immediate payment of rent and the hirer refuses to pay when the lessor demands the rent in ready money, the lessor has the right to repudiate the contract,[15] which would lead to the automatic dissolution of the contact. Similarly, if there is a stipulation that the price shall be paid at such a time (*khiyar al-naqd*) in a contract of sale and the purchaser fails to pay the price at such a time, the contract is dissolved.[16]

13.6.4 Destruction of the subject matter

If the thing sold is destroyed while in the hands of the vendor, before receipt by the purchaser, the loss does not affect the purchaser, it falls on the vendor.[17] The contract is automatically dissolved by such destruction of the subject matter.

13.7 Dissolution by revocation and termination (*al-Faskh*)

A contract may be dissolved in two ways; by the revocation of one of the parties and termination by operation of law. This is called *al-Faskh*. *Al-Faskh* is the Arabic term that adequately accommodates these two grounds of dissolution of a contract.

Al-Faskh's dissolution by revocation and termination is very well explained in detail in the article by Muhammad Wohidul Islam "Dissolution of contract in Islamic law (1998) 13, *Arab Law Quarterly*, 336–368.

In the following, we are reproducing the necessary parts from it.

13.8 Unilateral revocation of contract

A group of contracts susceptible to being dissolved by unilateral revocation is known as *'uqud ja'izah.* Mahmassani categorises them as non-binding contracts either from either side or only one side.[18] They may be terminated by the revocation of the party for whom they are licensed. If such contracts are non-binding for both parties, each of them is allowed to revoke the contract without the consent of the other. For instance, a partnership is dissolved by the revocation of one of the partners, but it is a condition that the other should know of its dissolution. If one has revoked his partnership, the dissolution of the partnership is not effected until the other knows of it.[19] Similarly, in the case of an agency (*wakalah*), the principal can dismiss his agent (*wakil*). However, he cannot dismiss him if there is a right of another related to the agency.[20]

13.8.1 Termination for nullity and illegality

As we know, constitutive elements or natural conditions are the foundation (*arkan*), without which a contract could not be validly concluded and if one of them were lacking, that contract would be non-existent in law. Such an act would be null and void. For example, if any of these elements, such as the meeting of minds, capacity of the parties, object of the contract and purpose or cause, are missing, then the contract is null and void.

Hence nullity and illegality are also the causes of the dissolution of a contract in Islamic law of contract. One of the general rules concerning nullity, as perceived by Ibn Taymiyyah, is that the absolute nullity must be based on either a pillar (*rukn*) or cause (*sabab*) of the contract, and this, as often as not, concerns either the offer and acceptance, or the object of the contact, or both.[21] Similarly, all unlawful contracts are liable to be dissolved.

13.8.2 Termination by options

The system of options (*khiyarat*, pl. of *khiyar*) in Islamic law of contract is aimed at removing as much risk as possible and realising the highest possible degree of certainty in the rights and obligations arising from a contract, that is to say, that a contract will not be legally binding without ascertaining the equality of counter values. Hence a contract is terminated by option.

13.8.3 Termination by non-approval to contingent contracts

Islamic law of contract recognises certain non-binding contingent contracts whose effects are suspended (*mawquf*) until ratification by the party who has been granted the option to terminate the contract.

13.8.4 Termination for breach

The general principle is that all valid contracts must be performed specifically. The contracting parties can oblige each other to perform the contractual obligation by force, through judicial order, in case of any breach of contract. Thus, under the traditional Islamic law, it is contended, specific performance and/or the equivalent in monetary compensation (damages), were the only two remedies available for failure to perform a valid contract.

13.9 Dissolution for the impossibility of performance of the contract (*istihalah*)

Muslim jurists used different legal terms for the same "doctrine" according to their different research. The same is the case with the doctrine of impossibility of performance of the contract. Some jurists use the term "frustration" while others use "supervening events" and other use "*force majeure*." Moreover, some call it "natural disaster" or *Afat samawi*, etc. Nevertheless, all terms possess the same meaning and the same effects. For example:

1. Mahmassani uses the term *Afat samawiyah*, misfortune from heaven, for the causes rendering the performance of contractual obligation impossible, such as rain, cold, drought or wind, earthquake, fire.[22]
2. Dr. Abdal Razzaq Sanhuri uses the term *sabab ajnabi*, "foreign causes," under which, according to him these external factors make the performance of the contract impossible.[23]
3. Rayner uses the term *quwah qahirah* or *quwah al-qanun* corresponding to the terms *force majeure*, etc.[24]

Impossibility of the performance of a contract can be regarded as having taken place when supervening events without default of the parties to the contract occur and make significant changes to the nature of the contractual rights and obligations arising out of that contract, and it would be unjust to hold or perform them. Moreover, it renders the performance of the contract impossible. In such a case the law permits both parties to discharge the contract. "As a right to dissolve a contact when unforeseen changes of circumstance made the contractual obligation more burdensome and difficult than expected at the time of the formation of a contract."[25]

13.9.1 Constituent elements of the doctrine of impossibility

The principle of supervening legal or factual impossibility cannot be applied unconditionally. The legal writers have worked out several constitutive elements that qualify an event as supervening to render the performance of a contract impossible. The constituent elements will be discussed below.[26]

(i) **The event must be exceptional:** An event is held to be exceptional when its occurrence is infrequent, irregular or rare.[27] The question of whether an event is of an exceptional nature can only be determined according to the circumstances of each case. For example, high winds, thunder and heavy rain leading to the destruction of crops may be.

(ii) **The event must be unforeseeable:** The event must not have been anticipated or foreseen at the time the contract was made. An event is unforeseeable if at the time of the conclusion of a contract, there are no immediate signs or particular circumstances which make it reasonably likely. The test which determines the element of absolute unforeseeability has been held to be that of a reasonable and diligent man. That is to say; the event must not have been foreseeable by the contracting parties, or by a reasonable and diligent person who might have been in the contracting parties' position.[28]

(iii) **The event must be unavoidable:** The unforeseeable event must also be unavoidable in the sense that it must not have been possible for a party claiming a supervening circumstance to have avoided or prevented the occurrence of the event or its consequences by taking all necessary steps to stop the event from occurring or to prevent its consequences.

(iv) **The event must occur during the performance:** The supervening event should occur while the contract is still being performed.

(v) **The event must render performance impossible:** An essential element of an event to be considered as supervening is that it must make the performance of the affected contract impossible.

(vi) **The event must be general in character:** The supervening event should also be general in character, that is to say; it should affect not only the contracting parties but also a wide spectrum of people.

Notes

1 Sobhi Mahmassani Rajab, *Al-Nazariyyah al-'Ammah Li'l-Uqud* (Beirut, Daral Ilm Lil-Malayin, 1983), p. 485.

2 'Abd al-Razzaq Sanhuri, *Masadir al-Haqq fi al-Fiqh al-Islami* (Cairo, *Daral Nahdah al-'Arabiyyah*, n.d.), vol. 6, p. 201f.

3 Dr. Liaquat Ali Khan Niazi, Islamic law of contract, p. 301.

4 The most matter is taken from a thesis for PhD degree by Abrahim Saad Alhowaimil on the topic "Frustration of performance of contract: A comparative and analytic study in Islamic law and English law."

5 Jamila Hussain, Islam its law and society. (The federation press 2004) 179.

6 Dr. Wahbah Al-Zuhaili, *al-Fiqh al-Islami wa Adillatuhu*, vol. 4 (Damascus, Daral Fikr, 1984) p. 277.

7 Ibn Najim, Zainul 'Abidin, *al-Bahr al-Ra'iq Sharh Kanz al-Daqa'iq*, vol. 4 (Egypt, 1334h), p. 277.

8 Sobhi Mahmassani Rajab, *Al-Nazariyyah al-'Ammah Li'l-Uqud* (Beirut, Daral Ilm Lil-Malayin, 1983), p. 486.

9 Sobhi Mahmassani Rajab, *Al-Nazariyyah al-'Ammah Li'l-Uqud* (Beirut, Daral Ilm Lil-Malayin, 1983), p. 486.

10 Bin Qudamah, p.96.
11 Also see Article 159 of the new Egyptian civil law.
12 Dr. Wahbah Al-Zuhaili, *al-Fiqh al-Islami wa Adillatuhu*, vol. 4 (Damascus, Daral Fikr, 1984), p. 277.
13 Uthman ibn Ali Al-Zaila'yi, *Tabyin al-Haqa'iq Sharh Kanz al-Daqaiq*, vol. 4 (Boulac, 1313–15h), p. 144; Al-Kasani, *'Alauddin, bada'I al-Sana'I fi Tartib al-Shari'i* (Egypt, 1327–28h), vol. 4, p.2–1.
14 Dr. Wahbah Al-Zuhaili, *al-Fiqh al-Islami wa Adillatuhu*, vol. 4 (Damascus, Daral Fikr, 1984), p. 277.
15 Article No. 648, *Medjelle al-Ahkam-ul-Adalia* English translated by W.E. Grigsby, London.
16 Article No. 313–4, *Medjelle al-Ahkam-ul-Adalia* English translated by W.E. Grigsby, London.
17 Article No. 293, *Medjelle al-Ahkam-ul-Adalia* English translated by W.E. Grigsby, London.
18 Sobhi Mahmassani Rajab, *Al-Nazariyyah al-'Ammah Li'l-Uqud* (Beirut, Daral Ilm Lil-Malayin, 1983), p. 487.
19 Article No. 1353, *Medjelle al-Ahkam-ul-Adalia* English translated by W.E. Grigsby, London.
20 Article No. 1521, *Medjelle al-Ahkam-ul-Adalia* English translated by W.E. Grigsby, London.
21 'Abd al-Rahman al-Jaziri, *Kitab al-Fiqh al-Madhahib al-Arba'ah*, vol. 3 (Beirut, 7th ed.) pp. 224–225.
22 Sobhi Mahmassani Rajab, *Al-Nazariyyah al-'Ammah Li'l-Uqud* (Beirut, Daral Ilm Lil-Malayin, 1983), p..485.
23 'Abd al-Razzaq Sanhuri, *Masadir al-Haqq fi al-Fiqh al-Islami* (Cairo, Daral Nahdah al-'Arabiyyah, n.d), vol..6, pp. 77–78.
24 Dr. S.R. Rayner, The theory of contracts in Islamic law (London, Graham & Trotman, 1st ed. 1991) p. 259.
25 'Abd al-Razzaq Sanhuri, *Masadir al-Haqq fi al-Fiqh al-Islami* (Cairo, Daral Nahdah al-'Arabiyyah, n.d.), vol. 6, pp. 77–78.
26 Adnan Amkhan, Force majeure and impossibility of performance in Arab contract law (1991), at 142.
27 Kuwaiti High Court of cassation judgement, Case No.1265/1970 (Commercial), 10/12/1970, reproduced in *Medjelle al-Qada'wa'l-Qanun*, 1970, No. 1, Year 3, p. 53.
28 'Abd al-Rashid Mamun, *Ilaqat al-Sababiyyah fi al-Masuliyyah al-Madaniyyah, Medjelle al-Qanun wal-Iqtisad* (1979), Nos. 3–4, pp. 581–675.

14 System of options under contract

14.1 Introduction

The topic of options is critical in the Islamic law of contract. After explaining the topic of cessation and termination of the contract, it is the right place to discuss the topic of options. We know that contracts are binding. However, the law provides the choice to opt out or cancel a contract before its finalisation. Hence, the system of "options" relates to confirm or cancel the contract in a different time frame, which is unique and differentiates the Islamic law of contract from its counterparts. This system of options protects the contracting parties before concluding the contract by giving them the right of inspection, and after the conclusion of the contract by giving the right of option. The right of options is accorded by the *Shariah* as a unilateral "choice" to cancel (*faskh*) or to ratify (*imda'*) a contract.[1] For example, in a revocable contract, the contractor has the right to withdraw his obligation if one or both parties stipulate this condition in the contract.[2]

Actually, the system of options (*khiyar*) is for the fulfillment of the interests of business transactions in Islamic law. These interests include the protection of benefits and wills of both parties in a contract and protects them from the possible danger that will harm their business in the future.[3] An option is one of the main financial securities that give the right to buy or sell an asset, with predetermined time and price.[4] The system of options is for removing as much risk as possible and ascertaining the equality of counter-values in the contract-making process. It often happens that an apparently lawful and voluntary contract involves a latent flaw or defect unknown to the parties at the time of formation.[5] The Islamic law of contract does not enforce such a defective agreement unless the defect is removed.

It is noteworthy that although Western law also has similar concepts to the system of options in Islamic law, Islamic law of contract is more extensive than its counterpart. For instance, the option of the session (*khiyar al-majlis*) (which we shall discuss in the following passages) is an option not so easily accepted by modern law. Accordingly, the act of inspection or investigation, such as wearing clothes or riding a vehicle, is recommended in order to ascertain the equality of counter-values.[6] This Islamic system is remarkably in favour of the purchaser. Goods and services must fulfil the proper expectation of the purchaser, or he has the right to terminate the contract.[7] It is again noteworthy that the Islamic law of contract has assumed a consumer protectionist character for more than ten centuries.[8] Thus, this idea of protecting the weak against exploitation by the strong led to the elaboration of a rule of general application, commanding that transactions should be devoid of uncertainty and speculation, and this could only be secured by the parties having a perfect knowledge of the counter-values intended to be exchanged as a result of their transaction; otherwise the purchaser can use a proper option for a respective reason[9] to terminate the contract.

Muslim jurists have suggested several devices to safeguard contracting parties against hasty undertakings. These devices give a party who signed a contract unwisely and then regretted his haste on seeing some lesion or fraud, an opportunity to ponder over his transaction and revoke the contract. These devices are called *khayarat* (plural of the word *khiyar*), i.e. options in Islamic law. They have been designed to maintain balance in transactions and to protect a weaker party from being harmed. They constitute preventive measures against error, defect in goods, want of knowledge concerning the quality of things, lack of desired quality.[10]

14.2 Kinds of options

Like other topics, the jurist described the different numbers regarding the kinds or categories of *khiyar*. Imam Hanafi divides it into 17 types, Shafi 16, Hambali 18 and Maliki 2.[11] Some jurisprudents mentioned 13 kinds,[12] while others distinguished only 7.[13] The *Medjelle* codified the different options in seven chapters.[14]

We shall limit our discussion to only the four most essential types widely discussed by jurists and authors in the following:

14.3 *Khiyar al-majlis* (during the sitting/meeting)

This refers to the right of choices during a particular ceremony.[15] It is defined as the right for both parties, between the seller and buyer to perform the transaction or cancel it as long as the ceremony of the transaction is still in place. When both have departed from the ceremony, then the right of the *khiyar* will be lost until there can be made no more changes to it.[16]

This right of *khiyar al-majlis* (of the sitting) is the inalienable right to cancel the contract concluded by both parties as long as they have not yet separated. "The right of option maintains for all agreements of the nature of a sale, e.g. exchange of gold or silver or of foodstuffs, contract of *salam*, mere transfer of a thing purchased, sharing compromise for an equivalent, etc."[17] it is also the period during which the contracting parties devote themselves to the business at hand and is terminated by any event, such as physical departure from the place of business which indicates that negotiations are concluded or suspended.[18]

There is an "option during meetings" as each one of the parties has the right to confirm or cancel the contract in the negotiation stage of the contract as long as the two parties are still there and have not left."[19]

The jurists based this right on the *hadith* where Ibn Umar reports that:

> The Prophet (PBUH) said, "If two men conduct a sale, each one of them has the right of choice until they part or until one of them gives a choice to the other, if one of them gives the right of choice to the other and they conclude the sale is then confirmed."[20]

Also another *hadith*: "The contracting parties have the right of the option until they separate."[21] The option of *majlis*, where it is recognised, exists during the period of meeting for bargaining (*majlis*), and commences with the offer, lasting for the period of the *majlis*.[22] The wisdom behind the option of meeting here is to give ample room for the parties to think before any decision is to be made regarding the contracts. This will give justice to both the contracting parties and will prevent them from regretting the decision made later.

However, the right of the option does not exist in the following two cases.[23]

14.4 When the parties declare their approval of the contract

If only one does so, then he loses his right of option, but the other party retains his right until he makes a similar declaration.

14.4.1 When the parties separate without any express reservation

The right of option remains, however, as long as the separation has not taken place, even though the parties remain together for a long time. Usually customary practice (*'uruf*) indicates what is to be understood by the word separation.[24]

14.5 Jurists view regarding *khiyar al-majlis*

There is disagreement among the jurists regarding *khiyar al-majlis*. Hanafi and Maliki hold a view that the contract is enforced through *'ijab* and *qabul* and *khiyar al-majlis* has nothing to do with it as it may become irrevocable. This is in line with the Qur'ānic verse which means: "O belivers! Fulfil (your) promises ..."[25] and in other places "Unless it is a trade by your mutual agreement ..."[26]

According to their view, if we depend on *khiyar* then we will deny the rights of the contracting parties to perform the contract. The contract is complete when both parties consent to it.

Whereas according to Shafi once there is an *'ijab* (offer) and acceptance (*qabul*) is made, the contract is not yet concluded because both parties still have the right of *khiyar* as long as they have not parted.

However, the option of the meeting is not applicable in contracts that do not involve mutual commitment like donation, usefulness and non-committing contracts and contracts which involve forced acquisition and licensing contracts. Thus, the following contracts do not have the option of meeting the contract of rent because it involves usefulness: the power of attorney, because it does not involve forced acquisition; and *hawalah* (remittance) as it is a form of licensing. The option of the meeting does not apply also in the following contracts: *nekah* (marriage), *khul'* (divorce agreement where the wife exempts the husband from paying alimony and other expenses or giving their additional payment), *hebah* (grant without compensation), *mosaqat* (agricultural partnership, where one party offers the land and water and the other party offers labour), *sharekah* (partnership), *Rahn* (mortgage) and *qerad* (loan).[27]

14.6 *Khiyar al-shart* (option of condition)

Khiyar al-shart is the option through which one party or both of them stipulate for themselves or someone else the right to remove the contract within a determined period.[28] The *Medjelle* states that "If at the sale the condition is fixed that within a definite delay the seller, or buyer, or both, have the option to make void, or ratify, the sale by their consent, this condition is lawful."[29] *Khiyar al-shart* gives the right to one of them or both of them or a third party to verify or cancel a specific contract in a certain period.[30]

This option is based on the following *hadith*:

> It is reported that the Holy Prophet (PBUH) granted this option to Hibban ibn Munzir who complained that he was defrauded each time he made a purchase. He was directed by the Holy Prophet (PBUH) to say whenever he made a purchase "No cheating, and I reserve option for three days."[31]

This is also called the option to withdraw. In a revocable contract, the contractor has the right to withdraw his obligation if one or both parties stipulate this condition in the contract.[32] The duration of this right must be known and made explicit in the contract,[33] and a period not specified will be ignored and considered unsound about any claim made over the finalisation of the contract.[34] The option to withdraw leads to a freezing of the consideration for the duration specified.[35] For example, in a contract of sale, if the buyer stipulates this condition, he can freeze the price and possess the property; and he can maintain the price until he is legally compensated.[36]

14.7 Contract in which *khiyar al-shart* is applicable

The option of the condition is also called the option of *tarawwi* (deliberation, reflection) because it involves thinking over things and consulting others. It should be made clear that this option of the condition is not applicable to all contracts. It applied to contracts that are binding, necessary and committing and which are cancellable. Examples of these contracts are a sale, rent, agricultural partnership, trade partnership, warranty, money transferring, capital-labour partnership and division, etc.

14.8 Contracts in which *khiyar al-shart* is not applicable

It is not applicable to contracts like a grant, power of attorney, will, lending and deposit also contracts of: marriage, divorce, *khul* and *eqrar* (avowal, admission) which do not allow the option of condition. These contracts are not able to be cancelled, so they do not admit the option of condition. Besides, contracts of *sarf* (exchange) and *salam* (advanced payment) and usurious contracts do not allow such an action. All these contracts stipulate receiving money, and this contradicts the option of condition.[37] As regards those contracts, which are revocable by nature like agency, and partnership, the stipulation of *khiyar al-shart* would be futile as they can be revoked at the will of either party. It is also not permitted in contracts of *salam* (sale of future goods).[38]

14.9 For whom the option is stipulated

The option of condition or deliberation may be given to both or either one of the parties, or it may be given by either one of the parties to a stranger or a third person.[39] Abu Hanifa, Maliki, Ahmad bin Hanbal,[40] the Zaidis[41] and al-Shafi (in one of his two statements) have all permitted that either one of the parties may delegate the option of condition to a third person (other than two parties).

Al-Shafi, in another statement, and Zufar state that it is not permissible to delegate the option of condition to a stranger. This is because the option was meant originally to be used by the two parties exclusively. The practice of delegating it to another person means transferring the power over the contract to a stranger, and this is illegal.[42]

14.10 Period of *khiyar al-shart*

There is disagreement among scholars on the period within which the option of the condition can be exercised:

1. Abu Hanifa, Zufar and al-Shafi state that the period should not exceed three days, and this period should be left to the parties to determine, provided that it does not go beyond three days. This is supported by the comment of ibn ‘Omar: “I find that the Prophet (PBUH) has given ample time to Habban; he gave him three days to make his choice; if he is satisfied, he can take it; if he is not satisfied, he can leave it.”[43]
2. Imam Abu Yusuf and Muhammad and the Hanbalis are of the opinion that it is permitted to lay down more than three days without any restriction of the maximum period.[44] They hold that the term should be unlimited.[45] According to them the reason behind the ruling of the option of the condition is to avoid unfair dealings in the sale; and wherever the reason applies, the option should be implemented and the period should be left to the contractors to determine.
3. Imam Maliki states that the period of the option was originally three days, but it can be extended to any sufficient time. According to the Malikis, the period of *khiyar* varies from case to case. Thus, it may be one day when a piece of cloth has been purchased and may be one or two months when a house has been purchased.[46]

14.11 Effect of the contract with *khiyar al-shart*

The difference between the jurists as regards the *hukm* of the contract can be reduced to two opinions:

First opinion: The effects do not come into operation during the period of the option. The contract remains suspended (*mawaquf*) during the period of the option or till such an option is exercised. Thus, right in the property is not transferred to one in whose favour the option has been stipulated.

Second opinion: The effects come into operation, but the contract is now not binding or *ghayr lazim* and can be revoked during the period of the option by the one in whose favour the option has been stipulated.

Baillie says about it:

> When delay as stipulated for in the delivery of the thing sold, and the thing is specific, the contract is invalid; but when delay is stipulated for in payment of the price, and the price is an obligation, and the period of payment fixed, the sale is lawful, and where the period is left uncertain, the sale is invalid.[47]

The option may be exercised expressly or impliedly. Revocation does not require the *hukm* of the court to become effective. Ratification may also be expressed or implied.[48]

14.12 End of the option

The option ceases to be applicable in the following cases:

i) **Death:** According to Hanafi and Humbali jurists, in such cases the option comes to end and cannot pass to the heirs.[49] According to Malikis and Shafis on the other hand, it is a right which can be inherited and the heirs can exercise the option within the stipulated period.
ii) **Expiry of the period:** For the beneficiary there is an exercise of option within the stipulated or legal limits.[50] On the expiry of the period, the contract becomes binding and irrevocable.
iii) **Destruction of the subject matter:** In this case, also the contract becomes binding.

14.13 *Khiyar al-ru'yat* (option of viewing)

This refers to the right of the party purchasing to view the property, which was described at the time of negotiation, but which he has been unable to see before deciding whether to finalise or revoke his contract. This is authorised by law and hence has the status of an implied clause. To view means to be made aware of and know about the consideration, which is ascertainable through one or more senses. Viewing is executed upon the whole or part of the property, as for goods that can be measured, weighed or numbered.[51] Knowledge of the subject matter at the time of the contract is an essential condition. Such knowledge is possible through an examination of the subject at the time of the contract or by the description in a manner which removes all kinds of *jahadah* (want of knowledge). "Viewing here does not mean looking with the eyes only. The quality of viewing depends on the nature of the thing to be seen. Thus the viewing should be understood to mean looking with the eyes along with experiencing with other senses. For example, if the subject matter is clothes, then viewing means also touching, if the subject matter is perfume, then viewing means smelling, and so on" [52]. It also means that where the parties are contracting *in absentia* or the object is not present at the *Majlis*, and the buyer has given valuable consideration, he is granted the right to rescind or confirm the contract by the option of inspection, when the object is eventually delivered into his possession and does not meet with his contractual expectations.[53]

This option is also known as the option of inspection. The purpose of this option is to avoid the injustice that may lead to ignorance and dispute among parties, to protect the interest (*Istihshan*) of Muslims and to prevent any disputes among them and to avoid unfairness when they have no experience or ability in the market place to buy things they have not seen.[54]

14.14 Contracts in which *khiyar al-ru'yat* is applicable

The option to view is applicable on a contract that is revocable and whose consideration requires it to be ascertained as to quality such as:

1. A contract of sale of real property, such as land or a house, where the consideration has unique features that need to be verified.
2. A contract of sale of personal property, such as goods, where the consideration has a required quality that needs to be ascertained.
3. A contract of exchange, where both parties need to verify the consideration exchanged.
4. A contract of hire, where the rental property, such as a car, needs to be ascertained.
5. A contract of reconciliation, where the consideration is compensation to the damaged party who needs to ascertain it.
6. A contract of company, where the consideration is assets that need to be verified.[55]

14.15 Opinions of jurists regarding option of viewing

The majority of jurists such as Hanafi, Hanbali and Maliki admit the legality of the option of viewing and consider inspection at the time of contract essential.

However, the Shafi are of the view that the contract in which the subject matter has not been examined is not valid.[56] Thus they reject the validity of *khiyar al-ru'yah*. They argue based on the tradition, "Do not sell what you do not have."[57]

The Hanafis argue that the tradition, "Do not sell what you do not possess" means "what you do not own." According to them, the more relevant *hadith* is "He who buys a thing which he has not seen has an option upon seeing it."[58]

They also base its legality on a judgement against Hadrat 'Uthman (R.A) who had sold land to Hadrat Talhah (R.A). Either had not seen the land. Someone said to Talhah: "You have made a bad bargain." He replied: "I have not seen the land and thus have an option." Jubayr ibn Mut'am arbitrated the dispute and allowed Talhah right of option. The course taken by this litigation without any objection on the part of the companions is said to have established the right of option of examination for the buyer.[59]

Both Malikis and Hanbali agree with Hanafi, with a little bit of difference, that when inspection at the time of the contract becomes difficult or impossible, they allow sale by description. In such a case, the buyer may exercise the option of inspection and reject the object if it does not conform to the description.[60]

14.16 Effects of the option of viewing

The option makes the contract non-binding. The seller cannot revoke such a contract, which is binding for him even if he has not seen his property. The property passes to the buyer, and the contract is non-binding.

14.17 *Khiyar al-'aib* (option of the defect)

Aib is defined as any defect existing in the goods at the time of the contract that will call for a reduction in value as recognised by the common standards of merchants.[61] Here defect also covers the manufacturing design and instruction defects.

Khiyar al-'aib is the right to cancel or continue a transaction when specific goods bought experience defects or damages, so the seller has the right to return the money of the buyer.[62] Islam emphasises perfection in the process of business and forbids actions that are related to the transaction to be done in an unlawful manner.[63] It would be considered fraudulent on a seller's part to intentionally conceal a defect.[64] It is a very well-recognised legal method under the Islamic law of contract that protects the consumer against the defective product.

> If the goods purchased prove unfit for use, the buyer is entitled to a full refund of the purchase price even in case of perishables, if a person purchases eggs, musk melons, cucumbers, walnuts or the like, and after opening them discover them to be of bad quality; in that case, if they are altogether unfit for use, the purchaser is entitled to complete restitution of the price from the seller, as the sale is invalid, because of the subject of it not being in reality property.[65]

The *khiar al-aib* is valid only after found the imperfection in the subject matter in the case of trading. Besides, everything that caused reduced in the value and as a result in the market. This option is valid when the purchaser comes to recognise some defects in the article of sale. Thus, he shall cancel the agreement or refund the price of trading.[66]

It is a right given to a purchaser in a sale to cancel the contract if he discovers that the object acquired has in it some defect diminishing its value.[67] It is noteworthy that this option has been imposed by the law itself in the case when consideration is generalised and the parties do not have to stipulate it. It is thus a necessary condition of the contract. However, this option can be stipulated if the consideration is nominated and has specific features. Thus, the option of fault can be stipulated such as in contracts that are revocable and when the consideration requires them to be ascertained as to quality. Some jurists described the following Qur'ānic verse as the base of *khiyar al-aib*:

يَٰٓأَيُّهَا ٱلَّذِينَ ءَامَنُواْ لَا تَأۡكُلُوٓاْ أَمۡوَٰلَكُم بَيۡنَكُم بِٱلۡبَٰطِلِ إِلَّآ أَن تَكُونَ تِجَٰرَةً عَن تَرَاضٖ مِّنكُمۡۚ وَلَا تَقۡتُلُوٓاْ أَنفُسَكُمۡۚ
إِنَّ ٱللَّهَ كَانَ بِكُمۡ رَحِيمٗا

> "O believers! Do not devour one another's wealth unlawfully amongst yourselves unless it is a trade by your mutual agreement and does not kill yourselves. Surely, Allah is Kind to you."[68]

This option is based on the following *ahadith*:

> "He who defrauds another is not from amongst us."[69]
>
> "It is not permitted for the seller to sell things which are defective unless he points it out to him."[70]
>
> "If the contracting parties speak the truth and reveal the defects of the goods then the contract will be beneficial for both. If they do not speak the truth and hide the defects of the goods they will (Allah will) diminish the benefit of the transaction."[71]

For the option of fault to be considered as grounds for revocation, the contract must have been liable to common rejection and the acceptance affected, had the fault been recognised before drawing up the contract.[72] Thus, the fault in consideration would have led to an unfair bargain in the price of the goods in a contract of sale, of a rent in a contract of hire, or of damage and compensation in a contract of reconciliation. Accordingly, a fault in consideration is grounds for stipulating the option of fault, and in a contract is either implied by law or explicit as a clause. However, there are certain conditions to be met for the option of fault to be valid.[73]

14.18 Conditions for exercising the option of defect

According to the *Medjelle*, there are three main conditions to implement *khiyar al-aib*. First, that defect occurs at contract time or before that. Second, this defect should decrease its price. Third, the customer must be uninformed about that defect before the delivery of the commodity.[74]

Along with above three, the fourth condition is that the buyer should have no knowledge of the defect at the time of the contract or at the time of delivering, and finally the fifth condition is that there should not be any agreement of non-guarantee expressly exonerating the seller of any responsibility for a defect in the article sold.

14.19 Effects of the option of defect

The contract with the option of defect is revocable. The affected party has the choice to confirm or to cancel the contract. This is the majority opinion. The Maliki jurists distinguish between the minor (*yasir*) defect and major (*fahish*) defect and propose that if the defect is minor, the buyer may confirm the sale while being returned part of the price paid in proportion to the extent of the defect. In the case where the defect is significant, he has the choice either to cancel it or conform it without compensatory restitution.[75] The Hanbali jurists hold that the buyer of an object with a defect, whether minor or significant, may conform to the sale while being paid the difference between the price of the article in perfect condition and its price with the defect.[76]

We have explained the above four kinds of options in detail. Following are other options which exist in Islamic law of contract; for the purpose of brevity no detail is being produced here:

i. *Khiyar al-Tayeen* (option to ascertain the subject matter).
ii. *Khiyar al-Ghabn.*
iii. *Khiyar al-Takhir.*
iv. *Khiyar Kashf al-Haal.*
v. *Khiyar al-Naqd.*
vi. *Khiyar al-Qabul.*
vii. *Khiyar al-Taghrir.*
viii. *Khiyar al-Ghalat.*
ix. *Khiyar al-Tadlis.*

Notes

1 Joseph Schacht, Introduction to Islamic law (Oxford 1964), p. 152.
2 Haji Hasan Abdullah Alwi, Sales and contracts in early Islamic commercial law, Islamabad, Islamic Research Institute, 1994, p. 41.
3 Muhammad Murshidi Muhammad Noor etc. The rights of *khiyar* (option) in the issue of consumerism in Malaysia printed in Middle-East Journal of Scientific Research, 2013.
4 Kamali, M. H. (1999). Prospects for an islamic derivatives market in Malaysia. Thunderbird *International Business Review*, Kuala Lumpur *41*(4–5), 523–540. https://doi.org/10.1002/tie.4270410413
5 Nabil A. Saleh, Financial transactions and the Islamic theory of obligations and contracts, Islamic law and finance (ed. London 1988) p. 93.
6 Hideyuki Shimizu, Philosophy of the Islamic law of contract, A comparative study of contractual justice (1989), p. 70.
7 Muhammad Wohidul Islam, Dissolution of contract in Islamic law, p. 356.
8 Noel J. Coulson, Commercial law in the Gulf States: The Islamic legal tradition (London, 1984), p. 67.

9 Hideyuki Shimizu, Philosophy of the Islamic law of contract, A comparative study of contractual justice (1989), p. 71.
10 Dr. Muhammad Tahir Mansuri, Islamic law of contracts and business transactions, p. 163.
11 Jabatan Kemajuan Islam Malaysia, 2011. Portal Rasmi Muamalat Dan Kewangagan Islam. [Online] Available: http://www.islam.gov.my/ muamalat/ sites/default/files/kertas_ilmiah/2011/03/khiyar....pdf20 (Nov. 20, 2011).
12 Sharh al-Azhar, vol. 3, p. 85.
13 Ibn Qodamah, al-Moghni, vol. 2, p. 33.
14 Article No. 355, *Medjelle al-Ahkam-ul-Adalia* English translated by W.E. Grigsby, London.
15 Nadratuzzaman, H.M. 2007, Kamus popular keuangan ekonomi syariah. PKES publishing, Jakarta, p. 43.
16 Nadratuzzaman, H.M. 2007, Kamus popular keuangan ekonomi syariah. PKES publishing, Jakarta, p. 43.
17 Mahyuddin Abu Zakariya Yahya, Minhaj et Talibin, Lahore, p. 130.
18 Haji Hasan Abdullah Alwi, Sales and contract in early Islamic commercial law, ch. 5, p. 37; Al-Mausuawa, al-Fiqhiya al-Kuwatiya, vol. 1, p. 205.
19 Ala' Eddin Kharofa, Transactions in Islamic law, 2000, p. 92.
20 Imam Muslim, Sahih Muslim, Vol.3, Sh. Muhammad Ashraf, Lahore, 1976; Sunan Bayhaqi.
21 Al-Bukhari, Sahih, Kitab al-Buyu', Hadith No.2079, vol. 3, 58, Maktabah Dar Tauq al-Najat, Beirut.
22 Article No. 82, *Medjelle al-Ahkam-ul-Adalia* English translated by W.E. Grigsby, London.
23 Sanhuri, Masadir al-Haqq, vol. 2, p. 59.
24 Hamid, Mutual assent in the formation of contracts in Islamic law, JICL, vol. 7, p. 52.
25 Qur'ān, 5:1 (Eng. trans. from 'Glorious Qur'ān' by Shaykh-ul-Islam Dr. Muhammad Tahir-ul-Qadri).
26 Qur'ān, 4:29 (Eng. trans. from 'Glorious Qur'ān' by Shaykh-ul-Islam Dr. Muhammad Tahir-ul-Qadri).
27 Prof. Dr. Ala' Eddin Kharofa, Transactions in Islamic law, pp. 96–97.
28 Zuhayli, al-Fiqh al-Islami wa Adillatuhu, vol. 4, p. 254; Zaydan, al-Madkhal, p. 377.
29 Article No.300, *Medjelle al-Ahkam-ul-Adalia* English translated by W.E. Grigsby, London.
30 Muhammad O., 1998. Financial engineering with Islamic options, Islamic economic studies, 6(1): 77
31 Shawkani, Nayl al-Awtar, vol. 5, p.182.
32 Haji Hasan Abdullah Alwi, Sales and contracts in early Islamic commercial law, Islamabad research institute, 1994, p. 41.
33 This is under Hanbalis school of law. Hanafi and Shafi schools consider three days and Maliki considers it to be decided by custom.
34 Comair-Obeid, Nayla, The law of business contracts in the Arab Middle East (Arab and Islamic law series), Springer, 1996, p. 211.
35 Ahmad Hidayat Buang, Studies in the Islamic law of contracts, Kuala Lumpur, Sole distributor, Golden Books Centre 2000, p. 109.
36 Ahmad Hidayat Buang, Studies in the Islamic law of contracts, Kuala Lumpur, Sole distributor, Golden Books Centre 2000, p. 109.
37 Prof. Dr. Ala' Eddin Kharofa, Transactions in Islamic law, p. 99.
38 Abu Zahrah, Al-Milkiyyah wa Nazariyyat al-Aqd, p. 393.
39 Sanhuri, Masadir al-Haqq, vol. 4, p. 220.
40 Al-Moghni, vol. 2, p. 36.
41 Al-Taj al-Mudhabhab, vol. 2, p. 404.
42 Prof. Dr. Ala' Eddin Kharofa, Transactions in Islamic law, p. 100.

43 Al-Shrah al-Kabir, vol. 4, p. 66; Abu Zahrah, p. 432.
44 Ibn Qudama, al-Mughni, vol. 3, p. 498; al-Kasani, Badai al-Sanai, vol. 5, p. 174.
45 Sarkhasi, Kitab al-Mabsut, (1324–1331) vol. 13, p. 41.
46 Ibn Rushd, Bidayah al-Mujtahid, vol. 2, p. 208; Sanhuri, Masadir-ul-Haqq, vol. 4, p. 221.
47 Neil B.E. Baillie, Muhammadan law of sale, pp. 208–209.
48 Hassan, al-Madkhal, pp. 456–457.
49 Marghinani, al-Hidaya, vol. 3, p. 24; Ibn Qadama, al-Mughani, vol. 4, p. 77.
50 Article No.307, *Medjelle al-Ahkam-ul-Adalia* English translated by W.E. Grigsby, London.
51 William Ballantyne, The Shariah and its relevance to modern transnational transactions, in International Bar Association, Arab comparative and commercial law—proceedings of the Arab regional conference 43, Cairo, 15–19 February, 1987.
52 Siti Salwani Razali, Islamic Law of Contract (2010), United Kingdom: Cengage Learning, p. 57.
53 Al-Kasani, Badai al-Sanai, vol. 5, p. 291.
54 Al-Zuhaili, al-Fiqh al-Islami wa Adillatuhu, vol. 4, p. 3125; al-Mausuawa' al-Fiqhiyya al-Kuwaitiya, vol. 1, p. 205.
55 William Ballantyne, The Shariah and its relevance to modern transnational transactions, in International Bar Association, Arab comparative and commercial law—proceedings of the Arab regional conference 43, Cairo, 15–19 February, 1987.
56 Shirazi, al-Muhadhdhab, vol. 1, p. 263.
57 Shawkani, Nayl al-Awtar, vol. 5, p. 164.
58 Madkur, al-Madkhal li al-Fiqh al-Islami, p. 686; Marghinani, al-Hidaya, vol. 3, p. 25.
59 Abu Zahra, al-Milkiyyah wa Nazariyyat al-Aqd, p. 398.
60 Ibd Rushd, Bidayat al-Mujtahid, vol. 2, p. 155.
61 Nabil Saleh, Remedies for breach of contract under Islamic and Arab laws, Arab law quarterly (1989) 4 269, 290.
62 Nasrul Hisyam, N., 2008. Aplikasi sains dan teknologi dalam transaksi muamalah Islam: Rujukan kepada rukun-rukun akad mengikut perspektif undang-undang kontrak Islam jurnal teknologi, 49€: 81–91.
63 Refer to verse in Qur'ān surah an-Nisaa.
64 Ibn Nujaim, al-Bahar al-Raiq, vol. 6, p. 36.
65 Al-Marghinani, Al-Hidaya, vol. 3, p. 39.
66 Dr. S.E. Rayner, The theory of contracts in Islamic law, pp. 327–328.
67 Al-Kasani, Badai al-Sanai, vol. 5, p. 247.
68 Qur'ān, 4:29 (Eng. trans. from 'Glorious Qur'ān' by Shaykh-ul-Islam Dr. Muhammad Tahir-ul-Qadri).
69 Imam Bukhari, Sahih Bukhari, Hadith No.4668; Muslim ibn al-Hajjaj, Sahih, Hadith No.101, vol. 1, p. 99, Dar Ihya al-Turath al-Arabi, Beirut.
70 Shawkani, Nayl al-Awtar, vol. 5, p. 224.
71 Al-Bukhari, Sahih, Kitab-ul-Buyu, Hadith No. 2082, vol. 3, p. 59.
72 M.E. Hamid, Does the Islamic law of contract recognize a doctrine of mistake?, p. 21.
73 Comair-Obeid, Nayla, Particularity of the contract's subject-matter in the law of the Arab Middle East, (1996), Legal journals Arab law quarterly, ALQ 11(4), p. 331–349.
74 Article No. 336, *Medjelle al-Ahkam-ul-Adalia* English translated by W.E. Grigsby, London.
75 Abul Qasim Al-Gharnati, al-Qawanien al-Fiqhiyya, vol. 1, p. 176.
76 Abdulsalam Majd al-Din, al-Muharrar fi al-Fiqh ala Mazhab al-Iman Ahmad ibn Hanbal, vol. 1, p. 324, Maktabat al-Marif, al-Riyadh.

15 Remedies for breach of contract

Breach of contract is generally described as the unjustifiable refusal or failure by one party to a lawful and enforceable contract to implement any of the express or implied duties incumbent on that party under the contract. Usually, a breach occurs by refusing to perform the contract, failing to perform, performing late or performing poorly. Breach of a contract purports the existence of a "lawful and enforceable" contract.

There are different remedies in the Western legal system for breach of a contract. The question may arise whether there are remedies for breach of contract available under the Islamic law of contract. The answer is yes.

The following remedies are available for breach of contract:

1. Rescission.
2. Damages.
3. Specific performance.
4. Injunctions.
5. Restitutionary remedies.[1]

15.1 Rescission

The first kind of remedy available is rescission. Islamic law of contract has given the right to rescind the contract to the affected parties when they feel that their rights are at stake. They can use this right by applying the system of options. In a case when it is known to the innocent party that the product sold to him is defected, for example, and may cause damage to him, he can rescind the contract. "Rescission is an equitable right to put an end to a contract and have the *status quo* restored."[2]

Zakhaili says:

> If the sale is valid, obligatory, free from option and the parties agree to abolish or terminate it, then its cancellation will be by way of rescission. Moreover, rescission, if it is separate from the sale of which is generally consists, will be allowed in all binding contracts, except marriage.[3]

In the words of Joseph Schacht:

> The right of rescission (*khiyar*, option) is the right unilaterally to cancel (*faskh*) or to ratify (*imda'*) a contract, and in particular a contract of sale; if it is not exercised within the proper time limit, the sale is complete (*tamm*), with a somewhat different meaning of the term. It can be conferred by law, or agreed upon by the contracting parties. The buyer has the right of rescission at the time at which he sees the object which he has bought, the act of 'seeing' not to be taken too narrowly (*khiyar al-ru'ya*); also in the case of a defect, i.e. everything that causes a reduction in price among traders (*khiyar al-'ayb*) or lack of a stipulated quality. The defect given only the right of rescission, not of abatement; this last arises only if the return of the object of the sale has become impossible, either by its loss or by the occurrence of a new defect after delivery but before recognition of the first defect (in which case return is possible only with consent of the seller), or by increase in value (such as the dyeing of cloth). If the seller delivered less than the stipulated quantity, the buyer has the choice between rescission of the sale and abatement of the price in proportion.[4]

The waiver of the *khiyar al-'ayb* by the buyer in a contract of sale is possible; the resulting absence of obligation is called *bara'a*. The buyer can stipulate the right of choosing from among several objects (*khiyar al-ta'yin*), and by agreement of the contracting parties there can be conferred on one or both or a third party the general right of rescission (*khiyar al-shart*) during a period of not more than three days (according to the prevailing opinion).[5]

15.2 Difference between rescission and repudiation

Rescission is often confused with repudiation. They have a common element in that restitution *in integrum* must be possible. However, rescission is more varied than repudiation for repudiation is only available for a breach of a condition which goes to the root of a contract but rescission is a general equitable remedy. It is a discretionary remedy.

Rescission can be granted on terms, but if grounds for repudiation are established, it is available as of right. In theory, there is no need to go to court in order to rescind a contract; an application to the court is prudent where there is some doubt, or when damages are sought, or where rescission is only one of many remedies being sought, or where assistance is required to restore the *status quo*.

15.3 Grounds for rescission

Following are the grounds for a rescission of a contract:

i) Fraud.
ii) Innocent misrepresentation. A false statement of fact not made fraudulently, inducing another to enter into a transaction.

iii) Constructive fraud. A miscellaneous collection of conduct which equity treats as if it were fraud, for example, undue influence; in these cases, equity ensures that the will of the subordinate party is not overborne, by insisting that the subordinate party receives separate advice.
iv) Mistake. Rescission will be available for a mistake where there has been a common misapprehension which is fundamental or where the mistake is unilateral, and there have been sharp practices.[6]

15.4 Damages

The second remedy available for breach of contract to an innocent party in Islamic law of contract is to claim damages for compensation.

Once a contract has been terminated by the breach, the correct action lies in damages. The object of the award of damages is to put the innocent party in the position he would have been in had the contract been performed. Generally, loss of bargain may be calculated by reference to the deficiency in value of the subject matter of the contract assessed at market value. In contracts for the sale of goods, where there is a readily available market, the loss will be the difference between the contract price and the market price at the date of the failure to accept or deliver the goods.

There is no link under the *Shariah* between the reciprocal obligations generated by a given contract. Contrary to positive law, Islamic law regards the obligation(s) of one contracting party as independent of the obligation(s) of the other contracting party. Consequently, a contract is not cancelled for breach by one party of its obligation(s).[7] On the contrary, such a contract remains valid, and the creditor is entitled to ask for its enforceability or damages when the debtor is deemed by law liable for the defect in or the loss of the subject matter of the contract (*daman*).[8]

Contractual liability for compensation in Islamic law is known as *dhaman-al-uqud*. When the subject matter of the contract is destroyed, as in the case where the sold property has been destroyed before delivery or when the hired subject matter is destroyed while in possession of the hirer, the concept of warranty (*daman al-aqd*) applies. This means that the holder of the subject matter in question in warranty (*daman al-aqd*) will be responsible for the destruction of the subject matter[9] and is liable to pay the damages. In this regard, the *Medjelle* states:

> A defect of long-standing is a fault which existed while the thing sold was in the possession of the vendor; any defect which occurs in the thing sold after the sale and before delivery, while in the possession of the vendor, is considered a defect of long-standing and justifies rejection.[10]

15.5 Kinds of damages

The contractual liability can be applied to the various kinds of damages that may be awarded to the party seeking remedy, i.e. compensatory damages, consequential damages, punitive damages and nominal damages. Islamic law too has no problem with these kinds of remedies in general and compensatory damages in particular. Compensatory damages are called *dhaman*, which means compensation. The value depends on the amount of performance promised in the contract. This may be the value of the commodity sold or services rendered or other considerations. Consequential damages occur as a result of the breach and are usually lost profits. These are also termed *dhaman al-uqud.*

Hence, damage is one of the essential elements of contractual liability in Islamic law. In order to satisfy this element, the consumer is only required to prove the link between the product and the manufacturer, i.e. the product is produced by a particular manufacturer. If this link is established, that is enough proof for the liability of the manufacturer.[11]

15.6 Specific performance

Specific performance is a third kind of remedy provided by the Islamic law of contract in cases of breach of some specific contracts only. If any party denies performing his part of the contract, he may be asked and forced to perform the contract according to the terms and conditions specified therein, if possible.

Specific performance is a discretionary remedy. Specific performance is an order of the court requiring the person to whom it is addressed to perform a contract.

Following are the principles which govern the specific performance:

(a) There must be an enforceable contract.
(b) The claimant must have given consideration.
(c) Damages must be an inadequate remedy—for example;
    (i) In contracts regarding any land. As all lands are unique, thus damages for breach of such contracts will always be an inadequate remedy. Where a contract for the sale of land is breached, the remedy for specific performance is always available.
    (ii) Similarly, where the contract of a loan is breached, damages will always be an adequate remedy; hence, remedy of specific performance is awarded.
    (iii) However, in the case where chattels are the subject matter of a breach of contract, then if chattels are not unique, so specific performance is not generally available. Where the chattels are rare or unique and are specifically ascertainable, then the remedy of specific performance may be granted.

Followings are the cases where no specific performance is available:

(a) Mistake: When a contract is rendered void at law, no specific performance of it may be granted.
(b) Hardship amounting to injustice: No specific performance will be granted in circumstances where specific performance of a contract may cause hardship to the party even if the plaintiff is not at fault.

15.7 Injunctions

The injunction is the fourth kind of remedy which is available to an affected party in case of breach of a contract.

An injunction is an order of the court to a party to the effect that he shall do or refrain from doing a particular act.

The court may grant any of the following injunctions:

(a) Mandatory—to compel the performance of some affirmative act.
(b) Prohibitory—to restrain the doing of some act.
(c) Perpetual—by way of final relief when the case has been tried.
(d) Interlocutory—to last only until the trial of the action.

It has been laid down in the *Medjelle*: "Excessive damage in whatever way it may be caused is to be removed."[12] It is further laid down: "Some people also, who are public harm, like unskilled doctors are restrained."[13]

Thus, courts in an Islamic country have full powers of granting injunctions.

15.8 Restitutionary remedies

The fifth kind of remedy available to the affected party is a restituting remedy. As regards remedies for other wrongs, restitution may be either by return (*radd*) of the thing, subject of the wrong or by delivery of a similar article (*itaua' mithlihi*). The first is the proper remedy in cases of usurpation or wrongful appropriation of all properties of dissimilar nature, but if in such cases the property cannot be restored or if the article in respect of which a wrong has been committed was similar, the defendant will be compelled to deliver a similar article to the plaintiff.

15.9 *Quantum meruit*

An alternative route to getting damages is an action for *quantum meruit* where damages cannot be claimed under a contract because no sum was set for the work to be done, or the contractual work has not been finished through no fault of the plaintiff. The award made will depend on the facts of the case.[14]

Notes

1 Dr. Liaquat Ali Khan Niazi, Islamic law of contract, p. 309.
2 Muhammad Ma'sum Billah, Shariah standard of business contract, p. 141.
3 Dr. Wahbah al-Zakhaili, al-Fiqh al-Islami wa Adillatuhu, p. 713.
4 Joseph Schacht, Introduction to Islamic law, p. 152.
5 Joseph Schacht, Introduction to Islamic law, p. 153.
6 Dr. Liaquat Ali Khan Niazi, Islamic law of contract, p. 309–310.
7 Chafik Chehata, Etudes de Droit Musulman, la Notion de Responsabilite Contractuelle, p. 15; al-Amrusi, al-Qanoun al-Madani al-Mu'addala, vol.1, p. 427 (Alexandria, 1983).
8 Sanhuri, Sadadir al-Haq, vol. 6, p. 230 (Beirut, n.d.).
9 F. Vogel & S. Hayes, Islamic law and finance, Brill, 2007, 112.

10 Article No.339–340, *Medjelle al-Ahkam-ul-Adalia* English translated by W.E. Grigsby, London.
11 Kahf Manzer, economics of liabilities: an Islamic view (2000) 8(2) Journal of economics and management, 85.
12 Article No.1200, *Medjelle al-Ahkam-ul-Adalia* English translated by W.E. Grigsby, London.
13 Article No.964, *Medjelle al-Ahkam-ul-Adalia* English translated by W.E. Grigsby, London.
14 Susan Blake, A practical approach to legal advice & drafting, Financial training publications, London 1985, p. 217.

16 Some important contracts

16.1 Contract of sale

The contract of sale is one of the most important contracts for the exchange of goods. It is classically defined as "an exchange of a useful and desirable thing for a similar thing by mutual consent in a specific manner."[1]

Some jurists have added the words "for the alienation of property"[2] to the above-mentioned definition to denote that the purpose of such a contract is to transfer property in goods to the buyer, and in price to the seller. Thus, the complete definition of sale will be as follows: "Exchange of useful and desirable thing for a similar thing by mutual consent for the alienation of property." It can also be defined as the "exchange of property for a property with mutual consent."[3]

The term "contract of sale"'[4] signifies the "delivery of a definite object which possesses legal value in exchange for something equivalent in a value called the price."[5] According to Ibn Arfa, a sale is a contract of obligation by which each party transfers to the other the property of something other than simple usage of pleasure. An additional limitation is that the contract is communicative, of which one of the considerations shall be legal tender, and the other shall be a specific object.[6] In other words, a contract of sale is an agreement of an exchange of goods by goods or goods by properties or properties by properties or goods by price or properties by price, between two or more contracting parties.

16.2 Conditions for validity of sale contract

1. Risk about existence and acquisition.
2. There should be an agreement.
3. Contracting parties should possess the legal capacity necessary for concluding the sale contract.
4. The commodity should be a thing whose transaction is permissible in the *Shariah*.
5. The commodity must be either in actual existence or it should be capable of being acquired and delivered to a buyer.
6. The transactions should not involve an element of uncertainty. Goods should be owned by the seller.

7. The goods should be possessed by the seller so that he can deliver them to the purchaser.
8. The goods should be ascertained and known to the contracting parties.
9. The sale contract should be absolute and not contingent upon a future event.
10. Free consent of the parties to the contract.
11. The price is fixed[7] or if the consideration is other than the price, then it should be ascertained.

16.3 Kinds of sale transactions

Following are essential kinds of the sale in Islamic law:

1. *Muqayadah*: The sale of goods for goods or barter trade.
2. *Bay' Mutlaq*: The sale of goods for money.
3. *Sarf*: The sale of money for money or money changing, i.e. the sale of absolute price for absolute price.
4. *Salam*: This is a sale in which the price is paid in advance, and the articles are delivered on a future date.
5. *Istisna*: A contract for manufacturing. It consists of ordering an artisan or manufacturer to make sure goods answer a given description. By *istisna*, one may engage, for example, a cobbler to make a pair of shoes for a fixed price or ask a tailor to make a suit to be delivered later.[8]
6. *Murabahah*: It is a sale of goods at a price covering the purchase price plus profit margin agreed upon between the contracting parties.
7. *Bay' al-mu'ajjal* (credit sale): It is a sale on a deferred payment basis.

We shall discuss all these kinds in a little bit more detail in the following passages.

16.4 *Musharakah*—the contract of partnership

16.4.1 Definition

The term *musharakah* derived from the word *sharikah*, the literal meanings of which are sharing, mixing or mingling.

Muslim jurists defined the "*sharikah*" in various ways. According to the Hanafi school of thought, "*Sharikah* is a contract between two or more people for participation in capital and its profit."[9]

A contract of partnership under Islamic law has been defined by the *Medjelle* as: "An agreement for the association on the condition that the capital and its benefit be common between two or more persons."[10]

Meanwhile, Ibn Arfa defined it as: "An agreement between two or more persons to carry out a particular business with the view of sharing profits by joint investment."[11]

According to Cowan, "*ishtirak* means partnership, participation, sharing and joining."[12]

According to him, "*shirkat* or *sharikah* means a partnership, association or commercial enterprise in Islamic law."[13]

> *Shirkat*, in its primitive sense, signifies the conjunction of two or more estates, in such a manner that one of them is not distinguishable from the other. In the language of the law, it signifies the union of two or more persons in one concern. The term *shirkat*, however, is extended to contracts, although there is no actual conjunction of estates because a contract is the cause of such conjunction.[14]

16.4.2 Qur'ānic and Sunnah basis of sharikah

According to the Qur'ān:

وَإِنَّ كَثِيرًا مِّنَ ٱلْخُلَطَآءِ لَيَبْغِي بَعْضُهُمْ عَلَىٰ بَعْضٍ إِلَّا ٱلَّذِينَ ءَامَنُوا۟ وَعَمِلُوا۟ ٱلصَّٰلِحَٰتِ وَقَلِيلٌ مَّا هُمْ

> "And it is true that most of the partners wrong one another except those who believe and do pious deeds, and such people are very few."[15]

According to *hadith*, the Holy Prophet (PBUH) said: "Allah Almighty is with the two partners unless they defraud each other."[16]

Musharakah is a very important and valid mode of business.

> A *musharakah* is a partnership between two or more entities or persons whereby each contributes cash or assets toward a venture. As a result, the profits are shared in pre-agreed proportions, and because of the prohibition on undue reward, the parties must assign each partner an award that corresponds to his contribution of the cash or asset warrants. However, scholars generally permit profit-sharing out of pro-rata proportion subject to certain requirements.[17]

As in all other usual partnerships and other kinds of business, in Islamic law *musharakah* losses and profits are shared in the same proportion that the assets are contributed by the parties involved.

Dr. Omar Chapra thus views that a contract of partnership does not only signify the sharing of profit over the business but also the sharing of loss and liabilities between the partners.[18]

16.4.3 Kinds of sharikah

There are two main kinds of *sharikah*:

1. *Sharikat al-Milk* (proprietary partnership).
2. *Sharikat al-'Aqd* (contractual partnership).[19]

1. ***Sharikat al-Milk***: *Sharikat al-milk* is defined by the *Medjelle*, as

    > the existence of a thing in the exclusive joint-ownership of two or more persons due to any reason of ownership, or it is the joint claim of two or more persons for a debt that is due from another individual arising from a single cause.[20]

    It means a combined partnership/ownership of two or more parties in a jointly established business in order to share profit and loss.
2. ***Sharikat-ul-Aqd***: It means a partnership/business created by a mutual contract. It is a partnership, which comes into being as a result of an agreement between two or more persons in order to share the profit.[21] It has a further three subdivisions:
    i) *Sharikat-ul-amaal.*
    ii) *Sharikat-ul-amwaal.*
    iii) *Sharikat-ul-Wajooh.*[22]

The following are some salient features of *musharakah.*

1. All the stringent conditions of the sale contract should be present in the *musharakah.*
2. All partners should invest their amount according to the agreed ratio of percentage.
3. The percentage of profit should be determined by mutual consent at the time of making a contract.
4. The profit is shared between the partners according to the agreed percentage of investment. In the case of any party remaining a sleeping partner throughout the contract, the profit should not exceed its investment.
5. The loss will be distributed according to the share of investment.
6. *Musharakah* can be terminated by any partner.
7. If any partner dies or becomes insane, then the contract is automatically terminated.

16.5 *Mudarabah*—limited partnership

Mudarabah, *qirad* and *muqaradah* are different terms used to express the particular type of business arrangement in which the capital is from one side while the labour or work is from the other side. The word *mudarabah* is derived from the phrase "*al-darb fil ard*" which means to make a journey.

It is also called a contract of co-partnership. A contract of co-partnership is an agreement between at least two parties of which one party provides capital while the other provides the labour and both parties will share the profit, loss and liabilities according to the proportion that they agree upon during the contract.

The *Medjelle* defines a contract on co-partnership as: "A kind of partnership on the condition that the capital is to be found by one and the labour and work by the other."[23]

16.5.1 Definitions of mudarabah

The following are the definitions of *mudarabah* in different schools of law.

Hanafi School: "It is a partnership (*sharikah*) for participation in profit in which capital is from one side, whereas labour or skill (*'amal*) is from the other side."[24]

Shafi School: "It is an agreement whereby an owner hands over the capital to a worker who trades with it and the profit is shared by the parties."[25]

Mudarabah (is a contract) or a partnership where one provides the capital and the other the labour.[26]

16.5.2 Modern definitions of mudarabah

A renowned scholar, 'Ali al-Khafif, has defined *mudarabah* as a "contract for sharing the profit of a business in which one party contributes with capital and other with his labour."[27]

Dr. Rashid Khalil, another scholar, has defined it as a contract whereby a legally competent person hands over known and defined capital to a person possessed with reason and discretion to trade with it for a part of profit defined in proportion."[28]

16.5.3 Qur'ānic and Sunnah basis of mudarabah

According to the Qur'ān: "And (some), others will be travelling in the land to look for Allah's bounty."[29] Abu Bakr Jassas explains that they seek the bounty of Allah through trade and disposition.[30]

The Holy Prophet (PBUH) is reported to have said: "There is a great blessing in three things: The credit sale, the *mudarabah* and mixing wheat and barley for domestic consumption, not for sale."

The Holy Prophet (PBUH) gave his tacit approval to the conditions imposed by Ibn 'Abbas (R.A) who used to give money based on *mudarabah*.

The Holy Prophet (PBUH) himself acted as *mudarib* (agent/manager) for Khadijah (R.A) before his marriage.

According to the *Medjelle*:

> The essence of a *mudarabah* is an offer and acceptance. For example: If the owner of capital says to the person who provides the labour "Take this capital and do the work and labour in return, on the terms that the profits are to be divided between us, half and half, or as two to one." Or if he says anything else which represents the meaning of a *mudarabah* like. "Take this money and make it capital and let the profit be in common between us in this proportion" and the *mudarib* (working partner) accepts a contract of *mudarabah* is concluded.[31]

16.5.4 Types of mudarabah

Mudarabah is of two types: unrestricted *mudarabah* and restricted *mudarabah*.

16.5.4.1 Unrestricted mudarabah

It is also called unlimited or perpetual or absolute *mudarabah.* According to the *Medjelle*:

> Unrestricted *mudarabah* is a *mudarabah,* which is not restricted in terms of time, place, kinds of trade or person from whom he is to buy and to whom he is to sell. However, if it is restricted to one of these, it is a restricted *mudarabah.* For example: if one says, "Buy and sell at such a time or in such a place, or sell such a kind of property, or trade with such person or with the inhabitants of such a town." It is a restricted *mudarabah.*[32]

16.5.4.2 Restricted mudarabah

Mudarabah is restricted when the liberty of action of the agent (*mudarib*) is restricted in terms of kind of trade, time and place. The restrictions allowed to be imposed by the investor are not a matter of agreement among the jurists. For example, the restriction to purchase from a particular person is permissible to Hanafis and Hanbalis but not permissible according to Shafi and Maliki.[33]

16.6 *Murabahah*—deferred payment sale

Murabahah is a sale of goods at a price covering the purchase price plus profit margin agreed upon between the contracting parties. In *murabahah,* the seller discloses the cost of the sold commodity. It is defined as: "*Murabahah* is a particular kind of sale where the seller expressly mentions the cost of the sold commodity he has incurred and sells it to another person by adding some profit."[34]

Murabahah is a trust sale (*bay' al-amanah*) in which the buyer depends on and relies upon the integrity of the purchaser as regards the cost of mentions to the buyer. Thus, it is the moral and legal obligation of the seller to be honest and truthful in stating the price at which he purchased the goods, and if he succeeded in obtaining a discount or rebate, it should also be acknowledged and accounted for the benefit of the purchaser.[35]

In Islamic law, the contract of sale about the cost of the sale's object to the seller is divided into three kinds:

i. *Tawliyah*: resale at the stated original cost with no profit or loss to the seller.
ii. *Wadi'ah*: resale at a discount from the original cost.
iii. *Murabahah*: the resale at a fixed surcharge or rate of profit on the stated original cost.

The main purpose of these sales is to "protect the innocent general consumer lacking expertise in the various items of trade from the wiles and stratagems of sharp traders."[36]

Technically, it is a deferred payment sale.

> *Morabahah* is the resale of a thing for a similar to its first price, with the same addition for profit.[37]

So, we can conclude by saying that this Islamic instrument is not a loan that bears interest, but it practised as a sale of the commodity by adding some agreed profit whose payment can be made in some future date.[38]

16.6.1 Conditions of murabahah

The conditions of a *murabahah* contract are as follows:

1. The seller should disclose the original price of the commodity to the purchaser. If the price is not disclosed, the contract will be invalid.
2. Parties should now exact cost, which should include all necessary expenses.
3. The profit over the original price should be fixed by any amount or in percentage and be mentioned in the contract by mutual consent of the parties.
4. Price should be specific for the validity of the sale.
5. Before sale, the commodity of sale has to be in the possession of the vendor.
6. If the sale is attributed to a future date or event, it will be regarded as void, and if parties want to effect a sale, a new sale contract is required.
7. The delivery of the commodities must be sure etc.
8. Payment can be made on a deferred basis with the mutual consent of both parties.
9. Commodity should be purchased from the third party.

16.7 *Ijara*—Contract of Lease

According to Patrick Hughes:

> The Arabic term, *ijarah* which means the use and enjoyment of the property for a time, includes hire, rental, and lease.[39]

Ijarah means rent, letting, leasing, hiring out or letting on lease.[40]

As mentioned by the Hanafi school of thought: "It is contract on usufructs for a known consideration."[41]

The word *ijarah* means to give something on rent. In the language of the law, it means lending of some object to somebody in return for some rental against a specified period. It can also be described as the sale of usufruct for consideration. It includes letting things moveable and immovable for hire and rendering services such as custody of property and professional services.

Hiring means a lease or hiring, and a contract of hiring[42] or leasing is an agreement between two parties on a particular subject matter to transfer the temporary title of that particular subject matter. For instance, one party offers a particular property to another who accepts it for a fixed period. In a contract of hiring, the person who offers the property is called lessor or hirer while the person who enjoys over the property after the acceptance is called lessee or hiree.

An *ijara* is an Islamic lease. This is often used as a financing lease. The parties agree to the lease terms, including the instalment amounts and payment dates. At the end of the term, the investor may sell the asset to a third party or to the lessee, depending on what arrangements the parties have made.

It is also a term used in Islamic *fiqh*, which means to give something on rent.

16.7.1 Qur'ān and Sunnah basis of ijara

Allah says:

> "Then if they suckle (the child) for your sake, pay them their recompense."[43]
> "One of those (girls) said: 'O my respectable father! Take him into your service. Surely, the best person you can employ is the one who is strong and trustworthy (and he is worthy of this assignment)."[44]

The Holy Prophet (PBUH) said: "Give wages of the person hired before his sweat dries up."[45] "If someone hires a person, let him inform him about the wages he is to receive."[46] Hadrat Sa'd ibn Abi Waqqas (R.A) reported that in the age of the Holy Prophet the owners of the land used to let their lands on rent.[47]

16.7.2 Kinds of ijara

Ijara has two different types, i.e. it can be used in two different situations.

1. It is related to engaging the services of a person on wages, if a person provides services, and wages are given as compensation against hired services. In this sense, the employee is called *Mustajir,* and the employee is called *Ajir*.
2. It is related to the usufruct of assets and properties. So *ijara* means "to transfer the usufruct of a particular property to another person in exchange for a rent claimed from him."[48]

In this sense lessor is called *Mujir,* and the lessee is called *Mustajir*, and the rent payable is called *Ujrah* (as analogies to the English term, leasing).

For the validity of a contract of hiring, the following elements must be available:

i. There must be at least two parties.
ii. There must be free consent of the parties.
iii. The price or remuneration of the hiring must be determined.[49]
iv. The object of the hiring must be ascertained.
v. The subject matter should be legal.
vi. The parties should have legal capacities.
vii. The period of hiring should be ascertained.

16.8 *Sukuk*—issuer's certificates

Sukuk is the plural of the Arabic singular *sakk* which means, certificate, legal instrument or a deed. In Islamic contract law, it refers to issuer's certificates representing an undivided share in the ownership of tangible assets, i.e. securities backed by real assets. Hence true *sukuk* are backed by tangible assets, usufruct or services.

Sukuk are financial instruments similar to bonds, hence referred to as Islamic bonds and also shared that the compliant with Islamic law. Since their inception in 2002, Sukuk markets have experienced dramatic growth rates attracting the attention of investors, analysts and researchers alike.

Sukuk are based on specific contracts borrowed from Islamic modes of financing: accounting and auditing organisation for Islamic financial institutions (AAOIFI). The AAOIFI, an Islamic international standard issuing institution that prepares accounting, auditing, governance and *Shariah* standards for the Islamic financial industry, defines Sukuk as being: "Certificates of equal value representing undivided shares in the ownership of tangible assets, usufructs, and services or (in the ownership of) the assets of particular projects or special investment activities."[50]

16.8.1 Requirements of sukuk

There are three requirements for a *sukuk* to be considered in compliance with the *Shariah* law.[51] First, the certificates must represent intangible ownership assets, usufructs or services from revenue-generating firms. Second, payments to the investor come from after-tax profits, and third, the value repaid at maturity date should follow the current market price of the underlying asset and not the initially invested amount.

The main difference between *sukuk* and conventional bonds is that *sukuk* does not involve any interest-based transactions because of their prohibition in *Shariah*. Like conventional asset-backed securities (ABS), *sukuk* is also backed by assets. However, the difference between *sukuk* and conventional ABS is that in the latter the underlying assets can be financial assets like loans or other receivables but in *sukuk,* only real assets can be used as collateral. The sale of debt is not permissible in Islamic finance, except when it is traded at par. This is the viewpoint of the majority of scholars. However, in Malaysia and some other countries discounted sale of debt is considered permissible.

16.8.2 Kinds of sukuk

Although initially various structures were employed for *sukuk, ijarah* (similar to a conventional operational lease contract) and *musharakah* (joint venture/ co-ownership) have become the most popular and commonly used *sukuk* because of their eligibility for trading in the secondary market according to Islamic jurisprudence.

Another popular *sukuk* structure is *musharakah* (joint venture/co-ownership).[52] The difference between *musharakah* and *ijarah sukuk* is that in the former the *sukuk* holders also share the ownership of the underlying *musharakah* assets with the originator of the assets which are used for business whereas, in *ijarah*, *sukuk* holders are the sole owner of the underlying assets. Both of the aforesaid *sukuk* types are backed by assets and are therefore called asset-backed *sukuk*.

There also exists another class of *sukuk*, the so-called asset-based *sukuk*, where the initial sale of the original assets by the originator to the S.P.V. does not take place, so the ownership (title) of assets remains with the originator of the *sukuk*.

16.8.3 Guidelines for Islamic sukuk

AAOIFI attempted to create guidelines for *sukuk* in accordance with *Shariah* principles:

1. *Sukuk* holders must own the real assets whether tangible, usufructs or services, capable of being owned and sold legally, with all rights and obligations of ownership in those assets. Transfer of the assets from manager/originator is ensured by writing them (*sukuk*) off its books.
2. *Sukuk*, to be tradable, must not represent receivables or debts except in the case of a trading or financial entity selling all its assets, or a portfolio with a standing financial obligation, in which some debts, incidental to physical assets or usufruct, were included unintentionally.[53]
3. It is not permissible for the manager of *sukuk* to undertake to offer loans to the *sukuk* holders when actual earnings fall short of expected earnings.
4. While issuing *sukuk*, it is also not permissible that the manager of *sukuk* undertakes to repurchase the assets from the *sukuk* holders at an initial value (face value), at the end of *sukuk*. However, it is permissible to repurchase the same at their market value, fair value or a price to be agreed, at the time of their actual purchase.
5. It is permissible for a lessee in an *ijarah sukuk* to undertake to purchase the leased assets when the *sukuk* are extinguished for its nominal value, provided he (lessee) is not also a partner or investment agent.
6. Besides issuing a *fatwa* (*Shariah* ruling) about the validity of *sukuk* structures, *Shariah* boards should also carefully review all the relevant contracts and documents related to the *sukuk* transaction and make sure that the actual means of implementation, operations and investments comply with *Shariah* standards.

16.9 *Takaful*—contract of insurance

There is a difference of opinion among jurists regarding *takaful* and insurance, and it is a critical and widely used method of business. Hence a detail discussion is required. In the beginning, it must be kept in mind that there is no harm in entering into an insurance policy with one of the numerous Islamic insurance companies that strictly observe *Shariah*-compliant standards.

Conventional insurance as practised in the advanced industrial societies is generally considered to be illegal by the majority of Islamic scholars. However, holding an insurance policy is allowable, according to some scholars. Still, it is better for the faithful to avoid this business, putting their trust in the Almighty, instead of putting faith in the insurance company and assuming that it would come to their rescue if there were a disaster.

Insurance policies provided by conventional banks and insurance companies have been receiving criticism among several Muslim scholars. Alternatively, Muslim jurists have introduced an alternative: *takaful*, an insurance system which complies with the principles of *Shariah*.

16.9.1 Definition

The word *takaful* is derived from the Arabic verb *Kafala*, which means to guarantee; to help; to bear responsibility for. In simple words, *takaful* means an agreement wherein participants (members) of a group jointly guarantee each other to meet a defined loss/damage suffered by anyone amongst them.

A contract of insurance is a mutual agreement.[54] *Takaful* is basically a system of Islamic insurance based on the principle of *Ta'awun* (mutual assistance) and *Tabarru* (voluntary contribution) and mutual guarantee, where the risk is shared collectively by the group. It is operated based on shared responsibility, brotherhood, solidarity and cooperation or assistance, which provides for mutual financial security and assistance to safeguard participants against a defined risk.

To sum up, *takaful* is a *Shariah*-compliant insurance scheme which is grounded in Islamic *muamalat*, observing the rules and regulations of Islamic law and operated on the basis of shared responsibility and mutual obligation to safeguard its participants against a defined risk:

> such contract is known as an agreement of mutual co-operation as the insurance policy is entertained into by the parties with the view of helping one another on the basis of brotherhood, mutual co-operation, goodwill and most importantly, such contract of insurance between the insurer and the assured operates based on the Islamic principles of co-operation.[55]

16.9.2 **Takaful***: an alternative to conventional insurance*

The English terms for *takaful* are "solidarity," "mutual guarantee" or "guaranteeing each other." Based on "social solitary, cooperation and mutual indemnification of losses of the members,"[56] *takaful* is Islamic insurance as it is run under the principles of Islamic finance. The system is a communal enterprise in which members pool their resources and help each other in case of loss or casualty. *Takaful* is *Shariah*-compliant insurance, a modern approach to reducing one's exposure to risks and ensuring social welfare.

Technically *takaful* means "a mutual guarantee or assurance based on the principles of al-aqd (contract) provided by a group of people living in the same society, against a defined risk or catastrophe befalling life, property or any form of a valuable asset."[57] Ayub defined the term *takaful* as follows:

> A form of Islamic insurance based on the principle of *Ta'awan* or mutual assistance. It provides for mutual assistance in cases of loss to life, assets and property and offers joint risk-sharing in the event of a loss incurred by one of the pool members.[58]

16.9.3 **Takaful** *and risk mitigation*

Takaful, an alternative to conventional insurance, is a means of mitigating the financial risk of loss through accidents, injuries and misfortunes. Muslims avoid taking precautionary measures before any undesired situation reaches them; this is because of their unveiled understanding of Allah's desire. The following verse explains the desire of Allah Almighty in relation to the acknowledgement of people worldly affairs.

إِنَّ ٱللَّهَ لَا يُغَيِّرُ مَا بِقَوْمٍ حَتَّىٰ يُغَيِّرُواْ مَا بِأَنفُسِهِمْ

> "Verily, Allah does not change the state of a people until they bring about a change in themselves."[59]

The verse cited and the following tradition instill the importance of hard work and endeavouring to find a means of avoiding unpleasant circumstances and lessening the risk of adverse conditions. Reliance on the Almighty means exerting oneself and then committing one's affairs to Him.

One day Prophet (PBUH) noticed a Bedouin who left his camel without tying it up. The Bedouin asked:

> "Holy Prophet (PBUH), shall I tie it and rely (upon Allah), or shall I leave it loose and rely (upon Allah)?"

He a replied:

> "Tie your camel (first), then put your trust in Allah."[60]

So the real meaning of reliance on Allah Almighty means making careful plans to attain good and avert misfortune to the best of one's ability. The Qur'ān tells us that the Prophet Yusuf e worked out a carefully considered strategy to save the citizens of Egypt from imminent famine.

قَالَ تَزْرَعُونَ سَبْعَ سِنِينَ دَأَبًا فَمَا حَصَدتُّمْ فَذَرُوهُ فِي سُنۢبُلِهِۦٓ إِلَّا قَلِيلًا مِّمَّا تَأْكُلُونَ٤٧ ثُمَّ يَأْتِي مِنۢ بَعْدِ ذَٰلِكَ
سَبْعٌ شِدَادٌ يَأْكُلْنَ مَا قَدَّمْتُمْ لَهُنَّ إِلَّا قَلِيلًا مِّمَّا تُحْصِنُونَ٤٨ ثُمَّ يَأْتِي مِنۢ بَعْدِ ذَٰلِكَ عَامٌ فِيهِ يُغَاثُ ٱلنَّاسُ
وَفِيهِ يَعْصِرُونَ٤٩

"Yusuf (Joseph) said: 'You will cultivate as usual, consecutively for seven years. So whatever you reap, keep it (in storage), leaving the grains in their ears except a small quantity (to thresh) for your (yearly) consumption. Then after this, there will come seven hard years (of drought) which will consume that (store) which you will have laid up for these years except a small quantity (which will fall surplus and) which you will keep in reserve. Then, following this will come a year during which people will be blessed with (plenty of) rain, and (the yield of fruits will be such as) they will press juices (of fruits that year)."[61]

16.9.4 Qur'ānic and Sunnah basis

The Qur'ān says to its believers to cooperate with each other: وَتَعَاوَنُواْ عَلَى ٱلْبِرِّ وَٱلتَّقْوَىٰ

"And always support one another in (the works of) righteousness and piety."[62]

Allah describes the character of the faithful in these words:

وَٱلْمُؤْمِنُونَ وَٱلْمُؤْمِنَٰتُ بَعْضُهُمْ أَوْلِيَآءُ بَعْضٍ

"The believers, men and women, are helpers and friends to one another."[63]

In ancient Arabia, it was a common practice for tribes to put their resources together to pay for blood money. The tribal tradition of pooling money among male relatives was known as *aqila*.

Ibn al-Musayyib and Abu Salama b. 'Abd al-Rahman related that Abu Hurayra (R.A) said:

Two women of Huhdayl fought, and one of them threw a stone at the other and killed her and what was in her womb. They took the dispute to the Prophet (PBUH), and he a judged that the blood money owed for her fetus was a good slave, male or female, and judged that the blood money for the woman is paid by the *'aqila*.[64]

The theme of extending help to fellow beings occurs in many prophetic traditions. According to al-Numan b. Bashir (R.A), the Prophet (PBUH) said:

"In their mutual love (and affection), their mutual mercy (and sympathy) and their mutual compassion, the true believers are like the physical body. If one of its organs is afflicted with paid, the rest of the body rallies to its with sleeplessness and fever."[65]

According to Abu Hurayra (R.A), the Prophet (PBUH) said:

> "If someone relives a believer of the agony of this world, Allah will relieve him of one of the agonies of the Day of Resurrection. If someone makes life easy for a person in distress, Allah will make life easy for him in this world and the Hereafter. If someone covers the faults of a Muslim in this world, Allah will cover his faults in this world and in the Hereafter. Allah does not cease helping His servant as long as His servant continues helping his brother."[66]

On the authority of Abu Musa al-Ashari (R.A), Prophet (PBUH) said:

> "The believer is related to the believer like a (fortified) wall; its one portion supports and strengthens the other," and he interlaced his fingers (to illustrate the point).[67]

If an individual is murdered and the identity of the murderer cannot be established, the heirs of the victim go to inspect the scene of the crime and adjure 50 residents of the locality to swear that they are not aware of the culprit nor have they sheltered him. Under the circumstances, either the people of the area or the swearers pay *diya* (blood money). Imam al-Sarakhsi has stated this principle of *Shariah* in the following words:

> When a man comes across the dead body of someone in an area where people reside, fifty of them must swear on oath, "By Allah, we have not murdered the man, and we do not know the identity of the killer either," and then they will make a compensatory payment.[68]

16.9.5 The structure of a takaful *company*

The structure of a *takaful* company is as follows: when a *takaful* company is formed, policyholders make contributions for their common good which the company maintains in individual accounts. Thus pooled funds are invested in sound financial products.

As part of the *takaful* contract, all policyholders agree that if any one of them is hurt or suffers a loss, they will make a proportionate gift from their accounts to cover that loss. Moreover, profits are shared by the *takaful* holders.

16.9.6 Various models of takaful

There are various models of *takaful* adopted in different Muslim countries. *Takaful* is based on various transactions accepted by the *Shariah*. The contemporary Islamic scholars mentioned that *mudarabah* or *wakalah* or *waqf*[69] or a combination of the three models is the most appropriate Islamic contract which should be employed in managing *takaful* business.[70] The contract of *ju'ala* (reward contract) has also been suggested as more suitable to be applied by *takaful* operators in order to defend their entitlement to performance-related fees provided that all of its specifications are carefully observed.[71] The following are the *takaful* models used worldwide.

1. ***Mudarabah* model:** The contract of *mudarabah* (trustee profit-sharing) is defined as a contractual agreement between the *Rabbul mal* (capital provider) and the *mudarib* (entrepreneur) for the business venture, whereby both parties agree on a ratio of pre-determined profit-sharing and losses in the business venture which is the sole responsibility of the *Rabbul mal* (capital provider) except where the losses are caused by the misconduct, negligence, violation of conditions by the entrepreneur.[72] If *mudarabah* is applied to the *takaful* contract, the *takaful* operator is considered as the entrepreneur who has the responsibility of carrying out the *takaful* business activities, where the participants as capital providers (*Rabbul mal*) donate the funds to the *takaful* operator. Generally, the contract specifies typically the proportion of profit (surplus) to be shared between the participants and the *takaful* operator.[73] *Mudarabah* means project-sharing, a special kind of partnership where policyholders give money to the *takaful* operators to manage investment activities on behalf of all policyholders.

   Under this model, the operators do not have to pay to commission but will receive a salary that will be paid from a share of profits made by the company. These same conditions apply to the management.[74]
2. ***Wakala* model:** The term *wakalah,* indicates performing an act on behalf of others, or delegation of a job or task to another.[75] *Wakalah* is "the act of one party delegating the other to act on its behalf in what can be the subject matter of the delegation."[76] The *wakalah* concept is essentially an agent–principal relationship, where the takaful operator acts as an agent on behalf of the participants and earns a fee for services rendered. Thus, where the *wakalah* model is applied, the operator (*wakil*) will manage the *takaful* fund as an agent of the participants where he will be given an upfront fee (*Ajr*) for his services. Any profit gained from the management of the *takaful* fund is entirely owned by the participants, and in case of loss, it has to be borne by the participants as well, unless where the losses are caused by the negligence or misconduct of the *takaful* operator.[77]
3. ***Waqf* model (*tabarru*):** It means detention, but its legal meaning refers to "the dedication of a property or to donate it in charity for a moral religious or charitable purpose."[78] Where *waqf* is made, the right of the *waqif* (dedicator) has been completely taken away, and ownership is transferred to Allah.[79] In the *waqf* model, the *takaful* operator will establish a *waqf* account from the *takaful* fund. Here, the operator will separate some money as *waqf* to operate the said *waqf* fund. The *waqf* fund shall be used to provide financial assistance to the members in case of losses, and the benefits are given strictly based on the *waqf* deed. All expenses, together with underwriting and operational cost of the *takaful*, are to be charged to the *waqf* fund. The *takaful* operator, as the manager, will carry out all necessary functions for the operations of the *waqf*

for a *wakalah* fee which should be deducted from the contribution donated by the participants.[80]

According to this model, a *waqf* fund is created as a separate legal entity with the contribution of the participant's amount and the amount deposited to this fund is considered as a *tabarru* donation. The aim of this fund is to provide relief to participants against defined losses according to the terms and conditions of the *waqf* fund. This is also called the *tabarru* model.[81]

4. ***Kafalah* model:** *Kafalah* generally means a guarantee. It is a contractual guarantee given by the guarantor to assume the responsibilities and obligations of the party being guaranteed on any claims. This principle is also applied in specific guarantees. The *takaful* operator acts as a guarantor and assumes the liability of the policyholder when the policyholder fails to discharge his obligation; then the *takaful* operator takes over the responsibilities of policies holders' obligation.[82]
5. ***Hawalah* contract:** *Hawalah* means shifting a thing from one place to another. Technically, as a term of law, *hawalah* means the shifting or assignment of debt from the liability of the original debtor to the liability of another person. *Hawalah* operates to release the original debtor from the debt. The *hawalah* model was suitable to cover life annuity contracts in which the policyholder (employer) has an obligation to pay the annuity to the participant (employee). The policyholder (employer) was transferred to the *takaful* operator and paid a contribution. The operator receives the obligation to pay the annuity to the participant (employee). Actuarial liabilities for *hawalah* are as follows:[83]
6. ***Wakala–waqf* model:** It is a *wakalah* model with a separate legal entity of *waqf* in-between. The relationship between the participants and the operator is direct with the *waqf* fund. The operator is the *wakeel*' of the fund, and the participants pay a contribution to the *waqf* fund by way of *tabarru*. The contributions received would also be a part of this fund and the combined amount will be used for investment and the profits earned would again be deposited into the same fund which also eliminates the issue of *gharar*. Losses to the participants are paid by the company from the same fund. Operational expenses that are incurred for providing *takaful* services are also met from the same fund.
7. ***Mudarabah–wakalah* model:** The *mudarabah–wakalah* is a hybrid model, which is a combination of *mudarabah* and *wakalah*. In this model, the *takaful* operator manages the investment activities on behalf of policyholders and takes investment risk. In this model, the operator will receive the agency fee as upfront charges from the *takaful* fund and will also get a share of the profit produced from the investment of the *takaful* fund based on the *mudarabah* contract.[84]
8. ***Ju'ala* model:** *Ju'ala*, literally means a reward given to someone for work he or she has done. Technically, it is defined as an undertaking by a person to give an identified reward to another for work he has done for him either within a specified time frame or so long as it provides benefit to another.[85] AAOIFI, in its *Shariah* Standard No.1, defines *ju'ala* as "a contract where

one of the parties (the *ja'il*) offers specified compensation (the *ju'l*) to anyone (the *Amil*) who achieves a finished result in a known or unknown period."[86] In this model, it has been suggested that a portion of the surplus distributable to the operators is considered as an incentive or reward from the participants for the effort put in registering a surplus to the PRF.[87]

It is pertinent to mention here that some more models of *takaful* are also described by some authors. A service contract is a contract that is related to the takaful management operations. It means that the contract dealt with the services offered by the Takaful company. The contracts have liabilities to policyholders as the operator of the *takaful* company. Regarding this, following are some more models of *takaful*:

9. ***Wadiah* contract:** *Wadiah* is safekeeping of a deposit; the takaful operator is only keeping some policyholders' money without any investment activities.
10. ***Al-Rahn* contract:** *Al-Rahn* or collateral is defined in Islamic jurisprudence as "possessions offered as security for debt so that the debt will be taken from it in case the debtor failed to pay back the due money." In the case of insurance, the *al-Rahn* contract is using a policies loan with cash value as collateral. Position of *al-Rahn (mortgaged asset)* is that it is an asset of *takaful* company. The policy loan can be categorised as an *al-Rahn* contract. An *al-rahn* contract can be placed in an investment contract.
11. ***Qardhul-hasan*:** *Qardhul-hasan* is defined as a loan from a *takaful* operator to cover deficit funds on the *takaful* contract or investment contract. In this condition, the *takaful* operator must provide *quardhul-hasan* without guarantee or interest. *Qardhul-hasan* granted unconditional terms of refund and without any service fee or expenses. The amount of *qardhul-hasan* is an asset on corporate funds and liabilities on *takaful* fund or investment fund.[88]

16.9.7 Islamic insurance vs. conventional insurance

Conventional insurance is not *Shariah*-compliant as it involves elements of deception, gambling, excessive uncertainty and interest. However, as elaborated earlier, *takaful* is *Shariah*-compliant, and is approved.

Although it is in its early stages of development and growth, *takaful* is a financially sound alternative to conventional insurance. This is substantiated by the fact that *takaful* is gaining currency currently across Muslim and non-Muslim countries, including Iran, Turkey, Malaysia, Sudan, the Middle East, the United States and the United Kingdom.

16.9.8 Difference of opinion

Jurists have different opinions regarding *takaful*. The jurists who declared *takaful*, i.e. insurance impermissible had based their opinion on the argument that alleviating future risk is uncertain, hence it is not permissible to conclude a *takaful* contract. Similarly, some have asserted that making a future provision through insurance is contrary to the will of the Divine. The jurists who declared it permissible, believe that alleviating risk is not necessarily contrary to the will of Allah and note the *hadith* and passages in the Qur'ān that suggest that believers should take a proactive approach to risk.

The solution to circumventing uncertainty has been for the insured to donate the premium (expecting nothing back) and the insurer to donate the event-of-loss amount back upon the occurrence of an insured event. Since two unilateral obligations are occurring—each in and of itself discrete—uncertainty is said to be avoided.[89]

According to them, *takaful* has an independent legitimate basis and does not require legal fiction to validate its existence. This stems from the golden rule that that which is not prohibited is permissible and is buttressed by verses and *hadith.*

16.10 *Istisna*—contract of manufacturing

Istisna consists of ordering an artisan or manufacturer to make certain goods answering a given description. By *istisna,* one may engage, for example, a cobbler to make a pair of shoes for a fixed price or ask a tailor to make a suit to be delivered later.[90]

A contract of manufacturing is an agreement between two parties in making or manufacturing a particular article of which one of the parties will offer a labourer or artist to make a particular article for a fixed price with a certainty of quality and quantities of articles within a prescribed period. The price of the article is to be paid once the article is ready.[91]

It is to be noted here that a contract of manufacturing is based on the custom or practices which originated from the period of the Holy Prophet (PBUH) and were justified by equity[92] and by the necessities of business.[93]

An *istisna* is the giving of an order to a workman to make a definite thing, with an agreement to pay a definite wage or price for that thing when made. In this form of sale, nothing changes hands immediately and is only valid in respect of those goods with respect to which custom is proved and is similar to the hire of a workman to do a job.[94]

According to Zakhaili, the contract of *istisna* is complete by offer and acceptance between the manufacturer and the customer.[95]

According to Baillie:

> *Istisna,* or made to order, is lawful with regard to everything in which it is customary, such as the making of turbans, boots, and vessels of copper or brass, and the like. *Istisna* is in its inception a contact of hiring; but it terminates by becoming a sale for an instant, as it were before the surrender or delivery. The workman has no option and may be compelled to do the work, but the person who gives the order has an option and may either take or reject the article as he thinks proper. According to the most correct view of the matter, the subject of the contract is the thing required to be made; for which reason, if the contractor bring an article manufactured by another

> person, or by himself at a time previous to the contract, it is lawful, and a sufficient compliance with the contract. The manufactured article also does not become specific to the contract until it has been actually approved so that if the manufacturer should sell the article to another party before an inspection by the person who gave the order, the sale would be lawful.[96]

Istisna is a mode of finance; it is defined as "kind of sale where a commodity is transacted before it comes into existence."[97]

It is used in financing goods that are not yet ready for sale and will have to be manufactured. An example includes tailoring services, architect services, etc. It is an order for the producer to manufacture a specific commodity for the purchaser. It is used in pre-shipment export financing and usable in all other situations where goods have to be manufactured before the sale.

It is important to note that when a manufacturer uses its material for the production, it is *istisnā*, otherwise the contract will be of *ijara* rather than *istisna*.

16.10.1 Conditions of istisna

Hanafi jurists acknowledge the following conditions for a valid contract of *istisna*:

1. The subject of *istisna* should be precisely mentioned in terms of its kind, quality and quantity.
2. There should be some work or performance involved in the commodity.
3. The time of the completion of work and delivery should not be fixed. This is the view of Imam Abu Hanifa. His two disciples disagree with his teacher and hold that time should be fixed.
4. The price or consideration should also be specified.[98]

There are some differences between *istisna* and *salam*:

1. In *istisnā*, manufacturing of the commodity is necessary.
2. In *salam*, the full price is paid in advance but in *istisna* there is no such condition.
3. Delivery time is essential in *salam* and not in *istisna*.[99]

16.11 Contract of *salam*

"In Arabic, the word *salam* means to advance. When a man advances the price for certain goods to be delivered in the future on a fixed date, the transaction is called *salam*." "*Salam* is a contract involving immediate payment of the price, and admitting a delay in the delivery of the articles purchased."[100]

"The *salam* or advance is a sale of goods that have not been seen, but are specified in the contract."[101] Duncan B. MacDonald defines *salam* as a "bargain with payment in advance."[102]

> The *Shariah* recognises two kinds of sale for delivery in future under strict safeguards against gambling in options. They are *salam* and *istisna*. In *salam*, the price must be paid in cash at the conclusion of the bargain. A bargain must be for definite delivery at a definite future date of a *res fungibilis* (i.e. of something which is not specific but is sold quantity by quantity).[103]

Similarly, *salam* is also based on some defined conditions against the rule that physical ownership is necessary for the seller.

Salam: "A sale whereby the seller undertakes to supply some specific goods to the buyer at a future date in exchange for an advanced price fully paid at spots."[104]

It is used in financing goods and services that are not ready for spot sale and will have to be delivered later. In *salam*, payment is the spot, but the delivery is deferred. It is used in exceptional cases to facilitate transactions.

16.11.1 Qur'ānic and Sunnah basis of salam

According to some jurists following Qur'ānic verse and *hadith* are the basis of *salam*.

يَٰٓأَيُّهَا ٱلَّذِينَ ءَامَنُوٓاْ إِذَا تَدَايَنتُم بِدَيۡنٍ إِلَىٰٓ أَجَلٖ مُّسَمّٗى فَٱكۡتُبُوهُۚ

> "O believers! Whenever you strike deals with one another for a fixed period, reduce the transaction to writing."[105]

Narrated by Ibn Abbas: "Allah's Apostle came to Medina, and the people used to pay in advance the price of fruits to be delivered within one or two years." (The sub-narrator is in doubt whether it was one to two years or two to three years). The Prophet said, "Whoever pays money in advance for dates (to be delivered later) should pay it for known specified weight and measure (of the dates)."[106]

Again, Holy Prophet (PBUH) also allowed *salam* on the following circumstances:[107]

1. Full payment should be made from the end of the buyer because *salam* is allowed with keeping in mind the unavailability of finance of sellers such as farmers.
2. *Salam* is available for those supplies for which quality and quantity can be differentiated separately.
3. It is compulsory to mention in the contract the accurate date and place of delivery.
4. The contract is not applicable in a particular field or commodity such as a particular land of rice or fruit because a particular field ban is destroyed.
5. While contracting, the number of commodities must be specified leaving no ambiguity in the mind of any party.

16.11.2 The conditions of a valid salam

A valid contract of *salam* sale requires the fulfilment of the following conditions, which are over and above the conditions of an ordinary sale:

1. It is necessary that the buyer pays the price of the object in full to the seller in advance.[108]
2. An outstanding loan due on the seller cannot be fully or partially fixed as price, nor can a loan outstanding on a third party be transferred to the seller in future adjustment towards the price.
3. A single amount for payment of different commodities or of the same commodity in different periods or at different places is not approved. It is necessary that the amount for each item and for each period of delivery be separately fixed.
4. The object of *salam* should be in existence and well defined by description. It includes genus, species, colour and country of origin and any other feature, which affects the price.
5. *Salamable* articles include fungible things, i.e. weighable, measurable and accountable by number. Non-fungible things cannot be sold based on *salam.*
6. A *salam* contract cannot be affected by things that must be delivered on the spot simultaneously in the same session of contract.
7. About the minimum period of delivery, the jurists have different opinions which vary from 1 month to 15 days, etc.
8. The time of the subject matter of *salam* should be fixed at the time of the contract.
9. Fixing the place of delivery is requisite if it entails extra expenses, or the place of contract is not a suitable place for delivery.

16.12 Contract of partnership

Another Muslim jurist, Muhammad Akram Khan, defines a *sharikah* or partnership as: "A contract between two or more persons who launch a business or financial enterprise to make a profit."

In all the above definitions, the idea of partnership is to share profit over the business with the share of loss. Thus, a partnership needs to be defined as a contract between two or more persons in carrying out a particular business with a view to not only sharing the profit but also loss and liability between the partners relying on the terms of the contract.

A contract of partnership can be formed in any of the following models:

i. Partnership of reciprocity.
ii. Limited partnership.
iii. Partnership in arts.
iv. Partnership upon credit.

16.13 Contract of agency

A contract of agency is an agreement between two parties in which one party will appoint another party to act on his behalf. The agreement is to authorise the power to represent him or to exercise power on his behalf in any matter that is instructed by him. In a contract of agency the person who authorises the power is called the principal and the person who is appointed to exercise power is called the agent, and the subject matter of which the authority is given to exercise power is called the object.[109]

In its operation, however, the power of exercise is not to be vested in the agent in any of the following circumstances:

i. If the agent takes an oath on behalf of the principal.
ii. If the agent has been appointed by the principal to perform an illegal act.
iii. If the agent has been instructed by the principal to divorce the principal's wife on his behalf.
iv. If the agent has been appointed by the principal to give consent to the marriage of the virgin daughter of the principal.
v. If the agent has been asked by the principal to sell his (the principal's) house.[110]
vi. Any other matter which is not covered by the condition of the agreement.

16.14 Contract of arbitration

A contract of arbitration is an agreement between the parties who enter into a mutual agreement on a particular subject matter that in the case of any dispute or disagreement that arises over the transaction, the dispute or disagreement will be settled through the appointment of a third party as an arbitrator.[111]

According to Ahmad Mustafa Zarqa, a contract of arbitration is: "A contract between two contending parties in which both agree to appoint a third person as an arbitrator to settle their dispute" and "it can be between more than two parties."[112]

16.15 Contract of gift

A contract of the gift is an agreement between two parties of an unqualified transfer of a particular object (such as goods, property, etc.) without any consideration. In a valid contract of the gift, the following elements must be available:

i. The subject matter must be ascertained and legal.
ii. The parties must have legal capacities.
iii. There must be free consent of the parties.
iv. The offer of the gift by the offeror should be made unqualified or without any view of consideration from the offeror.
v. The offer of the gift made by the offeror should be accepted by the offeree.
vi. The title of the object of the gift should be fully delivered by the offeror to the offeree.[113]

16.16 Contract of suretyship

A contract of suretyship is defined in the *Medjelle* as: "(Suretyship) *kafala* is to add obligation to obligation in respect of a demand for something that is to say it is someone adding himself to another person, and himself undertaking a demand which is binding on that person."[114]

There are usually five types of suretyship models, as seen below:

i. ***Kafala bin nafs*:** a surety for the person or a man.
ii. ***Kafala bil mall*:** a surety for the giving of property, goods or article.
iii. ***Kafala bil tasleem*:** a surety for the delivery of property.
iv. ***Kafala bil darak*:** a surety of the delivery of payment over a property, goods or article sold.
v. ***Kafala bil manjaza*:** surety is subjected to neither the condition nor time.[115]

In a contract of suretyship, the person who has undertaken the responsibility of transaction is called *kafil*, the person who is being undertaken by the *kafil* is called *makful anhu*, the person for who the *makful anhu* is being undertaken is called *makful lahu* and the subject matter of such contract is called *makful bihi*.

16.17 Contract of guarantee

In a commercial transaction, a contract of guarantee comprises two separate agreements between three parties on two separate subject matters. The first agreement is between two parties where one party agrees to supply goods or property to the other party on credit for a special price, in which the first party is called the creditor and the second is called the principal debtor. Meanwhile, the second agreement is between the creditor, and a third party is called surety or the guarantor who will undertake full responsibility of liability in case of any default in settlement of the debt by the principal debtor.

"A contract of guarantee is a form of contract by which a third party undertakes to be responsible or liable for the debt of another."[116] Hence, if the principal debtor in such a contract fails to settle the debt on time, the guarantor is bound to settle the debt on the debtor's behalf. However, if in a case where the guarantor dies before settling the debt, the debt will have to be settled upon his estate.[117]

16.18 C.I.F. contract

Cost, insurance and freight (C.I.F.) is a contract of international trade and shipping of the carriage of goods by sea which was introduced by English law. A C.I.F. contract is not contrary to Islamic provisions.

A C.I.F. contract means a contract for the price that the buyer has to pay for the cost of goods together with the insurance of the goods during the transit and the freight or carriage of the goods to the port of destination. In other words, in a C.I.F. contract,[118] usually there are two subordinate contracts made by the seller of which the first is a contract of affreightment or contract of carriage of the goods by sea where the shop owner (carrier) signs a document known as the bill of lading upon receipt of the goods, while the second is a contract of insurance in accordance with which the underwriter will deliver a policy of insurance.[119]

16.19 F.O.B. contract

The free on board (F.O.B.) contract is also another form of a contract of international trade, which is also not contrary to Islamic provisions. A F.O.B. contract is defined as follows:

> A contract of sale of goods where the seller pays the cost of the shipment and makes delivery as soon as the goods are placed on board, the buyer bearing the risk of whether there are lost or not. The seller must give notice to the buyer to enable him to ensure the goods. The risk does not pass to the buyer, nor does the property until the goods are actually on board.[120]

16.20 Contract of mortgage or bailment

A mortgage transaction is allowed in Islam, and it was widely practised during the period of the Holy Prophet (PBUH). It is still widely practised today, not only in Muslim societies but also in non-Muslim societies. Anwar Ahmad Qadri said that “Bailment is a deposit in which the owner of property places his property in the custody of another for safekeeping.” Anwar further explained that the property deposited in the contract is considered as a trust and therefore if the person holding it, negligently or deliberately, by wrongful action causes or allows that property to be destroyed or perish, that person will be responsible for that loss. However, if the loss of that property is not caused by any wrongful act of deliberate or negligence of the person, the person holding that property will not be held liable for that loss.[121]

A mortgage transaction is allowed by the Divine injunction in the Qur’ān when Allah u says to the effect:

وَإِن كُنتُمْ عَلَىٰ سَفَرٍ وَلَمْ تَجِدُوا۟ كَاتِبًا فَرِهَٰنٌ مَّقْبُوضَةٌ ۖ فَإِنْ أَمِنَ بَعْضُكُم بَعْضًا فَلْيُؤَدِّ ٱلَّذِى ٱؤْتُمِنَ أَمَٰنَتَهُۥ
وَلْيَتَّقِ ٱللَّهَ رَبَّهُۥ

> “And if you are on a journey and do not find a scribe, then take possession of a pledge in the mortgage. Then, if one of you trusts the other, so he whose honesty has been trusted should deliver his trust and fear Allah.”[122]

Thus, a contract of mortgage or bailment is an agreement between two parties of sound mind[123] on particular security, for a particular debt and a particular period. The person who gives the pledge and takes the debt is called mortgagor or pledge (*Rahin*)[124] or bailer while the person who takes the pledge and gives the debt is called (*Murtahin*) or mortgagee or pledged or bailee.[125] The person to whom the pledge and the pledged deposit the pledge is called (*'Adl*).[126] The pledged property, is called *Marhun* or *Rahn*[127] and the debt of that mortgage is called debt or *Marhun bihi*.

16.20.1 Mortgages

Mortgages for household, commercial or personal needs in non-Muslim societies are based on interest. What Allah has prohibited no one may legalise. If an individual attempts to legalise interest or any one of the Divine prohibitions, he or she is no longer within the ambit of Islam. In non-Muslim countries where Muslims are small in numbers, the issue of mortgage for them becomes an issue of *ijtihad* (independent reasoning of a jurist's mental faculty in deducing a solution to a legal question).

A pertinent juristic maxim worth citing here is that "injunctions change with the change of circumstances, places and ages."[128] As the conditions of Muslim minorities living in non-Muslim countries change and there is no alternative system available, the legal status of the prohibited thing becomes different. According to jurists, if Muslims are residents of land where the rules of *Shariah* are not in force—when they also pay taxes to the non-Muslim government—then they may make use of the available facilities. In such a situation, forbidden interest will not become lawful, but this injunction will not be applicable. To sum up, interest-based mortgages are acceptable until a viable Islamic solution is available, even though the status of interest remains categorically forbidden.[129]

16.21 Contract of compromise

A contract of compromise is an agreement between two parties and a disputed matter to be settled outside the court of law. The *Medjelle* defines such a contract as: "A resolving a dispute by consent (of both parties), and it becomes a concluded contract by offer and acceptance."[130]

It has been further defined by Mustafa Ahmad Zarqa as: "An agreement between two contenders to have the right to take the disputed matter to the court of law."[131]

A contract of compromise is allowed in the Islamic law of contract. Qur'ān says:

وَإِن طَآئِفَتَانِ مِنَ ٱلْمُؤْمِنِينَ ٱقْتَتَلُوا۟ فَأَصْلِحُوا۟ بَيْنَهُمَا ۖ فَإِنۢ بَغَتْ إِحْدَىٰهُمَا عَلَى ٱلْأُخْرَىٰ فَقَـٰتِلُوا۟ ٱلَّتِى تَبْغِى
حَتَّىٰ تَفِىٓءَ إِلَىٰٓ أَمْرِ ٱللَّهِ فَإِن فَآءَتْ فَأَصْلِحُوا۟ بَيْنَهُمَا بِٱلْعَدْلِ وَأَقْسِطُوٓا۟ ۖ إِنَّ ٱللَّهَ يُحِبُّ ٱلْمُقْسِطِينَ

> "And if two parties of the Muslims fight, make them reconcile. Then if either of these (parties) commits injustice and aggression against the other, fight against (the party) that is committing aggression till it returns to Allah's command (of establishing peace). When they revert and submit, make peace between them with equity. And put justice to work. Surely, Allah loves those who do justice."[132]

إِنَّمَا ٱلْمُؤْمِنُونَ إِخْوَةٌ فَأَصْلِحُوا۟ بَيْنَ أَخَوَيْكُمْ ۚ وَٱتَّقُوا۟ ٱللَّهَ لَعَلَّكُمْ تُرْحَمُونَ

"The truth is that (all) believers are brothers (to one another). So make peace between your two brothers and always fear Allah, so that you may be shown mercy."[133]

16.22 Contract of employment

A contract of employment is an agreement between the employers and the employee, master, and servant, or company and worker on a particular work for particular consideration. This kind of contract is well developed in Islam, whereby the Prophet (PBUH) had always emphasised in many traditions on the rights and duties of the employer and the employee. Hence, in one of his traditions, the Prophet (PBUH) said to the effect:

> Narrated by Ibn Umar (R.A) who said that the Holy Prophet (PBUH) said: "(Oh employer) you (have to) settle the salary of the employee before his sweat dries."[134]

Again, the Prophet (PBUH) says in another tradition of his to this effect:

> Narrated by Imam Abu Hurairah (R.A) who said: The Holy Prophet (PBUH) said: "Allah declared that there will be quarrel between three types of people in the resurrection day: One of them is the one who enters into a contract by My name and breached it, secondly the one who illegally caught a free man and sold it and consumed the money, and finally the person who used a worker for his work and did not pay his salary."[135]

Notes

1 Al-Kasani, Badai al-Sanai, vol. 5, p. 133; Ibn al-Humam, Fath al-Qadir, vol. 5, p. 73.
2 Shirbini, Mughni al-Muhtaj, vol. 2, p. 2; Ibn Qudama, al-Mughni, vol. 3, p. 559.
3 Dr. Muhammad Tahir Mansuri, Islamic law of contracts and business transactions, p. 187.
4 Article No.105, *Medjelle al-Ahkam-ul-Adalia* English translated by W.E. Grigsby, London.
5 Abd al-Raheem, Muhammadan jurisprudence, p. 358.
6 N. Siegnette, Code musalman par Khalil, as quoted in Dr. S.E. Rayner, The theory of contracts in Islamic law, p. 103.
7 Noel J. Caulson, Commercial law in the Gulf States, p. 20.
8 Al-Kasani, Badai al-Sanai, vol. 5, p. 133; Ibn al-Humam, Fath al-Qadir, vol. 5, p. 3.
9 Ibn 'Abidin, Radd al-Muhtar, vol. 3, p. 364.
10 Article No.1329, *Medjelle al-Ahkam-ul-Adalia* English translated by W.E. Grigsby, London.
11 Ibn Arfa, Mukhtesan of Sidi Khalil, p. 193.
12 Cowan, A dictionary of modern written Arabic, p. 469.
13 Cowan, A dictionary of modern written Arabic, p. 468.
14 The Hedaya, English translation by Hamilton, pp. 217–231.
15 Qur'ān, 38:24 (Eng. trans. from 'Glorious Qur'ān' by Shaykh-ul-Islam Dr. Muhammad Tahir-ul-Qadri).

16 Ibn Qudamah, al-Mughni, vol. 5, p. 3.
17 AAOIFI Standard 12, Sharika (*Musharakah*) and modern corporations 3.1,3.4,5.3,5.4,5.5 and 5.9 (1429H/2008G).
18 M. Omer Chapra, Towards a just monetary system, p. 63.
19 Article 1045, *Medjelle al-Ahkam-ul-Adalia* English translated by W.E. Grigsby, London.
20 Article 1060, *Medjelle al-Ahkam-ul-Adalia* English translated by W.E. Grigsby, London.
21 Article 1329, *Medjelle al-Ahkam-ul-Adalia* English translated by W.E. Grigsby, London.
22 Abu Bakr bin Masud al-Kasani, Bidai al-Sanai, vol. 6, p. 85; Ibne Qudamah, al-Mughni, vol. 5, p. 109, Dar al-Fikr, Beruit.
23 Article No.1404, *Medjelle al-Ahkam-ul-Adalia* English translated by W.E. Grigsby, London.
24 Ibn Abidin, Raad al-Muhtar, vol. 5, p. 645.
25 Kharshi, vol. 6, p. 2.
26 Anwar Ahmad Qadri, A sunni Shafi Code, p. 73.
27 Ali al-Khafif, al-Sharikat fi al-Fiqh al-Islami p. 65, Cairo: 1941.
28 Rashad Khalil, al-Sharikat fi al-Fiqh al-Islami, p. 154, Cairo 1979.
29 Qur'ān 73:20 (Eng. trans. from 'Glorious Qur'ān').
30 Jassas, Ahkam al-Qur'ān, vol. 3, p. 45.
31 Article No.1405, *Medjelle al-Ahkam-ul-Adalia* English translated by W.E. Grigsby, London.
32 Article No.1407, *Medjelle al-Ahkam-ul-Adalia* English translated by W.E. Grigsby, London.
33 Sarkhsi, al-Mabsut, vol. 22, p. 42; Ibn Qudama, al-Mughni, vol. 5, p. 69.
34 Muhammad bin Ali Haskafi, al-Dur al-Mukhtar, vol. 4, p. 171, H.M.Saeed Co. Karachi..
35 Dr. Muhammad Tahir Mansuri, Islamic law of contracts and business transactions, p. 187.
36 Marghinani, al-Hidayah, vol. 3, p. 56.
37 Neil B.E. Baillie, The Mohammudan law of sale, p. 250.
38 Ali bin Abi Bakr al-Marghainani, al-Hidayah, vol. 3, p. 70, al-Misbah, Lahore.
39 Patrick Hughes, Dictionary of Islam, pp. 175–176.
40 Cowan, A dictionary of modern written Arabic, see *Ijarah.*
41 Al-Kasani, Badai al-Sanai, vol. 4, p. 174; Zaylai, Tabyin al_Haqaiq, vol. 5, p. 105.
42 Nabil A. Saleh, Unlawful gain and legitimate profit in Islamic law, (1989), p. 97.
43 Qur'ān 65:6 (Eng. trans. from 'Glorious Qur'ān' by Shaykh-ul-Islam Dr. Muhammad Tahir-ul-Qadri).
44 Qur'ān 28:26 (Eng. trans. from 'Glorious Qur'ān' by Shaykh-ul-Islam Dr. Muhammad Tahir-ul-Qadri).
45 Sanani, al-Salam, vol. 3, p. 81.
46 Shawkani, Nayl al-Awtar, vol. 5, p. 292.
47 Nasai, Sunan (Urdu) vol. 3, p. 60, Qur'ān Mahal Karachi.
48 Al-Sarakhsi, al-Mabsut, vol. 15, p. 74, (1989) Dar al-Fikr Beruit.
49 Abd al-Rahman, Muhammadan jurisprudence, for (i–iii) p. 370.
50 The AAOIFI Shariah standard (17) on investment *Sukuk*, Article 2 of AAOIFI.
51 Godlewski, C. Turk-Ariss, R & Weill, L. Sukuk vs conventional bonds: A stock market.
52 El-Hawary, Grais and Iqbal (2004).
53 Mohamed Naim, A., Yazid Isa, M. and Liki Hamid, M. (2013), "The effects of new AAOIFI standards on Sukuk in choosing the most authentic Islamic principles", *Journal of Islamic Accounting and Business Research*, Vol. 4 No. 1, pp. 77–93.
54 Nabil A. Saleh, Unlawful gain and legitimate profit in Islamic law, (1989), p. 100.

55 Nik Ramlah Mahmood, Insurance law in Malaysia (1992), p. 245.
56 An introduction to Takaful—an alternative to insurance, http://www.sbp. org.pk/departments/ibd/Takaful.pdf.
57 Brain Kettel, Introduction to Islamic banking and finance, p. 129.
58 Muhammad Ayub, Understanding Islamic finance, p. 495.
59 Qur'ān, 13:11 (Eng. trans. from 'Glorious Qur'ān' by Shaykh-ul-Islam Dr. Muhammad Tahir-ul-Qadri).
60 Narrated by al-Tirmidhi in al-Sunan, 4:668 #2517.
61 Qur'ān, 12:47–49 (Eng. trans. from 'Glorious Qur'ān' by Shaykh-ul-Islam Dr. Muhammad Tahir-ul-Qadri).
62 Qur'ān 5:2 (Eng. trans. from 'Glorious Qur'ān' by Shaykh-ul-Islam Dr. Muhammad Tahir-ul-Qadri).
63 Qur'ān 9:71 (Eng. trans. from 'Glorious Qur'ān' by Shaykh-ul-Islam Dr. Muhammad Tahir-ul-Qadri).
64 Narrated by al-Bukhari in al-Sahih, 6:2532 #6512.
65 Narrated by al-Bukhari in al-Sahih, 5:2238 #5665.
66 Narrated by Imam Muslim in al-Sahih, 4:2074 #2699.
67 Narrated by al-Bukhari in al-Sahih, 2:863 #2314.
68 Cited by al-Sarakhsi in al-Mabsut, 26:109.
69 M.M. Khan, Comparative analysis of Islamic and prevailing insurance practices, International journal of business and social sciences 2011, 2 (10).
70 HuHtay, Viability of Islamic insurance (*takaful*) in India, 2013.
71 Kamaruzaman NoorDin A juristic evaluation of the application of *ji'alah* (reward contract) as the underlying basis for justifying surplus sharing practice, 1st insurance and *takaful* international symposium, Selangor, Malaysia, 2013.
72 Muhammad Ayub, Understanding Islamic finance, UK 2007.
73 Hassan Aznan, Fundamentals of Shariah in Islamic finance, Kuala Lumpur 2011.
74 M.M. Billah, Comment of Shaikh al-Azhar's fatwa against life insurance, New Horizon, 58, 3-6 (1996).
75 HuHtay, Viability of Islamic insurance (*takaful*) in India, 2013.
76 AAOIFI, Shariah Standard No.23, Shariah standards for Islamic financial institutions, Bahrain 2007.
77 HuHtay, Viability of Islamic insurance (*takaful*) in India, 2013.
78 HuHtay, Viability of Islamic insurance (*takaful*) in India, 2013.
79 Abdul Rahman Doi, Shariah: the Islamic law, Kuala Lumpur 1984.
80 HuHtay, Viability of Islamic insurance (*takaful*) in India, 2013.
81 A.R.A. Wahab, *Takaful* business models—*Wakalah* based on *WAQF*, presented at second International symposium on *Takaful* 2006, Malaysia.
82 Ocke Kurniandi, Classification of takaful contracts, p. 7.
83 Ocke Kurniandi, Classification of takaful contracts, p.
84 HuHtay, Viability of Islamic insurance (*takaful*) in India, 2013
85 Kamaruzaman NoorDin A juristic evaluation of the application of *ji'alah* (reward contract) as the underlying basis for justifying surplus sharing practice, 1st insurance and *takaful* international symposium, Selangor, Malaysia, 2013
86 Abdul Rahman Doi, Shariah: the Islamic law, Kuala Lumpur 1984.
87 Kamaruzaman NoorDin A juristic evaluation of the application of *ji'alah* (reward contract) as the underlying basis for justifying surplus sharing practice, 1st insurance and *takaful* international symposium, Selangor, Malaysia, 2013.
88 Ocke Kurniandi, Classification of takaful contracts, p. 9.
89 Oliver Agha, Islamic finance: principle before profit, p. 134.
90 Al-Kasani, Badai al-Sanai, vol. 5, p. 3.
91 Nabil A. Saleh, Unlawful gain and legitimate profit in Islamic law, (1989), p. 61.
92 Nabil A. Saleh, Unlawful gain and legitimate profit in Islamic law, (1989), p. 61.

93 Abd al-Rahman I. Doi, Muhammadan jurisprudence, p. 293.
94 Anwar Ahmad Qadri, Islamic jurisprudence in the modern world, p. 326.
95 Dr. Wahbah al-Zakhaili, al-Fiqh al-Islami wa Adillatuhu, p. 631.
96 Neil B.E. Baillie, The Mohammudan law of sale, pp. 297–298.
97 Abu Bakr bin Masud al-Kasani, Bidai al-Sanai, vol. 5, p. 3; Ibne Qudamah, al-Mughni, vol. 5, p. 109, Dar al-Fikr, Beruit.
98 Abdal Karim Kasib, Aqd al-Istisna fi al-Fiqh al-Islami, pp. 133–134.
99 A. El-Gamal Mahmood, Islamic finance, p. 90, (2006) Cambridge University Press.
100 Thomas Patrick Hughes, Dictionary of Islam, p. 561.
101 Nawawi, Minhaj Talibain, Eng. Translation by p. 147.
102 Duncan B. MacDonald, Development of Muslim theology, jurisprudence and constitutional theory (1903) p. 353.
103 Anwar Ahmad Qadri, Islamic jurisprudence in the modern world, p. 325.
104 Mansoor bin Younus Bahuti, Kishaf al-Qina la Matn al-Qina, vol. 3, p. 276. Dar Dar al-Kutab al-Ilmiah.
105 Qur'ān 2:282 (Eng. trans. from 'Glorious Qur'ān' by Shaykh-ul-Islam Dr. Muhammad Tahir-ul-Qadri).
106 Imam Muslim, Sahih, Eng. Translated by Muhammad Mohsin Khan, p. 243.
107 Muhammad bin Ismail Bukhari, al-Jami al-Sahih, Kitab al-Baya, Bab al-Salam.
108 Shawkani, Nayl al-Awtar, vol. 5, p. 165.
109 Article No.1449, *Medjelle al-Ahkam-ul-Adalia* English translated by W.E. Grigsby, London.
110 Abd al-Rahman I. Doi, Muhammadan jurisprudence, for (i–v), p. 367.
111 Minhaj, p. 181; Sharh al-Wiqaya, vol. 3, p. 740 as cited in Dr. Niazi, p. 350.
112 Ahmad Mustafa Zarqa, p. 555 as quoted in Dr. Niazi, p. 350.
113 Abd al-Rahman I, Doi, Muhammadan jurisprudence, for (v–vi) p. 334.
114 Article 612, *Medjelle al-Ahkam-ul-Adalia* English translated by W.E. Grigsby, London.
115 Article 613–17, *Medjelle al-Ahkam-ul-Adalia* English translated by W.E. Grigsby, London for (i–v).
116 Abd al-Rahman I, Doi, Muhammadan jurisprudence, p. 369.
117 Abd al-Rahman I. Doi, Muhammadan jurisprudence, p. 369.
118 Dr. Liaquat Ali Khan Niazi, Islamic law of contract (1991), p. 371.
119 Dr. Liaquat Ali Khan Niazi, Islamic law of contract (1991), p. 372.
120 John Burka, Obsorn's concise law dictionary, p. 84 as quoted in Dr. Niazi p. 372.
121 Anwar Ahmad Qadri, Islamic jurisprudence in the modern world, p. 328.
122 Qur'ān 2:283 (Eng. trans. from 'Glorious Qur'ān' by Shaykh-ul-Islam Dr. Muhammad Tahir-ul-Qadri).
123 Article No.708, *Medjelle al-Ahkam-ul-Adalia* English translated by W.E. Grigsby, London.
124 Article No.703, *Medjelle al-Ahkam-ul-Adalia* English translated by W.E. Grigsby, London.
125 Article No.704, *Medjelle al-Ahkam-ul-Adalia* English translated by W.E. Grigsby, London.
126 Article No.705, *Medjelle al-Ahkam-ul-Adalia* English translated by W.E. Grigsby, London.
127 Article No.706, *Medjelle al-Ahkam-ul-Adalia* English translated by W.E. Grigsby, London.
128 Abdul Azim Islahi, "Book review: Shariah maxims modern applications in Islamic finance" Islamic economic studies, vol. 21, No.2, (Nov. 1, 2013).
129 For details, see Zahid Latif and Muhammad Masud Ahmad 'Uthmani's Asr-ihadir kay jaded masail awr Dr. Muhammad Tahir-ul-Qadri, pp. 39-46.

130 Article No.1535, *Medjelle al-Ahkam-ul-Adalia* English translated by W.E. Grigsby, London.
131 Dr. Liaquat Ali Khan Niazi, Islamic law of contract (1991), p. 345.
132 Qur'ān 49:9 (Eng. trans. from 'Glorious Qur'ān' by Shaykh-ul-Islam Dr. Muhammad Tahir-ul-Qadri).
133 Qur'ān 49:10 (Eng. trans. from 'Glorious Qur'ān' by Shaykh-ul-Islam Dr. Muhammad Tahir-ul-Qadri).
134 Ibn Majah.
135 Bukhari.

Bibliography

'Abd al-Jalil al-Rawi, (1953–54). Principles on the Islamic Law of Contracts. *The George Washington Law Review*, XXII, p.38.

'Abd al-Rahman al-Jaziri, (2009). *Islamic Jurisprudence According to the Four Sunni Schools: Al-Fiqh 'Ala al-Madhahib al-Arba 'ah*, Fons Vitae, Bolesławiec, vol.3. pp.224–5.

'Abdullah Yusuf 'Ali, (1983). *The Holy Qur'an, Translation and Commentary*, al-Rajihi Company, Saudi Arabia, p.111.

AAOIFI, (2008). *AAOIFI Standard 12, Sharika and Modern Corporations 3.1, 3.4, 5.3, 5.4, 5.5 and 5.9*, AAOIFI, Bahrain.

Abd al-Rahman, I. D., (1984). *Shari'ah, the Islamic Law*, Ta-Ha Publishers, Lahore, p.355.

Abdal Karim Kasib, (2009). *'Aqd al-Istisna fi al-Fiqh al-Islami*, Maktaba, Beirut, pp.133–4.

Abdul Razzaq al-Sanhuri, (1998). *Wujub Tanqih al-Qanun al-Madani al-Misri wa'ala ay' Asas Yakun Hadha al-Tanqih, Maj. Al-Qanun wa al-Iqtisad*, Dar al-Fikr, Beirut, *6*(1), p.3.

'Abdul-Azeem Badawi, (2010). *Al Wajiz*, Rajab & Dar al-Fawa'id, Cairo, vol.1 p.49.

Abdulsalam Majd al-Din, (2008). *al-Muharrar fi al-Fiqh ala Mazhab al-Iman Ahmad ibn Hanbal*, Maktabat al-Marif, al-Riyadh, vol.1 p.324.

Abdurrahman, Y., (2010). *The Art of Islamic Banking and Finance*, Wiley, New York.

Abu Al-Barakat Ahmad Dardir, (1986). *Al-Shrah al-Kabir*, Dar Al-Kathir, Cairo, vol.4, p.66.

Abū Dāwūd, Sulaymān b. Ash'ath b. Isḥāq b. Bashīr al-Sijistānī (202–275/817–889). (1994). *Al-Sunan*, Dār al-Fikr, Beirut, Lebanon, 1414.

Abu Zahra, (2010). *al-Milkiyyah wa Nazariyyat al-Aqd*, Maktaba, Beirut, p.398.

Abubakr al-Jassas, (2001). *Ahkamul Quran*, Maktaba, Beirut, p.465.

Abul Qasim Al-Gharnati, (2003). *al-Qawanien al-Fiqhiyya*, Wazara tul Awqaf, Riyadh, vol.1, p.176.

Afzal-ur-Rahman, M. A., (1974). *Economic Doctrines of Islam*, Islamic Publication, Lahore, vol.111.

Ahmad abu al Fath, (1989). *Ziyadat ul-Mar'i fi-Dunyahi Nuqsan*, Lajna tu Ahya e Al Ma'arif Al Hind, Agra, vol.1, p.185.

Ahmad Ibn Taymiyah, (2006). *Majmu al Fatawa*, Saudi Arabia King Fahad Printing Complex, Macca, vol.3, p.333.

Al-Zubaidi, Tajal, (1996). *'Arus min Jawaher al Nafus*, Dar al-Kutab al-Ilmiah, Cairo, vol.2.

Ala'eddin Kharofa, (n.d.). *Philosophy of Islamic Law of Contract*, A.S. Nordeen. Kuala Lumpur, p.1–2.

Al-Amrusi, (1983). *al-Qanoun al-Madani al-Mu'addala*, Al Farooq Li Tabaa'at wal Nashar, Cairo, vol.1, p.427.
Albert H. Utney, (1908). *Introduction to the Study of Legal History*, Cree Publishing Co., Minneapolis, MN, vol.1, p.20.
Al-Dardir, A. A. B. A., (2015). *al-Sharh al-Kabir*, Ihya al-Kutub al-Arabiyyah, Cairo, vol. 2.
Alhowaimil, I. S., (2013). *Frustration of Performance of Contracts: A Comparative and Analytic Study in Islamic Law and English Law* (Doctoral dissertation) Brunel Law School, Brunel University, London.
Ali al-Khafif, (1941). *al-Sharikat fi al-Fiqh al-Islami*, Dar al-Ilm, p.65.
Ali bin Abu Bakr al-Marghainani, (2007). *al-Hidayah*, al-Misbah, Lahore, vol.3, p.70.
Al-Moghni, (1997). *Kitab Wafayat Ala'yan*, Dar ul Kutub Al Ilmiyah, Beirut, vol.2, p.36.
Al-Nawawi, (2001). *Fiqh Al-Zakāh*, Dar al-Fikr, Beirut, p.483.
al-Nawawi, A. Z. Y. S., (1996). *Minhaj al-Taliban wa'Umdah al-Muftin*, Dar al-Kutub al-'Ilmiyah, Cairo.
Al-Sanhuri, (1990). *Al Wasit*, Dar ul Kutub Al Ilmiyah, Beirut, vol.1, p.125.
Al-Sarakhsi, (1989). *al-Mabsut*, Dar al-Fikr, Beirut, vol.15, p.74.
Al-Shamrani, A. S., (2014). *Islamic Financial Contracting Forms in Saudi Arabia: Law and Practice* (Doctoral dissertation) Brunel Law School, Brunel University, London.
Al-Sharbini, (2004). *Sharia Transformations*, Dar al-Fikr, Beirut, vol.2, p.11.
Al-Shatibi, (1987). *al-Muwafaqat*, Dar al-Fikr, Beirut, vol.5, pp.305–7.
Al-Subki, (1994). *Al-Ibhai fi Sharh al-Minhaj*, Dar al-Fikr, Beirut, vol.1, p.39.
Al-Taj, (1996). *al-Mudhabhab*, Dar ul Gharb al Islami, Turkey, vol.2, p.404.
Al-Uzma Ayatullah, (1983). *Islamic Laws of Worship and Contracts*, Az-Zahra Islamic Foundation, Cairo, p.142.
Al-Zarkashi, Badr al-Din, (1992). *al-Manthur fi al-Qawaid al-Fiqhiyyah*, Wizarat al-Awqaf wa al-Shun al-Islamiyyah, Kuwait.
Al-Zarqa, M. A., (1993). Rafiq Yunus Al Masri: Diśtribution of Inheritance between Males and Females-Search for Officer and Wisdom-Comment: Muśtafa Ahmed Al-Zarqa رفيق يونس المصري: توزيع الميراث بين الذكور والإناث-بحث عن الضابط والحكمة-تعليق. *Journal of King Abdulaziz University – Islamic Economics*, *5*(1), 79–86.
Al-Zarqa, Mustafa, (1965). *Ahkam al-Awqaf*, University Press, Damascus, pp.194–5.
Al-Zuhaili, (2004). *al-Fiqh al-Islami wa Adillatuhu*, vol.4, p.315.
Amin Ahsan Islahi, (2000). *Islamic Law: Concept and Codification*, 1st ed., Islamic Publications Ltd., Lahore.
Amkhan, A., (1991). Force Majeure and Impossibility of Performance in Arab Contract Law. *Arab Law Quarterly*, *6*(3), 297–308.
Ammer, C., (1997). *The American Heritage Dictionary of Idioms*, Houghton Mifflin, Boston, p.175.
Antony Allott, (1980). *The Limits of Law*, UK Publications, London, p.5.
Arabi, O., (1998). Contract Stipulations (Shurut) in Islamic Law: The Ottoman Majalla and Ibn Taymiyya. *International Journal of Middle East Studies*, *30*(1), 29–50.
Askari, H., Iqbal, Z., and Mirakhor, A., (2014). *Introduction to Islamic Economics: Theory and Application*, John Wiley & Sons, London.
Ayad, M. B., (2009). International Commercial Arbitration Award Enforcement at the Crossroads of Sharia 1 Law and Ordre Public 2 in the MENA: 3 Paving the Golden Path towards Harmonisation 4. *The Journal of World Investment & Trade*, Kuala Lumpur, *10*(5), 723–51.
Ayatullah Sayyid Mahmud Teleghani, (1882). *Society and Economics in Islam*, (Trans. From Persian) by R. Cambell (2015), BookBaby, West Coast, Western US, p.31.

Ayub, M., (2013). *Understanding Islamic Finance*, Gramedia Pustaka Utama, Kuala Lumpur.

Badawī, Yūsuf Aḥmad Muḥammad, (1970). *Taarekh at-Tashree' al-Islami*, al-Maktabah al-Tijariyah al-Kubra, Cairo, p.19–20.

Baillie, N. B. E., (1873). *The Land Tax of India: According to the Moohummudan Law*, Smith, Elder, Company, London, pp.208–9.

Bakr b. 'Abdullah Abu Zaid, (1983). *Mawārid Ibn-al-Qaiyim fī kutubihi*. Maktabat, ar-Rušd, pp.99–100.

Billah, M. M., (1996). Comment on Shaikh Al-Azhar's Fatwa against Life Insurance. *New Horizons*, *58*, 3–6.

Bin Qudamah, (2001). *Mujallah u Dirasat Al Qur'aniyah*, Centre of Islamic Studies, University of Michigan, Ann Arbor, MI, p.96.

Blake, S. H., and Barrister, M. A., (1989). *A Practical Approach to Legal Advice & Drafting*, Blackstone, Ashland, OR, p.217.

Buang, A. H., (2000). *Studies in the Islamic Law of Contracts: The Prohibition of Gharar*, International Law Book Services, Kuala Lumpur, p.109.

Buckler, W. H., (1895). *The Origin and History of Contract in Roman Law: Down to the End of the Republican Period. (Being the Yorke Prize Essay for the Year 1893)*, CJ Clay and Sons, London, pp.3–8.

Bukhārī, Abū 'Abd Allāh Muhammad b. Ismā'īl b. Ibrahīm b. Mughīra al-. (194–256/810–870). (1989). *Al-Ṣaḥīḥ*, Dār al-Bashā'ir al-Islāmiyya, Beirut, Lebanon, 1409.

Campo, J. E., (2009). *Encyclopedia of Islam*, Infobase Publishing, New york.

Chapra, M. U., (1985). *Towards a Just Monetary System* (vol.8), International Institute of Islamic Thought (IIIT), Kuala Lumpur.

Chehata, C., (1973). *Etudes de droit musulman: La nation de responsabilité contractuelle*, Pr. Univ. de France, Paris, p.15.

Comair-Obeid, N., (1996). Particularity of the Contract's Subject-Matter in the Laws of the Arab Middle East. *Arab Law Quarterly*, *11*(4), 331–49.

Comair-Obeid, N., (1996). *The Law of Business Contracts in the Arab Middle East: A Theoretical and Practical Comparative Analysis (With Particular Reference to Modern Legislation)*, Brill, London, p.211.

Coulson, N., (1984). *Commercial Law in the Gulf States: The Islamic Legal Tradition*, Springer, New York.

Cowan, J. M., and Wehr, H., (1979). *A Dictionary of Modern Written Arabic: Arabic-English*, O. Harrassowitz, Wiesbaden.

Dahma bint Yahya, (1984). *Sharh al-Azhar*, Dar al-Kitab al-Arabi, Beriut, vol.3, p.85.

Daphne A. Dukelow and Betsy Nuse, (1991). *The Dictionary of Canadian Law*, "Bilateral contract." Carswell Legal Pubns, New York.

Darir, pp.4–5.

David M. Walker, (1980). *The Oxford Companion to Law*, Oxford University Press, New York, p.234.

De Bellefonds Y. Linant, (1955). *Traite de droit Musulman Compare*, Mouton & Co./The Hague, England, vol.3, p.57.

El-Gamal, M. A., (2006). *Islamic Finance: Law, Economics, and Practice*, Cambridge University Press, London, p.90.

El-Hawary, D., Grais, W., and Iqbal, Z., (2004). *Regulating Islamic Financial Institutions: The Nature of the Regulated*. The World Bank, Washington, DC.

Fallon, S. W., (2000). *Urdu, English, Law and Commercial Dictionary*, Sang-e-Meel Publications, Lahore.

Galwash, A. A., (1940). *The Religion of Islam*, al-Azhar Magazine, Cairo, p.30.

Ghadas, (2009). An Appraisal of Sections 175–191 Contract Act 1950, Paper presented at the *International Conference on Harmonization of Shariah and Civil Law*, International Islamic University, Malaysia.

Godlewski, C. J., Turk-Ariss, R., and Weill, L., (2013). Sukuk vs. Conventional Bonds: A Stock Market Perspective. *Journal of Comparative Economics*, *41*(3), 745–61.

Hamid, M. A., (1977). Mutual Assent in the Formation of Contracts in Islamic Law. *Journal of Islamic and Comparative Law*, *7*, 41.

Hamid, M. E., (1972). Does the Islamic Law of Contract Recognize a Doctrine of Mistake? *Journal of Islamic and Comparative Law*, *7*, 1–16.

Haqqi, A. R. A., (2017). Islamic Law In State Life of Brunei Darussalam. *Journal of Malay Islamic Studies*, *1*(2), 81–92.

Hasan, Aznan, (2011). *Fundamentals of Shariah in Islamic Finance*, Institute of Islamic Banking and Finance Malaysia (IBFIM), Kuala Lumpur. ISBN 978-967-0149-16-5.

Hashim Kamali, (1999). Uncertainty and Risk Taking (Gharar) in Islamic Law. *IIUM Law Journal*, *7*, 200.

Hassan, A. A. H., (2007). *Sales and Contracts in Early Islamic Commercial Law* (No. 92), The Other Press, New York, p.37.

Ḥassān, Ḥsān and ḤndānL, Ḥ dān, (2010). *An Introduction to the Study of Islamic Law*, Adam Publishers, Delhi.

Hassan, K., and Lewis, M. (eds.), (2009). *Handbook of Islamic Banking*, Edward Elgar Publishing, Cheltenham, United Kingdom, p.43.

Hassan, M. K., Kayed, R. N., and Oseni, U. A., (2013). *Introduction to Islamic Banking & Finance*, Always Learning, Pearson Education Limited, New York.

Hughes, T. P., (1895). *A Dictionary of Islam: Being a Cyclopaedia of the Doctrines, Rites, Ceremonies, and Customs, Together with the Technical and Theological Terms, of the Muhammadan Religion*, WH Allen & Company, London.

Hussain Hamid Hassan, (1979). *Li-Dirasat-il-Fiqh-al-Islami*, Maktabah al-Mutanabi, Cairo, p.235.

Hussain, J., (1999). *Islamic Law and Society: An Introduction*, Federation Press, Alexandria, NSW, p.58.

Ibd Rushd, (1996). *Bidayat al-Mujtahid*, Dar al-Fikr, Beirut, vol.2, p.155.

Ibn ʻAbidin, (1988). *Radd al-Muhtar*, Dar al-Fikr, Beirut, vol.3, p.364.

Ibn al-Humam, (1976). *Fath al-Qadir*, Dar ul Kutub Al Ilmiyah, Beirut, vol.5, p.3.

Ibn Arfa, (2001). *Mukhtesan of Sidi Khalil*, Dar ul Gharb al Islami, Turkey, p.193.

Ibn e Jarir, (2008). *Tafseer Ibn Jarir*, Dar al-Kutab al-Ilmiah,Cairo, vol.3, p.101.

Ibn Hajar Ahmed, (2016). *The Different Aspects of Islamic Culture: Islam in the World*, 1st ed., Dar –us-Slam Publications, Riyadh, vol.19 pp.156–7.

Ibn Hazm, (1954). *al-Muhalla*, Dar al-Afaq al-Jadid, Beirut, vol.8, p.343–89.

Ibn Hazm, (n.d.). *al-Ihkam fi Usul al-Ahkam*, Dar al-Fikr, Beirut, vol.5, p.305.

Ibn Manzur, (1985). *Lisan al-ʻArab*, Dar al-Fikr, Beirut, vol.3, p.462.

Ibn Najim, Zainul ʻAbidin, (1982). *Islamic Law and Finance*, Dar Al-Ilm, Cairo, vol.4, p.277.

Ibn Nujaim, (2003). *al-Bahar al-Raiq*, Dar al-Fikr, Beirut, vol.6, p.36.

Ibn Qayyim al-Jawziyyah, (n.d.). *Ilam al-Muwaqqiin An Rab al-Alamin*, Dar Al-Kathir, Cairo, vol.1, p.299.

Ibn Qodamah, (1978). *al-Moghni*, Dar al-Fikr, Beirut, vol.2, p.33.

Ibn Saad, (1980). *Kitab at-Tabaqat Al-Kabir*, Dar al-Fikr, Beirut, II, p.363.

Ibrahim, A., and Datuk, T. S., (1965). *Sources and Development of Muslim Law*, Malayan Law Journal, Kuala Lumpur.

Imran Ahsan Khan Nyazee, (2003). *Islamic Jurisprudence*, The Other Press, International Institute of Islamic Thought, Petaling Jaya, p.13.

International Bar Association, and International Bar Association. Arab Regional Conference, (1987). *Arab Comparative & Commercial Law*, Springer, UAE, vol.2.

Islam, M. W., (1998). Dissolution of Contract in Islamic Law. *Arab L Q*, *13*, 336.

J. Schacht, (1964). *Introduction to Islamic Law*, Clarendon Press, Oxford, United Kingdom, p.201.

Jabbar, H. S. F. A., (2009). Islamic Finance: Fundamental Principles and Key Financial Institutions. *Company Lawyer*, *30*(1), 23–32.

John Burka, (1927). *Obsorn's Concise Law Dictionary*, Sweet & Maxwell, London, United Kingdom, p.84.

Justice Aftab Hussain, (1982). *Sources of Islamic Law-Classicism and Contemporary Problems*, Pakistan France Colloquium, Islamabad, p.42.

Kahf, M., (2000). Economics of Liability: An Islamic View. *International Journal of Economics, Management Accounting*, *8*(2), Qum, Iran.

Kamal al-Din, (1989). *Sharh fath al-Qadir*, Dar al-Fikr, Deirut, vol.3, p.187.

Khan, M. M., Alam, H. M., Ahmad, N., Iqbal, M. S., and Ali, S., (2011). Comparative Analysis of Islamic and Prevailing Insurance Practices. *International Journal of Business and Social Science*, *2*(10), 282–286.

Kharofa, A., (2000). *Transactions in Islamic Law*, AS Noordeen, Kuala Lumpur.

Kharofa, A. E., (2007). *Transaksi dalam perundangan Islam*. ITBM, Kuala Lumpur.

Khurshid, A., (2000). Islam and Democracy: Some Conceptual and Contemporary Dimensions. *Muslim World*, *90*(1/2), 1.

Kuwaiti High Court of Cassation Judgment, (1970). Case No.1265/1970 (Commercial), 10/12/1970, reproduced in, 1970, No.1, Year 3, p.53.

L. B. Curzon, (2003). *Dictionary of Law*, 6th ed., International Law Book Services, Kuala Lumpur, p.72.

Liaquat Ali Khan Niazi, (1990). *Islamic Law of Contract*, Dyal Singh Trust Library, Lahore, p.1.

Lichtenstein, E. A., and Read, P. A. (eds.), (1995). *Contract Law: Textbook*, Hlt Publications, London.

Macdonald, D. B., (2020). *Development of Muslim Theology, Jurisprudence and Constitutional Theory*, Library of Alexandria, Alexandria, vol.1.

Mahmood, N. I. K., (1988). *Insurance Law in Malaysia* (Doctoral dissertation, Queen Mary University of London).

Maine, H., and Henry Sumner Maine, (2005). *Ancient Law*, Cosimo Inc., New York, pp.282–7.

Maitland, (1899). *The History of English Law before the Time of Edward-I*, vol.1, 2 CUP Archive, pp.1–2.

Mālik, Ibn Anas b. Mālik b. Abī'āmir b. 'Amr b. Ḥārith al-Aṣbaḥī (93–179/712–795). (1987). *Al-Muwaṭṭā'*, Dār Iḥyā' al-Turāth al-'Arabī, Beirut, Lebanon.

Mannan, M. A., (2015). *Islamic Banking in Bangladesh: Progress and Potentials*, Islami Bank Bangladesh Limited, Dhaka, Bangladesh, pp.5–7.

Mansoor bin Younus Bahuti, (1982). *Kishaf al-Qina la Matn al-Qina*, Dar al-Kutab al-Ilmiah, Cairo, vol.3, p.276.

ManERLI, M. T., (2001). *Islamic Law of Contracts and Business Transactions*, Shari'ah Academy, International Islamic University, Islamabad.

Masud ibn Umar Taftazani, (1975). *Sharh al-Wiqaya*, Maktabah Muhammad Ali Sabih, Cairo, vol.2, p.151.

Milliot, L., (1954). La pensée juridique de l'Islam. *Revue internationale de droit comparé*, *6*(3), 441–454.

Mohd. Ma'sum Billah, (2006). *Shari'ah Standard of Business Contract*, Islamic Banking and Finance Institute Malaysia (IBFIM), Malaysia.

Mozley, H. N., Whiteley, G. C., and Neave, F. G., (1908). *Mozley and Whiteley's Law Dictionary*, Butterworths & Company, Kuala Lumpur.

Muhammad Ameen Bin Muhammad Umar, (n.d.). *Tanqih al-Hamidiya*, Wazara tul Awqaf, Riyadh, vol.1, p.206.

Muhammad b. al-Hasan al-Shaybani, (1999). *Muwatta' al-Imam Malik*, Azamran, Muzaffarpur, vol.1, pp.65–6.

Muhammad bin Ali Haskafi, (1989). *al-Dur al-Mukhtar*, H.M.Saeed Co., Karachi, vol.4, p.171.

Muhammad Darir, (1999). *Muassasat al-Rsalah*, Dar Ilm, Beirut, p.35.

Muhammad, O., (1998). Financial Engineering with Islamic Options. *Islamic Economic Studies*, *6*(1): 77.

Muhammad Tahir-ul-Qadri, (2001). *Islamic Concept of Law*, Minhaj ul Quran Publication, p.1.

Muslim, (1992). Ibn al-Ḥajjāj Abū al-Ḥasan al-Qushayrī al-Naysābūrī (206–261/821–875). *Al-Ṣaḥīḥ*, Dār al-Iḥyā' al-Turāth al-'Arabī, Beirut, Lebanon.

Nadratuzzaman, H. M., (2007). *Kamus popular keuangan ekonomi syariah*, PKES Publishing, Jakarta, p.43.

Nadvi, S. H. H., (1989). *Islamic Legal Philosophy and the Qur'ānic Origins of the Islamic Law: A Legal-Historical Approach*, Department of Arabic, Urdu & Persian, University of Durban-Westville, Westville.

Nasā'ī, Aḥmad b. Shu'ayb Abū 'Abd al-Raḥmān al- (215–303/830–915). *al-Sunan*, Dār al-Kutub al-'Ilmiyya, Beirut, Lebanon, 1416/1995.

Nasr, S. H., (1991). *Sufi Essays*, Suny Press, Michigan.

Nasr, S. H., (2009). *The Heart of Islam: Enduring Values for Humanity*, Zondervan, Lahore, p.123.

Nasrul Hisyam, N., (2008). Aplikasi sains dan teknologi dalam transaksi muamalah Islam: Rujukan kepada rukun-rukun akad mengikut perspektif undang-undang kontrak Islam. *Jurnal teknologi*, *49*, 81–91.

Nawawi, R. H., (1993). *Commercial Transactions: Islamic Law Perspective* (Doctoral dissertation, International Islamic University Malaysia), p.59.

Noor, M. M. M., Suliaman, I., Ahmad, K., Deraman, F., Abdullah, M., Shah, F. A., ... and Nor, M. R. M., (2013). The Rights of Khiyar (Option) in the Issue of Consumerism in Malaysia. *Middle East Journal of Scientific Research*, *13*(2), 154–61.

Noordin, K., (2013). A Juristic Evaluation of the Application of Ji" alah (Reward Contract) as the Underlying Basis for Justifying Surplus Sharing Practice. In *1st Insurance and Takaful International Symposium, Puri Pujangga UKM Bangi*, Selangor, Malaysia.

Obaidullah, M., (1998). Financial Engineering with Islamic Options. *Islamic Economic Studies*, *6*(1), 73–103.

Ocke Kurniandi, (n.d.). Classification of Takaful Contracts. Retrieved from https://cas.confex.com/cas/ica14/webprogram/Handout/Paper2047/Paper_2047_handout_1193_1.pdf.

P. S. Atiyah, (1989). *The Law of Contract*, 4th ed., Oxford University Press, Oxford, pp.1–19.

Patrick Hughes, (1995). *Dictionary of Islam*, Asian Educational Services, New Delhi, pp.175–6.

Philips, A. A. B., (1988). *Evolution-of-Fiqh*, IslamKotob.

Qadir, U., (1994). *Al– Tasyri Al-jinai Al-Islami Muqarina Bil- Qanun Al-Wadhi*, Dar Nasyr Tsaqafah, Cairo, vol.1. p.292.

Qadri, A. A., and Tripathy, N. M., (1963). *ISLAMIC JURISPRUDENCE*, Modern World, Chicago, IL.

Rahim, A., (1911). *The Principles of Muhammad an Jurisprudence*, Luzac & Co., Lahore, p.50.

Rashad Khalil, (1979). *al-Sharikat fi al-Fiqh al-Islami*, Dar Al-Kathir, Cairo, p.154.

Rayner, S. E., (1991). *The Theory of Contracts in Islamic Law: A Comparative Analysis with Particular Reference to the Modern Legislation in Kuwait, Bahrain, and the United Arab Emirates*, Graham & Trotman, Limited, London, vol.5. p.90.

Rayner, S. E., (1991). *The Theory of Contracts in Islamic Law: A Comparative Analysis with Particular Reference to the Modern Legislation in Kuwait, Bahrain, and the United Arab Emirates* (vol.5). Graham & Trotman, Limited, London, p.91.

Razali, S. S., (2008, July). The Concept of Wa'ad in Islamic Financial Contract. In *Islamic Banking, Accounting and Finance Conference (iBAF 2008)*, Faculty of Economics and Muamalat, Universiti Sains Islam Malaysia, Kuala Lumpur, (pp.28–9).

Saleh, N., (1988). Financial Transactions and the Islamic Theory of Obligations and Contracts. *Islamic Law and Finance*, *4*, 13–29.

Saleh, N., (1989). Remedies for Breach of Contract under Islamic and Arab Laws. *Arab Law Quarterly*, *4*(4), 269–90.

Saleh, N., (2001). Freedom of Contract: What Does it Mean in the Context of Arab Laws? *Arab Law Quarterly*, *16*(4), 346–57.

Sanhuri, (1980). *al-Wasit fi Sharh al-Qanun al-Madani*, Dar al-Kitab al-Arabi, Beirut, vol.4, part.1, p.1.

Sanhuri, (1984). *Masadir al-Haqq*, Dar al-Kitab al-Arabi, Beriut, vol.3, pp.31–41.

Sarakhasi, (1987). *al-Mabsut*, Dir al-Maarif, Beirut, vol.13, p.194.

Shah, Z. A., (2009). *The Astronomical Calculations and Ramadan: A Fiqhi Discourse*, IIIT, Virginia, vol.6, p.2.

Shalabe Muhammad Mustafa, (1969). *al-Madkhal fee at-Tareef bil fiqh Islami*, Dar al-Fawa'id, Cairo, p.93.

Sharbiny, (1984). *Mughni Muhtaj*, Dar ul Gharb al Islami, Turkey, vol.2, p.106

Shawkani, (1974). *Ansar al-Sunnah al-Muhammadiyyah*, Dar al-Kutab al-Ilmiah, Beirut, vol.5, p.156.

Shimizu, H., (1989). *Philosophy of the Islamic Law of Contract: A Comparative Study of Contractual Justice*, Institute of Middle Eastern Studies, International University of Japan Working papers series, *15*, 1–131.

Sufi Hasan Abu Talib, (1990). *Tatbiq al-Shariah al-Islamiyyah fi al-Bilad al-'Arabiyyah*, Dar al-Nahdah al-'Arabiyyah, Beirut, pp.238–9.

Syed Riaz ul Hassan Ghilani, (1974). *Re-construction of Legal Thought in Islam*, Law Pub. Co., London, p.203.

The Encyclopaedia of Islam, (1965). Edited by: P. Bearman, Th. Bianquis, C.E. Bosworth, E. van Donzel and W.P. Heinrichs. Brill, Leidn, Netherlands, vol.3, p.1100.

Tritton, A. S., (1971). Knowledge Triumphant: The Concept of Knowledge in Medieval Islam. By Franz Rosenthal. pp.viii, 356. EJ Brill, Leiden, 1970. *Journal of the Royal Asiatic Society*, *103*(2), 188–189.

Venardos, A. M., (2012). *Islamic Banking & Finance in South-East Asia: Its Development & Future*, World Scientific, London, vol.6, p.73.

Vikør, K. S., (1999). The Sharia and the Nation State: Who Can Codify the Divine Law? *The Middle East in a Globalized World*, Oslo, p.220–50.

Vogel, F. E., and Hayes, S. L., (1998). *Islamic Law and Finance: Religion, Risk, and Return*, Brill, London, vol.16, p.112.

Wahab, A. R. A., (2006, February). Takaful Business Models-Wakalah Based on WAQF. In *Second International Symposium on Takaful*, Kuala Lumpur, (vol.4).

Weiss, B., (1978). Interpretation in Islamic Law: The Theory of Ijtihād. *The American Journal of Comparative Law*, *26*(2), 199–212.

Winkel, E., (1997). *Islam and the Living Law: The Ibn al-Arabi Approach*, Oxford University Press, Oxford, p.15.

Zada, S. Q., and Zada, M. Z. Q., (2016). Codification of Islamic Law in the Muslim World: Trends and Practices. *Journal of Applied Environmental and Biological Sciences*, *6*(12), 160–71.

Zanki, N., (2014). Codification of Islamic Law Premises of Hand Debates of Contemporary Muslim Scholars. *International Journal of Humanities and Social Sciences*, *4*(9), 127–37.

Zaylai, (1982). *Tabyin al_Haqaiq*, Dar Al-Kathir, Egypt, vol.5, p.105.

Zayn al-Din, (1981). *al-Qawaid*, Dar al-Kutub al-Ilmiyyah, Egypt.

Index

'Aāisha (R.A), Hazrat 47
abandonment 183
'Abbas (R.A), 'Abd Allah b. 170
Abd, Jabir b. 76
Abd Allah (R.A) 47, 48
Abd Allah (R.A), Jabir b. 9
'Abd Allah Mas'ūd (R.A) 48
Abd al-Rahman, Abu Salama b. 225
Abd Ghadas, Zuhairah Ariff 42
Abd Manaf, Hashim bin 15
Abdul Jawad, Muhammad 23
absoluteness 113
Abu Al-Minhal 144
Abu Bakr, Hazrat 16
Abu Bakr (R.A), Sayyidina 16
Abu Hanifa 5–6, 199
Abu Huraira (R.A) 76, 145, 162, 167, 226
Abu Sunnah, Ahmad Fahmi 23
Abu Zahrah, Mohammad 23, 35, 66
Abu Zubair 77
Abu Zuhrah, Muhammad 42
acceptance (*qabul*) 92–97, 118
accounting and auditing organisation for Islamic financial institutions (AAOIFI) 221
action, expressing consent 120
active or executive capacity (*Ahliyyah al-ada*) 101–103
acts: acceptance (*qabul*) 94; offer (*ijab*) 87
adl (justice) 52
advanced payment (*salam*) 199, 214, 231–233
Afat samawiyah 192
'Affan (R.A), 'Uthman 145
agency contract (*wakalah*) 15, 169
agents: acceptance (*qabul*) 94; contract of agency 234; expressing consent 120; offer (*ijab*) 88
Ahadith, coercion (*ikrah*) 133
'ahd 69
ah'l 100
Ahliyyah (legal capacity) 100; active or executive capacity (*Ahliyyah al-ada*) 101–103; factors which prevent legal capacity 106–109; receptive capacity (*Ahliyyah al-wujub*) 100–101
Ahliyyah al-ada (active or executive capacity) 101–103
Ahliyyah al-wujub (receptive capacity) 101
Ah'liyyat 100
aib 202
Aishah 16
al-'adl 53
al-Ahkam al-Shariyah fil-ahwal al-Shakhiah 26
al-ahliyyah (capacity) 42
Al-Ahw, Rifah 26
Al-Ansari (R.A), Abu Qatada 76, 161
Al-aqud-al-sowri 106
Al-Asfahani 124
A-Ashari (R.A), Abu Musa 226
Al-Bazdawi 124
al-Dhimma 42
al-Faskh (revocation and termination), dissolution of a contract 190–191
"Al-Fatawa al-Hindiyyah/al-Fatawa al-Alamgiriyyah" 24
Al-Ghamidi, Sakhr 9
Al-Huna, Yahya b. Abu Ishaq 144
'Ali, Syed Ameer 133
alienation of property 183
Al-Kabashi 42
Al-Khafif, 'Ali 23, 217
Al-Khattab (R.A), 'Umar b. 9, 49
Al-Khudrī (R.A), Abū Sa'īd 50, 145
Al-Mansur, Abu Ja 'far 23
Al-Marghnns Hidya 24

al-maslaha al-mursalah (public interest consideration) 97
Al-Miqdām (R.A) 47
almuatah 87
Al-mu'atach (display of goods) 89
Al-Muktadir, Muhammad b. 76
al-musaqah 113
Al-Musayyab (R.A), Said b. 76
Al-Qaradawi, Yosuf 23
Al-Rāghib al-Alfahānī 52
Al-Rahn contract 229
"*al-Risalah al-Yatimah*" (The Orphan Message) 23
Al-Sanhuri, Abdul Razzaq 35, 71
Al-Sarakhsi 42, 147, 226
Al-Shafi 199
Al-Shanhuri 67
Al-Sharbini 90
al-Wa'ad 70
al-wasiyyah (bequests) 113
Al-Zakhaili, Wahab 91, 207
Al-Zarqa, Mustafa Ahmad 41, 42, 234, 237
Al-Zuhayli, Wahbah 23, 67, 83, 85, 112, 189, 190
'Amr, Sulayman b. 144
Amr (R.A), Abdullah b. 76
Anglo-Muhammadan Laws 24
approval of contracts, options (*khiyar*) 197
aqd 34, 65–68
'aqd infiradi (unilateral contract) 175–176
'aqd thuna'i (bilateral contract) 176–177
arbitration 234
arkan 83
Arqam, Zayd b. 144
artificial contracts 106
"*Ashraf al-Makhluqath*" 77
assignment of debt (*hawalah*) 188–189
Audah, Abdul Qadir 41
Aufa, Abdullah bin Abu 162
Auf (R.A), Abd Al-Rahman b. 77
Autangzeb 'Alamgir, Muhammad 24
authorisation 183
automatic dissolution of contract 189–190
awareness of rights and duties, Islamic contract law 55–56
Awfa (R.A), 'Abd Allah b. Abi 161
ayan (delivery of specific property) 188
Azib, al-Bara b. 144

Babylonian law of contracts 17
Bahrain, contracts 68
bai' (sale) 168
Baille, Neil 24, 90–91
bankruptcy 108
bara'a 208
Bashir (R.A), al-Numan b. 225
batil (void) 129, 180–181
bay' al-mu'ajjal (credit sale) 214
bay' al-ta'ati (sale by delivery) 120
bay' mutlaq (sale of goods for money) 214
beneficial transactions 105
benevolence 52–54
benevolent loan (*qard*) 15
bequests (*al-wasiyyah*) 113
bilateral contract (*'aqd thuma'i*) 176–177
binding contract/enforceable contract (*nafidh*) 181
breach of contract 207; damages 209–210; injunctions 211; rescission 207–209; restitutionary remedies 211; specific performance 210; termination for 192
Buckler, W. H. 18
business, encouragement and development of 61

cancel (*faskh*) 195
capacity: determining 104–105; division of for purpose of transactions 105–106; factors which prevent legal capacity 106–109; stages of 103–104
cessation of contract 187–189
cheating 156–157; consent 121; prohibition of 59; Qur'ān 157–158; Sunnah 158–160
childhood stage 103
choice (*khiyar*) 124
classification of contracts 175; bilateral contract (*'aqd thuma'i*) 176–177; binding contract/enforceable contract (*nafidh*) 181; invalid or deficient contract (*fasid*) 179–180; by legal consequences 178–182; multilateral contracts 177–178; non-binding contracts 182; by purpose 183–184; quasi-contract (*shibh al-'aqd*) 178; time of completion 182–183; unilateral contract (*'aqd infiradi*) 175–176; valid contracts (*sahih*) 179; void contract (*batil*) 180–181
cleverness 104
code, defined 19
codification 19–20; efforts of 23–24; Egypt 26; Java, Indonesia 24–25; Ottoman Empire 25–26; reasons for no codifications till the date 20–22; Saudi Arabia 26–27; views of 22–23

coercion (*ikrah*) 108–109, 131–135; consent 121
commerce, importance of 7–9
commercial transactions: false oath 160–162; philosophy of 9–11; *see also* transactions
commitments 71
communication of offers 90–91
compensatory damages (*dhaman*) 210
compromise 237–238
concealing defects of commodity 162–163
conditional contracts 183
conduct: acceptance (*qabul*) 94; contracts 71; offer (*ijab*) 87
consensus ad idem (meeting of the minds) 117
consent 117–118; expressing 119–121; factors which vitiate 121–122; Islamic contract law 118
consideration 110
contingent contracts 167–170, 183
contract breachers 76
contract limiting the rights of others 183
contract of agency 234
contract of arbitration 234
contract of authorisation 183
contract of compromise 237–238
contract of deposits and bailments 184
contract of employment 238
contract of extinguishing rights 183
contract of gift 234
contract of guarantee 183, 235
contract of insurance (*takaful*) 222–230
contract of *istisna* 149–150
contract of lease (*ijara*) 219–220
contract of mortgage or bailment 236–237
contract of ownership 183
contract of partnership (*musharakah*) 184, 214–216, 233
contract of *salam* 149, 231–233
contract of sale 213–214
contract of suretyship 235
cost, insurance, and freight (C.I.F) contract 235–236
Coulson, N. J. 32
counter offers 88
Cowan, J. M. 214
creation of wealth 49–50

damages, breach of contract 209–210
dayan (delivery of non-specific property) 188
death: dissolution of a contract 189–190; options (*khiyar*) 200
death-illness 107
death of contracting party, termination of offer 91–92
deferred payment sale (*murabahah*) 218–219
De Glanvill, Ranulf 18
deliverability, subject matter 113–114
delivery of non-specific property (*dayan*) 188
delivery of specific property (*ayan*) 188
description, subject matter 115
destruction of the subject matter: dissolution of a contract 190; options (*khiyar*) 200; termination of offer 92
dhaman (compensatory damages) 210
dhaman-al-uqud 209–210
A Digest of Mohummaddan Law 24
discharge of contract 187
display of goods (*mu'atah*) 89–90
dispositions 70–71
dissolution of a contract 186–187; automatically 189–190; impossibility of performance 192–193; by mutual agreement (*iqalah*) 189; revocation and termination 190–191; unilateral revocation of contract 191–192
divorce 36
Doi, Abdur Rehman I. 86, 88
dotis dictio form of contract 18
drunkenness 107–108

earning a living 46–48
earning in moderation 48–49
earning one's keep 11
economising 48
Egypt: codification 26; "contracts" defined 68
elements of a contract 83–84; acceptance (*qabul*) 92–97; communication of offers 90–91; counter offers 88; offer (*ijab*); *see also* offer (*ijab*); offer and invitation to treat 88–90; *sigha* (form) 84; termination of offer 91–92
El-Gamal, M. A. 152
embryo (*janin*) stage 103
employment 238
encouragement and development of business 61
English Contract Act 39
English law of contract 17–19, 27
equality, Islamic contract law 56–57
equity, Islamic contract law 56–57
existence of, subject matter 112–113

exploitation 61–62
expressing consent 119–121
extinguishing rights 183

factors which prevent legal capacity 106–109
factors which vitiate mutual consent 121–122
false oath, commercial transactions 160–162
fasid (invalid or deficient contract) 179–180
faskh (cancel) 195
Fatwa Alamgryah 24
Fiducia 18
fiqh 1–4
F.O.B. contract *see* free on board (F.O.B.)
forbidden commodities, prohibition of 60
forbidden factors 138; cheating 156–157; contracts contrary to *maqasid al-Shariah* 166–167; fraud 154–155; *gharar* (risk) 146–151; inconsistent contracts 167–170; *maysir* (games of chance) 151–154; *qimar* (gambling) 151–154; *riba* (interest) 138–146
force majeure 192
forgetfulness 106
form (*sigha*) 84
fraud 154–155; consent 121; prohibition of 59; Qur'ān 157–158; Sunnah 158–160
freedom of contracts 35–40
freedom to work 49
free mutual consent 117–118; factors which vitiate 121–122
free on board (F.O.B.) contract 236
free will (*iradah*) 124
fuqaha' 105, 112; mistakes 128

gambling (*qimar*) 151–154
gambling, prohibition of 59
games of chance (*maysir*) 151–154
general permissibility 56
general theory of contract 32–35
gesture or signs: acceptance (*qabul*) 93–94; offer (*ijab*) 86–87
ghabn (*al-Naqs*) 121–122
ghair maljian 134
ghalat 128
gharar (risk) 113, 146–151; prohibition of 59
Ghilani, Syed Riaz-ul-Hassan 67
gifts, contract of gift 234
God-made laws 54–55
guarantee 235

hajj (pilgrimage) 8
Hamilton, Charles 24
Hanafis: choice (*khiyar*) 124; coercion 109; contingent contracts 183; display of goods (*mu'atah*) 89; *ijab* (offer) 85; *istisna* (manufacturing contract) 231; knowledge of subject matter 114; offer by writing (*kitabah*) 86; option of viewing (*khiyar al-ru-yat*) 201
Hanbal, Ahmad bin 6, 199
Hanbalis 68, 199; acceptance (*qabul*) 94; cleverness 104; display of goods (*mu'atah*) 89; knowledge of subject matter 114; offer by acts or conduct 87; signs 87; subject matter 112–113
harmful transactions 105
Hassan, Hussain Hamid 67, 84; subject matter 111, 113; void contract (*batil*) 180
Hassan, M. Kabir 67, 84
Hastings, Warren 24
hawalah (assignment of debt) 188–189
hawalah contract 228
hebah (grant without compensation) 198
hoarding 163–165
Hughes, Patrick 92
Hukm 6
Huquq Allah (Rights of Allah) 59, 166–167
hypocrites, contract breachers 76

Ibadah (worship and devotion practices) 2
Ibadat 24
Ibn Abbas 8, 232
Ibn 'Abbas (R.A) 9, 60, 76, 170, 217
Ibn Abidin 147
Ibn 'Abidin Shami 43
Ibn Affan, Hazrat Uthman 16
Ibn al-Muqaffa 23
Ibn al-Musayyib 225
Ibn Al-Qayyim 112, 122, 147
Ibn Arfa 213, 214
Ibn 'Awf, Hazrat Abdul Rehman 16
Ibn Hazm 123, 147
Ibn Jabal, Mu'adh 108
Ibn Majah 133
Ibn Rushd 24, 147
Ibn Taymiyyah 34–35, 147, 191
Ibn 'Umar (R.A) 48, 164, 196
Ibrahim, Ahmad 71
idiocy (*'Atah*) 106
ignorance (*jahalah*) 122
ih sān 52

'ijaara 113
ijab (offer) 84–85, 118
ijarah (leasing) 16, 168, 169, 219
Ijarah Muntahia-bi-Tamleek 168
'Ikalah (annul) 91
ikrah (coercion) 131–134; consent 121
ikrah bi ghayr haq (unjust coercion) 134
ikrah bi haq (just coercion) 134
Ikrah Naqis 134
Ikrah Tamm 134
'illah (legal effective cause) 113
illegality 191
imda' (ratify) 195
impossibility of performance 192–193
inability to deliver, subject matter 113–114
inconsistent contracts 59, 167–170
ininsivrandum form of contract 18
injunctions, breach of contract 211
insanity (*Junun*) 106
insolvency 108
insurance: contract of insurance (*takaful*) 222–230; Islamic insurance versus conventional insurance 229
intention to create legal relation, consent 122–124
inter absentees 96, 97
interest (*riba*) 138; prohibition of 58–59
intoxication 107–108
invalid or deficient contract (*fasid*) 179–180
invitation to treat 88–90
iqalah (mutual agreement), dissolution of a contract 189
iradah (free will) 124
Iraq, "contracts" defined 68
Islam 54–55
Islamic commercial law 55; profits and loss sharing 61
Islamic contract law 19, 39; consent 118; encouragement and development of business 61; equality 56–57; equity 56–57; general permissibility 56; justice 56–57; mutual consent 55; prevention of violence and excessive gains 57; principles of 54–60; relation between purposes and prohibitions 137–138; removal of difficulty 57–58; sanctity of contracts 55
Islamic jurisprudence 5–6; mistakes 128; subject matter 111
Islamic law 1; options 195–196
Islamic law of contract 137
issuer's certificates (*sukuk*) 221–222
istisna (manufacturing contract) 149–150, 214, 230–231

jahalah (ignorance) 122
Java, Indonesia, codification of Shariah 24–25
jins 129
joint-stock companies 42
Jordan, "contracts" defined 68
ju'ala model 228–229
Junun (insanity) 106
jurisprudence, Islamic jurisprudence 5–6
juristic persons 40–43
just coercion (*ikrah bi haq*) 134
justice 52–54, 56–57

kafalah (suretyship) 169, 235
kafalah model 228
kalam (verbal offer) 85–86
Khadij, Rafi' b. 9, 77
Khalifah 25
Khan, Muhammad Akram 233
Kharofa, Ala' Eddin 111
khata' 128
khiyar (options) 124, 195–197
khiyar al-'aib (option of the defect) 129, 202–204, 208
khiyar al-majlis (during the sitting/meeting) 196–198
khiyar al-ru'yat (option of viewing) 200–202
khiyar al-shart (option of condition) 198–200
khiyar syarat 198
khul' (divorce agreement) 198
King Abdullah 27
kitabah (offer by writing) 86
knowledge of subject matter 114–115
Kuwait, "contracts" defined 68

lapse of time, termination of offer 91
law, Islamic concept of 6–7
law of contracts 32
leasing (*ijarah*) 168, 219
legal capacity (*Ahliyyah*) 100
legal capacity (*zimmah*) 100
legal consequences, classification of contracts 178–182
legal effective cause (*'illah*) 113
legal effects: of contracts under fraud or cheating 165–166; of contractual mistakes 128; of *gharar* (risk) 150–151; of invalid contract 180; of

misrepresentation 131; of voidable contracts 181
legality, subject matter 115
legal relation, consent 122–124
Lex Mancipi 18
Libber, A. E. 10
limited partnership (*mudarabah*) 216–218
limiting the rights of others 183
loan (*qerad*) 198
lunacy (*'Atah*) 106

Ma Alayh 100
Macca 14–17
MacDonald, Duncan B. 231–233
Madinah 14–16
madum (non-existing object) 113
Mahmassani, Sobhi 6, 187, 191, 192
Maitland, Frederic William 17
majlis (meeting) 96–97
Makhluf, Hasanain 23
Ma Lahu 100
Malaysia, English law of contract 27
Malik, Anas b. 144
Maliki, Imam 6, 199; acceptance (*qabul*) 94; cleverness 104; offer by acts or conduct 87; offer by writing (*kitabah*) 86; signs 87
maljian 134
manual labour 47
manufacturing contract (*istisna*) 230–231
maqasid al-Shariah 59, 166–167
marriage (*nekah*) 197–198
Ma'tuh 106
maysir (games of chance) 59, 151–154
Medjelle Ahkam Adliya 25, 34, 35, 38, 67; acceptance (*qabul*) 93–94; *al-Baiy* 179; bilateral contract (*'aqd thuma'i*) 176; damages 209; dissolution of a contract by agreement 189; gesture or signs 87; *ijab* (offer) 85; *khiyar al-shart* (option of condition) 198; misrepresentation 131; mistakes 127; *mudarabah* (limited partnership) 216, 218; offer by agent/ representative 88; rendering contracts void 129; *sharikat al-Milk* 216; void contract (*batil*) 180
meeting of the minds (*consensus ad idem*) 117
milk in the udder, sale of 160
misrepresentation 130–131; consent 122
mistakes 127–130; consent 121
mithaq 69
moderation in earning 48–49
mortgages (*rahn*) 198; contract of mortgage or bailment 236–237
mosaqat (agricultural partnership) 198
Muamalat 24
mu'amalat (civil transactions) 2
mu'atah (display of goods) 89–90
mudarabah (limited partnership) 216–218
mudarabah (trust financing) 15, 169
mudarabah model 227
mudarabah-wakalah model 228
mukallaf (responsible for his act) 100, 104
multilateral contracts 177–178
mumamalt 56
mumayyiz stage 103
muqayadah (sale of goods) 214
murabahah (deferred payment sale) 214, 218–219
Murshid al-hayran ill ma'rifat abwal al-insah 26
musharakah (partnership) 15, 169, 214–216
Muslim jurists 42–43; acceptance 95; bilateral contract (*'aqd thuma'i*) 177; choice (*khiyar*) 124; classification of contracts 175–176, 182; consent 118–119, 122; dissolution of a contract 187, 192; *fiqh* 5; *gharar* 151; *inter absentees* 96; juristic persons 41–43; legally capable person 100; *maysir* (games of chance) 151; *sharikah* 214; subject matter 110, 112, 113; *takaful* 223; theory of contract 32–35
mutual agreement (*iqalah*), dissolution of a contract 189
mutual consent 117–118; factors which vitiate 121–122; intention to create legal relation 122–124; Islamic contract law 55; offer and acceptance 124
Muwa'adah 70

nafidh (binding contract) 181
najsh (type of fraud) 160
Name of Allah 161
naqs (reduction) 121–122
Nawawi, Imam 151
nekah (marriage) 197–198
nexum form of contract 18
Niazi, Liaqat Ali Khan 133, 187
nominate contracts 30–31
non-binding contracts 182
non-existence of subject matter, consent 122

non-existing object (*madum*) 113
non-performance, dissolution of a contract 190
nullity 191

Obaidullah, M. 152
objects of contracts 115–116
obligations 71–72
obligation to perform an act 188
offer (*ijab*) 84–85, 118; by acts or conduct 87; by agent/representative 88; gesture or signs 86–87; invitation to treat 88–90; offer by writing (*kitabah*) 86; termination of offer 91–92; verbal offer (*kalam*) 85–86
offer by writing (*kitabah*) 86
option of condition (*khiyar al-shart*) 198–200
option of the defect (*khiyar al-'aib*) 129, 202–204
option of viewing (*khiyar al-ru-yat*) 200–202
options (*khiyar*) 195–196; end of 200; *khiyar al-'aib* (option of the defect) 202–204; *khiyar al-majlis* (during the sitting/meeting) 196–198; *khiyar al-ru'yat* (option of viewing) 200–202; *khiyar al-shart* (option of condition) 198–200; when parties declare approval 197
oral declaration, consent 120
Ottoman Empire, codification 25–26
ownable subject matter 111

Pakistan, English law of contract 27
parties 100; inspection of subject matter 114–115
partnership (*sharikah*) 15, 198, 214–216, 233
partnership agreement (*musharakah*) 15
performance, cessation of contract 187–188
personal resources, sharing 50
Pollock, Frederick 17
possession, subject matter 113–114
post-Islamic era contracts 15–17
pre-Islamic era contracts 14–15
prevention of violence and excessive gains, Islamic contract law 57
principle of general permissibility 56
prodigality 107
profits and loss sharing 61
prohibition of 137–138; dealing in forbidden commodities 169–170; forbidden commodities 60; fraud and cheating 59; *gharar* (risk) 59; inconsistent contracts 59; *maysir* (games of chance) 152–153; *qimar* (gambling) 59, 152–153; *riba* (interest) 58–59, 138–146; trickery 60, 170
property, subject matter 111
prudence stage 104
puberty (*baligh*) stage 104
public welfare 61–62
purpose 137–138; of contracts, classification of 183–184; of prohibition of *gharar* 150

qabul (acceptance) 92–97, 118
Qanun al-adl wa al-insaf lil-qada ala mushkilat al-awqaf 26
"*Qanun Huquq al-'Ailah*" (family law) 26
Qanun Namahs 25
qard (a benevolent loan) 15
Qardhul-hasan 229
Qatar, "contracts" defined 69
qerad (loan) 198
qimar (gambling) 151–154
quantum meruit 211
quasi-contract (*shibh al-'aqd*) 178
Quraish 14–15
Qur'ān 3–4; bilateral contract (*'aqd thuma'i*) 177; capacity 104–105; coercion (*ikrah*) 132–133; commercial transactions 9–10; contract of compromise 237; contracts 72–75; false oath 161; *fiqh* 3–4; fraud and cheating 157–158; freedom of contracts 36–40; general theory of contract 32; *gharar* (risk) 148; hoarding 163–165; *Huquq Allah* (Rights of Allah) 166–167; *ijara* (contract of lease) 220; justice 52; *khiyar al-'aib* (option of the defect) 203; misrepresentation 130; mistakes 127–128; *mudarabah* (limited partnership) 217; mutual consent 118–119; prevention of violence and excessive gains 57; *qimar* (gambling) 153–154; quasi-contract (*shibh al-'aqd*) 178; relation between purpose and prohibition 137–138; *riba* (interest) 140–142; *salam* (advanced payment) 232; *sharikah* (partnership) 215; *takaful* (contract of insurance) 225–226; unilateral contract (*'aqd infiradi*) 176; valid contracts (*sahih*) 179
quwah qahirah 192

Rahim, Abdur 1, 67
Rahn (mortgage) 198
Ramli, Allama 43
ratify (*imda'*) 195
reasons for no codifications till the date 20–22
receptive capacity (*Ahliyyah al-wujub*) 101
refusal of offers 92
removal of difficulty, Islamic contract law 57–58
rendering contracts void, mistakes 128–129
rendering contracts voidable 129–130
replacement authority 183
representatives: acceptance (*qabul*) 94; expressing consent 120; offer (*ijab*) 88
repudiation 208
rescission, breach of contract 207–209
restitutionary remedies, breach of contract 211
restricted *mudarabah* 218
revocation: dissolution of a contract 190–191; termination of offer 91
riba (interest) 138–146; prohibition of 58–59
rida (mutual consent) 117, 118
riba al-buyu (sale transaction in which a commodity is exchanged) 143
riba al-duyun (interested eared on leading money to another party) 143
riba al-Fadl (riba in excess) 143–146
Riba al-Jahiliyyah 143
riba al-Nasia (riba in losses) 143–144
"*Risalat al-Sahabah fi Ta 'at al-Sultan*" (Message of Companions in the Obedience of the Sultan) 23
risk (*gharar*) 146–151; prohibition of 59
risk mitigation, *takaful* (contract of insurance) 224
Roman Empire, contracts 18
Rosenthal, Franz 152
rukn (pillar) 83
rules of acceptance 94–97

Sabi Mumayyaz (minor possessed with discretion) 105–106
Sadr-ush-Shariah 100
safah 107
sahih (valid contract) 179
salam (advanced payment) 199, 214, 231–233
salam (forward) contracts 16
Salam (R.A), 'Abd Allah 144
salam sale 149
sale (*bai'*) 32, 168
sale contracts 83
sale of debt 150
sale of milk in the udder 160
sale transactions 214
Salwani, Siti 87
sanctity of contracts 55
Sanhuri, Abdal Razzaq 20, 31, 187, 192
sarf (exchange of money) 16, 214
Saudi Arabia, codification 26–27
Schacht, Joseph 30, 32, 40, 208
security 183
Shafi, Imam 6
Shafis 68; acceptance (*qabul*) 95–96; knowledge of subject matter 114; offer by acts or conduct 87; offer by writing (*kitabah*) 86; option of viewing (*khiyar al-ru-yat*) 201
Shaibani, Muhammad 43
sharekah (partnership) 198
Shariah 1–2, 4, 20; acceptance (*qabul*) 94; commercial transactions 10; contracts 77–79; dissolution of a contract by agreement 189; exploitation 61–62; general theory of contract 35; intention 123; legality of subject matter 115; Saudi Arabia 27
Shariah ahkam (legal rules) 3
sharikah (partnership) 214–216, 233
sharikat al-Milk 216
sharikat-ul-Aqd 216
sharing personal resources 50
Shatibi, Imam 123
shibh al-'aqd (quasi-contract) 178
shirkah (partnership) 15, 169
shirkat (partnership) 215
Shirkat-ul-Amwal 42
Shirkat-ul-Mal 42
Shirkat-ul-Wujuh 42
Shu'ayb, Prophet 52
Shu'ayb people, cheating 156–157
sigha (form) 84
sighah, expressing consent 120
signs, expressing consent 120
silence 87, 121
social welfare 51–52
specific performance, breach of contract 210
sponso form of contract 18
stages of capacity 103–104
subject matter 110–111; existence of 112–113; knowledge of 114–115; legality

115; no charge 111–112; ownable 111; possession and deliverability 113–114; value 111
suitability, subject matter 115
sukuk (issuer's certificates) 221–222
Sunnah: capacity 104–105; contracts 75–77; *fiqh* 3–4; fraud and cheating 158–160; general theory of contract 33–34; *Huquq Allah* (Rights of Allah) 166–167; *ijara* (contract of lease) 220; mistakes 128; *mudarabah* (limited partnership) 217; mutual consent 118–119; prevention of violence and excessive gains 57; *riba* (interest) 142–143; *salam* (advanced payment) 232; *sharikah* (partnership) 215; *takaful* (contract of insurance) 225–226
surety-ship (*kafalah*) 169, 235

Tabarani 14–15
tafa'ul 117
Taghrir 121
Tahir-ul-Qadri, Muhammad 100
takaful (contract of insurance) 222–230
Taklif-i-Shari'i 100
Takwin al-Aqd 83
Tanzil-ur-Rehman, Dr. 23
Taqnin 20
taradi (mutual consent) 117
tawliyah 218
Teleghani, S. M. 60, 170
temporarily unenforceable 182
termination of contract 190–192
termination of offer 91–92
timely payment of wages 50–51
time of completion, classification of contracts 182–183
trade, importance of 7–9
transactions: division of capacity 105–106; subject matter 110–111
trickery 60, 170
trust financing (*mudarabah*) 15

Uadimonium 18
'Ubayd (R.A), Fadala 145
Ulma 27
Umar (R.A), Abdullah 76, 170
unenforceable contracts 182
unenforceable permanently 182
unilateral contract (*'aqd infiradi*) 175–176
unilateral revocation of contract 191–192
United Arab Emirates (UAE), "contracts" defined 68
unjust coercion (*ikrah bi ghayr haq*) 134
unrestricted *mudarabah* 218
us-l al-fiqh 128
usul 5
usul al-fiqh (legal theory) 5
usury 138–146

valid contracts (*sahih*) 179
validity of sale contract 213–214
value, subject matter 111
verbal acceptance 93
verbal offer (*kalam*) 85–86
vitiating factors, mistakes 127–128
void (*batil*) 129
void ab initio 128
voidable contracts 181
void contract (*batil*) 180–181

wa'ad 69–70
waaf 40, 42
waaf model 227–228
wadi'ah 218
wadiah contract 229
wages, timely payment of 50–51
wakalah (agency contract) 15, 169
wakala model 227
wakala-waaf model 228
Wa'la al-Saba'I, 'Abd al-Rahman 170
Watt, Montgomery 17
wealth creation 49–50
withdrawal of offer 91
writing, expressing consent 120
written acceptance 93

Yemen, "contracts" defined 69
Yusuf, Imam Abu 199

Zaidis 199
Zakāt 51, 75
Zaki 'Abdul Barr, Muhammad 23
zimman 100

For Product Safety Concerns and Information please contact our EU representative GPSR@taylorandfrancis.com
Taylor & Francis Verlag GmbH, Kaufingerstraße 24, 80331 München, Germany

www.ingramcontent.com/pod-product-compliance
Ingram Content Group UK Ltd.
Pitfield, Milton Keynes, MK11 3LW, UK
UKHW020149200926
475702UK00016B/2626
9781032005096